BLOOMSBURY
GOOD READING
GUIDE TO
BIOGRAPHY & AUTOBIOGRAPHY

BLOOMSBURY
GOOD READING
GUIDE TO
BIOGRAPHY
&
AUTOBIOGRAPHY

KENNETH AND VALERIE McLEISH

BLOOMSBURY

First published 1991 by Bloomsbury Publishing Limited, 2 Soho Square, London W1V 5DE

A CIP record for this book is available from the British Library

ISBN 0 7475 0906 9

Designed by Geoff Green
Typeset by Alexander Typesetting, Inc.
Printed in Great Britain by Clays Ltd, St Ives plc

CONTENTS

Contents

INTRODUCTION

More biographies and autobiographies are borrowed from libraries than any other kind of book except fiction. It seems that few reading pleasures surpass that of an interesting life well told. Browsing along the shelves, we meet the 'great and the good' (sometimes discovering that they were neither), a crowd of ordinary men and women (whose lives read like hilarious, tender or terrible equivalents of our own) and a fair number of people whose awfulness is their claim to fame.

This *Guide* is not to people, but to books. We have included only men and women who have had interesting books written about them; if there are no good books about someone, that person, however famous or deserving, does not appear. We were especially choosy with books by and about politicians and soldiers—too often, we found, they seem to refight old battles or debates, as if self-justification had become an art-form. For similar reasons, we cut book on books about stage and screen stars. Fans already know what to look for, and non-fans find many showbiz books little more than lists of parts played, critical successes and backstage, backscreen bitchery.

We were astonished by the way some people's biographies seem to come like London buses in the old joke; none for ages, then half a dozen all at once. Why were so many books published about X in the 1970s, or Y in the 1980s? is it Z's turn this decade–and who decides who Z will be? Where biographies clustered, we chose the ones we found most revealing, most enjoyable, or preferably both. We hope to add many more biographies and autobiographies, old and new, in future additions of the *Guide*. We welcome suggestions; please write to us, care of the publisher.

Scattered through the Guide are 'menus' of suggested reading: enjoyable biographies and autobiographies on one particular topic or another. They range from Country Childhoods (page 63) to Showbiz (page 239), from To boldly go . . . (page 259) to Women and children at War (page 284). As with the main entries, we welcome suggestons for new menus, or for additions to those already here.

One of our aims in this *Guide* was to choose books written not for specialists but for ordinary readers, and available either in bookshops or in local libraries. We combed the catalogues of two county library services in particular, Cambridgeshire and Lincolnshire, and also made full use of the inter-county loan system. Sue Richardson and Jackie Holding helped in this, locating and processing two or three boxfuls of books each week; we could not have written the *Guide* without them. To them, to Sarah Robinson (who word-processed many entries) and to Tracey Smith (who commissioned the book in the first place, encouraged us during the writing and saw it through the press), our warmest thanks.

Kenneth and Valerie McLeish
Spalding, 1991

HOW TO USE THIS BOOK

The entries are arranged by subjects, not by authors. For other books by this or that biographer, see his or her name in the index.

Each main entry contains three elements:

1. a few words on who the person was and what he or she did;
2. descriptions of the most recommended book(s) by and/or about the person;
3. a list of 'read ons', recommending other books on the same person, or books of related interest.

Throughout the *Guide* the symbol * before a name means that that person has his or her own entry.

A

ABELARD, Peter (1079–1142) French religious thinker

Abélard's religious ideas are important in the history of medieval Catholicism, but hard for non-theologians. Ordinary readers know him chiefly because of his love-affair with a pupil, Héloise, for her uncle's revenge on him (castration), and for the letters (a heady blend of passion with religious acceptance and renunciation) he and Héloise wrote to each other when they parted, to live as monk and nun respectively. Marjorie Worthington, *The Immortal Lovers* (1960) gives a clear account of the whole affair – not an easy task in view of the remoteness of medieval ways of thinking from our own. J.G. Sikes, *Peter Abailard* (1932) deals, in a comprehensible way, with Abélard's religious teaching, and the quarrel with the authorities which led to his trial for heresy. But the best accounts of all are novels: George Moore, *Héloise and Abélard* (1921) and Helen Waddell, *Peter Abélard* (1933).

◊ **READ ON**
Betty Radice (ed. and trans.),
The Letters of Héloise and Abélard
(which also includes Abélard's
autobiography).

ACTON, Harold (born 1904) English writer

Acton based much of his life in Italy, although he was a constant traveller, and writes especially well about 1930s China. He was well connected in English society, and his *Memoirs of an Aesthete* (1948) and *More Memoirs of an Aesthete* (1970) contain thumbnail sketches of, it seems, everyone and anyone who was both well-born and interested in the arts. (He is interesting, for example, on the *Sitwells and *Waugh.) His style is slow and florid, often verging on but never really straying into the bitchy. He writes short sections of 3–5 pages each – and

◊ **READ ON**
*James Lees-Milne, *Ancestral
Voices* (word-portraits, from a
different point of view, of many
of the same people as feature in
Acton's books).

this, coupled with the gossipy fascination of what he says, makes his books ideal bedtime reading.

⋄ ACTORS

Michael Billington, *Peggy Ashcroft*
John Gielgud, *Stage Directions*
Anthony Holden, **Olivier*
G. L. Hoskins, *The Life and Times of Edward Alleyn*
Geoffrey Kendal, *The Shakespeare Wallah*
Roger Maxwell, *Sarah Siddons: Portrait of an Actress*
Giles Playfair, *A Flash of Lightning* (*Edmund Kean)
Peter Raby, *Fair Ophelia* (*Harriet Smithson)
Joanna Richardson, **Sarah Bernhardt*
Anthony Sher, *Year of the King*
Maurice Solotow, *Stagestruck* (*The Lunts)
See also Applause! Applause!; Film Stars

ADAIR, (Paul) Red (born 1915) US firefighter

To the layperson, putting out fires in oil-wells sounds just about as possible, and certainly as difficult, as capping a volcano. Adair has spent his life doing it, and treats it as a step-by-step, almost military operation. He has been famous in the oil world for five decades; he became a household name when John Wayne played him in the film *Hellfighters* and when he dealt with the fire on the Piper Alpha oil-rig in the North Sea, one of the worst in oil-exploration history. Philip Singerman, *Red Adair: an American Hero* (1989) tells his story in a fast-moving, dialogue-packed style and with action scenes which beggar those in any fictional thriller.

⋄ READ ON
Ed Punchard (with Syd Higgins), *Piper Alpha – A Survivor's Story.*

ADAMS, Abigail (1744–1818) American matriarch

Adams is normally described as 'wife and mother', as if she existed only in the shadow of two American presidents, her husband John Adams and their son John Quincy Adams. In fact, although she followed the female convention of the time in not taking centre stage in public affairs, she was a guiding spirit of the American revolution and the first decades of the new republic. Her letters teem with family interest – but what a family! – and are also full of political shrewdness, comments on the momentous events through which she lived, and sharp assessments of such people as *Franklin, *Jefferson, *Washington, *Lafayette and even George III. Phyllis Lee Levin, *Abigail*

⋄ READ ON
Abigail Adams, *Letters of Mrs Adams*. John Adams, *Letters of John Adams Addressed to his Wife.* John Quincy Adams, *Memoirs.* See also *Henry Adams.

Adams (1987) makes full use of this material, both published and unpublished, and despite its flowery style ('Gray melancholy ignited to white fury when Abigail turned to the subject of William Blount') gives a wonderfully lifelike picture of both Adams herself and her enormous, talented brood.

ADAMS, Henry (1838–1918) US historian

↔ **READ ON**
J.T. Adams, *The Adams Family*.

Adams, great-grandson of the second American president and grandson of the sixth, taught history at Harvard and specialized in the early years of the Republic. (His nine-volume *History of the United States During the Administrations of Jefferson and Madison* is still a major work.) He is best remembered for his wry, mellow autobiography *The Education of Henry Adams* (1907), a classic. He writes of himself in the third person, and delights in portraying himself as someone of no importance or accomplishment, a mere fly on the wall at great events: a typical sentence reads 'Of the five . . . Adams alone added nothing to the wit or humor, except as a listener; but they needed a listener and he was useful.' Despite (or perhaps because of) his ability to listen, he was visited by most of the 'great and good' of his time, and his pen-portraits are as shrewd and sharp as any novelist's. A bonus for British readers is the unusual glimpse he gives of 1860s London, where he spent some years with his father, the US 'minister' (that is, ambassador).

↔ AFRICA

Vivien Allen, *Lady Trader* (*Sarah Heckford)
Daphne Anderson, *The Toe Rags*
D. Child, *Portrait of a Pioneer: the Letters of Sidney Turner from South Africa*
John Flint, *Cecil Rhodes*
Ruth First, *Oliver Schreiner*
*Beryl Markham, *West With the Night*
E. A. Ritter, *Shaka Zulu*
Pat Ritzenthaler, *Ach Trimbi II, Fon of Bafut*
Sylvia Ross, *Stepping Stones: Memoirs of a Colonial Nigeria*
*Wole Soyinka, *Ake*; *Isara*
Donald Woods, *Asking for Trouble*
See also Beyond the Horizon; To Boldly Go . . .

AGATE, James (1877–1947) English critic

↔ **READ ON**
Alexander Woolcott, *The Portable Woolcott* (anthology of reviews by Agate's US clone). Clive James,

In the years between the World Wars, there was an odd tradition in critical circles that a particular kind of truculent rudeness was the same thing as wit. Agate was its chief English champion, closing shows and demolishing careers with a flick of the pen, holding court in the Café Royal in London, and putting down anyone and everyone he could think of. He wrote nine volumes of journals, all called *Ego* (the first was published in 1935; the last in 1948). They are interesting less for Agate's personality than because they echo his reviews so closely, and so give a one-sided but still fascinating glimpse of London theatre in the 1920s–1940s. James Harding, *Agate* (1986) is a delightfully deadpan biography. Harding tells all, sometimes like a rabbit writing about a snake, but often with insight, as when he quotes Agate's own remarkable judgement, part of a projected self-obituary: 'His shop-window was superb, and perfectly concealed the meagreness of the academic stock within.'

May Week Was in June (Cambridge memoir by the 1970s–80s TV critic who was an Agate of his day).

AKHENATEN (14th century BC) Egyptian Pharaoh

Akhenaten ('Glory of the Sun') was the name taken by the Pharaoh Amenhotep IV, who abandoned the state religion, with its terror of death and hundreds of implacable gods, in favour of belief in one God only, the creator, the power of light, embodied in the Sun. He built a magnificent city, El-Amarna, and married a beautiful wife, Nefertiti. After his death his religion was abolished and his name erased from official Egyptian history – but the remains of his city, and the tomb of his wife, were rediscovered in the 20th century, and are among the glories of Egyptian archaeology. Joy Collier, *King Sun* (1970) combines biography of the gentle, mystic king himself with an account of the excavation of El-Amarna. The book closes, movingly, with Akhenaten's own poem to his God, an expression of wonder and faith as immediate as any of the extracts from the Psalms with which it is interleaved.

◇ **READ ON**
Mika Waltari, *Sinuhe the Egyptian* (historical novel).

ALCOTT, Louisa May (1832–88) US writer

Daughter of the educationalist and philosopher Bronson Alcott, friend of *Emerson and *Thoreau, Alcott grew up in an atmosphere of heady intellectual discussion and genteel poverty. She served as a nurse in the Civil War and was a tireless advocate of women's rights. She began writing to support her family, and her works include poems, articles, detective stories, romances and novels, not least the partly autobiographical *Little Women* (1868) and its sequels, among the best loved of all US children's books. Her *Recollections of My Childhood's Days* (1890) make fascinating reading against *Little Women*, and *Hospital Sketches* (1863) describes her work in the Civil War. Madeleine

◇ **READ ON**
E.D. Cheney (ed.), *Louisa May Alcott: Her Life, Letters and Journals* (published 1889, just after Alcott's death).

B. Stern, *Lousa May Alcott* (1952), the standard biography, gains from being in a romantic style close to Alcott's own.

ALEXANDER THE GREAT (356–323 BC)
Greek conqueror

Alexander thought himself the equal of Agamemnon, Achilles or the other heroes of Greek myth, and employed a bevy of historians to write up his exploits. Those exploits were indeed magnificent: he advanced from his home kingdom Macedonia (modern Albania) throughout the Persian empire (modern Turkey, Syria, Iraq, Iran and Afghanistan) as far as the Indus valley, taking Greek culture east and bringing Asian culture west. Peter Green, *Alexander the Great* (1970) and Robin Lane Fox, *Alexander the Great* (1973) are scholarly biographies accessible to non-classicists; Green is good on the terrain (which he retrod in person as part of his research), Lane Fox on the documents. Robin Lane Fox, *The Search for Alexander* (1980) is an astonishing, beautifully illustrated book about Alexander's legend: later generations credited him with magic powers, liaisons with devils and space-beings, and the ability to trawl jewels from the ocean floor in a glass sphere whenever he ran short of cash.

> ·> READ ON
> Mary Renault, *Fire from Heaven*; *The Persian Boy*; *Funeral Games* (atmospheric novel-trilogy); *The Nature of Alexander* (historical study).

·> AMERINDIANS

Alexander B. Adams, *Geronimo*
Sam Blowsnake, *Crashing Thunder: the Autobiography of an Amerindian*
Dee Brown, *Bury My Heart at Wounded Knee*
Lovat Dickson, *Wilderness Man*
James Thomas Flexner, *Lord of the Mohawks: a Biography of *Sir William Johnson*
Clellan S. Ford, *Smoke from their Fires: the Life of a Kwakiutl Chief*
Theodore Kazimiroff, *The Last Algonquin*; *Joe Two Trees*
Frances Mossiker, **Pocahontas*

ANDERSEN, Hans Christian (1805–75) Danish writer

A cobbler's son, Andersen hoped to become an actor, but shyness and lack of education made this impossible. A benefactor paid for his university education, and he began to write. He became a friend of *Dickens, and was an unsuccessful suitor of

> ·> READ ON
> Hans Andersen, *A Poet's Bazaar* (travels in the Balkans). Reginald Spink, *Hans Christian Andersen: the Man and His Work* (critical and psychological study).

Jenny Lind. He is known in Scandinavia for novels and travel books, and throughout the world for fairy tales such as *The Little Mermaid*, *The Emperor's New Clothes* and *The Tinder Box*. His autobiography, *The Fairy Tale of My Life* (1855) is characteristically lively and light-hearted, intended for children as well as adults. Darker themes appear in Reginald Spink, *The Young Hans Andersen* (1962) and *Hans Andersen and His World* (1972), making the distinction between the ugly duckling Andersen was in life and the swan he became whenever he took up his pen.

ANGELOU, Maya (born 1928) US writer and performer

In her 20s and 30s Angelou was a singer and actress, touring the world in *Porgy and Bess* and working in New York nightclubs. She became a Black rights activist, worked as journalist and educator in Africa, and now teaches creative writing in North Carolina. All this and more is described in her five-volume autobiography; the books, all self-contained, are *I Know Why the Caged Bird Sings* (1969), *Gather Together in My Name* (1974), *Singin' and Swingin' and Gettin' Merry Like Christmas* (1976), *The Heart of a Woman* (1981), and *All God's Children Need Travelling Shoes* (1986). The books were bestsellers not only for their lively style or extraordinary characters and locations, but also because Angelou makes her career seem emblematic of the way Black people have progressed in the USA from 1920s segregation and oppression (scathingly evoked in *I Know Why the Caged Bird Sings*) to equal opportunities, both political and social.

> **READ ON**
> Alice Walker, *Meridian*; *The Color Purple* (novels about Black US experience, similar in style and tone to Angelou's autobiographies).

◇ ANIMALS

Joy Adamson, *Born Free*
*Gerald Durrell, *Three Tickets to Adventure*
*Gavin Maxwell, *Ring of Bright Water*
*Len Rush, *Captain of the Queen's Flight*
*Derek Tangye, *A Cat Affair*
Henry Williamson, *Salar the Salmon*
*Virginia Woolf, *Flush*

ANTINOUS (112–30) Greek courtier

A handsome Greek, friend and catamite of the Roman Emperor Hadrian, Antinous was drowned in a boating accident when he was 18. Hadrian, broken-hearted, set up statues to him all over the Empire – and almost at once mysterious ap-

> **READ ON**
> Marguerite Yourcenar, *Memoirs of Hadrian* (historical novel).

pearances and miracle cures began to be reported. Antinous, nicknamed 'the last Olympian', was worshipped as a god for 400 years, and his cult was as widespread, as inexplicable to outsiders, and as comforting to millions of devotees, as that of any Christian saint. Royston Lambert, *Beloved and God* (1985) tells his extraordinary story in lucid, elegant prose, a pleasure in itself.

‹› APPLAUSE! APPLAUSE!

Hermione Baddeley, *The Unsinkable Hermione Baddeley*
*Josephine Baker and Marcel Sauvage, *The Memoirs of Josephine Baker*
*Colley Cibber, *Apology for the Life of Mr Colley Cibber, Comedian*
Hunter Davies, *The Grades*
Michael Freedland, *The Secret Life of *Danny Kaye*
Dan Mannix, *Memoirs of a Sword Swallower*
Hesketh Pearson, *Beerbohm Tree*
M. Peters, *Mrs Pat* (Mrs Patrick Campbell)
A. H. Saxon, *P. T. Barnum: the Legend and the Man*
Donald Sinden, *A Touch of the Memoirs*
Otis Skinner, *Footlights and Spotlights*
R. Gordon Thomas, *Bed of Nails: the Story of the Amazing Blondini*
See also Actors; Film Stars; Hollywood; Showbiz; The Silver Screen

---

ARENDT, Hannah (1906–75) German/US philosopher

When Arendt's German career was cut short by the Nazis, she escaped first to France and then to the USA. She was prominent in left-wing intellectual circles, and spoke and wrote trenchantly about such matters as racism in the USA, the Holocaust, the cold war, student unrest and Zionism (especially in the years surrounding the foundation of the state of Israel, the *Eichmann trial and the Yom Kippur War). Elizabeth Young-Bruehl, *Hannah Arendt, For Love of the World* (1982) is a massive, authorized biography, shirking none of the thorniness of Arendt's ideas, but balancing them against warm accounts of her friendships and family life. The book is also a portrait of a difficult quarter-century for US liberalism, with intellectuality and rationalism in disarray despite the high profile of Arendt and such friends of hers as *Auden, Jarrell, *McCarthy and Morgenthau. Derwent May, *Hannah Arendt* (1986) covers the

‹› **READ ON**
Hannah Arendt, *Men in Dark Times* (savage political and historical survey of the evil side of human nature).

same ground in a briefer, crisper way, and has the benefit of a European perspective on Arendt's life and outlook.

ARMSTRONG, Louis (1900–71) US musician

'Satchmo' (short for 'satchel mouth', a nickname given to Armstrong because of his enormous grin) became a star at 25, and his records of Dixieland jazz took the new music round the world. He went on playing trumpet and singing for 50 years: one of the 20th century's best-loved and most characteristic stars. M. Jones and J. Chilton, *Louis* (1971) is an affectionate memorial of the man. James Lincoln Collier, *Louis Armstrong* (1983), the standard biography, is especially good on his musical achievement.

> ⋄ **READ ON**
> Louis Armstrong, *My Life in New Orleans* (lively memoir of Armstrong's orphanage childhood and his musical apprenticeship).

ARNIM, Elizabeth von (1866–1941) New Zealand writer

Born Mary Beauchamp, and *Katherine Mansfield's cousin, she married a German count, and in 1898 published her first book, the witty, autobiographical novel *Elizabeth and Her German Garden* – at first anonymously, as Prussian ladies of the time did not write for money. After her husband's death she married Bertrand Russell's brother Francis, Earl Russell – and when she discovered that he was consistently unfaithful, she began affairs of her own, most notably with Bertrand *Russell and *H. G. Wells. In the 1920s–30s she was a bestselling novelist, a well-known wit and feminist, and a society darling – until she antagonized many of her friends by holding them up to ridicule in her books, most of which made fictional use of episodes from her own full life. Karen Usborne, *'Elizabeth': The Author of Elizabeth and Her German Garden* (1986) is well researched, and although flatly written it tweaks back the curtain on a riotous, all-but-forgotten corner of the English literary scene.

> ⋄ **READ ON**
> Leslie de Charmes, *Elizabeth of the German Garden* (memoir by one of her daughters). Elizabeth von Arnim, *All the Dogs of my Life* (revealing as much about herself as about her pets).

⋄ ART AND ARTISTS

Mariam J. Benkowitz, *Aubrey Beardsley*
John Chancellor, *Audubon*
Susan Chitty, *Gwen John*
Gay Daly, *Pre-Raphaelites in Love*
Françoise Gilot, *Matisse and Picasso*
James Hamilton, *Arthur Rackham: A Life with Illustration*
Hayden Herrera, *Frida* (*Frida Kahlo)
Sean Hignett, *Brett, from Bloomsbury to New Mexico*

*Oscar Kokoschka, *My Life*
Rose Lindsay, *Model Wife*
Edward Lucie-Smith, *Lives of the Great Twentieth Century Artists*
See also Painters

ASQUITH, Herbert
ASQUITH, Margot

Herbert Henry Asquith (1858–1929) was Liberal Prime Minister of Britain from 1908 to 1916, during the campaigns for women's suffrage and Irish home rule, and the first years of the First World War. He was eventually ousted by a coalition of Conservatives and his own Liberal opponents – led by Lloyd George – and has tended to benefit at biographers' hands ever since, in comparison with the less morally scrupulous Lloyd George. Rose-tinted spectacles are evident in Roy Jenkins, *Asquith* (1964), otherwise an expert and thoughtful biography, good on the politics. Stephen Koss, *Asquith* (1976), is less favourable, partly because he uses sources not available to Jenkins in the 1960s. Asquith's private life is charted, in part and in passing, in Daphne Bennett, *Margot: a Life of the Countess of Oxford and Asquith* (1984). **Margot Asquith**, née Tennant (1864–1945), was witty, lively and forthright, bouncing on to the London social scene and becoming one of the great hostesses of the century, influential in academic, artistic and high-society circles as well as behind the scenes in politics.

⋅> READ ON
H. H. Asquith, *Memoirs and Reflections*; *Correspondence With Venetia Stanley* (voluminous and indiscreet; fodder for the next generation of biographers).
Margot Asquith, *Autobiography*.

ASTOR family

The Astor wealth was founded (on fur and property dealing) by **John Jacob Astor** (1763–1848) and his son **William Astor** (1792–1895), nicknamed 'landlord of New York'. The US branch of the family specialized in property and shipping. They were also philanthropists, giving vast sums to charity. The English branch (led by **William Waldorf**, 1st Viscount Astor (1848–1919), and his son **John Jacob Astor** (1886–1971) owned newspapers, and several members – especially **William Waldorf**, 2nd Viscount Astor (1878–1952), and his wife **Nancy Astor**, 1879–1964) – were also active in politics. Nancy Astor, the first woman ever elected to the British Parliament, was a person of remarkable energy and courage but no sense of proportion – a combination which made her domineering, terrifying and unpredictable, likely to flare into a row, or break off in a flurry of giggles, for no visible reason at all. As hostess of the 'Cliveden Set', she was the hub of an important clique in British public life for 40 years.

⋅> READ ON
Brooke Astor, *A Patchwork Childhood*; *Footprints* (memoirs of a happy childhood as the daughter of an officer in the US Marines, and of the author's three marriages. Her third marriage, to Vincent Astor, took her into US high society, and she also spent many years using the Astors' money for imaginative charitable work: using the property income to improve slum housing, for example. A light, pleasant memoir to counterbalance some of the higher-profile Astor lives).

Virginia Cowles, *The Astors* (1979) is a sparkling biography of both branches of the family, well written and splendidly illustrated. Michael Astor, *Family Feeling* (1963) is an interesting follow-up, by one of the younger generation. John Grigg, *Nancy Astor, Portrait of a Pioneer* (1980), and Anthony Masters, *Nancy Astor, A Life* (1981) are the most enjoyable of many biographies of Nancy: fascinating about Cliveden, interesting on her forthright opinions on such matters as prohibition, Christian Science and appeasement, and good on her friendships with *T.E. Lawrence and *Shaw. Rosina Harrison, *Rose: My Life in Service* (1975), by Nancy Astor's maid of 40 years, is a blow-by-blow story of two strong-willed women who respected each other without ever being happy to yield dominance or hold back criticism.

AUBREY, John (1626–97) English writer

Aubrey's mind was like an overstuffed cupboard: whenever he reached for a specific piece of information, dozens of other facts fell out, littering his pages as clothes might strew a floor. He was interested in (among other things) alchemy, algebra, astrology, oratory, politics and the theory of education; he wrote books on British antiquities, folklore and strange phenomena ('prophecies, marvels, magic, apparitions, converse with Angels, second-sighted men in Scotland . . . '). His best-known book, *Lives* (1669–96), contains over 400 biographies, packed with digressions and anecdotes and ranging in length from 20,000 words (*Hobbes) to two words (Abraham Wheloc; the words are 'simple man'). Anthony Powell, *John Aubrey and his Friends* (second ed. 1963) is an affectionate, brief life of one of the most magpie-minded men who ever set pen to paper.

> **READ ON**
>
> François Rabelais, *Gargantua and Pantagruel* (satirical novel: the English translation by Thomas Urquhart is close in style to Aubrey's *Lives*, and even more crammed with anecdotes and dotty lists).

AUDUBON, John James (1785–1851) US painter and naturalist

In its day, Audubon's *The Birds of America* (1827–38), containing paintings of 1,065 birds shown life-size in their natural habitats, was one of the most expensive artbooks ever produced, and it is still one of the most beautiful. Until Audubon began travelling to sketch birds, he earned his living by hunting them, and as a painting teacher to the Louisiana bourgeoisie. His painting trips, begun in his mid-30s, took him to remote regions where he lived (somewhat self-admiringly) in frontiersman style – Fenimore Cooper was one of his favourite novelists. Lucy Audubon, *The Life of John James Audubon, the Naturalist* (1902) was compiled by his widow, using his own journals (*see* Read On). Alexander B. Adams, *John James Audubon* (1966), the standard modern biography, is excellent on

> **READ ON**
>
> Howard Corning (ed.), *Journals of John James Audubon*; *Letters of John James Audubon*.

Audubon's early life as well as on his painting trips. John Chancellor, *Audubon* (1978) makes up for a much briefer text by dozens of magnificent illustrations.

AUSTEN, Jane (1775–1817) English writer

Although Austen's life was uneventful, her personality irradiated everything around her: her inner life makes her as fascinating to read about as any character in her books. Jane Aiken Hodge, *The Double Life of Jane Austen* (1972) and John Halpern, *The Life of Jane Austen* (1988), the standard biographies, reflect this, using plentiful quotations from letters, memoirs and other documents (including Austen's novels) to flesh out the facts they (include useful bibliographies). David Cecil, *A Portrait of Jane Austen* (1978) sets Austen in the context of her times. The text is brief and to the point, and the main work is done by scores of well-chosen, magnificently printed illustrations. Park Honan, *Jane Austen, Her Life* (1987) is good on all parts of Austen's life, but beats all other books in its account of her childhood. Constance Pilgrim, *Dear Jane* (1971) recounts Austen's one and only serious love affair, hitherto 'nameless and dateless': a fascinating piece of literary detection.

◇ **READ ON**

William and Richard Austen-Leigh, *Jane Austen, Her Life and Letters* (an early account – 1913 – by members of her family and using family documents). R.W. Chapman (ed.), *The Letters of Jane Austen*.

◇ AUTOBIOGRAPHICAL NOVELS

Peter Ackroyd, *The Last Testament of* *Oscar Wilde
*James Baldwin, *Go Tell it on the Mountain*
Margaret George, *The Autobiography of* *Henry VIII
*Robert Graves, *Wife to Mr* *Milton
Malcolm Lowry, *Lunar Caustic*
Stephen Marlowe, *The Memoirs of* *Christoper Columbus
Robert Nye, *The Memoirs of* *Lord Byron
*Evelyn Waugh, *The Ordeal of Gilbert Pinfold*
*Antonia White, *Frost in May*

B

BACKHOUSE, Edmund (1873–1944) English adventurer

Until the 1970s Backhouse was remembered as an eccentric scholar, co-author of two standard books on China, and benefactor of the Bodleian Library, to which he gave some 30,000 Chinese books and manuscripts. But in 1973 Hugh Trevor-Roper, Oxford Professor of History, was asked to authenticate a document – Backhouse's memoirs – and found it scurrilous and unprintably pornographic. His subsequent investigations showed that Backhouse was a conman, forger, liar and possibly spy. Hugh Trevor-Roper, *Hermit of Peking: the Hidden Life of Sir Edmund Backhouse* (1976), recounting the quest and detailing Backhouse's life, is so bizarre that it reads at times like spoof.

▷ **READ ON**
A.J.A. Symons, *The Quest for Corvo* (a similar scholarly and unlikely quest: see *Rolfe). Anne Taylor, *Laurence Oliphant* (biography of an earlier charlatan: secret agent, entrepreneur and mystic).

BAKER, Josephine (1905–75) US/French dancer and singer

In the 1920s–30s Baker was the sensation of the *Folies-Bergère*. Black, beautiful and elegant, she appeared in spectacular 'oriental' or 'harem' numbers and sang in a smoky, husky voice, often ending her act by sitting on a trapeze, swinging over the audience and scattering white roses. She was prominent in society, a friend of *Colette, *Hemingway, *Picasso, and reputedly the lover of just about everyone from Maurice Chevalier to the Pasha of Marrakesh (who tried to spirit her away to his real-life harem). In the Second World War she worked for the French Resistance, and after the war, unable to have children of her own, she adopted a 'rainbow tribe', a family of refugee

▷ **READ ON**
Josephine Baker and Marcel Sauvage, *The Memoirs of Josephine Baker* ('as told to' showbiz memoirs, first published in 1927 and updated in 1947). Paul Derval, *Folies-Bergère*.

children of all races. In her 60s, bankrupt and ill, she re-energized her career to support this family, and made a second sensation. Lynn Haney, *Naked at the Feast* (1981) and Phyllis Rose, *Jazz Cleopatra* (1990) tell her story, equally good on her jazz-age goings-on and the tragedy and triumph of her last decade.

BAKER, Samuel
BAKER, Florence

Samuel Baker (1821–93) was a wealthy Englishman who set out for Africa to join *Livingstone and explore the interior. On his way, at a slave auction in Bulgaria, he bought a girl, renamed her Florence (**Florence Baker**, 1832–1916), took her as his companion and later married her. Abandoning the idea of joining Livingstone, the Bakers began searching instead for the source of the Nile, and discovered Lake Albert in Nyasa. They became two of Victorian England's favourite explorers, rivals of *Richard Francis Burton, friends of the Prince of Wales (though not of the Queen) and trusted 'Africa hands', sent to govern the Equatorial Nile and to stamp out the slave trade. Their fame ended in disaster, caused by a sex-scandal involving Samuel's brother Valentine. Richard Hall, *Lovers on the Nile* (1980) is a lively joint biography, as good on the risks of living in a London where the Queen disapproved of you as on crocodiles, tsetse flies and natives of a physically more threatening kind.

> **READ ON**
> Michael Brander, *The Perfect Victorian Hero* (less romantically written, but good on Samuel's big-game hunting, his anti-slavery work and his quarrels with other explorers and officials in London).

BALDWIN, Monica (1893–?) English nun and writer

Baldwin, niece of the politician Stanley Baldwin, entered a convent in 1914 and came out in 1941. *I Leap Over The Wall* (1949) is the story of her adjustment to life. She found the ways and manners of wartime Britain incomprehensible, and fascinatingly compares each new experience with its nearest equivalent in convent life. These reflective parts of the book contrast with moving descriptions of her feelings of confusion and inadequacy, caused by her total lack of relevant skills, so that even when labour was so short she was still unable to find suitable work. The book is sad on a personal level, but also remarkable for its insights into two vanished worlds (convent life in the 1920s–30s and wartime London), and for its character-sketches, most notably of Stanley Baldwin.

> **READ ON**
> Karen Armstrong, *I Leap Over the Wall* (1983 memoir by another former nun, of a later generation. She wrote a thoughtful foreword to the 1987 edition of Baldwin's book).

BANKS, Joseph (1743–1820) English scientist

Banks, a rich landowner, used his fortune to finance botanical expeditions, first to Newfoundland and Labrador, then (with *Cook on *Endeavour*) to the southern oceans, and finally to Iceland. He was President of the Royal Society for 42 years, established Kew Gardens as a world centre of botanical research, and in the 1790s proposed the establishment of a settlement in Botany Bay in Australia. J.C. Beaglehole (ed.), *The 'Endeavour' Journal of Joseph Banks* (2nd ed. 1963) is a sumptuously illustrated record of Banks' trip with Cook, fascinating not only for Banks' scientific work but for his descriptions of uninhibited Tahitian and Maori life – customs which later seduced the crew of the *Bounty* and led to the famous mutiny (*see* *Bligh). The standard biography, H.B. Carter, *Sir Joseph Banks* (1988) is superb on Banks the public man, documenting his years of service to the nation with exemplary thoroughness. Patrick O'Brien, *Joseph Banks: a Life* (1987) is shorter and jollier. It quotes revealing anecdotes from Banks' *Endeavour* journal, and is good on his London sponsorship of the delightful Tahitian Omai, and his part in the 1796 Lincolnshire riots.

⋄ **READ ON**
J.C. Beaglehole, *James Cook.*

BARNACLE, Nora (1884–1951) Irishwoman

In 1904 Nora Barnacle left her job as a chambermaid in Finn's Hotel, Dublin, to join her lover *James Joyce in Europe. She shared the rest of her life with him, marrying him in 1931. Their fiery relationship, a blend of heady sex and equally passionate argument, was vital to Joyce's creativity, and Nora inspired most of his female characters, notably Molly Bloom in *Ulysses*. Nora herself, though fiercely protective of Joyce's creative processes, had little interest in the actual books, and (it seems) never read *Ulysses* or *Finnegans Wake* complete. It was as if she were the life-force incarnate, and after Joyce's death she put her vitality equally to the service of their children Giorgio and Lucia, and of Joyce's brother Stanislaus. It is an extraordinary, unlikely story, unaccountably neglected in the thousands of books dotting Joyce's 'i's' and crossing 't's'. Brenda Maddox, *Nora* (1988) is the first biography to do Nora justice, and it is hard to see how the job could be done with more thoroughness or zest.

⋄ **READ ON**
Stanislaus Joyce, *My Brother's Keeper.*

BARNUM, Phineas T(aylor) (1810–91) US showman

Barnum began as an impresario when he was 24, touring the country exhibiting a negro slave he claimed had been *Wash-

⋄ **READ ON**
'Lord' George Sanger, *Seventy Years a Showman* (autobiography). R.J. Walsh, *Buffalo Bill* (life of Barnum's greatest rival, inventor of the

ington's nurse. Later, he ran freak shows (exploiting, among others, the dwarf 'General Tom Thumb'), managed Jenny Lind's first US tour, and in 1881 merged with his circus rival James Anthony Bailey to produce what he characteristically billed as 'The Greatest Show on Earth'. He was the originator of razzmatazz, carrying the selling of snake-oil to heights unequalled since, the Emperor of Hype. His *Autobiography* (1927) is a work of typical shy charm. A.H. Saxon, *P.T. Barnum, The Legend and the Man* (1990) digs deeper, but still misses nothing of the glorious, raucous glitter of Barnum's life.

BARRIE, J(ames) M(atthew) (1869–1937) Scottish playwright

Barrie is known for plays which explore worlds of fantasy, sentiment and innocence: *Dear Brutus*, *Mary Rose* and above all *Peter Pan*, about the 'boy who never grew up'. It seems that Barrie himself, in spirit, was a boy who never grew up: he was at ease only with children, and awkward and tart-tongued with adults. This is explored in Andrew Birkin, *J.M. Barrie and the Lost Boys* (1979), an excellently illustrated account of Barrie's life, centring on his relationship with the Llewelyn Davies brothers, whom he befriended as tiny children and whose guardian he became when their parents died. J. Dunbar, *J.M. Barrie* (1970) is a more conventional biography, good on Barrie's Scottish upbringing, his early journalism and his theatre work.

BARRY, James (1795–1865) Scottish doctor

Barry's story is one of the most bizarre in British army history. James Barry served all over the world as a doctor, rising to the rank of Inspector General of Hospitals – a role in which he sparred with *Florence Nightingale over standards of administration and hygiene. He seemed big and burly, and was nicknamed the 'Kapok doctor'. It was not until after his death that people discovered that 'James Barry' was actually a woman, Miranda Barry Stuart, and that she had borne a child. 'Kapok doctor' was literally true: she had stuffed her clothes to make herself look brawnier. Her masquerade apart, she did more to improve conditions in field medicine than anyone else of her generation, including Nightingale. Her story is told, in an enjoyable if slightly 'tabloid' way, in June Rose, *The Perfect Gentleman* (1977).

'Wild West Show').

> ✧ **READ ON**
> J.M. Barrie, *The Greenwood Hat* (reticent memoir – and perhaps therefore more revealing than he intended).

> ✧ **READ ON**
> Mary Seacole, *Wonderful Adventures of Mrs Seacole in Many Lands*. *Elspeth Huxley, *Florence Nightingale*.

> ◆ BATTLE SCARS *(professional soldiers)*
>
>
> Peter Earle, **Robert E. Lee*
> Peter Greenhalgh, **Pompey: The Roman Alexander; Pompey, the Republican Prince*
> Joseph Lehmann, *Remember You Are an Englishman* (**Harry Smith)
> William Manchester, *American Caesar* (**Douglas MacArthur)
> Donald Thomas, *Charge! Hurrah! Hurrah!* (**Lord Cardigan)
> Marina Warner **Joan of Arc*
> Jeremy Wilson, *Lawrence of Arabia* (**T.E. Lawrence)

BAUDELAIRE, Charles Pierre (1821–67) French poet

In his 20s Baudelaire was a rich young man-about-Paris, friend of artists and theatre people, known for outrageous opinions, affairs and a love of shocking the bourgeoisie. In the 1840s–50s he became obsessed with the work of Edgar Allan Poe, translating it, imitating it, and identifying with Poe's tormented heroes. Eventually his money ran out, and by his mid-30s he was deeply in debt – not to mention being reviled as a pornographer for his poetry collection *Flowers of Evil* (1857). He tried to escape soul-sickness (and the agonies of syphilis) by taking drink and drugs, and when he died at 46 he was physically destroyed, as withered as a man twice his age. Charles Baudelaire, *Intimate Journals* (Eng. ed. 1920) is a terrifying account of his descent into hell. Enid Starkie, *Baudelaire* (1957), in its day the standard English biography, gives a sympathetic account of his life, and is excellent on his poetry. Claude Pichois, *Baudelaire* (1987) contains less literary criticism, but is more up-to-date and makes outstanding use of letters and journals.

◆ **READ ON**
Charles Baudelaire, *Artificial Paradises* (account of the effects of drug-taking: partly a commentary on extracts from **De Quincey's *Confessions of an Opium Eater*).

BAUMANN, Janina (born 1926) Polish writer

Baumann was Jewish, and was already beginning to feel the barbs of anti-Semitism when Poland was invaded by Nazi Germany. She tells what happened in two books of autobiography, whose titles describe their contents: *Winter in the Morning: a Young Girl's Life in the Warsaw Ghetto and Beyond, 1939–45* (1986) and *A Dream of Belonging: My Years in Post-War Poland* (1988).

◆ **READ ON**
Elsbeth Rosenfeld, *The Four Lives of Elsbeth Rosenfeld* (about how the author chose to wear the yellow star, although she was only half-Jewish, and worked in the Munich ghetto. Shaming exposé of Second World War life, and of Kafkaesque bureaucratic harassment).

BEATON, Cecil (1904–80) English photographer

Beaton published six volumes of diaries *The Wandering Years* (1961), *The Years Between* (1965), *The Happy Years* (1972), *The Strenuous Years* (1973), *The Restless Years* (1976), *The Parting Years* (1978). They are more like biographical/autobiographical sketches than diaries, covering his career chronologically. Because he photographed many famous people, and travelled widely, he was at home in many of the social 'sets' of his time: the *Bloomsbury Group and Cliveden Set (*see* *Astor family), for example. His urbane pen-portraits include those of people as diverse as Garbo and the Duke of *Windsor, *Picasso and *Hearst, the British royal family and the Rolling Stones. Gentle wit enlivens every page, and so does his artistic eye: how interesting (if hardly earth-shattering), for example, to know that one of the Duke of Windsor's eyes was set lower than the other.

◇ READ ON
Eddie Marsh, *A Number of People* (autobiography of the rich civil servant, *Winston Churchill's private secretary for many years, who was the patron and friend of such people as Rupert Brooke, *Robert Graves, Paul Nash, Ivor Novello and Stanley Spencer).

BEAUHARNAIS, Joséphine (1763–1814) French empress

Daughter of a planter in Martinique, Joséphine married a visiting aristocrat and returned with him to Paris, just in time for the Terror. He was guillotined but she survived, to become a leading light of the dazzling society which emerged when the Terror ended. In 1796 she married *Napoléon, and when he became emperor she provided the gloss of culture and manners which his court might otherwise have lacked. Divorced in 1809 because she had borne no heir, she retired to Malmaison, where she laid out gardens which rivalled those of the Tuileries for imaginative design and for their collection of exotic plants and shrubs. E.J. Knapton, *The Empress Joséphine* (1963) is a scholarly biography, making good use of first-hand documents. Carola Oman, *Napoléon's Viceroy* (1966) is excellent on the way Joséphine created a court style for Napoléon to rival those of the most glittering European rulers of the past.

◇ READ ON
Nina Epton, *Joséphine* (good on Malmaison, and on Joséphine's affectionate relationship with her son and daughter by her first husband). Theo Aronson, *Napoléon and Joséphine*.

BEAUMARCHAIS, Pierre Augustin Caron de (1732–99) French adventurer and writer

Although Beaumarchais is remembered now as author of the satirical comedies on which *Rossini's *The Barber of Seville* and *Mozart's *The Marriage of Figaro* are based, he was actually one of the most extravagant adventurers of his time. Trained as a watchmaker, he wangled his way to court, taught the harp to Louis XV's daughters, married money, and became a secret agent, specializing in hushing up royal scandals. In the 1770s,

◇ READ ON
Edna Nixon, *Royal Spy: the Strange Case of the Chevalier d'Éon* (biography of one of Beaumarchais' secret-service colleagues, forced to spend much of his life lying low disguised as a woman).

seeing revolution in the air, he began arms dealing, first in America and then with both sides in the French Revolution. He was eventually arrested, and escaped the guillotine only because he was rescued by a mysterious woman who had adored him since she was 17. His life could be the plot of a novel by Dumas or Orczy, and Frédéric Grendel, *Beaumarchais, the Man Who Was Figaro* (Eng. ed. 1977) tells it with every bit of the swagger and swashbuckle that suggests.

BEAVERBROOK, William Maxwell Aitken, Lord (1879–1964) Canadian/English businessman and politician

Beaverbrook was a self-made millionaire who settled in Britain, became an MP, and served as Lloyd George's Minister of Information. In 1919 he founded the Express group of newspapers, whose editorial stance reflected his own maverick, Empire-loyal, crusading style. In the Second World War he was an outstanding Minister for Aircraft Production. A.J.P. Taylor, *Beaverbrook* (1972) is a masterly biography by a friend who said 'I loved Beaverbrook more than any human being I have ever known', but who still writes with incisiveness, historical objectivity and style.

⋄ **READ ON**
Logan Gourlay (ed.), *The Beaverbrook I Knew* (reminiscences by 34 people, touching on every aspect of Beaverbrook's life and personality). C.M. Vines, *A Little Nut-Brown Man* (funny memoir by one of Beaverbrook's secretaries). Janet Aitken Kidd, *The Beaverbrook Girl* (autobiography of Beaverbrook's daughter: an independent, extremely full life).

BECKWITH, Lilian (born 1916) English writer

Beckwith went to live on a small Hebridean island, for health reasons. In *The Hills is Lonely* (1959), the first of many humorous memoirs, she describes how her attempts to 'go native' usually failed, foiled by the ineffable good sense and politeness of the islanders.

⋄ **READ ON**
Angus MacVicar, *Salt in My Porridge.*

⋄ BEDTIME STORIES

(kissing and telling)

Lesley Blanch, *Game of Hearts: Harriet Wilson and her Memoirs*
Philippa Dullar, *F.H.* (*Frank Harris)
*Jakov Lind, *Numbers: a Further Autobiography*
Alan Lomax, *Mister Jelly Roll: the Fortunes of Jelly Roll Morton*
John Masters *Casanova
*Henry Miller, *Sexus*; *Nexus*; *Plexus*
Jean Prasteau, *The Lady of the Camellias*
*Georges Simenon, *When I Was Old*

BEECHAM, Thomas (1879–1961) English conductor

Heir to the Beecham's Pills fortune, Beecham used it to found his own orchestra, and to advance the cause of what were then avant-garde British composers, most notably Delius. He later championed Sibelius, and was also renowned for his silky-toned, beautifully shaped interpretations of *Mozart, *Schubert and Bizet. He was fond of acidly witty remarks, in rehearsal, in after-concert speeches and to the press, and his one-liners – which nowadays often seem plain rudeness rather than wit – salt biographies. A good example is Alan Jefferson, *Sir Thomas Beecham* (1979), an affectionate account (written for Beecham's centenary) of rehearsals and performances, spats with patrons, agents and soloists, and above all Beecham's relentless, and successful, struggle to bring grace and delicacy back to the 'land without music'.

▪> READ ON
Thomas Beecham, *A Mingled Chime* (purring, but clawed, autobiography, written in 1944). Bernard Shore, *The Orchestra Speaks* (includes some of the most memorable Beecham anecdotes).

BEERBOHM, Max (1872–1956) English artist and writer

A member of the 1890s set which also included Beardsley, *Wilde and Yeats, Beerbohm succeeded *Shaw as drama critic of the *Saturday Review*. He deployed his fastidious wit not only in journalism and essays but in caricatures for *Punch* and other magazines. He wrote one novel, the urbane satire *Zuleika Dobson* (1911), in which a beautiful girl causes havoc at Oxford University. His affable asperity is well caught in David Cecil, *Max* (1964), which is good on his life before the First World War and on his broadcasts in the 1930s. The book is illustrated with Beerbohm's own cartoons of the friends and acquaintances described.

▪> READ ON
Max Beerbohm, *Rossetti and His Circle* (biographical cartoons). Rupert Hart-Davis (ed.), *The Letters of Max Beerbohm*. Samuel Behrman, *Conversations with Max*.

BEETHOVEN, Ludwig van (1770–1827) German composer

The details of Beethoven's life are well known: his fiery youth as a piano virtuoso, his untidiness, his deafness, his abrupt, irascible manner. His quarrels with publishers, and his failed attempts to bring up his nephew Karl, are the stuff of comedy and tragedy respectively. Above all, his stature in the arts, as a creative giant on the level of *Shakespeare or *Michelangelo, leads memoir-writers and biographers to try to answer the questions 'where did his inspiration come from?' and 'how did he work?'.

Although Beethoven left no autobiography, F. Kerst and E. Krehbiel, *Beethoven: the Man and the Artist, as Revealed in his*

▪> READ ON
H.C. Robbins Landon, *Beethoven: a Documentary Study* (scholarly but absorbing collection of documents, on every aspect of Beethoven's life and work). E. and R. Sterba, *Beethoven and His Nephew*. Two standard biographies (which require some knowledge of the theory of music) are Alexander W. Thayer, *The Life of Ludwig van Beethoven* and Maynard Solomon, *Beethoven*.

Own Words (second Eng. ed. 1964) and A.C. Kalischer, *Beethoven's Letters* (second Eng. ed. 1972) are the next best thing, blunt or playful depending on Beethoven's mood. Emily Anderson (ed. and trans.), *The Letters of Beethoven* (three volumes, 1961) is complete, down to laundry lists and bills. Otto Sonneck (ed.), *Beethoven: Impressions By His Contemporaries* (second Eng. ed. 1967), chronologically arranged, is the source of most of the Beethoven anecdotes: stew in the piano, raging at thunderstorms, being turned at concerts to face the applauding audience he couldn't hear. Alan Kendall, *The Life of Beethoven* (1978) covers all such points, and is good on Beethoven's personality and the creation and reception of his music. It is well illustrated, and avoids technicality. Marion Scott, *Beethoven* (second ed. 1974) discusses Beethoven's main works (technically) in the context of his life.

BEETON, Mrs

'Mrs Beeton', author of *Mrs Beeton's Book of Household Management* (1859), was actually two people: the publisher **Samuel Beeton** (1831–77) and his wife and principal author **Isabella Beeton** (1836–65). Sam made his first coup at 21, securing the English rights to Harriet Beecher Stowe's *Uncle Tom's Cabin*, and used the money this brought in to set up a firm publishing guides, encyclopedias, humour, children's books and a weekly magazine, *Englishwoman's Domestic Magazine*. Isabella (who married him in 1856) wrote magazine columns and full-length books on cooking, gardening, etiquette and letter-writing, as well as children's stories and biographies and other entries for the encyclopedias. They worked 20 hours a day, building up a publishing empire and making a fortune which they had no time to spend. Sarah Freeman, *Isabella and Sam* (1977), their joint biography, is a tribute to Victorian energy and enterprise, but also shows how much it cost in terms of unhappy family life and ruined health: Isabella died at 28 and Sam at 46.

> **READ ON**
> Nancy Spain, *Mrs Beeton and her husband*. H. Montgomery Hyde, *Mr and Mrs Beeton: a Joint Biography*.

BEHN, Aphra (1640–89) English writer

Behn coped with contemporary views of what women should and should not do by ignoring them. In her early 20s she visited Surinam, was involved in a slave rebellion and discovered an Amerindian tribe no other European had ever seen. In the Dutch Wars which followed the accession of Charles II she acted as a royal spy. From 1670 onwards she earned her living as novelist and playwright. She had 17 plays performed in London: most of them bawdy, swaggering comedies. Her 'novels' (the first ever written in English) include *Orinooko*, a denunciation of slavery. Much attacked during her lifetime for

> **READ ON**
> Kathleen Jones, *A Glorious Fame* (about Margaret Cavendish, Duchess of Newcastle, a contemporary of Behn whose 'eccentricities', in male eyes, included writing books and plays).

lewdness which men declared unbecoming to her sex, she was honoured after death with a memorial in Westminster Abbey.

Behn's reputation lapsed until the 1920s, when *Virginia Woolf wrote admiringly about her (in *A Room of One's Own*) as the first professional woman writer in Britain. In the 1970s two biographies were published, Behn's work was rediscovered, and she was restored to her rightful place as a minor but lively figure in Restoration English literature. The books are Maureen Duffy, *The Passionate Shepherdess* (1977), which takes a British feminist point of view and is particularly good on Behn and the theatre, and Angeline Goreau, *Reconstructing Aphra* (1980), by a US specialist on 17th-century sexual and social attitudes to women.

BELL, Gertrude (1868–1926) English traveller

Bell used her wealth to travel. From her 20s onwards she explored Europe, climbed the Alps, and in particular spent years criss-crossing the Middle East. Wherever she went she wrote clear-headed, witty letters describing people, places, archaeological sights and politics. During the First World War she served as Political Officer in Baghdad and worked with *T.E. Lawrence's Arab Bureau; after the war she was one of those whose dream was realized by the creation of the state of Iraq. Her *Letters* (ed. Florence Bell, 1927) are difficult to get hold of, but repay the effort. Elizabeth Burgoyne, *Gertrude Bell* (two volumes, 1958, 1961) is a fair substitute, as it quotes copiously from the letters – a sensible, if self-immolating, choice on Burgoyne's part.

> ❖ **READ ON**
> H.V.F. Winston, *Gertrude Bell* (1978) (draws on many sources as well as Bell's letters, and has a good bibliography – but still, like Burgoyne, comes off second-best compared with Bell's own writing). Reader Bullard, *The Camels Must Go* (autobiography).

❖ BELOW STAIRS

(Domestic Service)

Céleste Albaret, *Monsieur Proust*
Hannah Cullwick, *Diaries of *Hannah Cullwick*
*Monica Dickens, *One Pair of Hands*
Michael Harrison, *Rosa* (Rosa Lewis)
*Margaret Powell, *Below Stairs*
Jean Rennie, *Every Other Sunday*

BENNETT, Arnold (1867–1931) English writer

Novelist (best known for the 'Five Towns' books), playwright and journalist (among other things, editor of *Woman*), Bennett was a popular figure in literary and theatrical circles, and was also a workaholic: he wrote some half a million words each

> ❖ **READ ON**
> James Hepburn (ed.), *Arnold Bennett: Letters* (three volumes, chatty, self-revealing and businesslike as anything else Bennett wrote). Marguerite

year, and published altogether over 100 books. He loved sailing, opera, the theatre and all things French. He wrote a series of ebullient *Journals* (for a good selection, see the years 1932–3), and several autobiographical articles (collected in James Hepburn (ed.), *Arnold Bennett: Sketches for Autobiography* (1979)). The standard biography, Margaret Drabble, *Arnold Bennett* (1974), assesses Bennett's character and writings so enthusiastically that you rush to read the man himself.

BENNETT, J(ohn) G(odolphin) (1898–?) English writer

Bennett had a distinguished career as a research scientist, and also led a second, parallel life as a searcher for mystical truth, for the wholeness of humanity which could only be found (he believed) by tapping into extra-sensory, extra-intellectual reality. He became a follower of Gurdjieff, whose disciples practised rituals and meditations to release themselves into higher states of understanding. Bennett's autobiography *Witness* (1962) gives an account of his two lives, and is particularly good at explaining how mystical experience, however baffling it may seem to outsiders, can illuminate and transform the believer's personality. As Hamlet says to Horatio, 'There are more things in heaven and earth . . . than are dreamed of in your philosophy': that is the area this book explores.

BERENSON, Bernard (1865–1959) US art historian

The cash value of artworks increases dramatically when they are attributed to a great painter. If, therefore, a collector buys cheaply an artwork of doubtful attribution, and then has it assigned to a famous artist, huge profits can be made. Berenson was renowned for the authority of his attributions, but after his death it became known that he had charged a large percentage of the upward-valued prices for his opinions, and accusations of shady dealing inevitably followed. Sylvia Sprigge, *Berenson, a Biography* (1960), written before all this came out, is awestruck both by 'BB' himself and by the actual work of fine-art dealing. Meryle Secrest, *Being Bernard Berenson* (1979) leaves no stone of business scandal unturned, and discusses Berenson's infuriating, amusing, egotistical personality in terms of his determined abandonment of his Jewish-Lithuanian heritage: an approach which would have turned the old man puce with rage.

BERLIOZ, Hector (1803–69) French composer

Berlioz was a typical early Romantic: a rebellious student, a

Bennett (his wife), *My Arnold Bennett*).

⋄ **READ ON**
J.G. Bennett, *Gurdjieff: Making a New World* (partly a biography of Gurdjieff, but also a lucid description of his ideas and beliefs). *Christmas Humphreys, *Both Sides of the Circle* (autobiography, in very similar terms to Bennett's, of an English judge who was also a leading Buddhist).

⋄ **READ ON**
Bernard Berenson, *Rumour and Reflection*; *Sketch for Self-Portrait* (reticent autobiographies). Nicky Mariano, *Forty Years with B. B.* (memoir by Berenson's assistant and possible lover of more than 40 years). Mary Berenson (his wife), *Mary Berenson: a Self-Portrait from her Letters and Diaries*).

⋄ **READ ON**
Peter Raby, *Fair Ophelia* (biography of the actress *Harriet Smithson, who inspired

traveller ever eager for new experiences, a composer whose works seemed to revel in free expression and in outraging the bourgeoisie. His dazzling *Memoirs* (trans. David Cairns, 1969) depict him as a swaggering, swashbuckling champion of new ideas, music's equivalent of Cyrano de Bergerac or one of the Three Musketeers. His *Letters* (good selection, ed. Humphrey Searle, 1966) similarly blend self-glorification, gush and wit. Zestful biographies are David Cairns, *Berlioz 1803–1832: the Making of an Artist* (1989), the first of a projected pair, and D. Kern Holoman, *Berlioz* (1990). A good study (sometimes technical) of Berlioz as a musician of his time is Jacques Barzun, *Berlioz and the Romantic Century* (second ed. 1969).

Berlioz's *Fantastic Symphony* and whom he later married). Michael Ayrton, *Berlioz: a Singular Obsession* (fascinating study, by another artist, of Berlioz's genius and creative methods).

BERNHARDT, Sarah (1844–1923) French actress

The greatest French classical actress of her day, Bernhardt was as famous for her tantrums, her love affairs and her zestful private life (travelling the world, sculpting, nursing during the siege of Paris, hamming it up in silent films) as she was renowned in such parts as Phèdre, the Woman of the Camellias and (in later life, playing in French while everyone else spoke English) Hamlet. She seemed larger than life, and the best biographies gush and throb appropriately: Joanna Richardson, *Sarah Bernhardt* (rev. ed. 1980), for example, is crammed with anecdotes, letters, reviews and evocative pictures. Its bibliography will lead to a dozen other books – Bernhardt lives.

⚬> READ ON
Sarah Bernhardt, *My Double Life* (no-holds-barred memoirs). Lysiane Bernhardt, *Sarah Bernhardt: My Grandmother*. Françoise Sagan, *Dear Sarah Bernhardt* (letters, all by Sagan: an imaginary correspondence with her lifetime's idol). Joanna Richardson, *Sarah Bernhardt and Her World*.

BERNSTEIN, Leonard (1918–90) US composer and conductor

As a conductor, Bernstein exuded energy, crouching, leaping, swaying and going into ecstasies to seduce the sounds he wanted from an orchestra. The same kind of passion and tension marked his compositions, whether 'serious' (*Mass*, *Chichester Psalms*, symphonies) or 'Broadway' (*West Side Story*, *Candide*, *On the Town*). From the moment of his debut, conducting the New York Philharmonic Orchestra at one day's notice, he was one of the world's most famous and flamboyant musicians, loved and scorned as only a superstar can be. Peter Gradenwitz, *Leonard Bernstein* (1987) tries to pin down Bernstein's qualities as performer and composer, and includes excellent (if partly technical) commentaries on his works. Michael Freedland, *Leonard Bernstein* (1987) and Joan Peyser, *Leonard Bernstein* (1987) are no-holds-barred 'intimate lives', stuffed with anecdotes about such subjects as Bernstein's bisexuality,

⚬> READ ON
Burton Bernstein, *Family Matters: Sam, Jennie and the Kids* (family memoirs by Bernstein's brother).

the good or bad ways he treated fellow-musicians, and his behaviour as a media personality, never out of the public eye.

BESANT, Annie (1847–1933) English mystic

Few people, even in a guide to biographies, can be more astonishing than Besant. A clergyman's wife in mid-Victorian England, she divorced him (causing scandal) and began lecturing
on atheism, free love and birth control. She became a Fabian,
and *Shaw said that she was the best speaker on socialism he
had ever heard. In 1889 she became a Theosophist, and in
1895 she settled in India, took up the causes of women's education and the abolition of the caste system, and preceded
*Gandhi as President of the Indian National Congress. In 1911
she identified a 15-year-old boy, *Krishnamurti, as the Star of
the East, the Universal Saviour. She went on preaching and
teaching for the Theosophical Society until she was in her 80s,
and her followers still believe that she is not dead but has
simply 'suspended her work', and will be reincarnated at some
future date. Arthur H. Nethercot, in *The First Five Lives of Annie Besant* (1961) and *The Last Four Lives of Annie Besant* (1963),
tells of this and much, much more. For believers, and certainly
for sceptics, they are compulsive.

> **READ ON**
> Annie Besant, *Autobiography*
> (1891 account of her years in
> England, and above all of her
> conversion).

BETJEMAN, John (1906–84) English poet

Betjeman as an 'aesthete' at Oxford comes over like one of the
minor characters in *Waugh's *Brideshead Revisited*: the
pampered middle- or upper-class Edwardian at play. Later, as
a friend of such people as the *Mitfords and *Randolph
Churchill, and as a cuddly TV pundit on things suburban, Victorian and Edwardian (*The Times* called him 'teddy bear to the
nation'), he continued to have a wonderfully jolly time. His poetry sends it, his fellow countrymen and himself up with a wist-
fulness, tartness and sensitivity seldom seen in his extrovert
public manner. He wrote a bestselling, blank-verse autobiography, *Summoned By Bells* (1960), about his childhood, his miserable schooldays and his happiness at Oxford. Bevis Hillier,
Young Betjeman (1988), covers similar ground affectionately, but
with a shrewd eye for the follies and excesses of the time.

> **READ ON**
> Bevis Hillier, *John Betjeman, A
> Life in Pictures* (splendid, well-
> captioned collection of drawings,
> snapshots and paintings from
> each stage of Betjeman's life).

BEVAN, Aneurin (1897–1960) Welsh politician

However high Bevan rose among the 'great and good', he never
forgot the privations of his early years in the mines, or the people who still endured them, and this awareness of ordinariness
made him stand out in a British political scene dominated by
ex-university smoothies, just as the force of his intellect was

> **READ ON**
> Aneurin Bevan, *In Place of Fear*
> (1952) (book of personal
> philosophy: Foot calls it a
> striking attempt to 'reconcile his
> individualism and his
> collectivism'). Jennie Lee

rare in the Labour Party of his day. He revelled in books, music and intellectual argument, and shared *Winston Churchill's love of rhetoric and debate – their verbal duels still leap from the pages of any biography.

Michael Foot, *Aneurin Bevan* is the standard, two-volume biography of Bevan. Volume one (1962) covers Bevan's life until 1945; volume two (1974) describes his years in government and opposition, giving particular attention to his work as post-war Minister of Health and creator of the National Health Service. Foot writes with eloquence and admiration which never slips into sycophancy. He explains complex, distant political intrigues with lucidity, going into minute detail without ever boring the reader or losing the thread of his overall design. Political biographies are commonplace; this book, thanks to Foot's writing and Bevan's personality, should fascinate even those who find all politics, and Labour politics in particular, not to their taste. Mark M. Krug, *Cautious Rebel* (1961) is shorter, but offers British readers especially the freshness of a US perspective on our politics, and is particularly good on Bevan's (often anti-American) foreign policy.

(Bevan's wife), *This Great Journey*; *My Life With Nye* (autobiographies).

> ⌁ BEYOND THE HORIZON
>
> *(travellers)*
>
> Robert Fortune, *A Journey to the Tea Countries*
> Margaret Fountaine, *Love Among the Butterflies*
> Peter Hopkirk, *Trespassers on the Roof of the World*
> Richard Humble, **Marco Polo*
> Fitzroy MacLean, *A Person From England*
> Frank McLynn, **Richard Burton*
> Eric Newby, *Traveller's Life*
> Peter Sackville, *Adventure Calling: a Chronicle of Some of the Wanderings of Anthony Tovens in Chile, Peru, Brazil and Most of the South American Republics*
> *Wilfred Thesiger, *Desert, Marsh and Mountain*
> H.V.F. Winston, **Gertrude Bell*
> *See also* To Boldly Go . . .

BIELENBERG, Christabel (born 1909) Irish/German housewife

Irish-born Bielenberg married a Hamburg lawyer, took German citizenship, and lived in Germany throughout the Nazi era and and Second World War. One of her husband's friends was Adam von Trott (one of those involved in the 1944 bomb plot against *Hitler), and after the plot Peter Bielenberg was ar-

⌁ **READ ON**
Christopher Sykes, *Troubled Loyalty: a biography of Adam von Trott du Solz.*

rested, leaving Christabel to manage alone. Her book *The Past Is Myself* (1968) is an unforgettable account of all that happened, and particularly of the way ordinary German civilians behaved and thought during the war. And not just civilians: some of the book's most moving pages tell how, on a train, she met an ex-SS officer who described how his original high ideals crumbled to self-disgust as he followed orders to kill Jews in cold blood, and how he was now hoping for honourable death at the front. Contents like this make the book a grim read, but its tally of ordinary human decency, in appalling circumstances, is also high – and heartwarming.

‹› BIG BUSINESS

Stanley Chapman, *Jesse Boot of Boots the Chemist*
Edwin Palmer Holt, * *'Commodore' Vanderbilt*
R. Miller, *Bunny: the Real Story of Playboy* (Hugh Hefner)

Patrick O'Higgins, *Madame* (Helena Rubinstein)
Andrew Sinclair, *Corsair: the Life of J. Pierpoint *Morgan*
William A. Swanberg, *Citizen Hearst* (*William Randolph Hearst)
Bob Thomas, *King Cohn* (Harry Cohn)
Joseph F. Wall, **Andrew Carnegie*
John Winkler, *Five and Ten: the Fabulous Life of F.W. Woolworth*

BIHALY, Andrew (1935–68) Hungarian/US writer

Anyone who believes that the 20th century has shown the human race at its rock-bottom worst will find proof in Bihaly's *The Journal of Andrew Bihaly* (1973). A Jew, Bihaly's father died on the *Eichmann Death March, and when the child (aged nine) was sent to a monastery to escape the Nazis, he was gang-raped and brutalized. Eventually escaping to the US, he became a beggar, thief and drug addict, a psychological waif pressing his nose against the window of psychedelic happiness – or at least forgetfulness – in the 1960s. Despairing and bereft, he committed suicide in 1968, leaving this horrifying book, a diary of his last two years which also recounts and reflects on the tragedy that was his life. This is one of those books blurbwriters call 'Dostoevskian' (that is, relentlessly horrific) and say 'you must read'. It may also devastate your sleep.

‹› **READ ON**

Jean Genet, *The Thief's Journal* (fantasy autobiography of a boy brutalized into crime). Ultra Violet, *Famous for Fifteen Minutes* (the 1960s New York drugs scene, from the point of view of one of *Warhol's 'stars').

> ❖ BIOGRAPHICAL NOVELS
>
> Alan Brien, *Lenin*
> Lloyd C. Douglas, *The Big Fisherman* (St Peter)
> Margaret Irwin, *Young Bess* (*Elizabeth I)
> Thomas Keneally, *Blood Red, Sister Rose* (*Joan of Arc)
> Sue Limb, *The Wordsmiths of Gorsemere* (the *Wordsworths)
> James Paterson, *Gerontius* *(Elgar)
> Josef Škvorecky, *Dvořák in Love*
> Irving Stone, *The Agony and the Ecstasy* (*Michelangelo); *Lust for Life* (*Van Gogh)

BISMARCK, Otto von (1815–98) German statesman

Bismarck's political achievement – uniting Germany – was immense, and the means he used were conceived on an equally vast canvas. His political principles and legacy make a happy hunting ground for historians, just as the character of a man who could redraw the map of Europe at will, and yet had no idea how to treat his own king, is a feast for biographers and their readers. A.J.P. Taylor, *Bismarck: the Man and the Statesman* (1955) is a classic historical account. It is short, but nevertheless guides us through the tricky political and philosophical country of what Bismarck actually did, and ends with a fascinating discussion of how later German generations saw him. Edward Crankshaw, *Bismarck* (1982) is more concerned with Bismarck's character-contradictions, and with the achievement, use and effects of power. Each book is a good read in its own right, and they work well in tandem.

> ❖ **READ ON**
> Otto von Bismarck, *Reflections and Reminiscences* (not the lightest of reads, but gives a fair idea of the 'Iron Chancellor's' manner and character).

BLACK, Shirley Temple (born 1928) US film star and politician

Shirley Temple first acted at three years old, was an Oscar-winning professional by six and made 40 films – her teenage roles less satisfying than her bouncy, unsentimental performances as a tot – before retiring at 21. She made a second career as wife and mother, a third as company director and a fourth as politician: US representative to the United Nations, ambassador to Ghana and Czechoslovakia. Her book *Child Star* (1988) was a deliberate counter to the nonsense written about her when she was 'the world's sweetheart' in the 1930s, or the speculation about her adolescent love-life in the

> ❖ **READ ON**
> Anne Edwards, *Shirley Temple* (sympathetic 1988 biography, excellent on Black's adult life).
> Marc Best, *Those Endearing Young Charms: Child Performers of the Screen*.

1940s. It is a witty, candid picture of life in the Hollywood dream-factory, and (unlike so many other accounts) rings true without losing a moment's fascination. It ends with her retirement from films, and the start of her marriage to Charles Black. A second volume, covering the rest of her busy life, is promised, but this book is complete in itself: a whole career, from apprenticeship to retirement, lived in the time it takes most of us just to discover who we are.

BLAKE, William (1757–1827) English artist and poet

Blake struggled all his life to express in words and pictures a vision of the universe which blended humanism and Christian mysticism, while rejecting the scientific and social rationalism of the time. His work uses simple means to express complex ideas, and his life has a similar blend of simplicity and elusiveness. While no book about him can be an easy read, *Jack Lindsay, *William Blake* (1978) comes close, thanks to elegant prose, thorough research and a clear-headed view of the relationship between Blake's life and work. Other books, concentrating on more specific matters, include J. Bronowski, *William Blake and the Age of Revolution* (1944 and 1965); D.V. Erdman, *Blake: Prophet Against Empire* (1954) and Harold Bloom, *Blake's Apocalypse* (1963).

⋄ **READ ON**
M. Bottrall (ed.), *William Blake: Songs of Innocence and Experience*. Geoffrey Keynes (ed.), *The Letters of William Blake*. A. Gilchrist, *The Life of William Blake* and M. Wilson, *The Life of William Blake* are standard and readable biographies.

BLAVATSKY, Helena Petrovna (Madam) (1831–91) Russian mystic

After travelling in the East (especially to Tibet, a country visited by few westerners in the 1860s), Blavatsky toured the world as a spirit medium. Although the Society for Psychic Research condemned her as a fraud, her followers never wavered, and she had over 100,000 clients, ranging from ordinary people to the Russian court. In 1875 she founded the Theosophical Society, devoted to spiritual (and spiritualist) exercises intended to lead to mystical understanding of, and union with, the divine. (This was the society later led by *Annie Besant.) John Symonds, *Madame Blavatsky* (1959) begins from scepticism: Symonds knew little more of Blavatsky than her name and her reputation outside Theosophical circles as an eccentric fraud. He investigates her life, meeting ever weirder characters at every turn, and ends up by telling us everything without ever abandoning his robust, good-humoured and objective stance. The book is a model of research, and reads like a traveller's tale from one of the most bizarre corners of the human psyche: not to be missed.

⋄ **READ ON**
Henry Steel Olcott, *Old Diary Leaves* (rambling memoirs, based on journals, by the ex-Civil War soldier, lawyer, private detective and spiritualist who became Blavatsky's most faithful US follower and companion).

BLIGH, William (1754–1817) English sailor

To film fans, Bligh is known as the tyrannical captain of the *Bounty*, whose injustice caused Fletcher Christian and the crew to mutiny. Navy records, by contrast, show him as a capable officer, a companion of *Cook, a governor of New South Wales (where there was a second mutiny against him, after a squabble over rum rations) and a reforming civil servant. The first mutiny is well described in Richard Hough, *Captain Bligh and Mr Christian* (rev. ed. 1979), the second in H.V. Evatt, *Rum Rebellion* (1947). Gavin Kennedy, *Captain Bligh: the Man and his Mutinies* (rev. ed. 1990) tries to sort out fact from legend, and is particularly good on the problems Bligh faced, not only because of conditions on board ship and in newly colonized Australia, but because of his own psychological inadequacy.

⊹ **READ ON**
Paul Brunton (ed.), *Awake, Bold Bligh!* (Bligh's letters describing the mutiny on the *Bounty*). Ida Lee (ed.), *Captain Bligh: Second Voyage* (Bligh's memoirs of the *Bounty* voyage, without a hint of self-justification or self-doubt).

BLISHEN, Edward (born 1920) English writer

Blishen, a broadcaster and children's writer, is also known for half a dozen books of memoirs. Instead of taking its place in a consecutive autobiography, each focuses on a different area of experience. Blishen's style is like good conversation, as if he were telling you every passing thought on music, books, buildings, the weather and above all the characters and turns of phrase of the people in his story. Autobiography which reads like a novel is an English speciality, and Blishen is one of its masters. The books include *Roaring Boys* (1955), about teaching in a tough secondary modern school; *Donkey Work* (1983), about what happened when *Roaring Boys* made him famous overnight, an educational pundit on two continents; *A Cack-Handed War* (1972), about his experiences as a pacifist during Second World War, *Sorry, Dad* (1978), centring on his relationship with his father, and *Shaky Relations* (1981).

⊹ **READ ON**
Edward Blishen, *A Nest of Teachers* (about training and practising to be a teacher); *The Disturbance Fee* (on his life as writer and broadcaster). Philip Oakes, *From Middle England*; *Dwellers All in Time and Space*; *At the Jazz Band Ball* (autobiographical trilogy, similar in style, tone and events to Blishen's books).

BLOOM, Fanny (1807–?) English parson's wife

Illegitimate daughter of a gypsy and a rich farmer, Fanny was brought up by her father, became a great beauty (nicknamed 'the Rose of Norfolk'), was presented at court and married a royal chaplain. She and her husband seemed set for a placid, devoted existence, but it turned out as lurid as any stage melodrama of the time: adultery, abandoned babies, lost fortunes, a mysterious servant (Fanny's mother, though Fanny's husband never knew), TB and a Dickensian court case. Ursula Bloom (Fanny's great-granddaughter), *The Rose of Norfolk* (1964) tells all: a historical romance in which every word is true.

⊹ **READ ON**
Ursula Bloom, *Parson Extraordinary* (biography of the author's father: the saga continued).

BLOOMSBURY GROUP

The Bloomsbury Group, a loose association of writers, artists and critics, was formed in 1905, when Thoby Stephen invited some of his university friends to an 'at home' in the house he shared with his brother and sisters in Bloomsbury, London. In the years that followed, at this and several other addresses, people came and went, forming a network of friendships, marriages and love affairs. Although several protested that there was no such thing as a formal 'group', they shared tastes, interests and an approach to the arts, politics and sociology which affected those areas of British life in the 1920s–40s and are still of interest today. The 'Bloomsberries' (as they were nicknamed) were also famed for obsessive self-documentation: diaries, memoirs, biographies and letters poured out as if on a production line. Another cause of interest is their freedom in sexual matters: in Bloomsbury bedrooms, every variety of sex was tried and the visitor's books were crammed. Our list of books here is the tip of a huge iceberg: to include everything written by everyone ever associated with Bloomsbury would have filled this book.

Composite books on Bloomsbury:
Leon Edel, *Bloomsbury: A House of Lions* (1979) (good on the early days)
Quentin Bell, *Bloomsbury* (1968) (insider's overview)
J.K. Johnstone, *The Bloomsbury Group* (1964) (critical overview)
Richard Shone, *Bloomsbury Portraits* (1976) (concentrating on the painters)

Books by or about the main members of the Bloomsbury Group:
Bell, Clive (1881–1964) (art critic, husband of Vanessa):
Clive Bell, *Old Friends: Personal Recollections* (1956)
Bell, Vanessa, née Stephen (1879–1961) (painter):
Frances Spalding, *Vanessa Bell* (1983)
Fry, Roger (1966–1934) (painter and critic):
Denyss Sutton (ed.), *Letters of Roger Fry* (1972)
Virginia Woolf, *Roger Fry: a Biography* (1940)
Grant, Duncan (1885–1978) (painter and critic):
Roger Fry, *Duncan Grant* (1930)
Raymond Mortimer, *Duncan Grant* (1948)
Keynes, John Maynard (1883–1946) (economist):
R.F. Harrod, *The Life of John Maynard Keynes* (1951)
F.A. Keynes, *Gathering Up the Threads: a Study in Family Biography* (1951)
Robert Skidelsky, *John Maynard Keynes* (1983)
MacCarthy, Desmond (1878–1952) (literary critic):
Desmond MacCarthy, *Memoirs* (1953)

‹› **READ ON**
S.P. Rosenbaum (ed.), *The Bloomsbury Group* (collection of writings by and about the group, some critical). Michael Holroyd, *Lytton Strachey* (contains superb description of the whole Bloomsbury phenomenon). Peter Quennell, *Customs and Characters: Contemporary Portraits* (autobiography, juicy with Bloomsbury personalities). Mary Ann Caws, *Women of Bloomsbury: Virginia, Vanessa and Carrington*.

Hugh and Mirabel Cecil, *Clever Hearts* (1990) (joint biography of Desmond and Molly MacCarthy)
Mary MacCarthy (Molly) (1882–1953) (writer; founder of the Memoir Club, supposed to be a diversion for the Group, but which became practically an industry):
Mary MacCarthy, *A Nineteenth-Century Childhood* (1924)
See also: *Strachey, Lytton; *Woolf, Leonard; *Woolf, Virginia.
Bloomsbury associates:
E.M. Forster (1879–1970) (novelist):
P.N. Furbank, *E.M. Forster*
David Garnett (1892–1981) (novelist):
David Garnett, *The Golden Echo* (1954); *Flowers of the Forest* (1955); *The Familiar Faces* (1962) (autobiographies); *Carrington: Letters and Extracts from her Diaries*
C.G. Heilburn, *The Garnett Family* (1961)
Angelica Garnett née Bell (born 1918) (daughter of Duncan Grant and Vanessa Bell; married the much older David Garnett):
Angelica Garnett, *Deceived With Kindness* (1984)
Lydia Keynes, née Lopokova (ballerina; wife of John Maynard Keynes):
Milo Keynes, *Lydia Lopokova* (1983)
See also: *Dorothy Brett, *Ottoline Morrell, *Frances Partridge and *Alison Waley.

BLYTON, Enid (1897–1968) English writer

In the 1940s–50s Blyton was the best known of all English-language writers for children. She published some 600 books, and her creations – Noddy, Bom, the Faraway Tree, the Famous Five – introduced millions of children to the pleasures of reading. In the 1960s her reputation began to slump among adults: her books were branded snobbish, racist and stylistically deplorable, and were banned from many bookshops and library shelves, though children still adored them. After her death rumours began to circulate that many of her books were ghosted, that she was an inadequate or harsh mother, and articles were published speculating about her psychology. Barbara Stoney, *Enid Blyton* (1974), the authorized biography, is bland on all such matters, but excellent on Blyton's public life (especially her charity and wartime work). It also contains a complete, staggering, list of Blyton's books. Imogen Smallwood, *A Childhood at Green Hedges* (1989), by Blyton's younger daughter, gives a more intimate, bleaker and far less flattering account.

‹› **READ ON**
Charles Osborne, *The Life and Crimes of Agatha Christie* (about another literary phenomenon; *see* *Agatha Christie).

BOGARDE, Dirk (born 1921) English actor and writer

Bogarde's early films were thrillers (for example *The Blue Lamp*) or lightweight comedies (for example *Doctor in the House*). Later, he went on to more substantial acting roles (for example, in *The Servant* and *Death in Venice*). Margaret Hinxman, *The Films of Dirk Bogarde* (1974) gives a good critical and biographical account. In the 1970s Bogarde began a second career as a writer, and published three volumes of memoirs: *A Postillion Struck By Lightning* (1977), a sensitive account of childhood and growing up; *Snakes and Ladders* (1978), about his switchback early career, and *An Orderly Man* (1983), about middle age and semi-retirement in his beautiful French farmhouse. There is nothing remotely showbizzy about these books: they are atmospheric and evocative, in a literary style somewhat like *Collette's.

> ⋗ **READ ON**
> Dirk Bogarde, *A Gentle Occupation; Voices in the Garden* (novels); *A Particular Friendship* (letters to an American pen-friend whom he never met: intimate and appealing, descriptions of his life and ideas from 1967 to 1972).

BOGART, Humphrey (1899–1957) US film star

Bogart began his film career playing sneering, psychotic gangsters, but in the 1940s became known for deeper roles: men of action who were also mysterious, vulnerable, troubled and self-mocking. In Hollywood he was notorious for his roistering lifestyle, and for his love for his wife Lauren Bacall. There are hundreds of biographies, ranging from scholarly studies of his work to sensationalism about his life. The best-balanced (including both comment and gossip, but going for facts and trying to account for Bogart's immense popularity, on and off the screen) are Nathaniel Benchley, *Humphrey Bogart* (1958) and Ezra Goodman, *Bogey: the Good Bad Guy* (1965). One of the most zestful 'kiss and tell' accounts is Verita Thompson, *Bogey and Me* (1979), about a professional relationship (she was a makeup artist) and love affair which lasted from 1942 until Bogart's death.

> ⋗ **READ ON**
> Clifford McCarthy, *Bogey: the Films of Humphrey Bogart*. Lauren Bacall, *Lauren Bacall*.

BOLIVAR, Simón (1783–1830) South American revolutionary leader

Inspired by the French Revolution, Bolívar set out to free South America from Spanish rule. In a series of dazzling campaigns, he and his generals liberated Chile, Colombia, Ecuador, Venezuela and Peru (part of which was renamed Bolivia in Bolívar's honour). It was Bolívar's dream to create a United States of South America, but political opposition and factional quarrels forced him to abandon this in favour of increasingly despotic personal rule: the first of the military

> ⋗ **READ ON**
> Gabriel García Márquez, *The General in His Labyrinth* (fictional meditation of Bolívar in his paranoid last years, by the dean of South American novelists).

dictatorships from which South America has never since been free. Salvador de Madariaga, *Bolívar* (1951) is a magisterial literary biography, a classic of the genre. D. Bushnell, *The Liberator: Simón Bolívar* (1970) is no match for de Madariaga in style, but is shorter and historically more objective.

BONANNO, Joseph (born 1904) US Mafia boss

What is the Mafia? How did the concept of the Family arise in well-mannered, pious Sicily, and what made it plant such strong roots in alien US soil? Joseph Bonanno (with Sergio Lalli), *A Man of Honour* (1983) gives a glimpse into the Mafia's terrifying but self-consistent world. Bonanno ('Joe Bananas') was the most honoured leader of the entire US Mafia, the Don of Dons, and this is his autobiography. The power of what he says is doubled by the smooth, 'crinkly-eyed old man' style in which he writes. 'Thank God I can still laugh!' he says in the introduction. Thank God indeed.

⊳ **READ ON**
Mario Puzo, *The Godfather* (novel about Don Corleone, the Mafia boss for whom Bonanno may have been Puzo's model). Denis Eisenberg, Uri Dan and Eli Landau, *Meyer Lansky, Mogul of the Mob* (biography, based on Meyer's own testimony, of the man at the heart of the US Mafia gambling operation in the 1930s–60s: not only mogul but banker to the Mob).

BORGIA family

Few ruling families of the Italian Renaissance have a worse reputation than the Borgias – and there are plenty of contenders. Three family members, Pope Alexander VI (**Rodrigo Borgia**, 1431–1503), his son **Cesare Borgia** (1476–1507) and his daughter (and supposed mistress) **Lucrezia Borgia** (1480–1519) have been accused of every conceivable crime: adultery, bribery, incest, mass murder. They were also extremely rich, patrons of the arts and experts at political intrigue – this last probably the cause of all the other stories about their ruthlessness. Biographies of the whole family, sorting out truth from fiction, are led by Marion Johnson, *The Borgias* (1981), accessible to the general reader and well illustrated, and Michael Mallett, *The Borgias: the Rise and Fall of a Renaissance Dynasty* (1969), more technical and more full of historical complexity. Biographies of individual members of the family: A.H. Matthew, *The Life and Times of Alexander Borgia* (1912); S. Bradford, *Cesare Borgia, His Life and Times* (1976); M. Bellonci, *The Life and Times of Lucrezia Borgia* (Eng. ed. 1953).

⊳ **READ ON**
R. Ridolfi, *Life of Girolamo Savonarola* (*see* *Savonarola).

BOSTON, L(ucy) M(aria) (1892–1990) English writer

Boston is best known for the *Green Knowe* children's books, about an old English manor house and the people who lived there. Her autobiography *Perverse and Foolish* (1979) describes her strict Methodist childhood, and how, through a combination of innocence and determination, she regularly strayed from

⊳ **READ ON**
L.M. Boston, *Memory in a House* (sequel, taking up her story from the 1940s, this time as seen through the 'glass' of the manor house at Hemingford Grey, for which she had deep affection. The book, essential background for the *Green Knowe* books,

the rigid tenets of her family. In her early 20s she went to nurse in France during the First World War, and her reactions are as deeply felt (though not in the same literary style) as *Vera Brittain's. Throughout the book, she writes with the same unaffected clarity as in her fiction, emphasizing events as she remembers them, not reordering them by hindsight.

describes the restoration of the house, her garden and her rose-growing, as well as carrying on, in a charming, spasmodic way, the story of her life).

BOSWELL, James (1740–95) Scottish lawyer and writer

Ambitious for fame, Boswell moved to London and talked himself into friendship with great and good men, and into bed with every woman he lusted after. He was opinionated, argumentative and inquisitive, insatiably visiting new places, seeing unusual sights and soliciting ideas and opinions from everyone he met. He wrote everything down, exactly (one imagines) as he received it: he was like blotting paper, sucking up all he heard or saw. His masterpiece is his *Life of *Samuel Johnson*, a monument to Boswell's note-taking as well as to the dazzle of his subject.

Boswell's genius as a recorder has encouraged biographers to take more interest in his character than it perhaps deserves: for most of this century, for example, a team of Yale scholars has worked to find out and publish all they can about him, to dot every 'i' and cross every 't'. Good examples of their work, scholarly, lucid and mercilessly revealing of Boswell's personal boringness, are Frank Pottle, *James Boswell, the Early Years* (1966) and Frank Brady, *James Boswell, the Later Years* (1984). Marlies K. Danziger and Frank Brady (eds.), *Boswell, the Great Biographer, 1789–1795*, about the climax of Boswell's life, is a much livelier affair, using Boswell's own letters, journals and other documents. For anyone looking for Boswell himself, this is the best place to start.

‑› **READ ON**
James Boswell, *London Journal, 1762–63*; *Account of Corsica* (partly travel, partly about the Corsican independence struggle, which Boswell supported to the hilt).

BOTHWELL, James, Earl of (1535–78) Scottish nobleman

One version of Bothwell's story is that he was ruthless for power. He seduced *Mary, Queen of Scots, murdered her husband and married her, whereupon his fellow lords deposed her and drove him into exile, where he died insane. Other accounts depict Bothwell and Mary as star-crossed lovers, doomed both by destiny and by the turbulent politics of their time: theirs is the greatest story *Shakespeare never told. The first view is persuasively put in R. Gore-Brown, *Lord Bothwell* (1937), and the second in Humphrey Drummond, *The Queen's Man* (1975). The story remains extraordinarily fresh, one of the

‑› **READ ON**
Margaret Irwin, *The Gay Galliard* (historical novel).

BOX   35

liveliest of historical controversies; all the evidence is here; the judgement rests.

BOTTOMLEY, Horatio (1860–1933) English journalist

Bottomley was one of the most flamboyant humbugs in English history. A journalist, he began on the sober *Financial Times*, but then founded and edited the scandal-sheet *John Bull*, which specialized in tittle-tattle about people in public life and in the exposure of crooks and frauds (many of them invented by Bottomley to boost circulation). Bottomley, not unnaturally, spent much time in court, defending himself in libel suits and being spectacularly rude to judges and lawyers. He floated dozens of companies, some genuine, some dubious (a dozen, for example, were set up to reopen exhausted Australian gold-mines). In the First World War he wrote and spoke some of the most jingoistic nonsense produced in Britain until modern tabloid times. He was a combination of bully, toady and yarnspinner, and had his comeuppance in the 1920s, when he was convicted of fraudulent conversion and sent to gaol. Julian Symons, *Horatio Bottomley* (1955) tells all.

> **READ ON**
> Hugh Trevor-Roper, *A Hidden Life* (about another early 20th-century conman, *Edmund Backhouse.

BOWLES, Paul (born 1910) US composer and writer

In the 1930s–40s Bowles was a leading theatre composer, writing music for everything from French farce to Greek tragedy. In the 1950s he left the USA for Morocco, and turned his creativity to fiction, writing novels and short stories. He was a particular influence on the 1960s Beat generation. Christopher Sawyer-Lauçanno, *An Invisible Spectator* (1989) is a fascinating, intimate biography, the research for which included many hours of interviews with Bowles himself. It deals briefly with Bowles' life – with amazing stories of such friends as *Gertrude Stein, William Burroughs and *Truman Capote – and also goes deeply into his complex, private personality, his marriage to the equally tormented writer Jane Bowles, and the reasons for his switch of career and his move to Africa.

> **READ ON**
> Paul Bowles, *Without Stopping* (reticent autobiography, most revealingly read after Sawyer-Lauçanno's biography, as you begin to speculate on why Bowles, writing in 1972, left so much out).

BOX, Muriel (born 1905) English filmmaker and writer

Alone or in collaboration with her first husband Sydney, Box wrote, produced and directed a dozen of the finest British films of the 1940s–60s, including *The Man Within*, *The Seventh Veil*, *The Brothers* and *Rattle of a Simple Man*. She was also a poet,

> **READ ON**
> Michael Balcon, *A Lifetime of Films* (autobiography of one of the leaders of the British film industry, the head of (among others) Gainsborough Pictures, Gaumont British Pictures and Ealing Studios).

feminist and politician (married from 1970 to the lawyer and Labour Cabinet minister Gerald Gardiner). Muriel Box, *Odd Woman Out* (1974) is her autobiography, good on growing up in the 1920s–30s, the British film industry, the fight for women's rights, and especially, her emotional devastation when she heard that Sydney, after 30 years of apparently happy marriage and close professional relationship, was seeing another woman.

BOYCOTT, Rosie (born 1951) English journalist

Boycott, co-founder of *Spare Rib* magazine and the feminist publishers Virago, left London in the 1970s to go on a spree in Asia. Her memoir *A Nice Girl Like Me* (1984) describes meeting gurus, throwing the ashes of a friend into the Ganges, editing a magazine in Kuwait – and also her painful, gradual self-rehabilitation after she realized that she was an alcoholic. The book is something of a roller-coaster read, interspersing third-person chapters on her life with more downbeat chapters on her cure.
See also *David Leitch (Boycott's husband).

> **READ ON**
> Tom Wolfe, *The Electric Kool-Aid Acid Test* (the 1960s quest for psychic experience, wittily dissected). Malcolm Lowry, *Lunar Caustic* (terrifying, autobiographical novel about 'drying out').

BRACKEN, Brendan (1901–58) Irish newspaperman and politician

Bracken was obsessively mysterious about his origins, education and early life, and ordered all his papers burned on his death. Born in Ireland, he moved to England after the First World War, and worked behind the scenes at the *Financial News* and *Economist*. From 1929 he was an MP, and was a zealous Minister of Information in the Second World War. Andrew Boyle, *Poor Dear Brendan* (1974) fleshes out what evidence there is about his early life, and is good on his public career, bizarre personality and idolization of *Winston Churchill. (The book's title quotes Churchill, on hearing of Bracken's death.) Boyle, a broadcaster, has robust things to say about Bracken's attempt to keep the BBC impartial during the war; other people's bias was as much a preoccupation then (with more urgent reason) as it is today.

> **READ ON**
> Charles Lysaght, *Brendan Bracken* (outstanding on Bracken's Irish background). John Colville, *Action This Day: Working With Churchill* (fascinating glimpses of Bracken). See also *Beaverbrook.

> **BRAVE NEW WORLDS – AND HOW TO GET THEM**

(campaigners)

Vincent Brome, *Havelock Ellis*
David Green, *Great Cobbett*
Ruth Hall, *Marie Stopes*
John Hammond, *James Stansfield: a Victorian Champion of Sex Equality*

Beatrice Kemp, *Suffragette for Peace* (Bertha von Suttner)
Alma Lutz, *Susan B. Anthony: Rebel, Crusader, Humanitarian*; *Created Equal* (Elizabeth Cady Stanton)
Charles McCarry, *Citizen Nader*
Jeanne MacKenzie, **Beatrice and Sidney Webb*
Stephen Oates, *Let the Trumpets Sound* (*Martin Luther King)
*Huda Shaarawi, *Harem Years*
Mary Whitehouse, *Who Does She Think She Is?*
Donald Woods, *Biko*

BRETT, Dorothy (1883–1977) English painter

The only person actually to join *D.H. Lawrence's utopian artists' community in New Mexico, Brett lived with him and Frieda there for a year, and stayed for the rest of her life after the Lawrences left in 1925. She was a fine painter, in a style blending English neatness (something like *Gwen John's) with the bright colours of Mexican folk art. She knew the members of the *Bloomsbury Group, the *Huxleys, the *Russells, Stanley Spencer – indeed the index to Sean Hignett, *Brett* (1984) reads like a list of everyone who was anyone in 1930s artistic circles. Hignett quotes lavishly from unpublished letters and journals, and from the mountain of published material by Brett's acquaintances and friends. Her life was a side road in the artistic history of her time, but in the manner of side roads, it was often far more scenic and extraordinary than many a main highway.

> ⋄ **READ ON**
> Dorothy Brett, *Lawrence and Brett: a Friendship*. D.H. Lawrence, *Mornings in Mexico* (travel book).

BRITTAIN, Vera (1893–1970) British socialist and writer

Brittain's generation of Europeans was devastated by the First World War. Her own brother, many of his friends and her fiancé were all killed in the trenches, and when she left Oxford she herself went to nurse in France. Her book *Testament of Youth* (1933) is the story of 'her' war, and the biography of her generation. Her rage at the suffering she saw, and at the way no one at home in Britain knew anything about it, moulded her character and her life. Her literary style is rather old-fashioned, but the feelings are timeless.

> ⋄ **READ ON**
> Vera Brittain, *Testament of Friendship* (about her friendship with the novelist Winifred Holtby, who wrote *South Riding*); *Testament of Experience* (final volume of autobiography, taking her through the 1930s and 1940s). Her diaries are published in three volumes, entitled *Chronicle of Youth 1913–1917*, *Chronicle of Friendship 1932–1939* and *Wartime Chronicle 1939–1945*, and are breathless but useful background to the *Testaments*.

BRONTE family

The story is well known: gentle widower **Patrick Brontë** (1771–1861) brings up his children **Charlotte** (1816–55),

> ⋄ **READ ON**
> F.W. Ratchford, *The Brontës' Web of Childhood* (fascinating account of the childhood

Branwell (1817–48), Emily (1818–48) and Anne (1820–49) in the parsonage at Haworth, high on the Yorkshire moors. The children compensate for physical isolation by inventing romantic kingdoms and fairy tales. As adults, the girls turn their attention inwards to their own psychological landscapes, writing novels (including Charlotte's *Jane Eyre* and Emily's *Wuthering Heights*) and poems, and the boy – once thought the most talented of them all – tries to make his way as a painter, fails and turns to drink and drugs.

Phyllis Bentley, *The Brontës and Their World* (1969) and Brian Wilks, *The Brontës* (1975) are good, well-illustrated introductions to this legend and the reality behind it. Winifred Gérin, *The Brontës* (two volumes, 1974) is the standard work on the family, interesting about the mother and deceased siblings as well as the survivors. Gérin has also written 'classic' biographies of all four Brontë children: *Branwell Brontë* (1961), *Charlotte Brontë* (1967), *Emily Brontë* (1971), *Anne Brontë* (second ed., 1976). These are detailed, sympathetic and fascinating masterpieces of the genre. Their only real rival is Mrs Gaskell, *The Life of Charlotte Brontë* (1857), written by the novelist who was Charlotte's friend; it is meaty and emotionally insightful. Other interesting books are Margot Peters, *Unquiet Soul* (1987) (about Charlotte); Edward Chitham, *A Life of Emily Brontë* (1987); Ada Harrison and Derek Stanford, *Anne Brontë: Her Life and Work* (1959); John Lock and W.T. Dixon, *A Man of Sorrow: The Life, Letters and Times of the Rev. Patrick Brontë* (1965); Joan Rees, *Profligate Son: Branwell Brontë and His Sisters* (1986).

romances written by the Brontës in exquisite, matchbox-sized notebooks, and of their relationship to the later work).

BROOKS, Louise (1906–88) US film star

In the 1920s Brooks was nicknamed 'the flapper supreme', and was famed as one of the sexiest women in the world. She had cropped, jet-black hair, eyes made up like the newly discovered statue of Nefertiti, sensous lips and a boyish figure dressed in sheer, black gowns. She starred in Hollywood comedies, and in the darkly erotic German film *Pandora's Box*. The papers were full of her escapades, including (it was said) affairs with both *Chaplin and Garbo. She fell into obscurity in the 1930s, but was rediscovered in the 1970s when *Pandora's Box* was restored and became a cult. Barry Paris, *Louise Brooks* (1990) tells Brooks' story; it is less pungent about film-world hype than Brook's own autobiography (with Hollis Alpert), *Lulu in Hollywood* (1982), but hardly less incredible.

⇢ **READ ON**
Dentner Davies, *Hollywood Comet* (about that sex-bomb from a decade later than Brooks, Jean Harlow).

BROWN, Christy (1932–88) Irish artist and writer

⇢ **READ ON**
Christy Brown, *Down All the Days* (novel); *Of Snails and*

Brown suffered from cerebral palsy, which left him unable to control almost all movement in his body. His autobiography *My Left Foot* (1954) tells how he fought against his disability and to express the personality trapped by the disease. The help of his large, loving family, the guidance of a sympathetic specialist, and above all his own incredible determination, led to him living as near a 'normal' life as possible. He became an artist and writer, unlocking his creativity, as the title of his book suggests, in a way healthy people might find almost impossible to believe.

Skylarks (poems).

BROWNING, Elizabeth Barrett (1806–61)
English poet

Thanks to the 1930s play and film *The Barretts of Wimpole Street*, the 'EBB' legend tells of a shy romantic heroine snatched by her poet-lover *Robert Browning from a tyrannical, overbearing father. In the 1960s, research into hitherto unpublished letters showed that this view was mistaken or exaggerated, and that the truth lay in her own physical and mental state. Margaret Forster, *Elizabeth Barrett Browning* (1988) is the standard biography, making all others out of date, entertainingly written and full of enthusiasm for EBB's poetry. It has a detailed and helpful bibliography. Philip Kelley and Ronald Huson (eds.), *The Brownings' Correspondence* is an ongoing, many-volume project which will eventually contain every letter of the thousands which survive. *The Letters of Elizabeth and Robert Browning* are available separately: impetuous and heady, source of the romantic story of their courtship and elopement.

·> READ ON
Margaret Forster, *Lady's Maid* (novel about Wilson, the Brownings' devoted servant). *Virginia Woolf, *Flush* (spoof 'biography' of EBB's beloved cocker spaniel, mute witness to all the romantic goings-on).

BROWNING, Robert (1812–89) English poet

In 1844 Browning began a friendship with Elizabeth Barrett (see *Elizabeth Barrett Browning) which led to love, elopement to Italy and a happy marriage ended by her death 15 years later. Apart from this, his life was uneventful, that of a typical Victorian man of letters. Biographies talk of his love for his and Elizabeth's son Pen, his admiration for *Dickens, his enjoyment of the theatre, suggesting that he put his passion into his work (for example the dramatic monologues in *Men and Women* or *Dramatis Personae*). William Irvine and Park Honan, *The Book, the Ring and the Poet* (1975) is the standard biography, good both on Browning's life and on his works. Betty Miller, *Robert Browning: a Portrait* (1952) puts Browning into his 19th-century English context, seeing his character and energy as typical of his time.

·> READ ON
T.L. Hood (ed.), *The Letters of Robert Browning*. Margaret Forster, *Elizabeth Barrett Browning*.

BRUMMELL, George (1778–1840) English dandy

'Beau' Brummell was a courtier of the Prince Regent, later George IV. Like the rest of the Prince's circle, he spent his time gambling, visiting the theatre, power-dressing (the slightest turn of a cuff or placing of a button was headline news), and above all endlessly, mercilessly cutting everyone else down to size in waspish epigrams. It was a society of butterflies, and depended entirely on the Prince's favour for survival. When Brummell and 'Prinny' quarrelled ('Who's your fat friend?' Brummell notoriously asked someone in George's hearing), that was the end of Brummell. He fell like Icarus; his last years were tragic and pitiful. Hubert Cole, *Beau Brummell* (1977) is sympathetic, lively and full of glorious anecdotes and quotations. It is, nevertheless, not starry-eyed: the impression it leaves is that both Brummell and the society he led were the heights not only of fashion but of futility, sterility and heartlessness.

> ❖ **READ ON**
> William Jesse, *Life of Beau Brummell* (1844; fine on Brummell's sad last years). William Thackeray, *The Four Georges* (good on the Regency, with a wit as acid as Brummell's own). Keith B. Poole, *The Two Beaux* (funny joint study of Brummell and his main rival, Beau Nash). Willard Connely, *Count d'Orsay* (biography of their successor, the 'Phoebus Apollo of dandyism' in early Victorian London). Philip Hoare, *Serious Pleasures* (about the 20th-century social butterfly Stephen Tennant).

BRUNEL, Isambard Kingdom (1805–59) English engineer

Brunel was one of the highest-profile engineers in Victorian England, a symbol of national enterprise and achievement. His works include track, stations and rolling stock for the Great Western Railway, the Clifton Suspension Bridge (hailed in its time and ever since as a work of art as well as a way to cross a river gorge), the enlarged Bristol docks, and three enormous ships, *Great Western* (the first transatlantic steamship), *Great Britain* (the first large ship to be propeller-driven) and *Great Eastern* (the first iron ship built with a double hull). Isambard Brunel, *The Life of Isambard Kingdom Brunel, Civil Engineer* (1870), by Brunel's son, deals more with the public than the private man, and gives copious engineering and technical detail. John Pudney, *Brunel and His World* (1974), well illustrated, sets Brunel in the context of his times. L.T.C. Rolt, *Isambard Kingdom Brunel* (1957) is good on Brunel's personality and private life.

> ❖ **READ ON**
> James Dugan, *The Great Iron Ship*.

BURNEY, Frances ('Fanny') (1752–1840) English writer

Daughter of a well-known musician, and a successful novelist in her own right, Fanny Burney spent her 20s and 30s in the company of such people as Burke, Garrick, *Johnson and their aristocratic patrons. In the 1790s she worked at court, during

> ❖ **READ ON**
> Sarah Kilpatrick, *Fanny Burney* (neat, crisp biography, placing Burney and her work precisely in each shifting historical and artistic context.)

George III's worst illness; in the 1800s, married to a French nobleman, she was interned by *Napoléon; in the 1820s she retired to Bath and began editing her journals for publication. Fanny Burney, *Early Diary 1768–78* (1889) is a lively account of her home life, early literary career and friendships. Her style is unaffected, but her character sketches are beady-eyed and witty. Fanny Burney, *Later Diary and Letters, 1778–1840* (1842–6) is good about George III's tragic court, and on her time in France. Christopher Lloyd (ed.), *The Diary of Fanny Burney* (1948) is a handy selection, especially from the early diaries.

BURNS, George (born 1896) US comedian

In the 1940s–50s Burns was half of one of the most popular acts in US comedy, Burns and Allen. When his wife Gracie Allen died in the 1960s he began a solo career, and continued to star well into his 90s. His four volumes of memoirs, *I Love Her, That's Why* (1955), *Living It Up* (1976), *The Third Time Around* (1980) and *All My Best Friends* (1988) combine autobiography, one-liners and showbiz gossip in the unpretentious, deadpan manner of his stage and TV act, as if he were talking to you direct. *The Third Time Around* is especially good on the great Burns and Allen years, and includes some of their best-loved sketches.

‹› **READ ON**
Similarly relaxed, wisecracking memoirs: Bob Hope, *Have Tux, Will Travel.*

BURTON, Richard (1925–84) Welsh actor

In his 20s Burton looked set to be a great classical stage actor, *Olivier's heir. But instead he went to Hollywood and became world-famous, partly through his films and partly because of his high living and his on-off, tempestuous relationship with *Elizabeth Taylor. Melvyn Bragg, *Rich* (1989) tells all.

‹› **READ ON**
Graham Jenkins, *Richard Burton, My Brother* (the family's-eye view). Brenda Maddox, *Who's Afraid of Elizabeth Taylor?*.

BURTON, Richard Francis (1829–90) English traveller and writer

Burton spent much of his life abroad, in the Indian army, exploring in Africa, and as British consul in Brazil, Trieste and Syria. He spoke 30 languages, and made translations of *The Arabian Nights*, the *Kama Sutra* and *The Perfumed Garden*. His travel books, despite old-fashioned English, give fascinating glimpses of how such 'exotic' places as Iceland, Goa, Arabia and Darkest Africa seemed to our Victorian ancestors. Best known is *A Personal Narrative of a Pilgrimage to Al-Madinah and Mecca* (1855–6): Burton was the first non-Muslim to visit the holy cities, disguised as a Pathan merchant. After his death his

‹› **READ ON**
J. Burton, *Life of Lady Burton* (good about her dissatisfaction with Victorian domesticity, and the way she coped with living in her husband's formidable shadow).

wife, Isabel Burton, wrote a biography (*Life of Sir Richard Burton*, 1893) which veers between hero-worship and disapproval of his drinking and his fascination with 'dirty books'. T. Wright, *The Life of Sir Richard Burton* (1906), the standard work, is more objective, and still readable despite its ponderous English. Fawn M. Brodie, *The Devil Rides* (1967) is the best of dozens of later books: lively and enthusiastic, but full of sharp analyses and comments on Burton's character.

BYRON, George Gordon, Lord (1788–1824) English poet

One of Lord Byron's lovers, Lady Caroline Lamb, called him 'mad, bad and dangerous to know', and he lived up to it, presenting himself as a brooding, unpredictable, heroic genius. He spent much of his life travelling in Spain, Portugal, Italy, Turkey and Greece, where he was a passionate supporter of the War of Independence against the Turks. He died in Greece (of malaria), and is remembered there as a national hero.

The first, best source for Byron's life and character is Leslie Marchand (ed.), *Byron's Letters and Journals* (12 volumes, 1973–82). They are witty, outrageously self-admiring and have the whiff not so much of truth as of self-inventing genius. Peter Quennell, *Byron: a Self-Portrait in his Own Words* (1989) is a useful anthology, arranged to tell Byron's life – a replacement, Quennell says, for Byron's own autobiography which his scandalized publisher burned. Leslie Marchand, *Byron* (three volumes, 1958), the standard biography, is rather stiff and formal in style: more zestful is his *Byron: a Portrait* (1970), condensed from it. Frederic Raphael, *Byron* (1982) is shorter, wittier and beautifully illustrated.

▷ **READ ON**
Recommended books about people in Byron's circle: Henry Blyth, *Caro, the Fatal Passion* (Caroline Lamb). T.A.J. Burnett, *The Rise and Fall of a Regency Dandy* (Scrope Davies). Claire Tomalin, *Shelley and His World*. Margo Strickland, *The Byron Women*. Edward J. Trelawney, *Records of Shelley, Byron and the Author* (chatty memoirs). Doris Langley Moore, *The Late Lord Byron* (about the stormy relationships and revelations of those left behind after Byron's death). Robert Nye, *The Memoirs of Lord Byron* (novel).

C

CADDIE: *see* **MacKAY,** Catherine Elliot

CAESAR, Gaius Julius (c101–44BC) Roman general and statesman

Captured at 23 by pirates, Caesar waited till the ransom was paid, then gathered an army, killed the pirates, and used the cash to pay his troops. From then on he had an army loyal to him personally, and used it as a powerbase in his struggle for political supremacy. He fought Rome's enemies brilliantly in Gaul and Spain, and then advanced on Rome, defeating his old colleague and rival *Pompey on the way. He was one of the most dazzling soldiers of his time, but suffered from the megalomania characteristic of so many generals: it was his arrogance and imperial ambition which led others to conspire against him, and to murder him, more or less as described in *Shakespeare's play. Michael Grant, *Caesar: Politician and Statesman* (1968) is thorough, competent, and makes ancient politics both clear and interesting.

⟶ READ ON
Caesar, *The Gallic Wars*; *The Civil Wars* (memoirs, typically pompous – Caesar talks of himself in the third person, and never puts a foot wrong in planning or tactics – but good on the strategy and minute-to-minute management of Roman battles). Thornton Wilder, *The Ides of March* (historical novel, in letter form, about the events leading up to Caesar's assassination).

CALLAS, Maria (1922–1977) Greek singer

At her best, Callas (born Maria Kalogeropoulou) could thrill the most exacting opera audience; her worst, by contrast, could be dire. She claimed that her singing depended on her happiness – but to judge by her private life and the quality of her performances, she must have risen above personal misery every time she went onstage. Arianna Stassinopoulos, *Maria: Beyond the Callas Legend* (1980) delves into the emotional disaster area that was her character, with such gusto that one tends to lose

⟶ READ ON
Giovanni Battista Meneghini, *My Wife Maria Callas* (lachrymose account of how the author tried, and failed, to keep Callas away from Aristotle Onassis). Evangelina Callas, *My Daughter, Maria Callas* (vicious 'feet of clay' book by Callas' estranged mother). Peter Evans, *The Onassis Line*. David A. Lowe

sight of Callas' art. Sergio Segalini, *Callas: Portrait of a Diva* (Eng. ed. 1981) is the complete opposite: ravishing photos with a brief, gushy text outlining the high place the author gives Callas in operatic history and suggesting that her 'less good' notes were vital to her acting. Segalini is as effusive as a schoolboy, but none the less manages the extraordinary trick of all but evoking the Callas sound in words alone.

(ed.), *Callas as They Saw Her* (reminiscences by fellow artists, reviews, plus Callas' own memoirs).

‹› CANADA

Mollie Gillen, *The Wheel of Things* (*L.M. Montgomery)
Martha Martin, *O Rugged Land of Gold*
Gene Stratton Porter, *The Life and Letters of Gene Stratton Porter*
Alfred M. Rehwinkel, *Dr Bessie*
Mordecai Richler, *Home Sweet Home: My Canadian Album*
Phyllis Taylor, *Buckskin and Blackboard: Teaching Experiences in British Columbia*

CANETTI, Elias (born 1905) Bulgarian writer

English writers about childhood often treat it as a kind of magical country, a garden of innocence we can never revisit and whose perfection makes adult experience seem flawed and strange. Most European writers take precisely the opposite view. For them, maturity is the true state of human beings, and the joys of childhood, however intense, are outweighed by the prospect of the grown-up excitements which are to follow. This feeling is magnificently caught in the first volume of Elias Canetti's autobiography, *The Tongue Set Free* (1988). He describes his first 17 years: travels round Europe (from Istanbul to Manchester), schooldays in Austria, awakening to literature, art, music – and anti-semitism. Above all, the book describes his devotion to his mother, and his appalling sense of loss (like Adam's on leaving Eden) when he realized, at 17, that he was master of his own self and had grown away from her.

‹› **READ ON**
Elias Canetti, *The Torch in My Ear, The Play of the Eyes* (sequels, about Canetti's artistic apprenticeship and maturity in 1920s–30s Vienna: less generally compelling, but wonderful for anyone interested in Canetti, Viennese culture or the sheer power of words).

CAPOTE, Truman (1924–84) US writer

As a young man Capote was a darling of the smart set: beautiful, witty, talented, enchantingly original in all he did or said. His books (like *Other Voices, Other Rooms* and *Breakfast at Tiffany's*) were hits; his friends included film stars, presidents, hostesses, ballet dancers and painters (notably *Andy Warhol). The media hung on his words, not least after he published *In*

‹› **READ ON**
Truman Capote, *In Cold Blood* ('faction' account of gruesome, motiveless murder in a small Kansas town: in effect, a biography of the murderers, and a composite picture of the lifestyle and thought patterns of the middle-class, mid-western US).

Cold Blood (*see* Read On). But in the late 1960s, things went badly wrong. He published a book pillorying his erstwhile friends, many of whom cut him; he turned to drink and drugs; he lost his looks and trebled in weight; he became obsessed by his own genius. His decline was long-drawn-out and miserable, a bleak mirror-image of his climb to fame. Gerald Clarke, *Capote* (1988) tells the story, much of it based on talks with Capote and those who knew him: a real-life morality, though Clarke is careful not to moralize.

CARDIGAN, James Thomas Brudenell, Lord (1797–1868) English soldier

Cardigan joined the army against his father's will – he was the only son and heir. He was a libertine and an adventurer, tried by his peers for killing a brother-officer in a duel, notorious for his sexual affairs, even burned in effigy. He bought himself command of the 11th Hussars, spending a fortune of his own money every year to make them a crack regiment. At the battle of Balaclava (1854) he was ordered to lead his men, armed only with swords, along a ravine into the mouths of the Russian guns. He queried the order twice, then obeyed, and 'All in the valley of Death/Rode the six hundred', as Tennyson later put it. Cardigan survived, and was fêted as a hero. At 60 he took a mistress of 22, marrying her as soon as his wife died. Social ostracism followed, the revenge the Establishment had been planning for 40 years of unconventional behaviour. Donald Thomas, *Charge! Hurrah! Hurrah!* (1974) tells Cardigan's story with enthusiasm and a fine eye for the nuances of humbug in Regency and Victorian high society.

> **READ ON**
> Joan Wake, *The Brudenells of Deene* (story of Cardigan's family to 1950). Cecil Woodham Smith, *The Reason Why* (about Balaclava).

CARLYLE, Jane (1801–66) Scottish housewife

Carlyle was a witty, well-educated woman who chose to subordinate her life to her husband *Thomas Carlyle. He loved her passionately and treated her abominably. She compensated by writing reams of letters to her friends and family, among the freshest correspondence in the language. J.A. Froude, *Letters and Memorials of Jane Welsh Carlyle* (two volumes, 1883) is the earliest collection, with notes, by Thomas Carlyle's friend and biographer. C.R. Sanders and K.J. Fielding (eds.), *The Collected Letters of Thomas and Jane Welsh Carlyle* (12 volumes, 1970–85) is a complete, monumental work of scholarship. Good selections are Trudy Bliss (ed.), *Jane Welsh Carlyle: A New Selection of her Letters* (1950) and A. and M. Simpson (eds), *I Too Am Here: Selections from the Letters of Jane Welsh Carlyle* (1977). Lawrence and Elisabeth Hanson, *Necessary Evil: the Life of Jane Welsh Carlyle* (1952) is a furious biography, vitriolic about

> **READ ON**
> Thomas Carlyle, *Reminiscences*.

Thomas' behaviour and baffled by Jane's. Virginia Surtees, *Jane Welsh Carlyle* (1986), by taking the Carlyles less seriously, gives a cooler, seemingly more likely account of one of the oddest, and best-documented, relationships in English literature.

CARLYLE, Thomas (1795–1881) Scottish writer

In Carlyle's own day he was revered as a historian, essayist and thinker, 'the sage of Chelsea'. His view was that society of his time was soulless, awash with materialism, over-reliant on machines, and forgetful of the spiritual values (not necessarily religious) which had inspired 'heroes' (famous doers and thinkers) of the past. Nowadays he is also known for the psychological tangle of his personality and the self-induced misery of his life. In particular, his relationship with his wife *Jane Carlyle, and his attitude to women in general, have been much criticized. He was the subject of one of the classics of 19th-century biography: J.A. Froude, *Thomas Carlyle* (four volumes, 1882–4). Froude took Jane Carlyle's part in his description of the marriage; but his account of Carlyle as a craggy, difficult thinker and philosopher is both moving and persuasive. His book (especially as abridged in John Clubbe, *Froude's Life of Carlyle* (1979), is easier to read than Carlyle's own *Reminiscences* (two volumes, 1881), which are in tortured, awkward prose. Fred Kaplan, *Thomas Carlyle* (1983) is a scholarly modern biography, good on Carlyle's ideas and his psychology: not a substitute for Froude, but a help if read first. J.S. Collis, *The Carlyles* (1971) is an objective account of the marriage.

CARNEGIE, Andrew (1835–1918) Scots/US businessman

At the time of the US railroad boom, Carnegie made a vast fortune in the steel industry. Believing that rich people were no more than trustees for their wealth, which should be used for the good of the human race, he retired in 1901 and spent his money on philanthropic projects: libraries, hospitals, schools, universities and peace foundations. Joseph F. Wall, *Andrew Carnegie* (1970), the standard biography, is long (1,100 pages) but fascinating, both on Carnegie's character and on some more unexpected topics: Scottish Calvinism as a moral force, the effects of the Civil War on American industry, the 'robber baron' world of US business in the 1870s–90s, and Carnegie's attitude to his rivals and to the thousands of people he employed.

⟶ **READ ON**
Julian Symons (ed.), *Selected Works, Reminiscences and Letters by Thomas Carlyle* (outstanding anthology). Virginia Surtees, *Jane Welsh Carlyle*.

⟶ **READ ON**
Andrew Carnegie, *Autobiography*.

CARRINGTON, Dora: *see* **STRACHEY,** Lytton

CARROLL, Lewis (1832–98) English writer

'Lewis Carroll', author of the Alice books and *The Hunting of the Snark*, was in real life Charles Lutwidge Dodgson of Christ Church, Oxford, a mathematics don and cleric. He was an amateur photographer, and told stories to his child models to keep them still – the origin of his nonsense fantasies. The two sides of his personality, and his (typically Victorian?) blend of repression and fantasy, are revealed in Roger Lancelyn Green (ed.), *The Diaries of Lewis Carroll* (1953) and M.N. Cohen and R.L. Green (eds.), *The Letters of Lewis Carroll* (1979). John Pudney, *Lewis Carroll and his World* (1976) is a well-illustrated, brief biography. Fuller studies are Stuart Dodgson Collingwood (Carroll's nephew), *The Life and Letters of Lewis Carroll* (1899, reissued 1967) and Anne Clark, *Lewis Carroll* (1979).

⋗ **READ ON**
Helmut Gernsheim, *Lewis Carroll, Photographer*. Colin Gordon, *Beyond the Looking Glass* (book about the Liddell family, including Alice; sumptuously illustrated from the hoard of family pictures and treasures released after the death of Alice's great-granddaughter).

CASANOVA, Giovanni (1725–98) Italian adventurer

Casanova trained for the priesthood, but spent his life travelling and taking whatever jobs chance offered: he was at one time or another alchemist, cardinal's secretary, card-sharp, fortune-teller, preacher and professional violinist. He spent time in prison; he ran the French state lottery; he ended his days as librarian to Count Waldstein. He also – if his scandalous, compelling *Story of My Life* (1826–38; English version by Willard Trask, 1967–9; far more accurate than the French adaptation in which the book was known till then) is to be believed – seduced some 10,000 women, beginning when he was 11 years old. John Masters, *Casanova* (1969) untangles Casanova's boasting, making the truth seem even wilder than the old man's invention. The book is magnificently illustrated, and has a wide-ranging bibliography.

⋗ **READ ON**
*Lorenzo da Ponte, *Memoirs* (different events, but the same late 18th-century atmosphere and the same amoral, cheerful approach to life).

CATHERINE II (1729–96) Russian empress (ruled 1762–96)

Catherine (later nicknamed 'the Great') took power when her feeble husband Peter III was killed in a coup organized by two of her lovers. She ruled at first as an enlightened despot, inspired by the ideas of *Voltaire and *Rousseau, but the older she grew the more dictatorial she became. She doubled the size of the Russian empire, was a substantial patron of the arts, and lived at the heart of a glittering, Europeanized royal court. John

⋗ **READ ON**
Isabel de Madariaga, *Catherine the Great* (crisp, notably good on the background history of Catherine's times).

T. Alexander, *Catherine the Great: Life and Legend* (1989) is the standard biography, supplanting the earlier (meaty but less stylish) I. Grey, *Catherine the Great: Autocrat and Empress of all Russia* (1961). Vincent Cronin, *Catherine, Empress of All the Russias* (1990) is a lively account of the intrigue and colour of Catherine's court. Henri Troyat, *Catherine the Great* (1977) is a floridly written but persuasive assessment of Catherine's personality.

CELLINI, Benvenuto (1500–71) Italian artist

As goldsmith and musician, Cellini served a succession of Popes, the king of France and the *Medici family in Florence. His *Autobiography* (1562), a classic of the genre, is a swaggering tale of wenching, duelling, spying and roguery in every palace and pothouse in Europe, interspersed with acid but astute comparisons between his own works and those of clay-footed rivals. He comes out as a kind of cross between Tom Jones and one of the the Three Musketeers. The book may be mainly fiction (who can say?), but Cellini's personality and his lively, self-delighted prose make it hard to resist.

▷ **READ ON**
*Giovanni Casanova, *Story of My Life* (Cellini's only rival for gusto, extravagance and conviction that you'll believe every word he writes).

CERVANTES SAAVEDRA, Miguel de (1547–1616) Spanish writer

In his 20s and 30s Cervantes was a soldier: he fought at the Battle of Lepanto, was captured by pirates and served five years as a slave in Algiers. On his return to Spain he tried to earn a living as a playwright and then as a tax-collector, only to be thrown into prison for false accounting. From 1595 he lived (mysteriously and in poverty) in Seville, while writing *Don Quixote*, the book which finally brought him fame. From then till the end of his life his public success was counteracted by private misery caused by the intrigues and love-affairs of his beloved daughter Isabel. Richard L. Predmore, *Cervantes* (1973) is a short, illustrated biography, teasing out the riddles of Cervantes' life and full of quotations from his works. Jean Caravaggio, *Cervantes* (1990), much longer, talks of the difficulty of pinning down facts in Cervantes' life, even imagining a homonym, a second 'Cervantes Saavedra' who led an alternative life for him. A difficult, teasing, enthralling book, at least for Cervantes fans.

▷ **READ ON**
Richard L. Predmore, *The World of Don Quixote* (on the Spanish background common to both Cervantes' life and his masterpiece).

CEZANNE, Paul (1839–1906) French painter

Art historians see Cézanne's work as a bridge between the Impressionists (whom he knew and admired as a young man) and

▷ **READ ON**
J. Rewald (ed.), *Correspondence of Paul Cézanne.*

the Cubists (whose earliest work he lived just long enough to see and on whom he was a great influence). Until he was in his 50s he was unrecognized, and his personal story is of a struggle to keep sane while working day and night to break the mould of artistic style. Hugh McLeave, *A Man and His Mountain* (1977) solves the problem of writing about a painter without being allowed one single illustration by treating Cézanne's life as if it were a novel by his friend Zola. The result is engrossing, moving and packed with dialogue. J. Rewald, *Paul Cézanne* (1948) is the standard 'normal' biography, making good use of letters and with fascinating comments on the art.

CHANDLER, Raymond (1888–1959) US writer

Chandler worked as a reporter, then as bookkeeper and accountant until 1933, when he began to write full-time. He invented the 'private eye' Philip Marlowe, and the quality of his prose delighted academic critics as well as the public. The more Chandler was hailed as a genius, the harder he found it to write at all, and his later years were marked by depression, alcoholism and loneliness. Frank MacShane, *The Life of Chandler* (1976) is lively and sympathetic, even when Chandler's moroseness makes this difficult. It is good on Chandler's early writing for pulp magazines, excellent on the novels and outstanding about his uneasy time writing for Hollywood and being bullied by everyone from studio bosses (who objected to the fees he asked) to actors (who famously wrote asking 'whodunnit?' about the ending of *The Big Sleep*, a question to which he had no answer).

◇ **READ ON**
Raymond Chandler, *Collected Letters*. Dorothy Gardner and Katherine Sorley Walter (ed.), *Chandler Speaking*.

CHANEL, Gabrielle (1883–1971) French fashion designer

'Coco' Chanel began her career designing hats for her lover's other mistresses – and the blend that suggests, of high fashion and the *risqué*, was characteristic of her whole life. Her friends were the France-based glitterati of five decades, and her lovers included artists, ballet dancers, poets, White Russian grandees and the then Duke of Westminster, who tried to whisk her into the English aristocracy. She is credited with inventing sportswear, the 'little black dress', costume jewelry and a perfume which was the one thing incoming Nazi soldiers wanted to loot in 1940s Paris, to prove to their wives they'd been there. During the Occupation she lived in the Ritz, which caused her problems later when she was accused of collaboration. But she rebuilt her career in the 1950s, becoming once more a leading couturier and socialite, and sparring with *Katharine Hepburn at rehearsals for *Coco*, a musical about her scandalous, delicious

◇ **READ ON**
Axel Madsen, *Yves St Laurent*. Arthur Gold and Robert Fizdale, *Misia: the Life of Misia Sert* (about 'the divine Misia', the Paris hostess who was Chanel's devoted, if fiery, friend for 40 years).

life (*see* *Spencer Tracy). Few stories could be more glamorously Parisian, more like a novel by *Colette – and Axel Madsen, *Chanel* (1990), the latest of a dozen biographies, treats it just like that. The names in its index alone are a galaxy of the 20th century's most glittering artistic, social and political stars.

CHANNON, Henry (1897–1958) English politician

'Chips' Channon was wealthy and gifted: he could have had any of half a dozen careers. But his main abilities were in sociability and gossip, and as he moved in a world where they were at a premium he never had to exert himself or move elsewhere. He became an MP and a minor member of the Chamberlain government. This was not high office, but thanks to his engaging personality and because he was on easy terms with most of the English Establishment and royal family, he was close to the centre of events, especially before and during the abdication crisis of 1936 (see *Windsor). His gossipy diaries, published as *Chips* (ed. Robert R. James, 1963) are as intriguing on this as on many other social and political matters of his time, and although his views were often against the grain of history – he supported Mrs Simpson and appeasement, for example – he never fails to be urbane, interesting and full of amiable self-deprecation.

⊹ READ ON
John Colville, *Footprints in Time* (entertaining high-society memoirs by a civil servant who started as a page at Buckingham Palace, went on to become private secretary to three prime ministers, and has the endearing and un-civil-service characteristic of being always, cheerfully, ready to admit that he was wrong).

CHAPLIN, Charles (1889–1977) English film-maker

Chaplin's *My Autobiography* (1964) is heart-rending about his childhood (in a still-Dickensian paupers' London of lunatic asylums, workhouses and debtors' prisons), rather more reticent about his Hollywood career. His *My Life in Pictures* (1974) is a superb book, using family photographs and film stills to tell the story of his private and public life. David Robinson, *Charlie Chaplin* (1988) is the standard work, scholarly about Chaplin's life and good on the Hollywood in which he worked. John McCabe, *Charlie Chaplin* (1978) is less rigorous, but covers the events of Chaplin's life and has the bonus of enthusiastic, detailed accounts of each of his major films. Its bibliography lists the most interesting books by others, ranging from 'tell-all' accounts (like Michael Chaplin, *I Couldn't Smoke the Grass on my Father's Lawn*, 1966, by a disaffected son) to idolatry (like Robert Payne, *The Great Charlie/The Great God Pan*, 1952).

⊹ READ ON
Gerald Mast, *The Comic Mind* (analysis of the work of many silent clowns, brilliantly recreating their work in words, with a fine, long chapter on Chaplin's films).

CHARLES I (1600–1649) British king (ruled 1625–49)

Charles, grandson of *Mary Queen of Scots, was as out of tune with his times as she was with hers. This is the case made out in Charles Carlton, *Charles I: the Personal Monarch* (1983), an exhaustively researched, excellently written dissection of Charles' character and actions, showing how he failed at every stage to understand the imperatives of history. In passing – and only a senior historian could risk this and succeed – Carlton makes challenging comparisons between Charles' England and the USA under Nixon: both countries embroiled in unwinnable, distant wars and having a chief executive temperamentally unsuited to high office. Pauline Greeg, *King Charles I* (1981) also uses first-hand documents, but less controversially, to discuss Charles' temperament and behaviour. Interestingly, neither book takes sides, treating Charles as saint or tyrant, a trap many earlier biographers fall into. Christopher Hibbert, *Charles I* (1965) belongs to the 'saint' category, telling the events of Charles' life clearly and simply but from the King's own point of view. It is beautifully illustrated, an excellent book to read first.

> ⊹ **READ ON**
> Biographies of all English Civil War participants, whether on the King's side or *Cromwell's, should be read against the background of C.V. Wedgwood's magisterial historical trilogy *The King's Peace 1637–1641*, *The King's War 1641–1647* and *The Trial of Charles I/A Coffin for King Charles*. For all their 20th-century prose, these books tell 17th-century words and deeds in 17th-century terms: they are the biography of a country and a people as much as of a king.

CHAUDHURI, Nirad C. (born 1897) Indian writer

Chaudhuri, a Bengali journalist and broadcaster, wrote a dozen books on India, concentrating in particular on the interaction of cultures and on politics before and during British rule. He has published two volumes of autobiography. *The Autobiography of an Unknown Indian* (1951) describes growing up in Bengal in the Edwardian autumn of the Raj. *Thy Hand, Great Anarch* (1987) covers the next 30 years, during which Chaudhuri worked as a government clerk before becoming a journalist and political commentator. Both books blend the commonplace – family life, schooldays, office squabbles – with a tartly independent view of Indian politics and history. The second, 1000-page volume has fascinating accounts of such people as *Gandhi, *Mountbatten and the Congress Party leaders at the time of Independence. Chaudhuri moved unobtrusively among the great, but his beady, sardonic eyes missed not a single nuance of what was going on.

> ⊹ **READ ON**
> Nirad C. Chaudhuri, *Clive of India* (massive biography, scholarly but immensely readable).

CHEKHOV, Anton (1860–1904) Russian writer

Chekhov was fascinated by the stage, and would have been an actor had his health permitted it (he had TB). Instead he be-

> ⊹ **READ ON**
> S. Kotelianski and P Tomlinson (eds.), *The Life and Letters of Anton Chekhov* (excellent

came a doctor, writing short stories to improve his income, and later feeding his theatrical hunger by writing plays. His existence was comparatively simple, dominated by his illness, but his inner life was complex and tormented, the root of his art. It needs another great writer to do it justice, as *V.S. Pritchett does in *Chekhov, a Spirit Set Free* (1988), an evocative account of Chekhov's life and work, paying particular attention to the stories. Ronald Hingley, *Chekhov* (1950) is more scholarly and more sober, making good use of Chekhov's letters.

selection of letters, and Chekhov's own autobiographical fragment).

CHESTERFIELD, Philip Dormer Stanhope, Lord (1694–1773) English statesman

Chesterfield, a prominent courtier, served as British ambassador to Holland and Lord Lieutenant of Ireland. He is remembered today for his *Letters* (ed. Bonamy Dobrée, 1932). These were written to his son and godson, to instruct them in morals, manners and attitude. They are humourless and sententious – *Dr Johnson said that they taught 'the morals of a whore and the manners of a dancing-master' – but despite their stodginess they give a fascinating picture of the 'ideal' young gentleman of the time of King George I. Willard Connely, *The True Chesterfield* (1939) is a detailed biography, examining Chesterfield's busy and honours-laden life in the light of his own instructions for behaviour.

⋗ CHILDHOOD

Anne Arnott, *The Brethren* (1930s Christian)
*Gerald Durrell, *My Family and Other Animals* (1930s Corfu)
Winifred Foley, *A Child in the Forest* (Forest of Dean)
*Maxim Gorki, *My Childhood* (bargehand on Volga River)

*Edmund Gosse, *Father and Son* (Victorian Christian)
Shusha Guppy, *The Blindfold Horse* (upper-class intellectual household in pre-revolutionary Tehran)
W.H. Hudson, *Far Away and Long Ago* (Argentina)
Valentin Katayev, *A Mosaic of Life* (pre-Revolutionary Russia)
*Laurie Lee, *Cider With Rosie* (1920s English village)
*Jack Lindsay, *Life Rarely Tells* (childhood and student days in Brisbane, 1900–26)
*Carl Nielsen, *My Childhood* (1870s Denmark)
*V.S. Pritchett, *A Cab at the Door* (1900s London)
Jean Rhys, *Smile Please* (1900s Dominica)

⋗ **READ ON**
Lord Halifax, *A Lady's New Year's Gift, or Advice to a Daughter* (parallel 'Miss Manners' advice, from the court of Charles II).

*Terence Stamp, *Stamp Album* (1940s–50s London)
*Flora Thompson, *Lark Rise to Candleford* (Oxfordshire)
Nancy Thompson, *At Their Departing* (Middlesborough, Yorkshire, between the wars)

⋗ CHOCKS AWAY

Donald Bennet, *Master Airman*
John, Duke of Bedford (ed.), *The Flying Duchess: the Diaries and Letters of Mary, Duchess of Bedford*
*Beryl Markham, *West With the Night*
Antoine de Saint Exupéry, *Wind, Sand and Stars*
Sheila Scott, *I Must Fly*
Elinor Smith, *Aviatrix*
Gilbert Thomas, *Shoulder the Sky: the Biography of a Fighter Pilot*

CHOPIN, Fryderyk (1810–49) Polish composer

Society darling, 'poet of the piano', composer, lover, TB sufferer – Chopin can seem more like the hero of some romantic melodrama than a real human being. He revolutionized the arts of playing and writing for the piano, and his Nocturnes, Waltzes, Studies and Mazurkas are some of the best-loved classical music ever composed. Ates Orga, *Chopin, His Life and Times* (1976) tells the whole story without too much musical technicality, and with well-chosen pictures. Arthur Hedley, *Chopin* (1947), the standard work, makes fuller use of letters and other documents, but its musical comments require knowledge. Arthur Hedley (ed.), *Selected Correspondence of Fryderyk Chopin* (1962) is a good anthology.

⋗ **READ ON**
*George Sand, *Winter in Mallorca* (memoir, by Chopin's mistress, of a stay on Majorca at the height of the stormy season – both in the weather and in their relationship. Romantic genius, red in tooth and claw).

CHRISTIE, Agatha (1890–1976) English writer

Christie fascinates as the 'Queen of Crime', the world's bestselling writer of 'whodunnits' for over 40 years, and author of the longest-running play (*The Mousetrap*) in theatre history. Her private life is equally interesting: happy childhood, passionate love affair, First World War service as a dispenser, nervous breakdown – involving 'going to ground' – in the mid-1920s, followed by a second happy marriage and 50 years of extreme reclusiveness. Her two books of memoirs, *Come Tell Me How You Live* (1946) and *An Autobiography* (1977) are reticent, leaving much deliberately unsaid. Janet Morgan, *Agatha Christie* (1984) gives a fuller picture of Christie's private life, sorting out the secrets and

⋗ **READ ON**
Max Mallowan, *Mallowan's memoirs* (by Christie's second husband, an archaeologist). Anne Hart, *Agatha Christie's Poirot: The Life and Times of Hercule Poirot* (a companion to the Poirot novels).

sympathetic to her character and need for privacy. Charles Osborne, *The Life and Crimes of Agatha Christie* (1982) is good on Christie as a bestselling novelist and playwright.

CHRISTINA (1626–89) Swedish queen

Christina succeeded to the throne when she was six, after her father, the soldier-king Gustavus II Adolphus, died in battle. She was educated as a boy, in both arts and sciences (her maths teacher was Descartes), and was nicknamed 'Minerva of the North' after the goddess of wisdom. She disliked the pomposity of court life, and outraged her officials by dressing either as a man or as an oriental belly-dancer, holding masques, routs and hunts instead of attending to state affairs. In 1654 she abdicated, and spent the rest of her life in Rome, where she was one of the most dazzling hostesses and patrons of the age. Paul Lewis, *Queen of Caprice* (1962) tells her story in a wide-eyed, fictionalized way (it begins with an orgy and ends with a deathbed confession), but is also sharp about male reactions to Christina's self-assertive brilliance: the way he places a quotation from Pope Innocent XI at the start of the book, 'Christina is a woman, and behaves as such – irrationally', is typical.

> **READ ON**
> Christina, *Correspondence*. Francis Gribble, *The Court of Christina of Sweden*.

CHURCH, Richard (1893–1972) English writer

Church worked as a clerk for 24 years before becoming a full-time writer at the age of 40. He wrote poetry, novels, and an autobiography which was a bestseller in its day but is now neglected. It is a beautifully written account of growing up in lower-middle-class London at the beginning of this century. Church and his brother Jack, though serious people, shared the outlook and aspirations of *Wells' Kipps or the heroes of Jerome's *Three Men in a Boat*, and Church writes well about his schooldays (not the bullying and buggery experienced by many English toffs who later wrote memoirs, but a gentler, saner business involving ordinary children in a friendly environment), of the first experience of work, of life in a loving family, of discovering theatre, music-hall and the city itself. There are two volumes: *Over the Bridge* (1955) and *The Golden Sovereign* (1957). *The Voyage Home* (1964) continues the story, but in a less focused way: it is mainly concerned with the pull, as he grew older, between his office work and his literary career.

> **READ ON**
> Jerome K. Jerome, *My Life and Times*. *V.S. Pritchett, *A Cab at the Door*.

CHURCHILL, Randolph
CHURCHILL, Jennie

Randolph Churchill (1849–1895) was a politician of dazzling

> **READ ON**
> Mrs George Cornwallis West (Jennie's second married name), *The Reminiscences of Lady Randolph Churchill*. Hesketh

promise, and was made Chancellor of the Exchequer at the young age of 37. But months after this appointment, he was diagnosed as incurably syphilitic, resigned, and went into a prolonged mental and physical decline. He is interesting in his own right – he was, for example, one of the first politicians actively to tout for public favour – and because of his cold, prickly relationship with his son *Winston Churchill. Winston Churchill, *Lord Randolph Churchill* (rev. ed. 1952) is highly flattering, as if making amends for their relationship in life. Robert Rhodes James, *Lord Randolph Churchill* (1959) and Randolph Churchill (his grandson), *Lord Randolph Churchill* (1965) take a similar line, though adding new material and discussing aspects of Randolph which Winston suppressed. R.F. Foster, *Lord Randolph Churchill: a Political Life* (1981) is far less tactful, and has an interesting introduction and epilogue on biographies in general and Randolph's in particular.

Jeannette (Jennie) Churchill (1854–1921) was an American heiress and a long-suffering wife. In spite of constant financial problems and social disappointment – she had expected her husband to become Prime Minister – she was never bowed down for long, and her charm made a striking contrast to Randolph's increasing moodiness. *Anita Leslie, *Jennie: the Life of Lady Randolph Churchill* (1969), full of family gossip, is an affectionate biography by her great-niece. Ralph G. Martin, *Jennie Churchill* (two volumes, 1971) is long, but in an airy, readable style. The first volume goes up to Randolph's death, the second covers Jennie's subsequent life and marriages.

Pearson, *Pilgrim Daughters* (accounts of marriages between British aristocrats and US heiresses, with a good chapter on Jennie). William Manchester, *The Last Lion* (about Winston, includes a good study of his parents).

CHURCHILL, Winston S(pencer) (1874–1965)
English politician

Churchill's towering, diverse personality has been well served by his official biographers, his son Randolph (who began the project) and Martin Gilbert, who took over when Randolph died. The books are *Youth 1874–1900* (1966), *Young Statesman 1900–1914* (1967), *Volume III 1914–1916* (1971), *Volume IV 1916–1922* (1975), *The Coming of War 1922–1939* (1976), *Finest Hour 1939–1941* (1983), *Road to Victory 1941–1945* (1986) and *Never Despair 1945–1965* (1988). Each has one or more companion volumes of reference documents, chiefly of specialist interest, and (confusingly) sharing the titles of the books they serve. The main books deal with Churchill's life day by day, almost minute by minute, and are consequently vast (*Finest Hour*, for example, runs to 1,308 pages plus photographs), but the writing is always to the point, and the indexes are magnificent. Martin Gilbert, *Churchill: A Life* (1991), at a thousand pages, is still no lightweight, but is a clear and definitive one-volume distillation.

‹› **READ ON**
Winston Churchill, *My Early Life* (2nd ed. 1958); *Thoughts and Adventures* (2nd ed. 1948); *The Roar of the Lion* (1969) (autobiographies). F.W. Heath, *A Churchill Anthology* (1962) (selections from speeches and writings). Richard Hough, *Winston and Clementine: the Triumph of the Churchills* (joint biography of Winston and his hardly less remarkable wife).

Churchill is well served by the US writer William Manchester. His Churchill books put British politics and institutions in a new perspective, and are full of insights which may surprise British readers. The three volumes are *The Last Lion: Visions of Glory* (1983), *The Caged Lion* (1988) and *The Lion Triumphant* (not yet published).

Two briefer books are worth recommending: Piers Brendan, *Winston Churchill, a Brief Life* (1987) and Elizabeth Longford, *Winston Churchill* (1979), which is excellent on Churchill's feeling for history. Character studies include R.W. Thompson, *The Yankee Marlborough* (1963), whose British approach usefully counterbalances the Manchester biography, and *Churchill: Four Faces and the Man* (1969), which contains five expert essays: A.J.P. Taylor on Churchill as statesman, Robert Rhodes James on the politician, J.H. Plumb on the historian, Basil Liddell Hart on the military strategist and the psychologist Anthony Storr on the man.

On a personal level, Churchill's secretary Elizabeth Nel, his bodyguard W.H. Thompson and his doctor Lord Moran have all written memoirs. John Colville, *The Churchillians* (1981) deals with his circle in splendid anecdotal detail. Kenneth Young, *Churchill and *Beaverbrook: a Study in Friendship and Politics* (1966) is a lively joint portrait of two crusty, wary giants.

CIBBER, Colley (1671–1757) English actor and writer

Cibber's *Apology for the Life of Mr Colley Cibber, Comedian* (1740) is a funny, amiable autobiography, one of the classic accounts of 18th-century London theatre. Cibber specialized in playing hammy villains (rewriting *Richard III* to make it more melodramatic) and foolish fops. He wrote plays, managed Drury Lane theatre, acted with some of the greatest figures in theatre history, and knew everyone about town. He also served as Poet Laureate, and was savaged by Pope (in *The Dunciad*) for the awfulness of his verse. His autobiography has the same effect as *Pepys's *Diary*: reading it is like throwing open a window and letting the sights and sounds of another age flood in. R.H. Barker, *Mr Cibber of Drury Lane* (1939) is an almost equally zestful, equally enthusiastic biography.

> ∘› **READ ON**
> Mary Nash, *The Provoked Wife: the Life and Times of Susannah Cibber*. *Michael Kelly, *Reminiscences*.

CLAIRMONT, 'Claire' (1797–1879) English freethinker

Clairmont was William Godwin's stepdaughter, and her stepsister Mary married *Percy Bysshe Shelley. At the same time

> ∘› **READ ON**
> Margot Strickland, *The Byron Women* (a sympathetic account of Clairmont, and of many others).

as the marriage, Shelley began an affair with Clairmont, and she, Shelley and Mary formed a *ménage à trois* until Shelley's death. Clairmont was also *Byron's mistress, and bore him a daughter, Allegra. Her *Journals* (ed. Marion Kingston Stocking, 1968) give a day-by-day account of her life, not the less extraordinary because she saw nothing odd in it at all. R. Glynn Grylls, *Claire Clairmont, Mother of Byron's Allegra* (1938) fills in the gaps.

CLARK, Kenneth (1903–1983) English art historian

Clark was a private man who overcame his shyness to pursue his aim of introducing as many people as possible to great art. He wrote many books, including *Leonardo da Vinci* (1939, but many later editions) an account of *Leonardo's development as an artist. In the 1970s he became well known when his TV series *Civilisation* was a worldwide success. His tart autobiographies *Another Part of the Wood* (1974) and *The Other Half* (1977) are heartbreaking about his loveless childhood and tempestuous marriage (both his father and wife drank to excess), and interesting on his career as director of the National Gallery (and promoter of the famous lunchtime concerts in the Second World War), chairman of the Arts Council and Surveyor of the Queen's Pictures.

◇ **READ ON**
Meryle Secrest, *Kenneth Clark* (sympathetic account of Clark's attempts not to lose dignity in such a busy, stormy life, and to cope with his own contradictory, complex character).

◇ CLASSICAL MUSIC

George Antheil, *The Bad Boy of Music*
*Hector Berlioz, *Memoirs*
John Bird, *Percy Grainger*
Peter Gradenwitz, *Leonard Bernstein*
Alan Jefferson, *The Life of *Richard Strauss*
Herbert Kupferberg, *Felix Mendelssohn, His Life, His Family, His Music*
Nancy B. Reich, *Clara Schumann: the Artist and the Woman*
Andres Segovia, *Segovia: an autobiography*
*Ethel Smyth, *Impressions that Remained; As Time Went On . . .*
Otto Sonneck (ed.) *Beethoven: Impressions by his Contemporaries*
Ronald Taylor, *Franz Liszt*

CLAUDIUS I (10BC-AD54) Roman emperor (ruled 41–54)

Claudius' family considered him a harmless imbecile; he thus escaped the bloody power-struggles of the first half-century of Roman imperial rule, and was unexpectedly made emperor himself in a palace coup when he was 51. He continued to be scorned or neglected for 1,900 years, until the publication of *Robert Graves' blockbusting novels *I, Claudius* and *Claudius the God*, 'autobiographies' leaving no scandalous stone unturned. Graves' books (based on scrupulous research, whatever fictional use he made of it) have spurred others on to more objective accounts. Barbara Levick, *Claudius* (1990), though full of dry classical detail, examines all the evidence, and presents an entirely reasonable picture of Claudius' achievements as emperor – ironically not a million miles from Graves' claims.

⋗ **READ ON**
Suetonius, *The Twelve Caesars* (gossipy Roman account of the early emperors. Source of Graves' most over-the-top anecdotes; a bloodthirsty, steamy soap opera of ancient times).

CLEOPATRA V (69–30BC) Egyptian queen

An astute politician, Cleopatra saw the Romans as allies in her struggle for the Egyptian throne with her brother Ptolemy, and seduced first *Julius Caesar and then his lieutenant Mark Antony. For their part, Caesar and Antony coveted not only Cleopatra's body, but the wealth of Egypt, granary of the Mediterranean world and gateway to Africa, over which the Romans had had imperial ambitions since the time of Hannibal. Unfortunately for Cleopatra, her and Antony's navy was defeated by the forces of Octavian (the future emperor Augustus), and she committed suicide.

Immediately after Cleopatra's death, the Roman publicity machine began showing her as a monster, a *femme fatale* using sex to trap the honest nobility of Rome. In the succeeding 2, 000 years, this legend has all but eclipsed Cleopatra's reality: the 'Serpent of the Old Nile' has been seen as the very emblem of seductive womanhood and of the mysterious, exotic East. Lucy Hughes-Hallett, *Cleopatra* (1990) deals with this legend, as shown in art, drama (the plays, among others, of *Shakespeare and *Shaw), films (starring everyone from Theda Bara to *Elizabeth Taylor, from *Vivien Leigh to Amanda Barrie in *Carry On Cleo*), novels, poems, adverts, even sermons. Hughes-Hallett's basic thesis is feminist – she sees the Cleopatra legend as symbolic of the way men need to visualize women's sexuality in order to cope with it – but Cleopatra's fascination overwhelms even that, and is the main interest in this fabulous, unusual book. Jack Lindsay, *Cleopatra* (1971) and Michael Grant, *Cleopatra* (1972) are more standard biographies, sober but elegant accounts of fact.

⋗ **READ ON**
Margaret Lamb, *Antony and Cleopatra on the English Stage*. Antonia Fraser, *Boadicea's Chariot* (study of 'warrior queens' in popular legend and imagination).

COBB, Richard (born 1917) English historian

When Cobb, a professor of history, retired, he made a second reputation as a writer of memoirs. His autobiographical books describe a calm, privileged British existence: prep and public schools, Oxford, 'interesting war', university teaching (where he specialised in French history), and so on. Cobb makes stylish prose out of even the most trivial events: what matters is not what happens but how he tells it. Some people find his style self-obsessed and arch, too full of sentences like 'about the only thing to be said in favour of *ces événements* of May-June 1968, is that they happened when they did, that is in the middle of the Oxford University term'. For others, this approach gives the books their unique appeal. They are *Still Life* (1983), about Cobb's childhood, *A Classical Education* (1985), about his schooldays and university life – this volume interweaves autobiography and murder mystery – and *Something to Hold Onto* (1988), more detailed accounts of key events in his life.

> **READ ON**
> Gwen Raverat, *Period Piece* (childhood in middle-class Cambridge in the last years of the 19th century).

COBBETT, William (1763–1835) English campaigner and politician

After army service in Canada, Cobbett worked as a journalist in the fledgling USA, writing under the name 'Peter Porcupine'. After 1800 he continued his career in England, starting *Cobbett's Weekly Political Register* and writing, in all, some 20 million words. Originally a Tory, he changed his politics completely after 1804 and became one of Britain's best-known radicals, a parliamentary reformer and a propagandist for the welfare and dignity of working people. His best-known book, *Rural Rides*, combines descriptions of the English countryside with condemnation of the poverty and oppression he found there. George Spater, *William Cobbett* (two volumes, 1982) is a sympathetic biography, especially good on his time in the USA. Daniel Green, *Great Cobbett* (1983) is shorter, more romantically written, and has excellent assessments – it is by a journalist – of Cobbett's writing.

> **READ ON**
> G.D.H. Cole, *Life of William Cobbett* (published in 1927, but still the best account of Cobbett's political work and the conditions in which he wrote). William Rietzel (ed.), *Autobiography of William Cobbett* (compiled from Cobbett's own writings).

COCKBURN, Patricia (born 1914) Anglo-Irish writer

Cockburn's autobiography *Figure of Eight* (1985) tells, with unselfconscious wit, of a busy and unusual life. Brought up in the Anglo-Irish milieu fictionalized by Somerville and Ross, she married first a descendant of *Byron's family and then the radical journalist Claude Cockburn. With him, she edited the political magazine *The Week*, and travelled all over the world, to places even now beyond the scope of tourism. Her book tells of

> **READ ON**
> Patricia Cockburn, *The Years of the Week* ('biography' of the magazine). Claude Cockburn, *In Time of Trouble.*

all this, and is particularly lively about the people she met, in all countries and at all levels of society.

COCTEAU, Jean (1889–1963) French writer and film maker

Cocteau was a leader of the avant garde through the 1910s–30s. His friends and collaborators included *Diaghilev, *Picasso, *Colette and *Stravinsky; he wrote poetry, plays, novels, newspaper articles, ballet scenarios and opera libretti. He drew, played jazz and directed films. He was notorious for his love affairs and for using opium to trigger creativity. His personality was so overwhelming that people found it hard to get the measure of his work until he died; it was only then that many of his creations (the novel *The Children of the Game*, the play *The Infernal Machine*, the films *Beauty and the Beast* and *Orpheus*) were reassessed quietly and discovered to be masterpieces.

Elizabeth Sprigge and Jean-Jacques Kihm, *Jean Cocteau: the Man and the Mirror* (1968) is a short, brisk introduction to both man and work. Francis Steegmuller, *Cocteau* (1970), the standard biography, gives more space to descriptions of Cocteau's work, and quotes letters and other documents. It is objective about Cocteau's work, but wide-eyed at his life, giving an impression of frantic, chaotic days and nights, life lived at fast-forward, which may have been how it was for Cocteau and his circle, but can leave the reader limp.

❖ **READ ON**
Jean Cocteau, *Journals* (interesting because of Cocteau's more considered work, but less informative than many people's journals: chiefly dates, reports of conversations and oblique, fragmented thoughts).

COLERIDGE, Samuel Taylor (1772–1834) English writer

One of the most unruly geniuses of English romantic literature, Coleridge wrote powerful, visionary verse and prose, but became an opium addict in the 1800s and destroyed his own creativity. His prose writings, *Biographia Literaria* (outstanding on his friendship with *William Wordsworth), *Table Talk* and *Confessions of an Enquiring Spirit*, give a lively impression of his teeming mind and busy, tormented life. Books by others give more balanced views, notably Molly Lefebure, *Samuel Taylor Coleridge: a Bondage of Opium* (1974), good, and grim, on his drug addiction; and Richard Holmes, *Coleridge: Early Visions* (1989), volume one of a magnificent, scholarly biography.

❖ **READ ON**
Samuel Taylor Coleridge, *Letters*. Sara Coleridge (his unhappy wife) (ed. Potter), *Minnow Among Tritons: Letters to Thomas Poole*. A.S. Byatt, *Wordsworth and Coleridge in Their Time*.

COLETTE, Sidonie Gabrielle Claudine (1873–1954) French writer

In her 20s Colette was a music-hall mime artist, and later she acted in stage adaptations of her books. In the 1930s she ran a

❖ **READ ON**
Several of Colette's novels are autobiographical: the four *Claudine* books (schooldays, arrival in Paris, marriage and love affairs of a young provincial

beauty salon. She was notorious for her love affairs, with people of both sexes, and for her friendships with such people as *Jean Cocteau. All the time she wrote novels, usually about love and often involving the 'sentimental education' of a young person by someone much older. Critics acclaimed her as one of the finest French writers since *Proust. Her novel *Gigi* was filmed (with Maurice Chevalier and Leslie Caron), and Hermione Gingold delighted French society by making her characterization of the elderly, unshockable old aunt a deliciously recognizable parody of Colette herself, the French bohemian Grande Dame.

Joanna Richardson, *Colette* (1983), the standard English biography, tells her life in a series of short, impressionistic scenes like those in Colette's own books – the biographer bewitched by her subject, as so many people were by Colette's personality. Maurice Goudeket, *Close to Colette* (1956) is a memoir by her third husband. Yvonne Mitchell, *Colette, a Taste for Life* (1975) has magnificent illustrations.

girl); *The Vagabond* (life in the music-hall); *My Apprenticeships* (based on her first marriage, and her beginnings as a writer); *Sido* (a beautiful memoir of her mother). Robert Phelps (ed.), *Belles Saisons: a Colette Scrapbook.*

COLUMBUS, Christopher (c1446–1506) Italian explorer

Sure that the world was round, and that he could reach the spice markets of India by sailing west, Columbus raised finance in Spain and set out to prove his point. He made four voyages in all, exploring the Caribbean and Central America. Gianni Canzotto, *Christopher Columbus: the Dream and the Obsession* (Eng. ed. 1986) gives lively accounts both of Columbus' explorations and his (often devious) adventures on land. Paolo Emilio Taviani, *Christopher Columbus: the Grand Design* (Eng. ed., much revised, 1985) is a scholarly book about Columbus' early years, his education and the formulation of his plans for the famous voyage. It ends in 1492, as Columbus' design is about to be fulfilled. It covers earlier voyages of exploration by others, Columbus' own seafaring experience, the state of shipbuilding and navigation in the mid-15th century, the social and economic reasons for the quest for new spice routes, and a thousand other matters. Few books so authoritative have ever been less stuffy: this is a masterpiece of scholarship. Salvador de Madariaga, *Christopher Columbus* (1949) is an earlier, much more flowery biography, viewing Columbus' discoveries and their aftermath from the Spanish point of view.

➤ **READ ON**
Christopher Marlowe, *The Memoirs of Christopher Columbus* (historical novel).

CONRAD, Joseph (1857–1924) Polish/English writer

Fascinated by boys' adventure stories, Conrad (born Konrad Korzeniowski) went to sea at 16 and was a captain ten years

➤ **READ ON**
Jessie Conrad (his wife), *Joseph Conrad as I Knew Him; Joseph Conrad and His Circle.* Frederick R. Karl and L. Davis (ed.),

later. He wrote his first novel in 1895, retired from the sea soon afterwards, settled in England and quickly became a pillar of the literary establishment. His autobiography, *A Personal Record* (1912) was rewritten from articles and essays and is somewhat bitty. Frederick R. Karl, *Joseph Conrad: the Three Lives* (1979), the standard biography, is a detailed, 1,000-page account: the three 'lives' are Conrad's childhood in Russian Poland, his years at sea and his life as a writer. The book includes much discussion of Conrad's writings, relating them both to his life and to novels by such other writers as *Flaubert, Dostoevski and *George Eliot.

Collected Letters of Joseph Conrad (several volumes). Norman Sherry, *Conrad and His World* (brief; superbly illustrated).

COOKSON, Catherine (born 1906) English writer

Cookson's stories tell of ordinary working girls, usually from the north of England, whose sparky, unconventional approach to life leads them into love affairs and adventures far beyond the poverty-ridden backstreets and farms where they were born. Her autobiography *Our Kate* (second ed. 1982) is a warm, witty story of a very similar kind. Cookson writes of family life and schooldays in north-east England during the Depression, of her work as a laundry checker, her marriage to her old schoolteacher, her war experiences and her second career (not begun till she was 44) as one of Britain's best-loved novelists. The book is also a portrait of her mother, the 'our Kate' of the title, and of her relationship with her ever-cheerful, ever-determined daughter.

·> READ ON
Catherine Cookson, *Cookson Country* (about the moors, hills and working towns of her beloved North-east). Also of interest may be Jane Aiken Hodge, *The Private World of Georgette Heyer*.

COOPER, Duff
COOPER, Diana

Duff Cooper (1890–1954) behaved like a grandee from a vanished age. He made a rigorous distinction between his public and private lives, spending his days in politics or diplomacy and his nights – if memoirs and the press are to be believed – drinking, gambling and womanizing. He was the only member of Chamberlain's cabinet to resign over Munich, and after the war was a notable ambassador to France. His autobiography *Old Men Forget* (1953) is a straightforward account of his life, mainly about its public side. John Charmley, *Duff Cooper, the Authorised Biography* (1986) gives an idea of the private man, and insight into his remarkable marriage.

Diana Cooper (1892–1986) was brought up to a privileged life, mainly in Belvoir Castle, and 'came out' just before the First World War. She married Duff Cooper in 1919, and became a well-known hostess and leader of London society, re-

·> READ ON
Artemis Cooper (ed.), *A Durable Fire: the Letters of Duff and Diana Cooper 1913–1950* (edited by their grand-daughter). Susan Mary Alsop, *To Marietta from Paris* (letters by a woman whose husband was Cooper's attaché in Paris: an insider's view of embassy life).

nowned for beauty, wit and charm. She wrote three volumes of autobiography, chiefly about the people she knew, her marriage and her public life: *The Rainbow Comes and Goes* (1958), *The Light of Common Day* (1959) and *Trumpets from the Steep* (1960). Philip Ziegler, *Diana Cooper* (1981) is somewhat purse-lipped about the kind of privilege she and her set enjoyed, but he equally obviously shares the world's captivation with his subject.

CORKE, Helen (1882–1978) English writer

As a young teacher in the 1900s, Corke was fascinated by history, drama and music, and spent her energy educating herself as well as her charges, absorbing sensations and information as flowers absorb sun. At 27, she fell in love with her violin teacher (an older, married man) and they spent a week together on the Isle of Wight. The lover, ashamed to have given in to 'male urges' in this way, committed suicide soon afterwards. Corke showed her account of the affair to her friend and fellow-teacher, *D.H. Lawrence, who made it the theme of his novel *The Trespasser*. Corke describes all this in the first volume of her autobiography, *In Our Infancy* (1975). She is excellent at showing the delight of a mind awakening to music and literature for the first time, and at describing a young Victorian's mixed feelings of terror and excitement at the thought of sex.

'CORVO, Baron': *see* ROLFE, Frederick

COSBY, Bill (born 1938) US comedian

In his TV series *The Cosby Show*, Cosby plays the wry, wisecracking father of a large and loving family. The show blends folksiness, sentiment, warmth and wit in a way which seems particularly true to one kind of US family life. In the 1980s, Cosby distilled its essence into several books, part autobiography (about his real-life family), part joke routines. *Love and Marriage* (1989) is typical: an account of awakening to sex, discovering (and courting) girls, falling in love and staying happily married.

> ❖ **READ ON**
> Helen Corke, *The Light of Common Day* (sequel, about war service and her years as a teacher, enabling other minds to flower).

> ❖ **READ ON**
> Bill Cosby, *Fatherhood; Time Flies*. Giovanni Guareschi, *The House That Nino Built* (family life, Italian-style). Biographies of Bill Cosby include Bill Adler, *The Cosby Wit: His Life and Humour* and Roland L. Smith, *Cosby*.

❖ COUNTRY CHILDHOODS

*Gerald Durrell, *My Family and Other Animals*
Winifred Foley, *A Child in the Forest*
Grace Griffiths, *Days of My Freedom*
*Laurie Lee, *Cider with Rosie*

---

*Carl Nielsen, *My Childhood*
Rosemary Sutcliffe, *Blue Remembered Hills*
*Flora Thompson, *Lark Rise to Candleford*
Nancy Thompson, *At Their Departing*
Laura Ingalls Wilder, *The Little House on the Prairie*
See also Growing Up; London Life; Russian Childhoods.

COWARD, Noël (1899–1973) English actor and writer

'Actor and writer' is hardly enough: Coward was also a composer, director, cabaret artist and international wit. Apart from *Cocteau, few people this century have combined showbiz dazzle with such wide-ranging, solid achievement. Coward's songs, films and, above all, his plays will long outlive his legend. He wrote two volumes of glittering, malicious autobiography, *Present Indicative* (1937) and *Future Indefinite* (1954), and Sheridan Morley (ed.), *The Noël Coward Diaries* were published in 1982. The latter's *A Talent to Amuse* (1969) is a big biography, crammed with anecdotes and benefiting from Coward's own comments. Cole Lesley, *The Life of Noël Coward* (1976), though it omits none of Coward's showbiz triumphs, is a more intimate memoir, by his secretary, friend and companion of many years.

> ❖ **READ ON**
> Patrick Braybrooke, *The Amazing Mr Noël Coward* (spectacularly gushy 1930s account of Coward at his peak). Sheridan Morley, Graham Pain and Cole Lesley, *Noël Coward and His Friends* (picture book, but with anecdote-packed text).

CRAWFORD, Joan (1906–77) US film star

Crawford made her name in films in which gorgeously dressed women live on the edge of their nerves, tormented by their own insecurity and/or the buffets of a heartless world. Her autobiography, *A Portrait of Joan* (1962) tells the public side of her life: acting successes, charity work, meetings with adoring fans. Christina Crawford, *Mommie Dearest* (1979) paints an entirely different picture. Crawford's adopted daughter describes her childhood with Joan, and shows her mother as an egotistical monster who treated the child in public like a publicity doll, dressing her in outfits which were miniature versions of her own, cuddling her, hugging her – and in private beat her with coathangers, locked her in closets and deprived her of all normal, human warmth. The book was a scorching bestseller, and set a trend for 'tell-all' memoirs by the children of famous stars. It makes compulsive reading, though you may never be able to face a Joan Crawford film again.

> ❖ **READ ON**
> Warren G. Harris, *Cary Grant: A Touch of Elegance* (Not *Cary Grant as well! Is nothing sacred?).

CREVECOEUR, Michel-Guillaume St John de (1735–1813) French traveller, farmer and politician

> ❖ **READ ON**
> St John de Crèvecoeur, *Sketches of Eighteenth Century America* (more essays, assembled from his

As a young army officer in Canada, Crèvecoeur spent several years exploring and mapping the St Lawrence. He then settled in New York State, married and lived as a gentleman farmer until the American Revolution, when he was exiled for supporting the English. Later, he went back to the fledgling USA as French consul. His *Letters from an American Farmer* (1782), describing his life before the Revolution, was a bestseller on two continents, and is still a classic account of New World pioneer and frontier life. Gay Wilson Allen and Roger Asselineau, *St John de Crèvecoeur: the Life of an American Farmer* (1987) is a detailed biography, providing excellent historical background and pointing up what makes Crèvecoeur's life so characteristic of early American experience.

CRISP, Quentin (born 1910) English writer

Instead of hiding his homosexuality (as was common in England in the 1930s–60s), Crisp put on a peacock display of camp: dyed hair, makeup, gaudy clothes and a flirtatious, eyelash-fluttering manner. In short, he lived up to the tabloid vision of the gay man as 'screaming queen'. He suffered for it, physically and socially, and lived a lonely, if flamboyant, life on the fringes of the London art world (where he worked as a life-class model). In 1974 he wrote a no-holds-barred, full-frontal autobiography, *The Naked Civil Servant*, which was made into a TV film and changed his life. A second volume, *How to Become a Virgin* (1981) tells what happened next, of how he coped with fame and travel, and of his new existence in New York. The books are written with exactly the same slow-paced, acid wit as Crisp deploys in lectures and chat shows. They are the man.

CROMWELL, Oliver (1599–1658) English soldier and Protector

Although Cromwell became the first commoner ever to rule Britain, for the first 30 years of his life he was content to live as a country gentleman, and showed no political ambition. This is not the only apparent contradiction in his character. He was decisive, even impetuous, in battle, but otherwise found making up his mind an agonizing job. He ordered the execution of *Charles I with equanimity, and is still remembered in Ireland as a butcher, but was a kind friend and an indulgent husband and father. If the politics of the English Civil War are historically fascinating, so too is Cromwell's own personality: a biographer's treasure-trove.

Of the hundreds of Cromwell biographies, one of the most monumental (still readable today) is C.H. Firth, *Oliver*

papers and first published in 1925). Thomas Philbrick, *St John de Crèvecoeur* (crisp, clear life).

⋄ **READ ON**
Quentin Crisp, *Love Made Easy* (comic novel of love in bomb-ruined London after the Second World War); *How to Go to the Movies* (witty, bitchy film reviews).

⋄ **READ ON**
C.V. Wedgwood, *The King's War, The King's Peace* (outstanding historical study of the Revolution); *Oliver Cromwell* (an excellent 128-page summary biography). John Gillingham, *Cromwell: Portrait of a Soldier* (concentrating on Cromwell's military genius, and comparing him in detail with *Caesar and *Napoléon I). Pauline Gregg, *Free-born John* (biography of John Lilburne, revolutionary who thought Cromwell's reforms too lily-livered and favourable to the aristocracy. Sympathetic to Lilburne – no easy task – and

Cromwell and the Rule of the Puritans in England (1900; rev. ed. 1938). Christopher Hill, *God's Englishman* (1970) is equally heavyweight, focusing Cromwell's character against the social, economic and religious temper of his times. Antonia Fraser, *Cromwell Our Chief of Men* (1973) concentrates on actions and character: it was Fraser's stated aim to 'humanize' Cromwell, and she succeeds. Pauline Gregg, *Oliver Cromwell* (1988) is less floridly written, but no less packed with facts. Gregg draws on her knowledge of Charles I (whose biography she wrote in 1981), and has also tramped the ground Cromwell lived and fought on, to excellent effect. Roger Howell, *Cromwell* (1977) is chiefly recommendable for its superb bibliography and commentary on the different Cromwells seen by other biographers, from Stuart pamphleteers ('Cromwell's Bloody Slaughterhouse') to humanizing Fraser. Perhaps, for anyone really interested in Cromwell, this is the book to read first.

marvellously evocative of the revolutionary and religious fervour of the time).

CROSBY, Bing (Harry) (1901–77) US singer and film star

In his work, Crosby was renowned for a laid-back, no-fuss style, and he put on this manner backstage as well, arriving at studios claiming to have no idea what he was to do that day, and saying that he'd rather be somewhere else, playing golf. He was a 'man's man', forever hunting, fishing or playing sports, leaving his brother to manage the business and his wife to run the family. His first wife died of alcoholism; his second wife worked to reconcile adoration of Bing with her need to fulfil herself as actress, mother, nurse and teacher. The Crosby parcel, in short, is tied with complicated knots, and his autobiography *Call Me Lucky* (1953) does little to loosen them, being chiefly for fans. Charles Thompson, *The Complete Crosby* (1978, updating the earlier book *Bing*) is more revealing about Crosby the man, but sparse on his work, and Kathryn Crosby, *Bing and Other Things* (1967), by his second wife, hints at darkness behind the dazzle, especially in Crosby's attitude to his children. The impression is that there was a mystery to Crosby which he was reluctant to think about, and which was vital to his work. He was a secretive man who pretended to be open – and perhaps invading his privacy is less illuminating than simply enjoying his films and records. We have the star; do we also need the man?

‹› **READ ON**
Gary Crosby, *Going My Way* (autobiography of Bing's eldest son, determined not to be swallowed by his father's publicity machine, and battling every inch of the way until he finally broke free).

CROWLEY, Aleister (1875–1947) English occultist

Crowley claimed to be the 'Great Beast' of the Book of Revelation in the Bible: Number 666, 'Ipsissimus', Antichrist. He be-

‹› **READ ON**
Francis King, *The Magical World of Aleister Crowley* (careful, objective account of Crowley's 'magick': a useful antidote for

lieved in a kind of mystical and sexual anarchy, not subject to the normal rules of human life, religion or philosophy. The tabloid newspapers, claiming to be shocked, gave lip-smacking accounts of him, saying that he was a pervert, a black magician, a conman and a fraud. But everything he did had serious, if sinister, undercurrents, ignored by the press. His *The Confessions of Aleister Crowley* (ed. John Symonds and Kenneth Grant, 1971) blends boastful autobiography with occult preaching: an absorbing, unsettling read. John Symonds, *The Great Beast* (1971) is the standard biography: long, detailed and appalled. To outsiders, the material in these books is some of the strangest human belief and behaviour ever put on paper. Readers easily revolted or terrified may prefer to avoid it.

anyone snake-bitten by the occult).

CULLWICK, Hannah (1833–1909) English servant

Cullwick went into service when she was eight years old. In 1854 she met Arthur Munby, an upper-class writer fascinated by the lives of working-class women. For the next 16 years she wrote *Massa*, a daily account of bed-making, coal-carrying, floor-scrubbing, carpet-beating and the rest of her domestic drudgery. In 1870 she married Munby, and each carried on life exactly as before, he going about literary and court London as an eligible if elderly bachelor, Cullwick continuing her work 'below stairs'. Hannah Cullwick, *The Diaries of Hannah Cullwick* (ed. Stanley, 1984) is a selection from her writings for him. It gives an unblinking picture of what was to all intents and purposes paid slavery, and an unconscious revelation of two odd people, in a relationship bizarre even by the standards of Victorian English eccentricity.

⋄ READ ON
Derek Hudson, *Munby: Man of Two Worlds* (biography of Munby, good on his psychology). Edward Carpenter, *My Dreams and Days* (by an Edwardian toff infatuated with working-class men, who went on to share their lives).

CUNARD, Nancy (1896–1965) English socialite, publisher and campaigner

Cunard's mother was Lady Cunard, Maud (Emerald), a society hostess with a horde of male admirers and lovers, but no idea how to care for a growing girl. Nancy grew up despising the conventions and hypocrisies of her circle, and rebelled publicly and violently, working hard for left-wing and anti-racist causes. Her writing on these matters was ahead of its time, anticipating 1960s attitudes, but it is hard to tell if she was devoted to a cause for its own sake or because it would offend her mother. Her pamphlet *Black Man and White Ladyship*, for example, was a public rubbishing of her mother's foibles and pursuits as well as of her horror at finding Nancy living with a black man. For some years Nancy ran the Hours Press, publishing (among

⋄ READ ON
Daphne Fielding, *The Rainbow Picnic* (biography of Nancy's friend Iris Tree, whose acquaintance ranged from *Oscar Wilde in the 1890s to such 1930s luminaries as the *Bloomsbury Group, Carrington, *Chaplin, *Dalí and *Krishnamurti).

others) *Acton, Aldington, Beckett, *Ellis and *Graves. Her
life, once so brilliant, ended in a fuddle of drink and mental
illness. Anne Chisholm, *Nancy Cunard* (1979) tells the whole
sad story, being particularly frank about Nancy's relationship
with her mother, the thing that made her and destroyed her.

CURIE, Marie (1867–1934) Polish/French scientist

Curie's scientific achievements are well known: co-discoverer
(with her husband, Pierre) of polonium and radium, tireless
worker on the properties of radioactivity, winner of two Nobel
prizes. Her life also fascinates because of her unstoppable progress in worlds which men had hitherto kept resolutely for
themselves. Robert Reid, *Marie Curie* (1975) tells her story in a
particularly readable way, making the science accessible to non-
physicists and giving full attention to Curie's personality and to
her unending battle with male-dominated society.

▸ **READ ON**
Ève Curie, *Madame Curie*
(admiring memoir by Curie's
daughter, published two years
after Curie's death).

D

DAHL, Roald (1916–90) English writer

Dahl was a bestselling writer of children's books (among others, *Charlie and the Chocolate Factory*), and of short stories for adults. His books also included two volumes of autobiography. *Boy* (1984), ostensibly written for children, about his childhood, is as full of grotesque adults and slapstick events as any of his novels, but contains horrific accounts of sadistic beatings at public school. *Going Solo* (1986), for adults, is blackly funny about Dahl's time as a Second World War fighter pilot, first training in Egypt then defending the British Expeditionary Force in Greece. His view of human beings is as mordant as ever, but he allows himself more psychological depth and considerably more pain than in his children's books.

⠷ **READ ON**
*Spike Milligan, *Adolf Hitler, My Part in His Downfall*.

DALI, Salvador (1904–89) Spanish painter

Painter, stage-designer, film-maker, surrealist and eccentric, Dalí was either a genius (his own view) or a half-crazed artistic showman. Are repeatedly throwing yourself downstairs to gain attention, or giving lectures in full diving gear (complete with helmet) rational actions? Are paintings of floppy watches true artistic statements or brilliant aesthetic con-tricks? Salvador Dalí, *The Secret Life of Salvador Dalí* (1942), *Diary of a Genius* (1965) and *Dalí by Dalí* (1970) put forward Dalí's vision of himself with a relentless poker-face, very funny if you are in the mood. Meryle Secrest, *Salvador Dalí, the Surrealist Jester* (1986) is cool about Dalí's eccentricity, warm about his paintings, and persuasive about his status as a genius. Tim McGirk, *Wicked Lady: Sal-*

⋗ **READ ON**
Alain Bosquet, *Conversations With Salvador Dalí*. Robert Descharnes, *Salvador Dalí, the Work, the Man*. Luis Buñuel, *My Last Sigh* (autobiography of the film director, Dalí's friend and fellow surrealist).

vador Dalí's Muse (1989) is about Dalí's obsessive, possessive 50-year marriage to Gala, his chief model and inspiration.

DALTON, Hugh (1887–1962) English politician

Like *Bevan, Dalton was a left-winger, important in the post-war Labour government, and a contradictory, complex character. He was a master of political scheming, and 'brought on' many younger politicians who went on to lead the 1960s Labour governments. Ben Pimlott, *Hugh Dalton* (1985) is a classic documentary biography, full of revealing anecdotes about Dalton's personality and engrossing for anyone interested in the political process in general, and backstage Labour Party machinations in particular.

⋅> READ ON

Hugh Dalton, *Call Back Yesterday 1887–1931*; *The Fateful Years 1931–1945*; *High Tide and After 1945–1960* (memoirs, read for maximum enjoyment after Pimlott). Harold Nicolson, *George V* (early chapters detail the education Dalton's father, the Canon of St George's Chapel, Windsor, gave to the future King, and explain, in passing, the genteel but uncompromising hostility the royal family always felt towards Dalton).

⋅> DANCERS

Richard Buckle, *Nijinsky*
Sarah Giles, *Fred Astaire*
Alan Ross MacDougall, *Isadora: a Revolutionary in Art and Love* *Isadora Duncan
Agnes de Mille, *And Promenade Home*
Keith Money, *Anna Pavlova: Her Life and Art*
George Perry, *Bluebell* (*Margaret Kelly, 'Miss Bluebell')

Phyllis Rose, *Jazz Cleopatra* (*Josephine Baker)
Moira Shearer, *Balletmaster: a Dancer's View* (Balanchine)

DA PONTE, Lorenzo (1749–1838) Italian poet and librettist

The world knows Da Ponte as librettist of *Mozart's operas *The Marriage of Figaro*, *Don Giovanni* and *Cosí fan tutte*, and as a kind of cut-rate *Casanova. But these elements are just part of a long and adventurous life, beginning in the Jewish quarter of Venice and ending as Professor of Italian at Columbia College, New York. His *Memoirs* (Eng. ed. 1929) are racy, boastful and full of anecdotes about his famous friends, his gambling, his womanizing and his battle to make a living by teaching and writing. (Their early chapters are the source of his reputation as a Casanova.) Sheila Hodges, *Lorenzo da Ponte* (1985) sets out in a scholarly way to set the record straight, and to its author's

⋅> READ ON

*Michael Kelly, *Memoirs* (good on operatic life in Da Ponte's time). *Casanova, *Memoirs*.

surprise, finds most of Da Ponte's stories true. April FitzLyon, *The Libertine Librettist* (1955) is more colourful, making Da Ponte seem like Bob Hope in some wisecracking Hollywood costume comedy.

‹› DARK BLUE, LIGHT BLUE

(Oxford and Cambridge)

*Ralph Glasser, *Gorbals Boy at Oxford*
Bevis Hillier, *Young Betjeman* (*John Betjeman)
*Carola Oman, *An Oxford Childhood*
John Pudney, *Lewis Carroll and His World*
Gwen Raverat, *Period Piece*
A.N. Wilson, *C.S. Lewis*

DARWIN, Charles (1809–82) English scientist

After a five-year voyage round the world as naturalist on the survey ship *Beagle*, Darwin settled down to a quiet life of thought, scientific experiment – for 30 years, for example, he measured the distribution of worm-casts on the same square metre of his grounds – and writing, surrounded by a large, happy family. Poor health made him reclusive, so that others (notably *T.H. Huxley) took up the cudgels on behalf of his theory of evolution by natural selection and its corollary, that the human species was just one among many, not specially created or favoured by God.

Darwin's own writings include *Diary of the Voyage of HMS Beagle* (ed. Nora Barlow, 1933), part scientific diary part travelogue, and a hefty *Autobiography* (ed. Nora Barlow, 1958). Francis Darwin (ed.), *Darwin's Life and Letters* (1887) is a useful early source, edited by his son. Standard modern biographies are Peter Brent, *Charles Darwin: A Man of Enlarged Curiosity* (1981), fat, full of documents and good on the controversy over evolution, and Gavin de Beer, *Charles Darwin* (1963), setting Darwin's theories in the scientific context of their time. John Chancellor, *Charles Darwin* (1973) is a sumptuous, large-format book, with over 100 evocative illustrations. John Bowlby, *Charles Darwin* (1990) is fascinating about Darwin's health, from virile young naturalist on the *Beagle* to querulous, self-absorbed hypochondriac almost as soon as he returned to England.

‹› **READ ON**
Richard Dawkins, *The Blind Watchmaker* (elegant explanation of how Darwin's theories work). W. Irvine, *Apes, Angels and Victorians* (lively account of the Darwinian controversy). H.E.L. Mellersh, *Fitzroy of the Beagle* (biography of the navy officer who captained Darwin's voyage round the world). Harry Clements, *Alfred Russel Wallace: biologist and social reformer* (biography of the unorthodox scientist whose ideas on evolution prefigured and inspired Darwin's). Edna Healey, *Wives of Fame* (includes a section on Emma, Darwin's brilliant, self-effacing wife). Irving Stone, *The Origin* (historical novel).

DAVIES, W(illiam) H(enry) (1871–1940) Welsh writer

When Davies was 20 he left home to live on the road, and

READ ON
W.H. Davies, *Young Emma* (the story of his courtship and marriage, shown only to friends

travelled all over the USA and Canada before returning to England. He spent some years in dosshouses, publishing a book of poems at his own expense and sending it to famous people (for example *Shaw) asking them to pay by return. He wrote over 600 poems, chiefly lyrics about nature, and two novels. In 1908 his account of his wanderings, *Autobiography of a Super-Tramp*, was a huge literary success. He wrote a sequel, *Later Days (1925), describing London literary life with the same wry matter-of-factness as he had the drunks, dosshouse-keepers and pan-handlers of his youth.*

DAVIS, Bette (1908–90) US film star

Famous for playing strong, domineering women in films, Davis was equally hard-hitting in real life. Her way with studio bosses, directors, writers and fellow actors was notorious. Her friends said that it was the result of applying the same high standards to every-one else as to herself; her enemies gave a very different explana-tion. Barbara Davis Hyman, *My Mother's Keeper* (1985) is a no-holds-barred account of what it was like to be Davis' daughter. The clash of wills was such that the book might just as well have been called *Fifteen Rounds With the Champ and Still a-Punchin'*. Who won? Who always won a Bette Davis fight?

DE BEAUVOIR, Simone (1908–86) French writer

De Beauvoir is remembered for novels, for her lifelong associa-tion with *Sartre, for her philosophical work and for *The Second Sex*, (1949), a study of women which was one of the pillars of the feminist movement. She wrote four books of autobiography, par-ticularly good on growing up, on relationships (with her parents, with Sartre) and on political and philosophical work in the 1930s and 1940s. The English titles and publication dates are *Memoirs of a Dutiful Daughter* (1958), *The Prime of Life* (1960), *The Force of Circumstances* (1963) and *Final Account* (1974). Deirdre Bair, *Simone de Beauvoir* (1990) is a detailed, scholarly biography, by far the best of many available. It places de Beauvoir in the intel-lectual life of her time, deals well with her writing, her feminism and her relationship (physical and intellectual) with Sartre, but also shows her, with sympathy and conviction, as a complex, troubled and inconsistent human being.

DE QUINCEY, Thomas (1785–1859) English writer

A (sometimes extremely trying) friend of *Coleridge and

during his life and published after his death). Manfri Frederick Wood, *In the Life of a Romany Gypsy* (sharing Davies' feeling for the open road).

⋄ **READ ON**
Roy Moseley, *Bette Davis: an Intimate Memoir*. Shaun Considine, *Bette and Joan: the Divine Feud* (account of one of the most high-octane battles in movie history).

⋄ **READ ON**
De Beauvoir, *Letters* (1990, ed. recommended); *A Very Easy Death* (moving memoir of her relationship with her terminally ill mother).

⋄ **READ ON**
Hunter Davies, *William Wordsworth*. *Maxim Gorki, *My Childhood*.

Wordsworth, De Quincey published a fascinating, self-serving account of their relationship, *Recollections of the Lake Poets* (1834–9). He also wrote *Confessions of an English Opium Eater* (1822), a painful story of his childhood, adolescence and growing dependence on the drug which was to destroy his life. The books are classics, on a par with *Gorki's autobiographies, but they need to be read with the pinch of salt supplied in Edward Sackville-West, *A Flame in Sunlight: the Life and Work of Thomas de Quincey* (1974), an account of squandered talent no less harrowing because its viewpoint is objective.

⋅> DERRING-DO

L. Alder and R. Dalby, *The Dervish of Windsor Castle*
Frédéric Grendel, **Beaumarchais, the Man Who Was Figaro*
Fitzroy Maclean, *A Person From England*
Gilbert Ronay, *The Tartar Khan's Englishman*
'Ronald Sinclair' (*Reginald Teague-Jones) *Adventures in Persia*
N. St Barbe Sladen, *The Real *Le Queux*
Arthur Swinson, *Beyond the Frontiers: a biography of Frederick Marsham Bailey, Explorer and Special Agent*
H. Winstone, *Captain Shakespeare*

DIAGHILEV, Sergei (1872–1929) Russian impresario

As art critic, manager of the Mariinsky Theatre in St Petersburg and founder of the Ballets Russes, Diaghilev introduced more people to modern art, music and theatre than almost anyone else this century. He had a gift for finding genius, and creating circumstances which would trigger great work. His protégés included Balanchine, *Cocteau, Pavlova, *Picasso, Rimsky-Korsakov, *Stravinsky and *Nijinsky (whom he loved). He knew everyone, and drew patrons and audiences from the grandees of half Europe. Richard Buckle, *Diaghilev* (1979) is a zestful biography, crammed with anecdotes and comments by everyone who knew, loved, hated or lent money to Diaghilev. It reads at times like a glitteringly bitchy, name-dropping charade, a cavalcade of camp. But given the lifestyle of its subject, how could things be otherwise?

⋅> **READ ON**
Boris Kochno, *Diaghilev and the Russian Ballet* (a feast for ballet fans). Alexandre Benois, *Memoirs*. Richard Buckle, *Nijinsky*. Caryl Brahms and S.J. Simon, *A Bullet in the Ballet* (comic novel spoofing the backstage tantrums of the Ballets Russes: murder happens during rehearsals for *Petrushka* in a company run by the explosive showman Vladimir Stroganoff).

> ‹› DIARIES AND JOURNALS
>
>
> *Fanny Burney, *Early Diary*
> *Henry 'Chips' Channon, *'Chips'*
> *Hannah Cullwick, *The Diaries of Hannah Cullwick*
> *Anne Frank, *The Diary of Anne Frank*
> *Edmund Goncourt and Jules Goncourt, *Journals*
> *Alice James, *Diary*
> *Samuel Pepys, *Diary*
> William Plomer (ed.) *Kilvert's Diary 1830–1879*
> *Dorothy Wordsworth, *Journals*

DICKENS, Charles (1812–70) English writer

If many events of Dickens' life seem familiar, it is because he reworked them and stitched them into his novels; *David Copperfield* and *Little Dorrit*, are particularly autobiographical. One of the best straightforward biographies is also the earliest: John Forster, *The Life of Dickens* (1874), in sturdy Victorian prose, as filling as dumplings. Peter Ackroyd, *Dickens* (1990), 1,212 pages long, is the best modern equivalent. It is excellent on Dickens' character and outstanding on the real London scenes transmuted in his books. Shorter 20th-century accounts, dwarfed but not eclipsed by Ackroyd, are Hesketh Pearson, *Charles Dickens, His Character, Comedy and Career* (1949) and Edgar Johnson, *Charles Dickens: His Tragedy and Triumph* (1952). Because of the way Dickens worked, the most revealing books about him usually blend biography with references to his novels. Particularly recommended are Michael Slater, *Dickens and Women* (1983), and Philip Collins, *Dickens and Crime* (1962) and *Dickens and Education* (1963).

‹› **READ ON**
Walter Dexter (ed.), *The Letters of Charles Dickens* (three volumes). Henry F. Dickens, *Memories of my Father*. Angus Wilson, *The World of Charles Dickens*. Jerome Meckier, *Innocent Abroad: Charles Dickens in America*.

DICKENS, Monica (born 1915) English writer

Dickens, the great-granddaughter of *Charles Dickens, wrote her autobiography *An Open Book* in 1978. She describes her secure childhood in a large family, her coming-out as a débutante, and her feelings of being engulfed by social inadequacy. In an effort to feel needed she took jobs as cook, nurse and journalist, and turned her experiences into the amusing books *One Pair of Hands* (1939), *One Pair of Feet* (1942) and *My Turn to Make the Tea* (1951), as well as several novels. The books' tone seems more superficial than it is; she appears reticent about her emotions, but each time she records some sad or

‹› **READ ON**
*Betty MacDonald, *Anybody Ca Do Anything; Who, Me?*.

appy event, we realize that we have been secretly prepared to now exactly how she feels.

DICKINSON, Emily (1830–86) US poet

As a girl, Dickinson was rich, sociable and outgoing. But in her mid-20s she began to retreat from the world, and by her 40s he lived as a recluse, writing letters and tending her garden ut never going out. This seclusion seems to have fed her inner ife and her mystical, nature-haunted poetry. Her poems were not published complete until the 1950s, and she was seen to be one of the USA's major writers. R.B. Sewell, *Emily Dickinson* (two volumes, 1974) is the standard biography, outstanding on Dickinson's life and work and on the relationship between them. Richard Chase, *Emily Dickinson* (1952), an earlier biogra-phy, suffers because many of Dickinson's papers were not available until after it was written, but is enthusiastic and per-ceptive, a splendid introduction. It was originally published in a series on 'American Men of Letters', something which would infuriate Helen McNeil, author of *Emily Dickinson* (1986), a scholarly, feminist study, published under the equally irritating series banner 'Virago Pioneers'.

> **READ ON**
> Emily Dickinson, *Letters* (ed. T.H. Johnson and T. Ward, three volumes 1958) (difficult, intensely personal, but vital to understand both Dickinson's poetry and her life).

DIGBY, Jane (1807–81) English adventurer

Digby never met *Byron, but Margaret Fox Schmidt, *Passion's Child* (1977) claims that she was his female equivalent. She cuckolded her husband, the politician Lord Ellenborough, with an Austrian diplomat, and after a scandalous divorce case fol-lowed Digby's lover to Paris, where she bore him two children. He spurned her in the end – it took him years – and she took two further husbands (a German baron and a Greek count) and had an affair with an Albanian bandit before settling in Syria with a sheikh who matched her passion. She spent some of each year in the desert and the rest in Damascus, where she lived a life closely resembling that of her gentrified childhood in Norfolk: riding, shooting, gardening. Balzac used her story in the novel *The Lily in the Valley*. Fox Schmidt has a wonderful time with all these events, delving into the documents to dis-cover the secret of her passionate, unconventional character.

> **READ ON**
> Margaret Fountaine, *Love Among the Butterflies: the Travels and Adventures of a Victorian Lady*; *Butterflies and Late Hours: the Further Travel Adventures of a Victorian Lady*.

DISRAELI, Benjamin (1804–1881) English politician

Disraeli was charming, clever and ruthless, and used all three abilities to get precisely what he wanted. In spite of the un-thinking anti-semitism of his time, not to mention his lack of

> **READ ON**
> D.C. Somervell, *Disraeli and Gladstone* ('duo-biographical sketch': old (1932) but still revealing). Christopher Hibbert, *Disraeli and His World* (good pictures; clear-headed, short

inherited cash or land and the facts that he was a novelist and a 'damnfool wit' (cleverness was not at a premium in the Parliament of his time) he rose to become leader of the Tory Party and Prime Minister. He is credited with 'modernizing' his party, preventing it fostering the interests of the privileged classes and making it support political and social reform. His private life was blessed by a long, happy marriage with Mary Anne Lewis, and by friendship with Queen *Victoria, who was captivated by his charm and intellectual dazzle. Robert Blake, *Disraeli* (1966) leads the biographical field with a large, scholarly tome which pays equal attention to Disraeli's private and public lives. R.W. Davis, *Disraeli* (1976) is concise and clear, and does not shirk such nastier failings in Disraeli as self-centredness and willingness to whip up religious intolerance for political ends. Hesketh Pearson, *Dizzy* (1951) combines a solid account of Disraeli's life with excellent Victorian background. Cecil Roth, *Benjamin Disraeli, Earl of Beaconsfield* (1952) tackles Disraeli's Jewishness. Sarah Bradford, *Disraeli* (1982) is hampered by its tiny, eye-straining type size, but is worth the effort for its character-analyses of Disraeli and Mary Anne, and its insights into their relationship.

text). Mollie Hardwick, *Mrs Dizzy*. John Vincent, *Disraeli* (heavyweight political study, showing parallels between Disraeli's ideas and late 20th-century Tory thought). Daphne *Du Maurier, *Mary-Anne* (historical novel). Caryl Brahms and S.J. Simon, *Don't, Mr Disraeli* (spoof).

> DOING GOOD

Mary Bodley, *Don Vesuvio: the Story of Father Borelli*
M.J. Patrick Caroll-Abbing, *But for the Grace of God: the Story of an Irish Priest who Became a Resistance Leader and Later Father to Thousands of Children in Boy's Towns of Italy*
Stephen Clissold, *St Teresa of Avila*
J. Green, *God's Fool - the Life and Times of St Francis of Assissi*
Sergei Hackel, *One of Great Price: the Life of Maria Skobiskova, Saint of Ravensbrück*
Lynn Haney, *Naked at the Feast* (*Josephine Baker)
Geoffrey Hanks, *A Home for all Children - the Story of Dr Barnado*
*Vita Sackville-West, *Joan of Arc*
Ann Stafford, *Bernadette of Lourdes*
Anne Vernon, *A Quaker Businessman* (Joseph Rowntree)

DOYLE, Arthur Conan (1859–1930) English writer

> **READ ON**

Sherlock Holmes's inventor felt dwarfed by his own creation. He wanted to be remembered as a serious novelist, politician or

Roger Lancelyn Green, *Sherlock Holmes Letters* (dotty letters: to newspapers about details in the books, to Holmes by people wh thought that he really existed, b

propagandist for spiritualism, and was also a keen sportsman (among other things, he was the first Briton ever to ski in Switzerland). This 'real' life is covered in his autobiography *Memories and Adventures* (1924), and in a score of biographies, of which the most zestful – because they never take Doyle as seriously as he did himself – are Hesketh Pearson, *Conan Doyle, His Life and Art* (1961 ed.) (good on Doyle the professional writer) and Ronald Pearsall, *Conan Doyle, a Biographical Solution* (1977) (good on Doyle the Edwardian Englishman). Geoffrey Stavert, *A Study in Southsea* (1987) describes Doyle's penniless, ambitious early years, and is evocatively illustrated. S.C. Roberts, *Holmes and Watson* (1953) relates Doyle to his most famous creation, and Adrian M. Conan Doyle, *The True Conan Doyle* (1943) is a memoir by Doyle's son.

'Moriarty', 'Watson' and 'Lestrade'. Ridiculous and delightful; British eccentricity at full gallop).

DRAKE, Francis (c1540–96) English sailor

Drake went to sea at 15, and spent 20 years in the slave trade, plying between West Africa and the Caribbean. He was also a pirate, raiding Spanish ships and attacking Spanish cities in the New World – an activity officially disowned but privately encouraged by his patron *Elizabeth I. In four years in the 1570s, in a ship (the *Golden Hind*) no bigger than a modest family house, he sailed round the world, an exploit outranking even his part in the defeat of the Spanish Armada in 1588. John Sugden, *Sir Francis Drake* (1990) sees him as a typical Elizabethan: mercurial, entrepreneurial, patriotic, untroubled by conscience, a dazzler. Sugden describes the sailing magnificently (especially the 'Great Circumnavigation'), and sheds unexpected light on Drake's popularity with the peoples of Central America and Africa, and on his formidable reputation (halfway between Tamerlane and Mephistopheles) in Europe.

⊹ **READ ON**
J.A. Williamson, *Hawkins of Plymouth* (biography of Drake's cousin and colleague, who shared many of his exploits and died with him on a voyage to plunder the Spanish Main).

⊹ DREAM TIME AND AFTER

(Australians)

David Adams (ed.), *The Letters of Rachel Henning*
Max Brown, *Ned Kelly: Australian Son*
'Caddie' (*Catherine Elliott KacKay), *Caddie - The Autobiography of a Sydney Barmaid*
Bruce Chatwin, *The Songlines*
Verna Coleman, *Her Unknown (Brilliant) Career* (*Miles Franklin)
Geoffrey Dutton, *Australia's Last Explorer - the Life of Ernest Giles*
*Donald Horne, *The Education of Young Donald*
Douglas Lockwood, *The Aboriginal* (Waipuldanya)

*Alan Marshall, *I Can Jump Puddles*
Graham McInnes, *Humping My Bluey*
Sally Morgan, *Wanna Murraganya - the Story of Jack McPhee*
Hal Porter, *The Watcher on the Cast-Iron Balcony*
Tom Ronan, *Packhorse & Pearling Boat: Memories of a Misspent Youth*

DRIBERG, Tom (1906–76) English journalist and politician

Driberg faced in all directions at once. He was a snob committed to the Left, a compulsive homosexual 'cottager' who pontificated on morals, a charming companion who treated his wife abominably. He moved easily from Establishment circles to East End gangland, from MI5 to writing a tabloid gossip column. After his death it was claimed (on doubtful evidence) that he had been a Soviet agent. Francis Wheen, *Tom Driberg: His Life and Indiscretions* (1990) patiently tracks down the facts, concentrating on Driberg's public career, but also, fastidiously, describing his private life (if 'private' is right for such a lover of the one-night stand.)

> **READ ON**
Tom Driberg, *Ruling Passions* (autobiography whose sub-text – more relevant when it was written than nowadays – was to show that homosexuals could have 'useful' careers and hold high office. Apparently frank, but casting yet more veils over this complex man).

DUMAS, Alexandre (1802–70) French writer

Dumas swaggered, whored and drank his way through life in the same 'devil take the hindmost' spirit as the heroes of his novels *The Three Musketeers* or *The Count of Monte Cristo*. He had dozens of mistresses, made and spent several fortunes, was a secret agent in the 1830 Revolution and fought for Garibaldi during the 1860 siege of Naples. In his spare moments he poured out plays, novels, pamphlets and essays, sometimes as many as 40 works a year. He had so many assistants that people claimed he ran a prose-manufacturing business called 'Dumas and Co.'. His *Memoirs* (Eng. ed. 1907–9) seem as richly imaginative as any of his novels, until you read Michael Ross, *Alexandre Dumas* (1980), and find that objective research proves most of Dumas' anecdotes true.

> **READ ON**
André Maurois, *The Three Musketeers: a Study of the Dumas Family*. Edmond and Jules *Goncourt, *The Goncourt Journals* (about the Paris literary and theatrical worlds in which Dumas was such a star).

DU MAURIER family

George Du Maurier (1834–96) was a cartoonist for *Punch*; he drew those thin-lined, figure-packed cartoons with pieces of dialogue underneath which now seem so typical of Victorian middle-class humour. He also wrote three novels, one of which, *Trilby*, was a bestseller. His son **Gerald Du Maurier** (1873–1934) was an actor-manager, well known for society comedies –

> **READ ON**
Daphne Du Maurier (ed.), *The Young George Du Maurier* (letters). Angela Du Maurier, *It's Only the Sister*.

he always seemed to act in evening dress – and for playing such debonair 'villains' as Raffles, the 'Amateur Cracksman'. His daughter **Daphne Du Maurier** (1907–89) was a popular novelist (author of *Rebecca, Frenchman's Creek, Jamaica Inn* among others), and chief chronicler of her gifted, charming family. She wrote a family history, *The Du Mauriers* (1937), tracing them back to their ancestors in the French Revolution, a biography of her father, *Gerald: a Portrait* (second ed. 1966), and two volumes of autobiography, *Growing Pains* (1977) and *The Rebecca Notebooks and Other Memories* (1981). Leonee Ormond, *George Du Maurier* (1969) completes the picture.

DUNCAN, Isadora (1878–1927) US dancer

In days when even ballet dancers wore stays, Duncan performed in loose, flowing robes without underclothes. Her movements were as free-form and flowing as her costumes. She claimed to be reinterpreting the dance styles shown on ancient Greek vases, and caused a sensation. Her private life was equally headline-worthy: tantrums, eccentric pronouncements and a string of lovers. She died when the long scarf she was wearing caught in the wheel of an open car, and strangled her. Isadora Duncan, *My Life* (1955 ed.) is a gushy autobiography, and Alan Ross MacDougall, *Isadora: a Revolutionary in Art and Love* (1960) matches it exactly. Even Victor Seroff, *The Real Isadora* (1971), the standard biography, is compelling, since after six decades Duncan's vivacity and bizarreness leap from every page. Fredrika Blair, *Isadora: Portrait of the Artist as a Woman* (1987) is soberer about Duncan's life, but good on her work and her influence on dance.

> **READ ON**
> Francis Steegmuller (ed.), *Your Isadora* (collection of Duncan's letters to the theatre designer Gordon Craig, and his terse replies). Gordon McVay, *Isadora and Esenin* (about Duncan's impetuous, brief marriage to a Russian poet 20 years her junior, with whom she had a passionate understanding but no common language).

DU PRE, Jacqueline (1945–87) English cellist

Du Pré was renowned alike for the fire and passion of her performances (many preserved on records), and for irrepressible high spirits. Her marriage to the pianist and conductor Daniel Barenboim took her to the heart of a golden generation of classical musicians; it was like a court, and they were its queen and king. Then Du Pré was struck down by multiple sclerosis, and spent 15 years in a darkening, ever-sadder private world. Carol Easton, *Jacqueline Du Pré* (1989) is a moving biography, by a US journalist who befriended her in her last tragic years. Easton is no musician, and her descriptions of how Du Pré played in her prime and how her technique withered with illness are not persuasive. But she has marvellous sympathy for Du Pré as a person, and puts on the page exactly the qualities which made her so beloved. The book is rackingly sad, but unforgettable.

> **READ ON**
> Joseph Heller and Speed Vogel, *No Laughing Matter* (account of novelist Heller's fight against, and recovery from, near-fatal illness).

DURRELL, Gerald (born 1925) English naturalist and writer

Durrell's *My Family and Other Animals* (1956) describes his idyllic boyhood on Corfu, discovering wonders of the animal kingdom and surrounded by eccentric relatives and their adult friends. He followed it with a series of books about animal-collecting in exotic parts of the world – and as in *My Family and Other Animals* he is unfailingly serious about wildlife, uproarious about the humans. Typical books are *The Bafut Beagles* (1953), *The Drunken Forest* (1955) and *A Zoo in My Luggage* (1966). *Island Zoo* (1961) and *The Stationary Ark* (1975) are more serious, about establishing and running the Wildlife Preservation Trust on Jersey.

> **READ ON**
> Gerald Durrell, *Birds, Beasts and Relatives*; *Fillets of Place* (sequels to *My Family and Other Animals*). Jacquie Durrell, *Beasts in My Bed*; *Intimate Relations* (engaging memoirs, by Gerald's first wife, of life married to an impoverished, animal-obsessed young genius). *Lawrence Durrell (Gerald's brother), *Prospero's Cell* (another view of Corfu life).

DURRELL, Lawrence (1912–90) English writer

Author of poems and novels (including *The Alexandria Quartet*), Durrell lived most of his life in Greece, Egypt or Southern France. His non-fiction includes books describing his time spent on three Greek islands, Corfu (*Prospero's Cell*, 1945), Rhodes (*Reflections on a Marine Venus*, 1953) and Cyprus (*Bitter Lemons*, 1957). They blend accounts of landscape, customs and politics with philosophical and personal memoir in sensuous, poetic prose, among Durrell's finest work. He was a friend of *Henry Miller, and reading his and Miller's letters (for example in *Lawrence Durrell and Henry Miller: a Private Correspondence*, 1963) is like eavesdropping on a rambling, opinionated conversation between two drunken philosophers in some all-night bar in the Elysian Fields.

> **READ ON**
> *Gerald Durrell, *My Family and Other Animals* (includes a magnificent debunking, by his younger brother, of Lawrence as a self-obsessed 23-year-old genius).

DVORAK, Antonín (1841–1904) Czech composer

A country butcher's son who became an orchestral violinist, Dvořák combined love of the folk music of his native Bohemia with solid, Brahmsian skills in composition and orchestration. His music is both 'learned' and tuneful, among the friendliest in the repertory. His life, likewise, was a blend of the academic (honorary doctorates, teaching posts at this or that conservatory, conducting tours) and the ordinary (he had a large, loving and not particularly reverential family). John Clapham, *Antonín Dvořák* (1980) is the standard scholarly work, sometimes technical. Hans-Hubert Schönzeler, *Dvořák, His Life and Work* (1980) uses first-hand documents to excellent effect, and is interesting on the academic side of Dvořák's life. Neil Butterworth, *Dvořák, His Life and Times* (1980) is a short introduction, with well-chosen illustrations.

> **READ ON**
> Antonín Horějš, *Antonín Dvořák, The Composer's Life and Work in Pictures* (dry text; superb photos). Otokar Šourek, *Antonín Dvořák, Letters and Reminiscences* (1954). Josef Škvorecky, *Dvořák in Love* (novel, as engagingly absurd as a Hollywood biopic – 'Come quickly, Daddy. Mr Tchaikovsky's being sick again!').

E

EARHART, Amelia (1898–1937) US aviator

Fifty years ago, when Earhart vanished on a round-the-world flight, she was one of the best-known women in the world, famous not just for her flying records but as a speaker and fundraiser for women's rights and for pacifism. George Palmer Putnam, *Soaring Wings* (1939) is an upbeat story of her life by her husband and chief publicist. A more balanced account, good on Earhart's early life, and on her political and social work, is Doris L. Rich, *Amelia Earhart* (1989).

> ◇ READ ON
> Muriel Earhart Morrissey (Earhart's sister), *Courage is the Price: the Biography of Amelia Earhart*. Frederick A. Goerner, *The Search for Amelia Earhart* (account of the activity and speculation after Earhart disappeared. Could she be rescued? Had she been stolen by aliens? Was she working for the CIA? It depended which paper you read). George Palmer Putnam, *Wide Margins: the Story of a Publisher* and *Last Flights* (autobiography). Sheila Scott, *I Must Fly*.

◇ ECCENTRICS

Robert Baldick, **Huysmans*
J. Bird, **Percy Grainger*
Desmond Chapman-Houston, *Bavarian Fantasy: the Story of *Ludwig II*
Tom Cullen, *The Prostitutes' Padre: The Story of the Notorious Rector of Stiffkey*
Brian Fothergill, *The Mitred Earl: an Eighteenth Century Eccentric* (Frederick Hervey, Earl of Bristol)
Janet Hobhouse, *Everybody Who Was Anybody: a Biography of *Gertrude Stein*
Johanna Johnston, *Mrs Satan: the Incredible Saga of *Victoria Woodhull*
*Edith Sitwell, *English Eccentrics*
*Ethel Smyth, *Impetuous Heart*
Robert Lewis Taylor, **W.C. Fields: His Follies and Fortunes*

EDGEWORTH, Maria (1767–1849) Anglo-Irish novelist

Edgeworth's novels about Anglo-Irish life (for example *Castle Rackrent* and *The Absentee*), are something like *George Eliot half a century earlier. She travelled widely, writing tart, funny letters about the places and people she encountered. A good sample is in *Letters from England* (ed. Christina Colvin, 1971), as fascinating about the effects on the Midlands of the Industrial Revolution as it is on the gossip and power parties of literary and political London. Marilyn Butler, *Maria Edgeworth, a Literary Biography* (1972) is good on her life, and outstanding on her books: it makes you want to read everything she wrote.

⋄ **READ ON**
Desmond Clarke, *The Ingenious Mr Edgeworth* (biography of Edgeworth's father: educational pioneer, friend of *Wedgwood and fanatical inventor, deviser among other things of carriage springs, caterpillar tracks and a road-construction system far better than Macadam's).

EDISON, Thomas Alva (1847–1931) US inventor

Edison is popularly known as the inventor of the light bulb, phonograph and moving-picture camera. But he is far more interesting because of the way he worked. In 1876, having made a fortune from improvements to land telegraph systems, he set up an 'invention factory', forerunner of the research and development departments of modern large companies. Edison sat in his office having ideas, and a team of scientists and technicians worked on them, developed them and made prototypes. Edison's firm patented some 1,300 inventions, and he became one of the most famous people of his time, a confidant of presidents who was always ready to leave a White House dinner, roll up his sleeves and set to work to mend a fuse or fix a faulty bicycle. Ronald W. Clark, *Edison: the Man Who Made the Future* (1977) is brief but packed, good on Edison's personality. André Millard, *Edison and the Business of Invention* (1990) concentrates more on Edison's work: not only inventing, but patenting, marketing and making legal war on rivals.

⋄ **READ ON**
Henry Ford, *Edison as I Know Him/My Friend, Mr Edison* (unique memoir, interesting for what it reveals of the author as well as its subject).

EDWARD VII (1841–1910) English king (ruled 1901–10)

However much biographers disapprove of Edward's gambling, womanizing and other excesses as Prince of Wales, they usually find explanations: the effect his well-meaning but misguided parents had on his emotional development, or his education (quite unsuitable for his future regal role), or the pressure of having to wait for rule until he was 59 years old. Because of Edwardian codes of conduct, many facts and pieces of gossip have had to wait until the people concerned are dead: this means that books date quickly, and the most recent tend to be

⋄ **READ ON**
Ursula Bloom, *Victoria and Edward*. (Indeed all biographies of *Victoria). Ben Pimlott, *Hugh Dalton* (Edward asked Dalton's father to supervise the education of the future George V, with results as disastrous as his own upbringing was for him). David Duff, *Alexandra, Princess and Queen*; Georgina Battiscombe, *Queen Alexandra* (good biographies of Edward's tolerant,

most complete. Giles St Aubyn, *Edward VII, Prince and King* (1979) is a thorough account, dry but readable, and crammed with references. Kinley Roby, *The King, The Press and the People* (1975) is outstanding on the relationship between Edward and the British public. At times the press treated Edward with a venom rare even today, though he does seem to have escaped the treacly trivialization modern royals endure.

EICHMANN, Adolf (1906–62) Austrian Nazi war criminal

During the Second World War, as head of the Gestapo's Jewish Extermination Department in Germany, Eichmann ordered the deaths of hundreds of thousands of people. After the war, he escaped to Argentina, but was tracked down by the Israeli secret service, taken to Israel and tried. His defence was that he was a mere functionary, obeying orders from above; he was none the less found guilty and executed. *Hannah Arendt, *Eichmann in Jerusalem: a Report on the Banality of Evil* (1963) is an account of the trial, with pointed, anguished reflections on the Holocaust, the philosophical validity of Eichmann's defence, and the darkness inherent in the human soul.

⁃> READ ON
Elizabeth Young-Bruehl, *Hannah Arendt, For Love of the World*. George Steiner, *The Portage to San Cristobal of A.H.* (novel, in which *Hitler himself, captured in old age, talks of the Holocaust and of the nature of guilt and retribution). Simon Wiesenthal, *Nazi-Hunter*.

EINSTEIN, Albert (1879–1955) German/US scientist

Any biography of Einstein should come to terms not just with his science and with his political work for the control of atomic and nuclear weapons, but also with his wild-haired, shaggy-moustached public personality which, coupled with his thick accent, made him the prototype for the 'mad scientist' figure of comedy. Peter Michelmore, *Einstein: Profile of the Man* (1963) deals well with all this, and makes Einstein's science comprehensible to lay people, a major achievement. Abraham Pais, *'Subtle is the Lord . . . '* (1982) is a magisterial combination of personal reminiscences, biography and technical discussion of Einstein's work. The author, a physics professor, was Einstein's friend and colleague. The science is separated from the biography, section by section: an unusual solution to the problem of describing the achievements of someone whose work can be so difficult to understand, even if it does mean that the level of concentration needed to read the book zooms up and down like a fever-chart.

⁃> READ ON
Albert Einstein, *Out of My Later Years* (autobiography). Laura Fermi, *Atoms in the Family* (dazzling biography of *Enrico Fermi, as man and scientist, by his wife).

EISENHOWER, Dwight D(avid) (1890–1969) US soldier and 34th president

⁃> READ ON
Lester and Irene David, *Ike amd Mamie* (1981) is the story of a

liberal and charming wife).

As General in overall charge of Allied forces, and as US President from 1952 to 1960, Eisenhower was a key figure in the Second World War and the cold war which followed. S.E. Ambrose, *Eisenhower* (two volumes, 1983) is a standard, straightforward account of his life and work. Alan Wyks, *Eisenhower* (1982), one of a series on 'The Commanders', understandably devotes most of its space to Eisenhower in the Second World War. Marquis Child, *Eisenhower, Captive Hero* (rev. ed. 1959) discusses the US people's need for Eisenhower as a popular hero, and goes on to show how such a personality was incompatible with politics and politicians, and why Eisenhower's star faded so fast and far. Piers Brendon, *Ike* (1987) takes a similarly sharp look at Eisenhower's character, trying to find out if he was ditherer, political Svengali, or somehow both.

deep but difficult married relationship, and a sentimental rebuttal of the claim by Kay Summersby (in Kay S. Morgon, *Past Forgetting*) that she was not only Eisenhower's wartime driver but his mistress. Arthur Krock, *Memoirs: Twelve US Presidents from Roosevelt to Richard Nixon* (good on Eisenhower's presidency, though it assumes a fair knowledge of 1950s US politics).

EISENSTEIN, Sergei (1898–1948) Russian film director

Eisenstein was a pioneer, inventing ways of montage (story-telling by the choice of images) which have been part of film 'grammar' ever since. He also made acknowledged masterpieces: *Battleship Potemkin, Alexander Nevsky, Ivan the Terrible.* He was an eager Communist whose early films celebrated the Revolution and who later found himself at odds with the Soviet state machine. He flirted with Hollywood and struggled to film the tragedy and poverty of peasant lives in Mexico. His autobiography *Immortal Memories* (Eng. ed. 1983) is full of anecdotes and crammed with theories and ideas, but its avant-garde form (short, unrelated sections like sequences of film) needs concentration. Marie Seton, *Sergei M. Eisenstein* (rev. ed. 1978) is the standard biography, fat with quotations from Eisenstein's own writings, and full of 'backstage' glimpses of the master at work and battling Stalin's bureaucrats.

⋄ READ ON
Ivor Montagu, *With Eisenstein in Hollywood* (funny account of Eisenstein in 1930s Hollywood, totally at odds with the studio system).

ELEANOR of Aquitaine (c1122–1204) French duchess and queen

At 15 Eleanor inherited Aquitaine, the south western third of France. At once, she was courted on all sides, and married successively Louis VII of France and Henry II of England. Her children included Richard the Lionheart and King John of England, and she was prominent in European politics for 60 years. Without sacrificing a jot of historical accuracy, Marion Meade, *Eleanor of Aquitaine* (1978) makes Eleanor leap to life, simply by treating her as one might a modern woman, a modern politician. It's not blowing dust from the 12th century,

⋄ READ ON
Alfred Duggan, *Devil's Brood* (novel about the Plantagenet line).

more behaving as if there were no dust at all. If only all historical biographies were written as well as this!

ELGAR, Edward (1857–1934) English composer

Elgar's *Pomp and Circumstance March No 1* (also known as *Land
of Hope and Glory*) seems, to people throughout the world, a
kind of unofficial British national anthem, a symbol of the Imperial swagger and brash self-confidence of the Edwardian age.
Elgar did become a grandee, loaded with honours and intimate
with the good, the great and the royal, but all the evidence is
that he hated it. He was a self-made man, and his first 40 years
as a small-town violin teacher and all-purpose composer are as
interesting as anything from his later life. His insecurity and
melancholy are just as much part of the Edwardian picture as
pomp and circumstance. In this respect, as with *Kipling,
books about him are also biographies of an age. Jerrold Nor-
throp Moore, *Edward Elgar: a Creative Life* (1989) is particularly
good on this, while Michael Kennedy, *Edward Elgar* (1968) is
an intimate portrait of the man. Percy M. Young (ed.), *Letters of
Edward Elgar* (1956) offers (well-annotated) business and private correspondence.

> ⋄ **READ ON**
> William H. Reed, *Elgar As I
> Knew Him*. Jerrold Northrop
> Moore, *Elgar: a Life in
> Photographs*. James Paterson,
> *Gerontius* (novel, about the aging,
> lonely Elgar on a trip up the
> Amazon).

ELIOT, George (1819–80) English writer

'George Eliot' (Marian or Mary Ann Evans) was one of England's finest and bestselling novelists. She also led an unconventional private life, living for 23 years with G.H. Lewes, a
married man unable, under 19th-century law, to divorce his
wife. After his death she proposed to, and married, John Cross,
who was 20 years younger and so afraid of not being able to
live up to her that he tried to commit suicide on their honeymoon. She died a few months after the marriage, and Cross
compiled a biography by making a collage of lines and
paragraphs from her writings: J.W. Cross, *George Eliot's Life as
Related in Her Letters and Journals* (1885). Because, technically,
every word was by 'Eliot' herself, the book was accepted as fact
for 85 years, even by Gordon S. Haight, the author of the
once-standard biography, *George Eliot* (1968). More recent research has, however, shown a different Marian Evans entirely:
not the brilliant bluestocking of legend but a woman whose
powerful literary personality was balanced by a craving for just
the kind of respectable Victorian domesticity from which her
life with Lewes debarred her. It is a less flattering portrait, but
rings true to life, and is set out with conviction and sympathy in
Ina Taylor, *George Eliot, Woman of Contradictions* (1989).

> ⋄ **READ ON**
> Gordon S. Haight (ed.): *The
> Letters of George Eliot*. A.T.
> Kitchell, *George Lewes and George
> Eliot*.

ELIOT, T(homas) S(tearns) (1881–1965) US/ English poet

Eliot was a reclusive, ascetic man, physically tough but prone to minor ailments and a regular sufferer from creative block. His first marriage was unhappy; he was depressed and lonely for 20 years after it ended, finding happiness only when he remarried in 1956. His chief 'public' pleasure seems to have been one shared by several other shy writers: the unfussy friendship of the actors who performed his plays. It is a triumph of biography to make an interesting book about such a person, and Peter Ackroyd, *T.S. Eliot* (1984) makes us feel so much sympathy and fascination for Eliot that we turn the pages eagerly to share his each and every day. This is the standard work, scholarly and authoritative; it is also as compulsive as a novel.

> **⟶ READ ON**
> Lyndall Gordon, *Eliot's Early Years* (about Eliot's youth in Massachusetts); *Eliot's New Life.*

ELIZABETH I (1533–1603) English queen (ruled 1558–1603)

The facts of Elizabeth's life are well documented. There is no doubt about either the glories of her reign, in the arts, exploration, enterprise and national self-confidence; or about its barbarities, hanging, drawing and quartering, for example; or its unappealing mixture of glitter and squalor. Biographers of Elizabeth deal with all these things, and also try to answer the 'chicken and egg' question 'was Elizabeth's reign a golden age because of Elizabeth, or did she just happen to be on the throne at the time?' Her character is as fascinating as *Victoria's, and seems in a similar way to have moulded the style of her age.

Jasper Ridley, *Elizabeth I* (1987) is one of the most recent and best of hundreds of books about Elizabeth. It combines sound political and historical discussion with descriptions of bear-baitings, progresses and revels, and relishes every aside, comment or anecdote which bring Elizabeth and her courtiers to life. Its 250-book bibliography contains enough historical follow-up suggestions to last for years. Elizabeth Jenkins, *Elizabeth the Great* (1958) is not a conventional biography, but sets out to answer some of the most interesting questions about Elizabeth, not just such big issues as 'what did she think of Papists?', or 'why did she never marry?', but smaller, equally burning questions like 'was she really bald?'

> **⟶ READ ON**
> Maria Perry, *The Word of a Prince* (biographical collage of Elizabeth's own writings, with good linking commentary). Edith *Sitwell, *The Queens and the Hive* (spectacularly cranky biography, crammed with Sitwell's own opinions, dazzling language and glorious accounts of the eccentricities of Elizabeth and her court – historically unreliable, but 110% enjoyable). G.B. Harrison (ed.), *Letters of Queen Elizabeth*. Robert Carey, *Memoirs of Himself*. Margaret Irwin, *Young Bess*; *Elizabeth, Captive Princess*; *Elizabeth and the Prince of Spain* (novel trilogy).

ELLIS, (Henry) Havelock (1859–1939) English writer

Ellis devoted his life to the mystery of sex. He wrote about its

> **⟶ READ ON**
> Geoffrey Dutton, *Kanga Creek: Havelock Ellis in Australia* (extracts from Ellis' own

mechanics (which caused his books to be banned and burned) and speculated about its psychological and mystical importance. He was the great-grandfather of the sexual revolution of the 1960s, and – being a true Victorian at heart – he would have hated as well as enjoyed every part of that. His autobiography, *My Life* (1939) is a typical blend of defiance, reticence and mysticism. Phyllis Grosskurth, *Havelock Ellis* (1980), the standard biography, is fat with letters and other documents, and superb on Ellis' relationships with women (his lesbian wife, the three great loves of his life, and dozens, hundreds of eager young disciples). Grosskurth also charts the ups and downs of Ellis' relationship with Freud: an intellectual tragicomedy.

accounts of his three years teaching in the bush, during which, Ellis says, he decided who he was and what he wanted to do with his life). Peter Fryer, *The Birth Controllers*.

EMERSON, Ralph Waldo (1803–82) US philosopher and poet

‹› **READ ON**
Bliss Percy (ed.), *The Heart of Emerson's Journals* (useful anthology).

Emerson believed that the Divine is present in nature, and that if we immerse ourselves in nature we can contact the Divine. He also taught that America should free itself from the shackles of European thought, creating and exploring a culture of its own. These ideas helped to form the intellectual climate of the USA: he is part of what all later US thinkers know. His *Journals* (ed. J. Porte, 1982) are a good way into his mind and thought. Good biographies are by Richard Garnett, *The Life of Ralph Waldo Emerson* (1888), concise and still readable, and R.L. Rush, *Ralph Waldo Emerson* (second ed. 1967).

ERASMUS, Desiderius (1466–1536) Dutch theologian

‹› **READ ON**
Erasmus, *Letters* (fascinating for their insight into Erasmus' thought, and also for their lively accounts of his travels, the abbeys and courts he visited and the prelates and politicians he conversed with. Little known, but some of the most revealing and personal of all Renaissance writings).

Like *Luther, Erasmus was appalled by the corruption and ignorance of those who ruled the Roman Catholic Church of his time. But instead of breaking away, he tried to reform from within. He produced scholarly editions of the Bible and the works of the early Church Fathers, and wrote more than 16 million words of his own setting out his views on Christ's teaching and the inner truths of the Christian religion. He travelled widely, preaching and teaching, and was one of the most cultured and authoritative people of the Renaissance. George Faludy, *Erasmus of Rotterdam* (1970) and R.H. Bainton, *Erasmus* (1970) are good, readable lives, not overburdened with theological or philosophical detail, showing the lively, friendly human being Erasmus was behind the somewhat austere facade.

> ❖ EUREKA!
>
> *(inventors)*
>
> Catherine Drake Bowen, *The Most Dangerous Man in America* *(Benjamin Franklin)
> Desmond Clarke, *The Ingenious Mr Edgeworth*
> Gerald Fairlie, *George Cayley: the Life of a Genius*
> John Golley, *Whittle: the True Story*
> W.P. Jolly, *Marconi*
> Matthew Josephson, *The Man Who Made the Future* *(Edison)
> J.E. Morpurgo, *Barnes Wallis*
> Ian McNeil, *Joseph Bramah: a Century of Invention*
> L.T.C. Rolt, *James Watt*
> Werner von Siemens, *Inventor and Entrepreneur*
> Gary Webster, *Journey Into Light: the Story of Louis Braille*

EVELYN, John (1620–1706) English diarist and writer

A man of means and a Royalist, Evelyn spent most of the 1640s prudently on the continent, and when he returned home he devoted himself to a quiet life of gardening, studying plants and trees, and writing on such subjects as smoky chimneys, navigation, the history of religion, and wood engraving. For 20 years he was secretary to the Royal Society, encouraging scientific research, and he also worked as a courtier. He is chiefly remembered for his *Kalendarium* (good version, ed. E.S. de Beer, 1959), a composite of diary and memoirs, as meaty and wide-ranging as *Pepys' *Diary*, but with pithier entries which are not so much fun to read. Biographers make more of Evelyn's life and character than he did himself: the standard work, John Bowle, *John Evelyn and his World* (1981), for example, sets Evelyn's own record in its historical and social perspective, to fascinating effect.

❖ **READ ON**
Arthur Ponsonby, *John Evelyn* (intimate portrait of Evelyn as a family man; outstanding on his gardening, which is described at every opportunity with enthusiasm, knowledge and conspiratorial zest).

⋄ EXTRAORDINARY CHILDHOODS

*Shirley Temple Black, *Autobiography*
*Maxim Gorki, *My Childhood*
Shusha Guppy, *The Blindfold Horse*
W.H. Hudson, *Far Away and Long Ago*
*Alan Marshall, *I Can Jump Puddles*
*Ved Mehta, *Vedi*; *The Ledge Between the Streams*
*R.K. Narayan, *My Days*
Jean Rhys, *Smile Please*
*Han Suyin, *A Mortal Flower*
Florence Hays Turner, *Days of Elk and Buffalo, a Colorado Childhood*

EYRE, Edward John (1815–1901) Anglo-Australian explorer

Eyre was an intrepid explorer and, unusually for his time, was a friend and ally of the Aborigines. Later, as Governor-General of Jamaica, he suppressed a rebellion, only to be arraigned for murder by libertarians led by John Stuart Mill. His trial was one of the sensations of the age, and his supporters included *Carlyle, Ruskin and Tennyson. Geoffrey Dutton, *The Hero as Murderer* (1967) is a fascinating study, by one of Australia's leading biographers, of this extraordinary man and his treatment by the English establishment.

⋄ **READ ON**
Geoffrey Dutton, *Colonel William Light – Founder of a City* (portrait of the attractive, multi-talented man who founded Adelaide); *Australia's Last Explorer – the Life of Ernest Giles* (study of the explorer whose *Journals* are among the liveliest, wittiest surviving accounts of 19th-century Australia).

F

FACEY, A.B. (1894–1984) Australian bushman

Facey spent his life doing back-breaking work in the bush, apart from his years with the Anzacs in Gallipoli during the First World War. His autobiography *A Fortunate Life* (1981) is simply told, unsentimental and remarkably free from self-pity. Not everyone living such a life, or reading about it, might agree with the assertion in its title, and yet a feeling of being specially chosen, specially lucky, shines from the book.

⋗ **READ ON**
Sally Morgan, *Wannamurraganya: the Story of Jack McPhee* (biography of the author's 'uncle', who worked all his life as a stockman. As a child he was taken from his Aboriginal mother and raised by whites to join a pool of well-trained, cheap labour – a shameful but common practice at the time).

> ⋗ FEET OF CLAY
>
> Richard Aldington, *Lawrence of Arabia* (*T.E. Lawrence)
> Evangelina Callas, *My Daughter*, *(Maria Callas)
> Gina Campbell, *Bluebirds: the Story of the Campbell Dynasty*
> Christina Crawford, *Mommie Dearest* (Joan Crawford)
> Kathryn Crosby, *Bing and Other Things*
> Albert Goldman, *Elvis*
> Roland Huntford, *Scott and Amundsen*
> Fiona MacCarthy, *Eric Gill*
> Imogen Smallwood, *A Childhood at Green Hedges* (*Enid Blyton)
> Arianna Stassinopoulos, *Picasso*

FERMI, Enrico (1901–54) Italian scientist

Fermi, a particle physicist, won the Nobel Prize in 1938 and took the opportunity to escape from Fascist Italy (where he and

⋗ **READ ON**
Leslie R. Groves, *Now It Can Be Told: the Story of the Manhattan Project*.

his wife were being harrassed because she was Jewish) to the
USA. There he built the first atomic pile, allowing the splitting
of the atom, and was one of the team which developed the
atomic bomb. His horror when bombs were dropped on Japan,
against all scientific expectation, is well told in the final
chapters of his wife Laura Fermi's *Atoms in the Family* (1955) –
one of the most readable of all scientific biographies, catching
the fiery, affectionate flavour of Fermi's family life, and notably
clear-headed when it comes to explaining his scientific work
and what he achieved.

FIELDS, W(illiam) C(laude) (1879–1946) US comedian

Fields' fuddled, slow-paced screen personality, and his surrealist one-liners ('There's an Ethiopian in the fuel supply';
'I must have a drink of breakfast') were matched in real life
by self-delighted eccentricity. When he took friends on a
picnic in his silver-plated Rolls Royce, he ended the day by
buying each of them six clocks at a goldsmith's, 'to tell time
for the next 300 years'. When a hotel manager refused him
the honeymoon suite because he had no bride, he replied,
'Pardon me while I step outside and find one.' The best
book about him, Robert Lewis Taylor, *W.C. Fields: His Follies and Fortunes* (1950), both tells his life and conjures up
his personality with affection and good humour, warts and
all, without ever trying to explain.

> ⟶ **READ ON**
> W.C. Fields, *Fields for President*;
> *W.C. Fields by Himself: an
> Intended Autobiography*.

FIGES, Eva (born 1932) German/English writer

Until Figes was seven, she lived in Berlin. Her family belonged
to the Jewish upper-middle class, and were harried by the
Nazis until, in 1939, they emigrated to London. A year later,
Figes was evacuated to Cirencester to escape the blitz. Eva
Figes, *Little Eden: a Child at War* (1978) is a deeply felt account
of how she settled down to life with strangers, in an English
country town where war might be remote but where social, religious and cultural attitudes had hardly changed since Queen
*Victoria's time. Figes was happy in Cirencester, and at school
– not a common thing in books by evacuees – and writes evocatively of an idyllic, pastoral existence like a happier *Thomas
Hardy story lived for real. Even so, a book which could be just
one more piece of English nostalgia for a country childhood is
given an edge by Figes' insistent memory of her Berlin past,
her consciousness of wider cultural horizons than rural England had to offer.

> ⟶ **READ ON**
> Ben Wicks, *The Day They Took
> the Children* (anthology of
> evacuees' memoirs). *Laurie
> Lee, *Cider With Rosie* (childhood
> in a Gloucestershire village).

> FILM STARS

Melvyn Bragg, *Rich* (*Richard Burton)
Simon Callow, *Charles Laughton, a Difficult Actor*
Minty Clinch, *Robert Redford*
Bill Davidson, *Jane Fonda: an Intimate Biography*
*Bette Davis, *This 'n That*
Ezra Goodman, *Bogey: the Good Bad Guy* (*Humphrey Bogart)
Fred Laurence Guiles, *Legend: the Life and Death of *Marilyn Monroe*
Warren G. Harris, *Cary Grant: a Touch of Elegance*
Charles Higham, *Kate* Katherine Hepburn, *see* *Spencer Tracy)
Laurence Leamer, *As Time Goes By: the Life of Ingrid Bergman*
Sheridan Morley, *James Mason: Odd Man Out*
David Shipman, *Marlon Brando*
Hugo Vickers, *Vivien Leigh*
See also Hollywood; The Silver Screen

FITZGERALD, F(rancis) Scott (1896–1940) US writer

Fitzgerald's novels and stories described the hectic, empty lives of rich young people in the 1920s, the period he christened 'the Jazz Age'. He and his wife *Zelda Fitzgerald were leaders of the society he wrote about, partying the nights away. Drink, drugs, frantic dancing and easy sex: it was a sensualist's dream of paradise. But fate was waiting to mug them: Zelda went mad, the couple separated, and Fitzgerald became an alcoholic wreck, doing Hollywood hack work to make ends meet. James R. Mellow, *Invented Lives* (1984) is a dazzling, tragic biography of both Fitzgeralds, and Matthew J. Bruccoli, *Some Sort of Epic Grandeur* (1981), the standard book on F. Scott Fitzgerald, is fat, readable and good not only on the sad side of Fitzgerald's life but on his work. Its long bibliography leads to most other entries in the field.

> **READ ON**
Andrew Turnbull (ed.), *The Letters of F. Scott Fitzgerald*. Sheila Graham, *The Real Scott Fitzgerald* (memoir by a journalist who was Fitzgerald's friend and confidante in his last miserable years in Hollywood). Aaron Latham, *Crazy Sundays: F. Scott Fitzgerald in Hollywood* (genius engulfed by the studio system).

FITZGERALD, Zelda (1900–48) US socialite

Zelda Sayre married *F. Scott Fitzgerald when she was 20, and became queen of the smart 'Jazz Set' of which he was such an eager member and about which he wrote so acidly. She could not match his creativity, though she worked at

> **READ ON**
Zelda Fitzgerald, *Save Me the Waltz* (autobiographical novel). Matthew J. Bruccoli, *Some Sort of Epic Grandeur* (biography of F. Scott Fitzgerald).

painting, dancing and writing, but she was his equal partner
in every folly and extravagance of the next decade. In the
1930s her mental health declined, and the couple's story ended with separation: she entered a mental home and tried to
rebuild her personality. In the 1940s, though saner, Zelda
was as frail as a woman twice her age; her death was mysterious. She was a sad, doomed soul – the title of one of Fitzgerald's early books, *The Beautiful and Damned*, sums her up exactly. Nancy *Mitford, *Zelda Fitzgerald* (1970), the standard
biography, is sympathetic but remorseless, a desperately sad
read, especially about Zelda's last unhappy years. James R.
Mellow, *Invented Lives* (1984), a joint study of both Fitzgeralds, is more objective, but – the lives being what they were –
hardly more upbeat.

FLAUBERT, Gustave (1821–80) French writer

Flaubert's novels, such as *Madame Bovary*, are known for their
pure style, and for the precision with which he describes both
natural sights and sounds and the feelings of his characters.
His working life was a constant struggle to get such matters
right, and his private life was bedevilled by financial incompetence and by the effects of a lawsuit over alleged 'immorality' in
Madame Bovary. His life and work were even more entwined
than those of most writers, and biographers usually discuss
them both together. Enid Starkie, *Flaubert* (two volumes: *The
Making of the Master*, 1967; *The Master*, 1971) is particularly
good at this, and contains outstanding comments on Flaubert's
work. Herbert Lottman, *Flaubert* (1989), using much new material, and in a livelier style, is a double portrait of the writer
and the 'interesting times' he lived in. Philip Spencer, *Flaubert*
(1962) is brief and brisk: more an *apéritif* to Starkie or Lottman
than a substitute for them.

> ⋗ **READ ON**
> Julian Barnes, *Flaubert's Parrot*
> (novel about a man, researching
> a biography of Flaubert, who
> becomes obsessed to the point
> where his own personality
> vanishes into Flaubert's: a
> challenging, dazzling read).

⋗ FORCES OF EVIL,

John Beattie, *The Life and Career of Klaus Barbie*
Jean Benedetti, *Gilles de Rais: the Authentic Bluebeard*
Michael Grant, **Nero*
Raymond T. McNally, *Dracula Was a Woman*
R.J. Minney, **Rasputin*
Tadeusz Parlovich, *Commissar: the Life and Death of
Laurenty Beria*
John Symonds, *The Great Beast: the Life and Magick of
Aleister Crowley
Donald Thomas, *The Marquis de Sade*
Marina Warner, *The Dragon Empress* (*Tz'u-Hsi)

FORRESTER, Helen (born 1919) English/Canadian writer

Forrester's *Twopence to Cross the Mersey* (1974) tells in simple, unaffected language of her childhood in Liverpool during the Depression. Her family had no money whatever: if by some miracle there was enough for either coal or food, Forrester says, they bought coal because it was better to starve to death than to freeze. In *Minerva's Stepchild* (1979) she is adolescent, able to go out to work and earn money – if her parents will let her. In *By the Waters of Liverpool/Liverpool Miss* (1981) she finally conquers illness and parental opposition, and goes to work; and in *Lime Street at Two* (1985) we see her beginning an independent life, harassed this time not just by poverty and her parents' endless quarrelling, but by German air-raids in the Second World War. The harshness of Forrester's story is balanced by her eye for detail: she records the brand-names, speech-patterns and social attitudes of the past in a way which makes what she describes seem instantly familiar to anyone over 60, and fascinatingly nostalgic to their juniors.

▷ **READ ON**
The Latchkey Kid; *Liverpool Daisy* (novels about very similar ordinary life in Liverpool).

FRAME, Janet (born 1924) New Zealand writer

Frame is a poet, short-story writer and novelist (of titles like *State of Siege*; *Faces in the Water*; *Living in the Maniototo*). Her autobiography is published complete as *An Autobiography* (1990), and in three separate volumes. *To the Is-land* (1982), describing her childhood in New Zealand, is a memoir of picnics, pets, seaside and country, tumultuous family life and escape to a 'private place' of her own imagination. *An Angel at My Table* (1984) is harsher. Its chief subject is the eight years Frame spent in a mental hospital in the 1940s, and it balances accounts of her own painful self-adjustment with moving descriptions of the lives and characters of other residents, often long-term, elderly and alone. (This book was successfully made into a film in 1990.) *The Envoy from Mirror City* (1985) begins with Frame's voyage to England in search of fame and fortune, and sees her starry-eyed but hungry in Clapham and Soho, in love and happy in Ibiza, and finally back in New Zealand, her first work published and ideas for more books teeming in her mind.

▷ **READ ON**
To the Island: *Miles Franklin, *Childhood at Brindabella*.

FRANK, Anne (1929–45) Dutch diarist

The story of Frank, who hid from the Nazis in Holland for three years before being betrayed and taken to a concentration camp, is one of the best-known episodes in the Second World War, solely because of her *Diary of a Young Girl/The Diary of*

▷ **READ ON**
Janina Bauman, *Winter in the Morning: a Young Girl's Life in the Warsaw Ghetto* (published in 1986, and also about the confrontation between war and the innocence of adolescence.

Anne Frank (1947), found and published after her death. It is less an account of persecution than of adolescence, of the adventure of growing up in a secret place, of the kindness of friends and neighbours, and of the agonies and delights of calf-love, intensified by Frank's terrible situation.

Bauman's autobiography continues in *A Dream of Belonging: My Years in Postwar Poland*).

FRANKLIN, Benjamin (1706–90) American journalist, scientist and statesman

Franklin made a fortune by writing, printing and publishing *Poor Richard's Almanac*. He founded and ran societies to discuss philosophy, science and politics, fought against the Mohawks and the French, served as Deputy Postmaster for the British in America, tried to mediate between the British and their increasingly edgy colonists, and finally worked for independence, helping to draw up the Declaration of Independence, the Treaty of Versailles and the Constitution. In his spare time he investigated electricity, and was fond of music, literature and conversation. He was a self-proclaimed happy man, an emblem both of the European Age of Enlightenment and of American 'get up and go'.

Franklin's *Autobiography* (1771) is an American classic, a zestful account of his life until 1757; the edition completed by William Macdonald (1908) continues the story to his death. Carl van Doren, *Benjamin Franklin* (1938) is the standard popular biography, good on Franklin as thinker and experimenter, and outstanding on his private life and feelings. Catherine Drinker Bowen, *The Most Dangerous Man in America* (1974) is a series of biographical 'snapshots', word-pictures of crucial moments in Franklin's life. R.W. Clark, *Benjamin Franklin* (1983) is scholarly, complete and up to date.

⊳ READ ON
Alistair Cooke, *America* (outstanding on all the Founding Fathers, including Franklin).

FRANKLIN, Miles (1879–1954) Australian writer

(Stella) Miles Franklin is known for stories of the outback (published under the pen-name 'Brent of Bin Bin') such as *Gentlemen at Gyang Gyang* and *Up the Country*, and for the first-person novels *My Brilliant Career* and *My Career Goes Bung*, about an excitable, naive and determined girl at the start of this century who breaks away from outback society to make her career as a writer. How close (or not) these come to true autobiography is shown by Franklin's evocative memoir, *Childhood at Brindabella* (1963), and by Verna Coleman, *Her Unknown (Brilliant) Career* (1981), which describes Franklin's second life in the USA, where she worked in the 1920s–30s as trades unionist, columnist and feminist activist. A feature of Coleman's

⊳ READ ON
Bread and Cheese Club, Melbourne, *Miles Franklin: a Tribute By Some of her Friends*. Ray Matthew, *Miles Franklin* (good study of Franklin's books).

book, showing Franklin at her most typical, is descriptions of her Sunday tea-parties, whose guests included 'social reformers, socialists, millionaires, muck-rakers, singers, writers, overseas visitors' and ordinary working girls.

FREUD, Anna (1895–1982) Austrian psychoanalyst

Freud, youngest daughter of *Sigmund Freud, was devoted to her father both – if one can so put it – as human being and intellect. As a child she wheedled him, sat on his knee while he told her fairy tales; as an adolescent she allowed him to psychoanalyse her; as an adult she studied psychoanalysis herself and became a major advocate of the technique in Austria. When the Freuds escaped to London from Nazi persecution, she put aside her own flourishing career to look after him. After his death she turned to war work, running a residential home for orphans. This led to her major achievement, the development of child psychology, of which she was a pioneer and in which her reputation still stands supreme. Elizabeth Young-Bruehl, *Anna Freud* (1989) is a scholarly biography, not shirking the intricacies of Freud's work, but readable and excellent on her private life and personality before and after her father's death.

ᐅ **READ ON**
Peter Gay, *Freud: a Life for Our Time* (biography of Sigmund Freud).

FREUD, Sigmund (1856–1939) Austrian founder of psychoanalysis

Of all recent thinkers, only *Marx and *Einstein have had as much influence as Freud on 20th-century ideas and way of life, and few thinkers, apart from Marx and Einstein, have been more thoroughly misunderstood. Freud also suffers, from the biographical point of view, because he was the subject of one of the most magisterial 'lives' ever written: Ernest Jones, *Sigmund Freud, His Life and Work* (three volumes, 1953–7; one-volume abridgement, 1961). Although (to the lay person at least) this seems to say the last word on Freud, it is monumentally hard to read. Peter Gay, *Freud: a Life for Our Times* (1988) is both shorter and more comprehensible, using facts and anecdotes about Freud's personality to leaven the (still somewhat daunting) exposition of his ideas. It has a full bibliography. Jonathan Miller (ed.), *Freud* (1972) contains a dozen essays on Freud's life, background, theories and effect on our century, written by experts but perfectly accessible. It is illustrated, with everything from photographs of the Vienna street where Freud was born to Hieronymus Bosch's picture *The Garden of Earthly Delights*,

ᐅ **READ ON**
Vincent Brome, *Ernest Jones* (life of one of the few biographers to rate a biography on his own account). Penelope Balogh, *Freud* (good, brief introduction to Freud's ideas).

whose inspiration was 'Freudian' 400 years before Freud was born.

G

GABLE, Clark (1901–60) US film star

Gable was one of those stars whose real life seemed to disappear into his own legend: a macho, devil-may-care rake who took a two-fisted approach to life's difficulties, won any woman he wanted with a raised eyebrow and a drawled 'Frankly, my dear, I don't give a damn', and lit the screen in every role he played. Lyn Tornabene, *Long Live the King* (1977), a classic Hollywood biography, sets out to find the human being behind the legend, and by diligent research, an objective and witty tone, and a refusal to be dazzled by either Gable or Hollywood, makes the man a hundred times more hypnotic than any of the roles he played.

⋄ **READ ON**
Nathaniel Benchley, *Humphrey Bogart* (similar treatment of another legendary star).

GAGE, Nicholas (born 1939) US journalist

Gage was christened Nikola Ngagoyeanes, the youngest child of a Greek peasant family. His *Eleni* (1984) movingly describes the privations of village life during the 1940s Greek Civil War, and how his mother sacrificed her own life to save her children. *A Place for Us* (1990) continues the story, describing the children's 1949 voyage to America to join their father, Nick's rebellious childhood and adolescence, and his gradual coming to terms with the prickly, bewildered father he blamed for indirectly causing Eleni's death.

⋄ **READ ON**
*Anne Frank, *The Diary of Anne Frank* (classic account of trying to live 'ordinary' life in wartime). Jerome Weidman, *Fourth Street East* (autobiographical novel about growing up as an immigrant in the USA).

GALBRAITH, J(ohn) K(enneth) (born 1908) Canadian/US economist

A leading US economist, Galbraith wrote such standard books

⋄ **READ ON**
J.K. Galbraith, *Ambassador's Journal* (account of his year as US Ambassador to India during the *J.F. Kennedy

on his subject as *The Affluent Society* and *The Great Crash*. He worked in universities, and also moved in and out of the Washington political scene, acting as adviser to several Democratic presidents, and on terms with most of the 1940s–80s 'great and good'. His memoirs, *A Life In Our Times* (1981) tell with passion and humour of his busy public life. He is that rare breed, a political memoirist happy to admit mistakes and repeat stories against himself. And he is also candid, in a refreshing, Olympian way, about the people he knew and worked with. There is some economic theory in the book, but (as always with Galbraith) it is clearly explained and easy to understand.

administration).

GAMBLE, Rose (born 1920s) English writer

Rose Gamble, *Chelsea Child* (1979) is a searing memoir of urban poverty before the Second World War. There is no softening, no analysis by hindsight: just the story of a family (two adults, five growing children) battling to survive in a single Chelsea room. Two things stand out: the relentless struggle against debt and the inadequacy of Rose's father. Unable to cope, he turned to violence – described, like everything else, without pity, sentimentality or artifice.

> **READ ON**
> Phyllis Willmott, *Growing Up in a London Village* (working-class life in Lee, London, between the wars); *A Green Girl* (sequel, about her 'escape' to grammar school, and her work for the Times Book Club). Angela Rodaway *A London Childhood* (slightly earlier and better-off than Gamble; similar milieu).

GANDHI, Mohandas Karamchand (1869–1948) Indian leader

After studying law in England, Gandhi worked in South Africa for 21 years, campaigning against laws which discriminated against Indians. In 1915 he went home to India to work on behalf of 'untouchables', and gradually broadened his activities to lead the independence campaign. After independence he opposed the foundation of Pakistan, advocating instead the peaceful unity of Moslems and Hindus, a stand which led to his murder, at a prayer meeting, in 1948.

Gandhi's own writings are chiefly philosophical or political: even his *Autobiography* (1948) is subtitled *The Story of My Experiments With Truth*. There are many collections of his letters, of which *Selected Letters* (1962) is the most interesting to non-specialists. D.G. Tendulkar, *Mahatma* (eight volumes, 1951–4) and Pyarelal, *Mahatma Gandhi* (1958–90) are the main Indian biographies, epic, scholarly and exhaustive. Pyarelal's two volumes on the independence struggle, *Mahatma Gandhi: The Last Phase* (1956, 1958) are particularly accessible to non-Indians. Robert Payne, *The Life and Death of Mahatma Gandhi* (1969) and Judith M. Brown, *Gandhi: Prisoner of Hope* (1990), the standard western biographies, are objective, fluent accounts of Gandhi's life and philosophy, making sense of the politics and dealing well with his place on the larger stage of world

> **READ ON**
> Homer A. Jack (ed.), *The Gandhi Reader* (useful anthology of Gandhi's writings). Alan Campbell-Johnson, *Mission With *Mountbatten* (the independence debate, from the other side of the table). Louis Fischer, *The Life of Mahatma Gandhi* (1951).

affairs. Ved *Mehta, *Mahatma Gandhi and His Apostles* (1977) is an account of Gandhi's life based on interviews with people who knew him or were influenced by him.

❖ GARDENERS AND PLANT COLLECTORS

Alan Bloom, *Prelude to Bressingham*
Susan Chivers and Suzanne Woloszynska, *The Cottage Garden: Margery Fish at East Lambrook Manor*
Robert Fortune, *A Journey to the Tea Countries*
Thomas Hinde, *Capability Brown: the story of a master gardener*
Prudence Leith-Ross, *The John *Tradescants*
Betty Massingham, *Miss Jekyll*
Marianne North, *Recollections of a Happy Life*
Patrick O'Brian, *Joseph Banks: a Life*
H.J. Samuel, *Wild Flower Hunter* (Ellis Rowan)
Arthur Swinson, *Frederick Sander: the Orchid King*

GARVEY, Marcus (1887–1940) Jamaican reformer

One of the first and most influential workers for racial equality in America, Garvey founded UNIA (Universal Negro Improvement Association) in 1914, and worked tirelessly to develop black self-awareness, black pride and black culture. Inevitably, books about him tend to be both political and polemical: good examples are E.D. Cronon, *Black Moses: the Story of Marcus Garvey and the Universal Negro Improvement Association* (1968) and Tony Martin, *Marcus Garvey, Hero – a First Biography* (1983). Rupert Lewis, *Marcus Garvey* (1987), though its politics are densely argued, is more accessible to non-specialists, showing Garvey less as symbol or saint than as a human being working against the odds for what must have seemed an impossible dream.

❖ **READ ON**
Amy Jacques-Garvey, *Garvey and Garveyism* (scholarly book by Garvey's wife, a leading authority on his work). James R. Hooker, *Black Revolutionary: George Padmore's Path from Communism to Pan-Africanism*).

GELDOF, Bob (born 1952) Irish singer

In the 1970s Geldof and his band the Boomtown Rats had huge success, and he also starred in the anti-establishment films *The Wall* and *Number One*. In the 1980s he made a second reputation as organizer of Live Aid, the pop-based charity which galvanized people round the world to send aid to the starving in Africa. For this Geldof was knighted by the British Queen, the first rock musician ever to be so honoured. His autobiography (with Paul Vallely) *Is That It?* (1986) describes

❖ **READ ON**
Bob Geldof and Paul Vallely, *With Geldof in Africa* (about working for Live Aid). Bernie Taupin, *A Cradle of Haloes* (childhood memoirs, close in mood and period to Geldof's, by Elton John's lyricist).

all this and is also superb about growing up as a rebellious teenager in Ireland, discovering culture, politics and sex in the teeth of adult disapproval. The book's openness about sex, and its language, may upset some readers – but then so did some teenagers at the time Geldof is describing.

GILBERT and SULLIVAN

↔ **READ ON**
Raymond Mander and Joe Mitchenson, *A Picture History of Gilbert and Sullivan.* Leslie Baily, *Gilbert and Sullivan and Their World.*

As working partners, **William Schwenck Gilbert** (1836–1911) and **Arthur Sullivan** (1842–1900) were fire and ice. Their joint work was better than anything either of them wrote separately, and yet each was convinced that he was the junior partner, that the other was doing him down. They fought chiefly by letter – in days when there were four postal deliveries a day, not counting telegrams and private messengers, a row could begin, run its course and blow itself out between dawn and sunset – and argued over everything from jokes about elderly females to theatre carpets and the allocation of rehearsal time.

The Gilbert and Sullivan story is told in some of the most enjoyable biographies mentioned in this Guide. Caryl Brahms, *Gilbert and Sullivan* (1975) is the sharpest and funniest, followed closely by Leslie Baily, *The Gilbert and Sullivan Book* (1952). Hesketh Pearson, *Gilbert: His Life and Strife* (1935) is fat with anecdotes and witty, peppery quotations from the great man himself. Percy M. Young, *Sir Arthur Sullivan* (1971) is good on the 'other side' of Sullivan: the English *Mendelssohn, as he liked to imagine himself, composer of symphonies, oratorios and other such 'serious' works.

GILL, Eric (1882–1940) English artist

↔ **READ ON**
Eric Gill, *Autobiography* (boastful, inaccurate and entirely fascinating, so long as you read MacCarthy first).

Gill saw himself as *William Morris' heir, both in art and ideals. He was a distinguished type-designer, stonemason, wood-engraver and architect, and he set up groups devoted equally to craftwork and to communal living. After his death it was suggested that he had combined this austere, lofty approach to life with sexual aggression and domestic tyranny, not least towards his sisters and daughters. Fiona MacCarthy, *Eric Gill* (1989) tells every detail of his life, and in the process makes him seem consistent if seldom likeable, driven by idealism and tragically confused by the pull between head and heart.

GLASSER, Ralph (born 1920) Scottish writer

↔ **READ ON**
Ralph Glasser, *Gorbals Voices, Siren Songs* (more intimate memoir, talking of Glasser's

Glasser grew up in the Gorbals, the area of central Glasgow which, in the 1920–40s, was the largest slum in Europe. His memoir *Growing Up in the Gorbals* (1986) is an unsparing account of tenement life, as raw as *Gorki's or Zola's accounts of their childhoods, but enlivened with classic examples of Glaswegian – Gorbals? – acid wit. *Gorbals Boy at Oxford* (1988) carries the story on, showing Glasser confronting the manners and ideals of gilded privilege, befriending (among others) Beveridge, Laski, Tynan and *Betjeman and gaping, like a horror-struck Martian, at the university's fizz of champagne socialists.

postwar London life, but devoting time to his political and philosophical beliefs, his sense of Jewishness and his family and married life).

GLENNIE, Evelyn (born 1966) Scottish musician

Glennie is a virtuoso percussion player, one of the world's leading young performers. To make a solo career in percussion is unusual enough, but she is also profoundly deaf. Evelyn Glennie, *Good Vibrations* (1990) tells, movingly, how music threw open the windows of her soul, gave her self-confidence and let her make her way without difficulty in the hearing world. It also explains, in passing, how you can play instruments, with soloists and with orchestra, when you cannot 'hear' sounds in the same way as other musicians.

❖ READ ON
James Blades, *Drum Roll* (effervescent autobiography, by another percussionist – and one of the happiest people who ever set stick to drum or pen to paper).

GODDEN, Rumer (born 1907) English writer

Godden's autobiography, *A Time to Dance, No Time to Weep* (1978) is a fascinating companion to her books. In her novels she conveys atmosphere or relationships in small, subtle touches, hardly seeming to mention them, and she uses the same skill here. She is particularly good at evoking places, and as her story is set in various locations – France after the First World War, Cornwall, on board a ship in the Second World War, and above all India, where she spent several years as a child, and later ran a school – it is an exotic, ever-surprising treat. Some chapters share the names of her novels, showing where she picked up an idea, an atmosphere or a character-hint for her fiction: an added bonus for lovers of her books.

❖ READ ON
Rumer and Jon Godden, *Two Under the Indian Sun*; *Shiva's Pigeons* (memoirs of India, written with her sister). Rumer Godden, *The Greengage Summer*; *Black Narcissus* (novels with strong autobiographical elements).

GOGOL, Nikolai (1809–52) Russian writer

A restless aristocrat, Gogol worked as an actor, a civil servant and a university teacher before becoming known as a satirical writer. He is remembered today for two works above all, the stage farce *The Government Inspector* and the novel *Dead Souls*. In later years he became a religious maniac, convinced himself that his work was sinful, burnt his manuscripts and starved himself to death. Henri Troyat, *Gogol: the Biography of a Divided Soul* (1971) is written in flowery style, but gets to the heart of his bleak, manic-depressive nature, and is full of interesting detail about Russian official and literary life in Gogol's time.

❖ READ ON
*Vladimir Nabokov, *Nikolai Gogol* (eccentric, funny biographical/literary study, which starts by telling Gogol's life in reverse order, ends with an interview between Nabokov and his unsatisfied publisher – and on the way gives a thousand insights into Gogol, his work and the whole nature of Russian literature and humour).

GOLLANCZ, Victor (1893–1967) English publisher

Gollancz founded the Left Book Club, was a major propagandist against Fascism, capital punishment and nuclear arms, and built a fiction list which included such authors as A.J. Cronin, *George Orwell and Kingsley Amis. Ruth Dudley Edwards, *Victor Gollancz* (1987), the authorized biography, catches his intellectual integrity and pugnacity, his charm and his pigheadedness (not least over the matter of retiring and leaving the firm in other hands). Gollancz was a vital influence on British political thought in the Second World War and the Labour administration which followed, and discussion of this is the core of Edwards' book. Biographies of publishers can be tedious accounts of power lunches and squabbles with authors over proofs. This is an exception: book-making, for Gollancz, was merely the activity which allowed him to transmit ideas, and Edwards sees his intellectual ferment and passion as typical not only of the man himself but of his generation. Their feeling was that 'something could be done', and that they were the people to do it.

> **READ ON**
> Victor Gollancz, *Journey Towards Music* (memoir about Gollancz's second intellectual passion after politics: classical music); *Reminiscences of Affection* (about his family and friends). Richard Joseph, *Michael Joseph, Master of Words* (about another influential English publisher).

GONCOURT brothers

Edmond Goncourt (1822–96) and **Jules Goncourt (1830–70)** were devoted equally to each other and to writing. They collaborated on realistic novels of contemporary life, on art and literary criticism, and above all on their *Journals*, in which they took turns, day by day, to record every detail of people visited, food eaten, books read, music heard, pictures seen and their views on the 'great and good' of French artistic life. They knew many of the literary people of the time, from *Flaubert to Zola, from Daudet to Turgenev – and had robust ideas about everyone else. Their *Journals* are as meaty as *Pepys' *Diary*, a factual equivalent of what *Proust later did in fiction. André Billy, *The Goncourt Brothers* (Eng. ed. 1960) is a detailed, affectionate biography, especially moving about Edmond's loneliness after Jules died.

> **READ ON**
> R.B. Grant, *The Goncourt Brothers* (less about the brothers' lives than a study of the literary and artistic background to their work.)

GORKI, Maxim (1869–1936) Russian writer

Orphaned at the age of 5, Gorki was brought up by his grandparents, a brutal bargee and a terrified wife who escaped from reality with the child by telling folk-tales. At 12 he ran away, and spent his adolescence among what he later called society's 'lowest depths': criminals, tramps, drunks. He began his adult life as a journalist, took up revolutionary politics in the early years of this century, and went on to become the leading writer of the fledgeling USSR, a man whose avowed ambition

> **READ ON**
> Jean Genet, *The Thief's Journal* (parallel account of growing up among thieves, pimps and derelicts – this time in France).

was to be the 'Communist Tolstoy'. His best-known work is the classic three-part autobiography, – *My Childhood* (1913), *My Apprenticeship* (1916), *My Universities* (1923) – which tells in unsparing detail of the horrors of his youth in the Tsarist underclass. Dan Levin, *Stormy Petrel* (1965), the standard biography, picks the bones of truth from these accounts, adds details of Gorki's life after the Revolution, and is outstanding on his work.

GOSSE, Edmund (1849–1928) English writer and critic

Gosse's father, a Christian fundamentalist, struggled all his life to balance his beliefs with his profession (science): he was particularly racked when *Darwin's *The Origin of Species* was published. He brought up his son with love and gentleness – until Edmund was old enough to think for himself, and began to reject Christian dogma. Gosse's memoir *Father and Son* (1907) is an autobiographical classic, charting the affection between the two, Gosse senior's early indulgence as his son's mind developed, and his eventual, regretful decision that if the young man would not accept the Lord, their relationship must end. It is a quiet, wistful book, as much about the evolution in Victorian Britain from the Age of Faith to the Age of Scientific Reason as it is about the love between two intelligent, stubborn people.

> ⋗ **READ ON**
> Ann Thwaite, *Edmund Gosse* (about the whole of Gosse's life: especially good on his literary and theatrical work).

GRADE family

The brothers **Lew Grade** (born 1906), **Bernard Delfont** (born 1909) and **Leslie Grade** (1916–79) were the sons of Russian emigrants to the East End of London who began as dancers, then became agents, impresarios and finally film and TV moguls. Between them, they controlled much of British popular entertainment in the 1950s–80s, and their story is a rags-to-riches saga stuffed with some of the best-known names in British variety. Hunter Davies, *The Grades* (1981), the authorized biography, is good on the family's early life and the boys' start in music-hall. Rita Grade Freeman, *My Fabulous Brothers* (1982) is a memoir overflowing with family sentiment and anecdotes of such stars as Carol Channing, Judy Garland, Harry Secombe, Barbra Streisand and Adam Faith.

> ⋗ **READ ON**
> Lew Grade, *Still Dancing: My Story*. Bernard Delfont, *East End, West End*. Ian Beaver, *Top of the Bill; The Story of the London Palladium*.

GRAHAME, Kenneth (1859–1932) English writer

Grahame's *The Wind in the Willows* (1908) is a hymn to the Edwardian longing for an escape from the modern world, for a rural paradise where, as Grahame himself put it, 'all vestiges of

> ⋗ **READ ON**
> Anne Thwaite, *A.A. Milne, His Life* (about an equally ill-at-ease children's writer, unhappy in his personal relationships and depressed by the way his 'Winnie the Pooh' books so

sordid humanity disappear'. It has been a bestseller since it was published, and sells some 80,000 copies every year. Grahame's life after its publication is a sad obverse of the happy escape of his fiction: unable to cope with fame or public life, he and his wife retreated into an eccentric isolation which became more and more paranoid. Grahame longed, like the Water Rat in the story, to 'escape to the South', but in the end all he did was walk alone on the Downs, read books and endlessly turn in upon himself until at last he died. Peter Green, *Kenneth Grahame, a Biography* (1959) is detailed, well written and – because of Green's sensitivity to Grahame's mental plight – desperately sad. A fine illustrated edition, with shortened text, was published in 1982 as *Beyond the Wild Wood*.

GRAINGER, Percy (1882–1961) Australian musician

Grainger was a formidable concert pianist, though he never made much of a living at it because he used to perform free, on condition that the orchestra also played pieces by himself or his friends. He was a composer and folk-song collector, publishing hundreds of 'dishings-up' (as he called his arrangements), as well as original pieces such as *Country Garden* and *Handel in the Strand*. He was a friend of Grieg, Delius and Britten. He was also a one-hundred-and-ten-per-cent eccentric, determined to purge food, language, lifestyle and music of everything artificial and so to return to a kind of 'garden of Eden' innocence of which (he wrote) folk tunes were a last remaining glimpse. For 50 years he worked to invent new instruments on which music of the future would be played. They were made from items salvaged from junk shops, and had names like 'The Inflated Frog Blower' and 'The Kangaroo-pouch Free Music Machine'. John Bird, *Percy Grainger* (1982) is a glorious biography, detailing Grainger's (substantial) musical achievements, relishing his oddity and giving a clear impression of his gentle, life-enhancing charm.

> ◆ **READ ON**
>
> Percy Grainger, *The Furthest North of Humanity* (Grainger's own diaries and letters, making a different impression entirely from Bird's account). George Antheil, *The Bad Boy of Music* (autobiography of another musical eccentric, whose attempts to produce 'the music of the future' were all the rage in 1920s smart-art circles, and who went on, wide-eyed, to write for films in Hollywood).

(easily obliterated every other word he wrote).

◆ GRAND PASSIONS

Henry Blyth, *Caro; the Fatal Passion* (Lady Caroline Lamb)
Margaret Fountaine, *Love Among the Butterflies*
Charlotte Haldane, *The Galley Slaves of Love* (*Liszt and Marie d'Agoult)
Royston Lambert, *Beloved and God* (*Antinous)
Norah Lofts, *Emma Hamilton*
*Nancy Mitford, *Voltaire in Love*

*Vita Sackville-West, *Daughter of France* (La Grande Mademoiselle)
Margaret Schmidt, *Passion's Child* (*Jane Digby)
Helen Waddell, *Peter Abelard*

GRANT, Cary (1904–88) US actor

Grant, born Archie Leach in England, became one of the screen's best-loved stars, expert in light comedy and known for such films as *Bringing Up Baby*, *The Philadelphia Story*, *Indiscreet*, *Arsenic and Old Lace* and *North By Northwest*. He seemed as ageless as he was charming – when a newspaper cabled him 'How old Cary Grant?' he cabled back 'Old Cary Grant fine. How you?' – and when he retired at 62 he still looked and sounded 20 years younger. Warren G. Harris, *Cary Grant: A Touch of Elegance* (1988) covers this side of Grant, but also takes the lid off 'Archie Leach', a lothario (rumoured to be bisexual), depressive, a skinflint and a domestic tyrant – such are Harris' claims – who finally sorted out his problems thanks to LSD therapy. Anyone who likes their idols with feet (legs, arms, torsos, heads) of clay will enjoy this book; if you prefer to remember Grant as he was on screen, it is not for you.

> **READ ON**
> William Currie McIntosh and William Weaver, *The Private Cary Grant* (intimate memoir by Grant's secretary and business partner).

GRAVES, Robert (1895–1985) English writer

Graves wrote poetry, novels, literary criticism and books on myth and anthropology. Several of his novels are fictional 'biographies' or 'autobiographies' of real people: *I, Claudius* (about the fourth Emperor of ancient Rome); *Wife to Mr Milton*; *Sergeant Lamb of the Ninth* (set during the American Revolution). He wrote three volumes of autobiography: *Goodbye to All That* (1929; including a lacerating account of his service during the First World War), *But It Still Goes On* (1930), and *Occupation, Writer* (1950). Martin Seymour-Smith, *Robert Graves* (1982) is a sober-toned biography, reticent about some of the more turbulent parts of Graves' life, but full of insightful comments on his works. Richard Perceval Graves, *Robert Graves: The Assault Heroic* (1986) and *Robert Graves: The Years With Laura* (1990) are lively accounts by Graves' nephew of the poet's first five decades, using family documents and fleshing out Graves' own autobiographies.

> **READ ON**
> Siegfried Sassoon, *Memoirs of an Infantry Officer* (heartfelt narrative of his time as a young officer in the First World War). Charles Graves, *The Bad Old Days* (lively account, by Robert's brother, of Fleet Street life in the 1920s–40s, plus fascinating detail of his and Robert's childhood).
> Thomas Stanley Matthews, *Under the Influence: Recollections of Robert Graves, Laura Riding and Friends*.

GREEN, Michael (born 1927) English writer

Green is a comic writer best known for his 'Art of Coarse . . .' series: *Art of Coarse Rugby*, *Art of Coarse Acting*, *Art of Coarse Sex* and so on. They explain how to succeed while being totally

> **READ ON**
> Michael Green, *Art of Coarse Moving*; *Don't Print My Name Upside Down* (novel).

useless: a coarse actor, for example, wears a costume made for someone three sizes bigger, remembers all the lines of the play just before the one they should be saying, and steals the limelight by coming on as Fu Manchu when actually playing Second Footman. Green's autobiographies are in the same brisk, brash mood: *The Boy Who Shot Down an Airship* (1988), about growing up in 1930s Leicester, and *Nobody Hurt in Small Earthquake* (1990), chiefly about working on a decrepit provincial newspaper.

GREENE, Graham (1904–91) English writer

Until Greene was over 70 he avoided photographers, never appeared on TV and gave press interviews with extreme reluctance. He published two books of memoirs, *A Sort of Life* (1971) and *Ways of Escape* (1981), excellent on his manic-depressive personality when he was young and on his travels, but tight-mouthed about the fripperies of an author's life – publishers' parties, meetings with X or Y, reactions to critics – which pad out some other writers' autobiographies. Then, in the 1980s, he finally agreed to a biography, and gave its author his full collaboration. Norman Sherry, *The Life of Graham Greene; volume 1: 1904–1939* (1989) is fat (750 pages), full and immensely readable, a classic in the making. Sherry writes especially well about Greene's schooldays and his Roman Catholicism, showing their influence on many passages in Greene's own work. The book drives you back to Greene's novels, time after time – and perhaps this explains Greene's former reticence about biography: his life was in his work.

> **READ ON**
> Graham Greene, *Journey Without Maps* (about his travels in Africa in the 1930s).

GREER, Germaine (born 1939) Australian writer

Best known for the feminist classic *The Female Eunuch* and for her outspoken lecturing and journalism, Greer has also published *Daddy, We Hardly Knew You* (1989). This is part autobiography, part biography of her inadequate, runaway, yearned-for father, and part a meditation on psychological and cultural rootlessness, especially in her two homelands, Australia and Britain. Like all Greer's writing, it is densely packed and needs concentration, but is also (if you're in the mood) a witty and rewarding read.

> **READ ON**
> Sally Morgan, *My Place* (a similar quest, though in different circumstances: Morgan was raised to believe that she was half-Indian, discovered in adulthood that her mother was actually an Aborigine, and set out to discover her own true identity, the nature of her people and their relationship over the years with the white Australians who shared, or occupied, their land).

GREGORY, Maundy J. (1877–1941) English titles broker and conman

Tom Cullen's *Maundy Gregory, Purveyor of Honours* (1974) is

> **READ ON**
> Hugh Trevor-Roper, *Hermit of Peking: the Hidden Life of *Sir Edmund Backhouse*.

to be believed, Gregory was Lloyd George's honours broker, selling peerages for cash. After Lloyd George fell from power, Gregory invented and sold honours of his own, until he was arrested. His clients (now peers of the realm) arranged a deal, he was set free and went to live in France. He was interned in the Second World War and died in a German prison camp. Other stories about him are that he was a secret agent in the First World War, and that he murdered the woman he lived with and stole her cash. Cullen ferrets out evidence for all this, and tells Gregory's story with a wide-eyed relish which exactly suits the plot.

GREY OWL (1888–1938) Scottish/Canadian campaigner

Grey Owl was an early campaigner for understanding between the Amerindian peoples and the Europeans who had settled and ruled their lands. He wrote books and gave talks about his life as a woodsman, trapper and fire ranger, and on Amerindian ways and beliefs, always beginning 'My name is Wa-Sha-Quon-Asin, Grey Owl. I come in peace'. In later life, he turned to animal conservation, and began teaching the mystical harmony between human beings and the environment which was an essential part of Amerindian culture, then virtually unknown to whites. After his death it was revealed that he was not of Amerindian descent at all, but a Scots adventurer called Archie Belaney. Lovat Dickson, *Wilderness Man* (1973) tells his story, and also contains fascinating sidelights on the wild Canada and the Amerindian ways Grey Owl talked about.

⋄ **READ ON**
Grey Owl, *Pilgrims of the Wild* (best known of Grey Owl's own books: the story of how he fell in love with a beautiful Iroquois girl, Anahareo, who persuaded him to give up trapping and to treat the environment and its creatures with proper respect).

⋄ GRIEVING

*Simone de Beauvoir, *A Very Easy Death*
John Hillaby, *Journey Through Love*
David Jacobs, *Caroline*
*Rosamund Lehmann, *The Swan in the Evening*
*C.S. Lewis, *A Grief Observed*
*Georges Simenon, *Intimate Memoirs*

⋄ GROUP BIOGRAPHIES

Alexander B. Adams, *The Eternal Quest* (14 great naturalists, including *Audubon, *Darwin, Linnaeus, Lyell and Mendel. Science lucidly explained.)

*John Aubrey, *Lives* (over 400 people)
Piers Brendon, *Eminent Edwardians* (Northcliffe, Balfour,
*Pankhurst, Baden-Powell)
Alistair Cooke, *Six Men* (*Chaplin, *Edward VIII,
Mencken, *Bogart, Stevenson, Russell)
Michael Foot, *Debts of Honour* ('intellectual heroes' of the
author, including Swift, Hazlitt, *Paine, *Disraeli,
*Russell and Silone)
Robert Gray, *The King's Wife: Five Queen Consorts*
Edna Healey, *Wives of Fame* (Mary Livingstone; *Jenny
Marx; Emma Darwin)
Peter Hopkirk, *Trespassers on the Roof of the World*
(travellers to Tibet); *Foreign Devils on the Silk Road* (pre-
20th-century travellers to China)
*Samuel Johnson, *The Lives of the Most Eminent English
Poets* (52 poets, including Donne, *Milton, Dryden)
Leane Jones, *A Quiet Courage* (Second World War
women agents in the French Resistance)
Charles   Moran,   *Black   Triumvirate*   (*Toussaint
l'Ouverture, Dessalines, Christophe)
Jane Robinson, *Wayward Women* (potted biographies of
some 400 women travellers, from the fourth-century
Abbess Etheria to the present day)
Anthony Smith, *Explorers of the Amazon*

⋅> GROWING UP

*Richard Church, *Over the Bridge*
*Anne Frank, *The Diary of Anne Frank*
*Maxim Gorki, *My Apprenticeship*
*Jack Lindsay, *Life Rarely Tells*
*Mary McCarthy, *Memoirs of a Catholic Girlhood*
*Finlay J. MacDonald, *Crotal and White*
*Ved Mehta, *Sound-Shadows of the New World*
*V.S. Pritchett, *A Cab at the Door*
*Sarah Shears, *Tapioca for Tea*
*Terence Stamp, *Stamp Album*
*Phyllis Willmott, *Growing Up in a London Village*

GUINNESS, Alec (born 1914) English actor

Guinness is known to world audiences for his film roles, which
include all eight murder victims in *Kind Hearts and Coronets*, the
ramrod-backed English officer in *Bridge On the River Kwai* and
Obi Wan Kenobi in *Star Wars*. On stage he has played an

⋅> **READ ON**
Ronald Harwood (ed.), *Dear Alec*
(celebration, by Guinness'
colleagues and friends, of his
75th birthday in 1989).

equally wide range of parts, from Hamlet and Macbeth to
*T.E. Lawrence. He is one of those actors who seem unrecognizable in real life, but who totally become each role on screen
or stage: as he puts it in his autobiography *Blessings in Disguise*
(1985), he 'donates his face'. This book is the most intimate
volume which exists about him, and even it is reticent about his
private life. In compensation, books about his art are thorough
and searching, giving insight into how he transforms himself,
performance by performance, into someone else. Kenneth
Tynan, *Alec Guinness* (1953) is especially good on this. John
Russell Taylor, *Alec Guinness* (1984) covers a wider range of
performances, and also gives more (a little more) about Guinness' life offstage.

H

HAHN, Otto (1879–1968) German scientist

Hahn studied chemistry and then, inspired by the work of *Curie, did research into radioactivity. He was also involved in work which led to others developing the mustard gas used in the First World War. In 1938 he and others discovered that the nucleus of the uranium atom could be split – work, again, which others developed for war purposes (the fission bomb). Interned after the Second World War, Hahn returned to Germany in the 1950s, and spent the rest of his life working for the peaceful uses of nuclear energy and campaigning against nuclear weapons. His autobiography *My Life* (1968) is fascinating (but not incomprehensible) about the science, interesting about his family and friends, and remorseless about the political and military background to his life. Every so often there is a chapter of interrogation, a question-and-answer session in which Hahn discusses scientific and political ethics – not the least agonising sections in this tormented, thought-provoking book.

⊹> **READ ON**
David Irving, *The Virus House* (history of German atomic research in the 1930s–40s, and of the Allied response). Werner Heisenberg, *Physics and Beyond* (scientific autobiography paralleling Hahn's).

HALL, Radclyffe (1886–1943) English writer

Hall and her friend Una Troubridge (wife of a high-ranking naval officer) made no secret of their lesbianism, and society never forgave them for it. The chance for public revenge came in 1928, when Hall published her novel *The Well of Loneliness*, about a 'Sapphic' relationship. There was an instant court case, with the 'great and good' of English letters queuing up to support, or damn, the book. The whole story – a notorious example of humbug, but with a tragic outcome – is told in Lovat

⊹> **READ ON**
Una Troubridge, *The Life and Death of Radclyffe Hall*. Michael Howard, *Jonathan Cape, Publisher* (history of Hall's publisher, including an interesting section on the *Well of Loneliness* case).

Dickson, *Radclyffe Hall at the Well of Loneliness* (1975), as dramatic as any novel.

HAMMETT, Dashiell (1894–1961) US writer

Hammett worked as a detective for the Pinkerton Agency, whose symbol was a staring eye. He wrote stories of self-employed detectives ('private eyes') for pulp magazines, and in the 1930s published two novels, *The Maltese Falcon* and *The Thin Man*. These were later filmed, and Hammett went to work in Hollywood. He was famous as one of the glitterati of the day, a hard drinker and hell-raiser. He supported left-wing causes when that was as risky in the USA as 'tramping down mean streets for ten dollars a day plus expenses'. William F. Nolan, *Dashiell Hammett: a Life at the Edge* (1983) does Hammett's career full justice, and is particularly good on his work, his creative blocks, his war service and his politics in the McCarthy years. Diane Johnston, *The Life of Dashiell Hammett* (1984) covers the same ground, but benefits from the input and approval of *Lillian Hellman, Hammett's long-time colleague and companion. Julian Symons, *Dashiell Hammett* (1985) has a brief, no-nonsense text – one suspects that Hammett would have approved – and dozens of illustrations.

> **READ ON**
> *Lillian Hellman, *Scoundrel Time* (account of the McCarthy years, and Hammett's part in them).

HANCOCK, Tony (1924–68) English comedian

In the 1950s few British entertainers rivalled Hancock: he was a 'comedian's comedian', widely regarded as a genius, and tapes of *Hancock's Half Hour* (radio and TV shows) show him at his peak. In the 1960s, after a car accident, he lost the ability to remember lines, took to drink, and his career collapsed. It is a common story, and the tale of Hancock's decline makes familiar if depressing reading. But nothing dims the dazzle of his great decade, and this is well caught in Roger Wilmut, *Tony Hancock, 'Artiste'* (1978), which quotes from Hancock's scripts, evoking his performances as if he were there in person. Philip Oakes, *Tony Hancock: a Biography* (1975) is the standard 'life', by a man who knew Hancock and wrote for him at the turning-point of his career.

> **READ ON**
> Freddie Hancock and David Nathan, *Hancock* (harrowing memoir of Hancock's decline co-written by his second wife). The happier side of the world of British comedy is portrayed in *There's No Answer To That!!*, an autobiography written (with help from Michael Freedland) by Eric Morecambe and Ernie Wise. Also of interest is Joan Morecambe and Michael Leitch, *Morecambe and Wife*.

HANFF, Helene (born 1916) US writer

Helene Hanff's, *84, Charing Cross Road* (1971) was a runaway bestseller: a series of witty, warm-hearted letters written over 20 years between the author and the owner of a London second-hand bookshop. Each of Hanff's other books is a straightforward memoir, open and funny about one particular aspect of her life. In *Underfoot in Show Business* (1961) she is a

> **READ ON**
> Helene Hanff, *The Apple of My Eye* (affectionate portrait of the author's life in New York).
> *Betty Macdonald, *Anyone Can Do Anything* (comic account of a young woman trying to make her way in the Big City – Seattle, in

starry-eyed young playwright reaching for success on Broadway. *The Duchess of Bloomsbury Street* (1974) is about her first visit to London, after the success of *84, Charing Cross Road*. In each of them, nothing particularly extraordinary happens, but Hanff's friendly, cheerful personality transforms everyday events to gold.

HANNIBAL (247–152 BC) Carthaginian general

In the third century BC the only power which seriously challenged Rome was Carthage. Hannibal, the most charismatic and successful Carthaginian general, did the hitherto unthinkable: he led an army (including cavalry and elephants) from Spain to Italy, and defeated every Roman force sent against him. Hannibal marched south – and if he had captured Rome, the entire history of western civilization would have been different. But the Romans defeated his head-on drive by guerrilla tactics. Ernle Bradford, *Hannibal* (1981) has the knack – absent in both Roman writings and those of most modern historians of classical times – of making ancient history, and ancient battles in particular, throb with life.

this case – during the Depression).

⏵ **READ ON**
Livy, *The Punic Wars* (books 21–45 of Livy's *History of Rome*: jingoistic stuff, still raging 200 years later at the enormity of what Hannibal nearly did). Bernard Levin, *In Hannibal's Footsteps* (eccentric travel-book by a journalist who set out, in knee-length shorts and accompanied by a TV crew, to retrace Hannibal's route in modern times).

⏵ HAPPY LIVES

*Christmas Humphreys, *Both Sides of the Circle*
*Geoffrey Kendall, *The Shakespeare Wallah*
Hesketh Pearson, *The Smith of Smiths* (Sydney Smith)
*Richard Rodgers, *Musical Stages*
*Artur Rubinstein, *My Young Years*
*Len Rush, *Captain of the Queen's Flight*
*Ben Travers, *A-Sitting on a Gate*
*Peter Ustinov, *Dear Me*
*Molly Weir, *Stepping Into the Spotlight*
*P.G. Wodehouse and Guy Bolton, *Bring on the Girls*
*William Carlos Williams, *Autobiography*
*Fay Wray, *On the Other Hand*

HARDY, Oliver: *see* LAUREL AND HARDY

HARDY, Thomas (1840–1928) English writer

For the first half of his career Hardy wrote powerfully emotional novels set in 'Wessex', a version of the rural Dorset of his childhood. In 1897, dismayed by hostile reviews, he abandoned novels for poetry, and went on writing and publishing well into his 80s. His first wife died when he was 73, and he

⏵ **READ ON**
Michael Millgate (ed.), *Thomas Hardy: Selected Letters*. Hugh Brasnett, *Thomas Hardy: a Pictorial Guide*. Denys Kay-Robinson, *The First Mrs Hardy* (sensitive account of Hardy's

married a woman nearly 40 years younger. On the surface, his life was marked by placid, comfortable routine. But in underlying obsession and pessimism he yielded nothing to his own fictional characters. Little of this is revealed in Florence E. Hardy, *Thomas Hardy: the Early Life* (1928) and *Thomas Hardy: the Later Life* (1930), a bland, third-person autobiography Hardy wrote in old age, to be published under his second wife's name. But his life is covered in detail and with great sympathy in Robert Gittings, *Young Thomas Hardy* (1975) and *The Older Hardy* (1978): the standard biography, a monument to scholarly thoroughness and a classic.

HARRIS, Frank (1856–1931) Irish journalist

Harris was an influential London editor, encouraging (among others) *Beerbohm, *Shaw, *Wells and *Wilde, and editing several newspapers and magazines including the *Evening News*, *Saturday Review*, *Hearth and Home* and *Vanity Fair*. He was a brash, opinionated man, who delighted in outraging Victorian and Edwardian society – in the 1890s by championing socialism and sexual freedom, and during the First World War (which he spent in the USA) by supporting Germany rather than the Allies. His *My Life and Loves* (four volumes, 1922–7) is a lively autobiography, trumpeting his views on every conceivable subject, quoting liberally from his speeches and articles and notorious for its sexual boasting. It is one of the 'great' autobiographies, a match for *Casanova's or *Cellini's and just about as reliable: huge fun, if you can take the pace or stand the man. Philippa Pullar, *Frank Harris* (1975) gives a more sober account – and paradoxically makes Harris seem far more intriguing than he does himself.

love-hate relationship with his first wife). Robert Gittings and Jo Manton, *The Second Mrs Hardy* (brief account of Florence Hardy before, during and after her marriage to a man six years older than her own father).

> ⬦ **READ ON**
> Hugh Kingsmill, *Frank Harris* (written the year after Harris died: part biography, part personal memoir by a friend and colleague who also published lives of *Dickens, Matthew Arnold and *D.H. Lawrence).

⬦ THE HEALING ART

R.W.S. Bishop, *My Moorland Patients by a Yorkshire Doctor*
Richard B. Fisher, *Joseph Lister*
Hugh McLeave, *McIndoe: Plastic Surgeon*
Charles William Mayo, *Mayo: the Story of my Family and my Career*
F.N.L. Poynter (ed.), *The Journal of James Yonge 1647–1721, Plymouth Surgeon*
Alfred M. Rehwinkel (ed.), *Dr Bessie*
Geoffrey Robertson, *A Gorbals Doctor*
George Sava, *The Healing Knife*
Constance Babington Smith, *Champion of Homeopathy: The Life of Margery Blackie*

> Dorothy Clark Wilson, *Lone Woman*
> Wu Lien-Tem, *Plague Fighter: the Autobiography of a Modern Chinese Physician*

HEARST, William Randolph (1863–1951) US journalist

If anyone was the grandfather of today's tabloid press, Hearst was that man. He believed that newspapers should not merely record events, but should be entertaining, polemical, sensational. He pioneered such ideas as banner headlines, chequebook journalism, 'agony aunts' and editorial opinions in news reports. His enemies called his papers 'the yellow press' and claimed that his reporters invented news. There were circulation wars and lawsuits. In the 1910s–30s Hearst, one of the most influential people in the USA, yearned to be taken seriously. He hobnobbed with presidents, collected artworks and built palaces to house them, and poured money into the film career of his protégée Marion Davies. His life reputedly inspired *Orson Welles' film *Citizen Kane*, about a megalomaniac newspaper owner for whom 'ethics' and 'conscience' were words unknown. W.A. Swanberg, *Citizen Hearst* (1961) writes about Hearst in a wide-eyed, dropped-jaw way, claiming that the man's flamboyance makes 'true' biography virtually impossible, and – an amazing assertion – that things have changed in newspapers since Hearst's time.

⋄ **READ ON**
R. O'Connor, *Ambrose Bierce* (biography of Hearst's star columnist of the 1900s). Marion Davies, *The Times We Had: My Life With William Randolph Hearst*. Fred Laurence Guiles, *Marion Davies*.

HECKFORD, Sarah (1839–1903) Anglo-Irish philanthropist and campaigner

Heckford's is one of the least known 'strange but true' stories of the 19th century. She and her husband worked for child welfare in the slums of East End London, and when he died she worked on alone to fulfil their dream, the foundation of the East London Children's Hospital in Stepney. Then, still not 40, she went as a nurse to India and South Africa, financing herself from private means. When the money ran out (much of it given away) she began trading and farming in the Transvaal. She was a friend of Modjadje (the queen who was the inspiration for H. Rider Haggard's 'She'), and encouraged her to found schools and educate her people's children, girls equally with boys. In the Boer War she worked to help Blacks caught up in the struggle, and after the war she went back to London to campaign against the Pass Laws and other Boer infringements of Black rights. Vivien Allen, *Lady Trader* (1979) tells her story plainly and simply, and it is a gem.

⋄ **READ ON**
Sarah Heckford, *A Lady Trader in the Transvaal* (memoir, hard to find but worth the search).

HELLMAN, Lillian (1907–84) US writer

Hellman was a dramatist and screenwriter, known particularly for *The Little Foxes* (about a smothering Southern family), and for plays and films about 'issues': *Watch on the Rhine*, about Fascism, and *The Children's Hour*, about a small community hounding two teachers for lesbianism. Her memoirs – *An Unfinished Woman* (1969), *Scoundrel Time* (1976), and the pen-portraits in *Pentimento* (1973) – were among her most successful works, and were reissued as *Three* in 1979. (Their fame was, if anything, enhanced when *Mary McCarthy said that every word in them, including 'and' and 'the', was a lie.) They describe Hellman's childhood (divided between New Orleans and New York), her literary apprenticeship, her theatre and film work, her relationship with *Dashiell Hammett, and, most pungently, the anti-left witchhunts of the McCarthy years. Hellman's skill is partly in describing issues and passions of the past, partly the playwright's ability to bring people vividly to life in a very few words: not only such famous names as *Dorothy Parker or *F. Scott Fitzgerald, but unknowns as well. The impressionistic nature of the memoirs – sketches rather than a consecutive autobiography – is compensated for, and background is generously supplied, in William Wright's sympathetic biography *Lillian Hellman* (1987).

> ⬧ **READ ON**
> Bernard F. Dick, *Hellman in Hollywood*.

HEMINGWAY, Ernest (1899–1961) US writer

Hemingway served in the First World War and Spanish Civil War; he was devoted to boxing, bullfighting, hunting and deep-sea fishing; his macho image was vital to him, and when illness began to sap his powers he shot himself. He-man attitudes pervade his work, both journalism and fiction (in which the heroes often stand for Hemingway himself).

Hemingway's autobiography, *A Moveable Feast* (1964) is laconic about feelings, but strong on places visited, things seen and above all on his friends, both in 1920s–30s Europe and in the USA. Carlos Baker, *Ernest Hemingway: A Life Story* (1969) is the standard scholarly biography, full of detail about Hemingway's working life and good on the complex psychology which underlay his apparently simple approach to life. Jeffery Meyers, *Hemingway* (1986) and Kenneth S. Lynn, *Hemingway* (1987) take a more engaged, critical look at Hemingway, both as man and writer. Both books are immensely readable, and will appeal especially to those who agree with the authors that Hemingway was a good writer until he became famous, but then became obsessed with the darker side of his own nature (Lynn), or a self-glorifying braggart (Meyers), and threw his talent out of the window.

> ⬧ **READ ON**
> Ernest Hemingway, *Selected Letters*. Anthony Burgess, *Hemingway and His World* (brief, insightful text and good illustrations). Charles Whiting, *Papa Goes to War: Ernest Hemingway in Europe, 1944–1945*.

HENREY, Mrs Robert (born 1906) French/ English writer

Henrey was brought up in poverty in Paris, moved to England when she married, and became a well-known journalist. She wrote 14 autobiographical books, beginning with *The Little Madeleine* (1951), about her childhood and relationship with her mother. It is atmospheric without being romantic about Paris, and loving and honest about her mother. In each of her books, Henrey likes to centre on one subject but jump around in her life, so that there is no consecutive thread between the books. Her relationship with her mother-in-law, for example, is the main subject of *Green Leaves* (1976), but also features in *Madeleine Grown Up* (1952), *Madeleine Young Wife* (1960) and *London Under Fire* (1969).

❖ **READ ON**
Mrs Robert Henrey, *The Virgin of Aldermanbury* (about the rebuilding of the City of London after the Second World War); *Spring in a Soho Street* (about people she knew when she lived in Soho).

HENRY VIII (1491–1547) English king (ruled 1509–47)

Myth-makers to the Tudor court, including *Shakespeare, put a pattern on Henry's life and character which has survived for four centuries. He is 'bluff king Hal', the much-married, merry monarch whose will it was death to cross. The problem for biographers is that historical reality tends to lack the narrative shape and the fascination of such legends, and the books therefore disappoint. Jasper Ridley, *Henry VIII* (1984) is an exception. Ridley untangles all the complications of Henry's life, especially his religious and dynastic politics, in a thorough and scholarly way. He surveys Henry's psychology, and considers the various reasons – anything from syphilis and minor strokes to nervous breakdown – given for Henry's increasingly unpredictable behaviour as he grew older. But he is well aware of Henry's legend, and keeps referring to its details as one strand in the tapestry of a genuinely multi-talented and multifarious personality. The book is long and dense, but repays perseverance: the more often you read it, the more it seems to tell. There are hundreds of books on Henry; none equals this.

❖ **READ ON**
Margaret George, *The Autobiography of Henry VIII* (superb historical novel: the legend in full cry).

❖ HENRY VIII'S WIVES

Margaret Campbell Barnes (novel), *My Lady of Cleves*
Frances Clark (novel), *Mistress Jane Seymour*
C. Erikson, *Anne Boleyn*
Julia Hamilton (novel), *Anne of Cleves*
Mary M. Luke, *Catherine, the Queen* (Catherine of Aragon)

> Irene Mahoney, *Madame Catherine* (Catherine Howard)
> Anthony K. Martienssen, *Queen Katharine Parr*
> Paul Rival, *The Six Wives of Henry VIII*

HEPBURN, Katharine: *see* TRACY, Spencer

HERSCHEL family

William Herschel (1738–1822), a German bandsman, settled
in England in 1755 and worked as a performer and teacher until
1781. His hobby was making and using telescopes, and in 1781
he discovered the planet later called Uranus. In 1782 George III
appointed him his private astronomer, and Herschel went on to
build ever-larger telescopes (the biggest was 13m long) and to
map the sky. Caroline Herschel (1750–1848), his sister, is generally, unjustly, pushed into the wings in books about the family.
She worked with her brother from 1772: they made telescopes,
scanned the skies and drew meticulous maps for which he usually took public credit. After William's death Caroline worked on
her own and with William's son John Herschel (1792–1871),
who went on to pioneer celestial photography.

   There is, alas, no satisfactory modern study of all three Her-
schels: the only book recommendable, A.M. Clerk, *The Her-
schels* dates from 1896. J.B. Sidgwick, *William Herschel, Explorer
of the Heavens* (1963) does discuss the whole family's astro-
nomical work, but gives William pride of place. Constance
Lubbock, *The Herschel Chronicle* (1933) skimps William, but is
good on John and Caroline. Other recommended books are
Mrs John Herschel, *Memoir and Correspondence of Caroline Herschel* (1876) and M.A. Hoskin, *William Herschel and the Con-
struction of the Heavens* (1964).

⋄ **READ ON**
G. Buttmann, *The Shadow of the
Telescope* (history of astronomy,
strong on John Herschel and his
work).

HEYER, Georgette (1902–74) English novelist

Heyer wrote bestselling detective stories and Regency romances
(a genre she perfected). In private life she combined reclusiveness (refusing, for example, ever to give press interviews or be
photographed) with sharp business sense and a tart tongue (especially to her publishers). Jane Aiken Hodge, *The Private World
of Georgette Heyer* (1984) takes us through Heyer's life, concentrating especially on her writing, book by book. The illustrations
are spectacular: cartoons and drawings of Regency scenes like
those in Heyer's books, and many of Heyer's own research
sketches of such things as carriages, dress styles and types of hat.
Anyone who enjoys Heyer's work will be instantly absorbed; for
outsiders, the book is an unusual glimpse of how one of this
century's best-loved writers did her work.

⋄ **READ ON**
Barbara Stoney, *Enid Blyton*
(about a woman with a
remarkably similar character and
approach to the craft of writing,
despite the difference in the
books she wrote).

HEYERDAHL, Thor (born 1914) Norwegian anthropologist and traveller

Heyerdahl believes that there are cultural links between the peoples of Polynesia, Central America and North Africa, and that sailors of these ancient civilizations crossed the Atlantic and Pacific, taking implements, myths and customs with them. He made several voyages in replicas of ancient craft, writing a bestselling book about each of them: *The Kon-Tiki Expedition* (1948), *The Ra Expeditions* (1971), *The Tigris Expedition* (1980). Arnold Jacoby, *Señor Kon-Tiki* (Eng. ed. 1968) is an amiable biography by an old friend, filling in Heyerdahl's personal story, and good about his wartime work. Christopher Ralling, *The Kon-Tiki Man* (1990), based on a TV series, covers much of the same ground, contains interviews with Heyerdahl, commenting on his younger self, and brings the story up to date.

> **READ ON**
> Thor Heyerdahl, *Fatu-Hiva: Back to Nature* (about the year Heyerdahl and his first wife spent in the Marquesas Islands just before the Second World War, 'in search of paradise', as the book's Norwegian title put it); *Aku-Aku: the Secret of Easter Island* (about an expedition to investigate Easter Island religion, customs and history).

HILLARY, Edmund (born 1919) New Zealand mountaineer

Hillary and Norgay Tenzing were the first human beings to reach the summit of Mount Everest; Edmund Hillary and George Lowe, *East of Everest* (1956) and John Hunt, *Ascent of Everest* (1953) are accounts of that triumph. Edmund Hillary, *Nothing Venture, Nothing Win* (second ed. 1988), Hillary's autobiography, tells of his life before and after 1953: his childhood, his climbing in New Zealand and in the Alps, how he climbed Everest (and coped with worldwide fame afterwards), his subsequent expeditions, his family life and his many years of work in Nepal to better the lives of the Sherpa people.

> **READ ON**
> J.R. Ullman, *Man of Everest* (biography of Norgay Tenzing, much of it in his own words). Edmund Hillary and Vivian Fuchs, *The Crossing of Antarctica* (story of the 1958 expedition which made Hillary the first person since *Scott to reach the South Pole overland).

HIMES, Chester (1909–84) US writer

Himes is best known for nine funny, violent crime novels set in Harlem and starring detectives Coffin Ed Johnson and Gravedigger Jones. In fact they were something of an afterthought: he wrote the first when he was 50 years old and living in poverty in Paris. He had spent most of the 1930s in prison, and then moved abroad, sickened by the racism and lack of opportunity in the USA. His autobiographies, *The Quality of Hurt* (1973) and *My Life of Absurdity* (1976), are grimly funny accounts of a man with a huge chip on his shoulder, wandering Europe like a mixture of *Henry Miller and Jean Genet, trying to make a success both of writing and of life. In Himes' hands, his own life becomes a kind of surrealist farce, simmering with violence – exactly the mood of his more famous books.

> **READ ON**
> Henry Miller, *The Tropic of Cancer* (a similar worldview, and a similar tale, though this down-at-heel US writer is white, and is in Europe a generation earlier than Himes).

HITCHMAN, Janet (born 1916) English writer

An intelligent child, Hitchman knew that something was lacking in her life, but she was grown-up before she realized that it had been love: she had had no one who loved her or whom she could love. She was an orphan, shunted from one set of foster parents to another at the whim of the Ministry of Pensions. She was never constantly ill-treated (except for the years she spent in a hospital for senile old ladies) and admits to being a difficult child, but the emotional coldness of her upbringing makes her autobiography *The King of the Barbareens*, (1960) a bleak if compelling read. Eventually she went to a Barnardo's home, where she still felt unloved, but was encouraged to learn. In adult life she became a writer, and her books include *Such a Strange Lady* (a biography of *Dorothy L. Sayers) and a moving novel about two Quaker friends, *Meeting for Burial*.

‹› **READ ON**
*Sarah Shears, *Tapioca for Tea* (rural childhood of a different kind, though just as bleak).

HITLER, Adolf (1889–1945) German dictator

Hitler worked as an architect's draftsman until the First World War, when he served in the Bavarian Army and won an Iron Cross. In the 1920s he transformed the German Workers' Party into a powerful political force, the National Socialist (Nazi) Party; by 1932 he was Chancellor; by 1934 he was President. The steps from there to attempts at world domination, to dreams of a Third Empire to equal those of Rome and Charlemagne, are small, seemingly inevitable and irrevocable. Hitler's own progression, from obsessive ambition to dictatorship and (possibly) paranoia, is less inevitable but just as compelling, and the power of his personality still remains, leading to a kind of numbed shock on the one hand, and on the other to idolatry by a sinister and persistent worldwide minority.

Hitler's own *My Struggle* (*Mein Kampf*, 1925) blends autobiography with exposition of his political ideas. There are shelves of books about him, by everyone from scholarly historians to his cook and his chauffeur. All are dwarfed by Alan Bullock, *Hitler, a Study in Tyranny* (1952), which is both a readable history and a compulsive psychological 'explanation' of why, and how, Hitler did what he did. Hugh Trevor-Roper, *The Last Days of Hitler* (fifth ed. 1978) is a sober record of precisely what the title says. Robert Payne, *The Life and Death of Adolf Hitler* (1973) is outstanding on Hitler's private life and personality. Other books spotlight specific periods of Hitler's life: Eugene Davidson, *The Making of Adolf Hitler* (1978); Hans Staengel, *Hitler: the Missing Years* (1957); August Kubichek, *Young Hitler: the Story of Our Friendship* (1973).

‹› **READ ON**
Heinrich Hoffmann, *Hitler Was my Friend* (memoir by the photographer who became an intimate member of Hitler's entourage: personal, unpolitical and illustrated with photographs both official and candid). Bridget Hitler, *Memoirs*. Nerin Gun, *Eva Braun, Hitler's Mistress*.

✧ HOLLYWOOD

W.N. Beath, *Death of James Dean*
*Louise Brooks, *Lulu in Hollywood*
Shaun Considine, *Bette and Joan: the Divine Feud* (*Davis
and *Crawford)
Garson Kanin, *Tracy and Hepburn*
John McCabe, *Charlie Chaplin*
Brenda Maddox, *Who's Afraid of *Elizabeth Taylor*
*David Niven, *The Moon's a Balloon*
*Fay Wray, *On the Other Hand*
Adolf Zukor, *The Public is Never Wrong*
See also Film Stars; The Silver Screen

HOLMAN HUNT, William (1827–1910) English painter

With *Rossetti, Millais and others, Holman Hunt was a
founder-member of the Pre-Raphaelite Brotherhood. His autobiography, *Pre-Raphaelitism and the Pre-Raphaelite Brotherhood*
(second ed. 1913) gives one version – the serious one – of the
Brotherhood's aims, methods and lives. Diana Holman-Hunt,
My Grandfather: His Wives and Loves (1969) gives the other
side: it reads like a spoof of high seriousness, high art, high
Victorianism, high religion and high pretension – and it is all
based on letters and the recollections of people who were there.
'Another glass of gin for Sarah!' 'Hunt got up and left without
a word.' 'He had no need to *summon* the Devil. That hairy
beast had haunted and tormented him uninvited for years.'
Novelists would eat their hearts out for such material.

✧ **READ ON**
Gay Daly, *Pre-Raphaelites in Love*
(group biography). Diana
Holman-Hunt, *My Grandmothers
and I* (fictionalized
autobiography: growing up in a
'big house' filled with echoes of
the eccentric Victorian past).

HORNE, Donald (born 1921) Australian writer

In his time, Horne has been academic, journalist, arts council
official and social commentator. *The Education of Young Donald*
(1967) is a wonderfully funny account of his childhood and
growing up, a classic of the 'how could I have been such a
pompous ass?' school of autobiography.

✧ **READ ON**
Donald Horne, *Confessions of a
New Boy*; *Portrait of an Optimist*
(sequels, equally enjoyable).

HSIAO CH'IEN (born 1910) Chinese writer

Hsiao began his working life as a goatherd; he educated himself, and eventually became one of China's leading journalists.
During the Second World War he worked in England; he reported the Potsdam Conference and the Nuremberg trials. In

✧ **READ ON**
Elias Canetti, *The Tongue Set
Free* (equally lively and
perceptive about the harshnesses
and joys of life, this time in
Bulgaria before WWI).

the 1950s, back in China, he was declared a 'stinking intellectual' and sent to a labour camp until 1979. His life centred on
politics, and his autobiography, *Traveller Without a Map* (1990),
does not shirk them. But each page also swarms with other
things: accounts of the books Hsiao read, the conversations he
had, the jokes he told, the wine he savoured, the smell of blos-
som in Cambridge or Heidelberg, and above all, always, the
way the world, East and West, seems to a man of enormous
humour and endless cultural curiosity. It is an unusual, ebullient and life-enhancing read.

HUBBARD, L(afayette) Ron (1911–86) US
writer and religious leader

In 1954 Hubbard, a block-busting SF author, founded the
Church of Scientology. He claimed that by following his teaching people could be cured of all disease, and that the world
itself would be saved. Despite disapproval by the authorities
(whose attentions led him to spend his time at sea, in international waters), he attracted six million followers. In 1980 he
vanished entirely from view. Russell Miller, in *Bare-faced Messiah* (1987), maintains that he was a fraud or madman, who
tried to take over countries, who claimed to have visited heaven
and whose disciples believed that he had messianic powers.
The Church of Scientology tried (and failed) to have the book
banned. So far as Hubbard's status is concerned, the jury of
world opinion is still out.

⋄ READ ON
L. Ron Hubbard, *Mission Earth*
(Hubbard's major fiction work,
claimed as the biggest decalogy
ever written).

HUGO, Victor (1802–85) French writer

Hugo's plays made him a leader of French Romanticism by the
time he was 30, and he went on to write poetry and two of the
major novels in the language, *Notre Dame de Paris* and *Les Mis-
érables*. He had a stormy second career as a politician: he was
elected in 1848, banished by Napoléon III in 1851, and made a
senator after the 1870 Revolution, to serve until his death. His
autobiography and several volumes of journals and letters are
still to be translated. André Maurois, *Victor Hugo* (Eng. ed.
1956) is a classic of French biography, strong on Hugo's politics and on his interest in the occult. Joanna Richardson, *Victor
Hugo* (1976) rounds out the picture: it is scholarly, good on
Hugo's works and easy to read, except that none of its quotations are translated. Readers vaguely interested in Hugo should
get most from Maurois; anyone drawn to read deeper will find
Richardson's bibliography first-class.

⋄ READ ON
André Maurois, *Victor Hugo and
his World* (stiff text – possibly
the translation is at fault – but
fine illustrations, evoking not
only Hugo but the spirit of
France before, during and after
the Second Empire).

HUMBOLDT, Alexander von (1769–1859)
German explorer

A Prussian nobleman, Humboldt devoted himself to science. His ambition was to write a complete encyclopedia of the physical universe, and to that end he studied astronomy, botany, geology, medicine, meteorology, mineralogy and zoology. He made exhaustive field trips, gathering specimens and making drawings, notes and maps, in Europe, South America and Central Asia. His work in geophysics and physical geography was fundamental to those sciences, and is still valuable today. Douglas Botting, *Humboldt and the Cosmos* (1973), a lively biography, is enriched by Botting's own travels on Humboldt's routes, and by some 200 illustrations ranging from Humboldt's own drawings to contemporary sketches, paintings and cartoons.

HUMPHREYS, Christmas (born 1901) English judge and writer

Humphreys rose to the height of his profession, playing a leading part in such famous cases as the trials of Klaus Fuchs and Ruth Ellis, and working backstage during the 1936 abdication crisis (*see* Windsor) and the Japanese war-crimes tribunal in the late 1940s. From the age of 20 he led an eventful parallel life as a leading western convert to and exponent of Buddhism. He wrote 15 books about Buddhism, travelled the world studying and explaining it, and was friend and adviser to the Dalai Lama and the royal families of Nepal, Sikkim and Thailand. His autobiography, *Both Sides of the Circle* (1978) describes all this, and is clear-headed about those twin mysteries, Buddhist philosophy and the workings of the English legal system. He writes well about his Edwardian childhood, his fascination for Jung's philosophy and alternative medicine, and his long and happy marriage. He regarded this life as just one in a series of reincarnations – and if any of his other existences equalled this one, he was a lucky man indeed.

HUNTER, Rita (born 1933) English opera singer

Hunter sang from childhood, disconcerting her teachers by volume alone, and performing in the family charity act 'Hunter's Modern Minstrels'. She went on to music college, served time in the chorus, and eventually became a leading dramatic soprano, noted for such heavyweight roles as Brünnhilde and Turandot. Her autobiography *Wait Till the Sun Shines, Nellie* (1986) is gloriously giggly and gushy, and is that rare thing, a showbiz book by someone who has had a fulfilled, happy life and is not afraid to say so.

> **READ ON**
> Lotte Kellner, *Alexander von Humboldt* (account of Humboldt's work, both in the context of its time and in the light of modern science: tough but rewarding).

> **READ ON**
> Agehananda Barrett, *The Ochre Robe*.

> **READ ON**
> John Culshaw, *Ring Resounding* (a treat for opera buffs: the story of the making of the first-ever recording of Wagner's *Ring* cycle, for Decca. Nothing to do with Hunter, but a perfect match for her zest for the profession.

HUSTON, John (1906–88) US film director

Huston directed a dozen masterpieces, such as *The Maltese Falcon*, *Fat City* and *The Dead*, and a number of spectacular duds, such as *Beat the Devil*, *The Kremlin Letter*, *Annie*. In private life he was a roaring boy: he drank, womanized, gambled, hunted, brawled and told tall tales in a way which was lovable or repulsive according to your mood. His autobiography *An Open Book* (1981) is full of the authentic tone of his voice (it was dictated), and has a kind of wide-eyed, 'what d'you mean you don't believe this?' candour which was characteristic of the man. Lawrence Grobel, *The Hustons* (1990) is large (812 pages), full of good stories (not always the same ones), and excellent on Huston's family: his father Walter and his children Anjelica, Danny and Tony.

> **READ ON**
> Lillian Ross, *Picture* (account of Huston wheeling and dealing, sweating and swearing as he made *The Red Badge of Courage*. A classic 'back of camera' book).

HUXLEY family

Thomas Henry Huxley (1825–95), a marine biologist, did work anticipating *Darwin's theory of evolution, and later became one of Darwin's most vigorous and outspoken supporters. He pioneered the addition of science to the educational curriculum, and gave public lectures on science and religion which outraged the authorities as much as they delighted his audiences. Cyril Bibby, *Scientist Extraordinary* (1972) is a good biography. **Julian Huxley** (1887–1975), T.H. Huxley's grandson, was a zoologist, director of the London zoo and pioneer conservationist. Julian Huxley, *Memories* (two volumes, 1970–73) is his autobiography, and J.R. Baker, *Julian Huxley, Scientist and World Citizen* (1978) is a biographical memoir, good on his work for UNESCO after his retirement from academic science. **Aldous Huxley** (1894–1963), Julian's brother, prevented by poor eyesight from scientific study, became one of Britain's most savage satirical novelists. Sybille Bedford, *Aldous Huxley* (two volumes, 1973–4) is magisterial and thorough; the first volume is on Huxley's years among the British glitterati, the second about his travels and his final years in Hollywood.

> **READ ON**
> Ronald W. Clark, *The Huxleys* (family biography). *Juliette Huxley, *Leaves of the Tulip Tree* (autobiography by Julian's wife). Laura Archera Huxley, *This Timeless Moment* ('personal view' of Aldous Huxley in the last years of his life, by his second wife).

HUXLEY, Elspeth (born 1907) English writer

Huxley was brought up in Kenya and has written novels, travel books and other accounts of the life and people there, especially white settlers of the first half of the 20th century. *The Flame Trees of Thika* (1959) is a memoir of her childhood, an account of white farmers trying to keep up 'civilized standards' (that is, the manners and attitudes of the suburban British middle class) in an entirely inappropriate environment. Huxley's early years were a blend of acute social anxiety (when should a

> **READ ON**
> Daphne Anderson, *The Toerags* (similar memoir of life in colonial Southern Rhodesia, now Zimbabwe). Elspeth Huxley, *White Man's Country* (biography of the pioneer Kenyan settler Lord Delamere, called in its day 'probably the best exposition of the case for white settlement in Kenya'. Unfashionable attitudes,

child be seen but not heard in adult company?) and exploration of the marvellous creatures and countryside all round her. *The Mottled Lizard* (1962) continues the story between the wars, and is enriched by Huxley's adult understanding of people's problems and absurdities, and of the African and European politics of the time.

HUXLEY, Juliette (born 1896) Swiss/English hostess

Brought up in a poor, Calvinist family, Juliette was pitchforked into a totally different milieu at 19, when she moved to England to become governess to the daughter of *Ottoline Morrell. She spent two years at Garsington, watching the antics of the *Bloomsbury group, and later married the brilliant young scientist Julian Huxley (*see* Huxley family). *Leaves of the Tulip Tree* (1986), her autobiography, is very much the story of this marriage, and of the couple's struggle to cope with Julian's stressful public life and his periodic nervous breakdowns. As well as of Julian, there is an intimate portrait of his brother Aldous, and other well-known people – *Wells, *Russell, the *D.H. Lawrences – appear off-duty. Juliette has a gentle but devastating line in social criticism. She doesn't mind the way the Bloomsberries sponged off Ottoline Morrell, repaying her by writing gushy bread-and-butter letters, but she makes a point of mentioning the way they also wrote to one another, vying to be bitchiest about their hostess.

⋄ **READ ON**
Julian Huxley, *Memories*. Sarah Jobson Darroch, *Ottoline* (Morrell).

intelligently and persuasively expressed).

HUYSMANS, Joris Karl (1848–1907) Dutch/French writer

Huysmans' early novels are harshly realistic, in the manner of Zola. But in the 1880s he became notorious as a decadent, determined to break through the barriers of inspiration by breaking down the constraints of 'normal' life and exploring every possible mental and physical sensation. His novel *Against Nature* (1884) is almost a self-portrait: the study of a neurotic, self-indulgent individual who turns from the world and tries satanism, masochism, sensual indulgence, sadism and mysticism in a doomed attempt to unlock his own soul. Later, Huysmans became a Roman Catholic convert, and wrote a memoir (*En Route*, 1895) and several novels outlining this progression. He was admired by such creators as *Wilde, Beardsley, *Rolfe and the surrealists, especially *Cocteau. James Laver, *The First Decadent* (1964) tells his bizarre, somewhat nasty but engrossing story.

⋄ **READ ON**
Pierre Loti, *Portrait of an Escapist* (about another experimental, sensualist writer, whose works, for example the erotic, fragmented *Chansons de Bilitis*, inspired Debussy).

I

❖ INDIA

Sasthi Bata, *Traitor to India: a Search for Home*
Tyndale Biscoe, *Tyndale Biscoe of Kashmir*
*Nirad Chaudhuri, *The Autobiography of an Unknown Indian*
*Rumer Godden and Jon Godden, *Two Under the Indian Sun*
Sanrepalli Gopal, *Nehru: a Biography* (two volumes)
M.M. Kaye, *The Sun in the Morning*
John Masters, *Bugles and a Tiger*
*Ved Mehta, *Vedi; The Ledge Between the Streams*
*R.K. Narayan, *My Days*
Percival Spear, *Master of Bengal: Clive and his India*
Francis Tuker, *The Yellow Scarf*
Angus Wilson, *The Strange Ride of *Rudyard Kipling*

❖ IRELAND

Brendan Behan, *Confessions of an Irish Rebel*
Elizabeth Bowen, *Seven Winters: Memories of a Dublin Childhood*
*Christy Brown, *My Left Foot*
Oliver St. John Gogarty, *As I Was Walking down Sackville Street*
Anita Leslie, *The Gilt and the Gingerbread*
Dervla Murphy, *Wheels Within Wheels*

Donough O'Brien, *History of the O'Briens from Brian Boroimbe 1000–1945*
Edna O'Brien, *Mother Ireland*
Sean O'Faolaoin, *Vive Moi: an Autobiography*
*Violet Powell, *Five Out of Six*
Edith Somerville and Martin Ross, *Irish Memories*
C.C. Trench, *Great Dan: a Biography of *Daniel O'Connell*

ISHERWOOD, Christopher (1904–86) English/US writer

Isherwood took part in two 20th-century events which seemed incredible at the time but are now old news: the discovery in 1930s Germany that the Nazis were both dangerous and sinister, and the 'coming out' of homosexuals in 1960s California. He wrote a dozen books around these themes, chiefly autobiographical stories such as *Goodbye to Berlin* (Germany) and *A Single Man* (USA). His *Christopher and His Kind* (1977) is a Berlin memoir, irritatingly moving between first person ('I', the elderly writer remembering) and third ('Christopher', the innocent experiencing), but a fascinating counterpart to the fictional *Mr Norris Changes Trains* and *Goodbye to Berlin*, not least because of its greater openness about homosexuality. *Lions and Shadows* (1938) is fictionalized autobiography from the same period, giving glimpses of such friends as Auden and Spender under different names. John Lehmann, *Christopher Ishwerwood* (1987) is an affectionate memoir by a friend of 35 years' standing.

◊ **READ ON**
Christopher Isherwood, *Kathleen and Frank* (memoir of his parents); *Ramakrishna and His Disciples* (biography of the Indian mystic who influenced Isherwood's thought in the 1940s and beyond). Dodie Smith, *Look Back in Astonishment* (struggles in Hollywood: good glimpses of Isherwood, a friend).

J

JAMES, Alice (1848–92) US diarist

James' father told his children 'to be extraordinary', to have a
unique perception of the world and to live by it. Two of his
sons took this advice intellectually: William James became a
psychologist and philosopher fascinated by individuality, and
Henry James became a novelist interested in how cultural experience affects character. Alice James, their sister, was
trapped in the upper-class 19th-century convention that
females had no need of intellectual distinction. As bright as
her brothers, she was forced to reconcile two warring ideas
about 'individuality' in her own personality. The struggle affected her health; she was a perpetual invalid, and died
young. Her *Diary* (ed. Leon Edel, 1964) gives tragic, inspiring glimpses of how she coped, and succeeded in being at
once her own woman and the model person her family and
society required. Jean Strouse, *Alice James* (1980) gives a partisan but readable account of her life, making scholarly use of
diaries, letters and other documents.

‣ **READ ON**
F.O. Matthiessen, *The James
Family* (good account of this
awkward, brilliant group,
determined to live by rationality,
and so tormented when the
attempt broke down). Leon Edel,
Henry James (five-volume 'life',
daunting but authoritative).

‣ JAZZ

Count Basie, *Good Morning Blues*
James Lincoln Collier, **Louis Armstrong*
Miles Davis, *Miles: The Autobiography*
Elaine Fernstein, *Bessie Smith*
Gary Giddins, *Celebrating Bird: the Triumph of Charlie
Parker*
Billie Holiday, *Lady Sings the Blues*
**Peggy Lee, *Miss Peggy Lee*

> Alan Lomax, *Mister Jelly Roll: the Fortunes of Jelly Roll Morton*
> B. Priestley, *Mingus: a critical biography*
> Jay D. Smith, *Jack Teagarden: the Story of a Jazz Maverick*
> W.T. Kirkeby ed., in collaboration with Duncan Schiedt and Sinclair Traill, *Ain't Misbehavin', the Story of 'Fats' Waller*

JEFFERSON, Thomas (1743–1826) third US president

Even among the indefatigable, multi-talented founders of the USA, Jefferson stands out. He spoke half a dozen languages, was interested in philosophy, literature and music, followed the latest ideas in science and was a skilled architect and craftsman, designing his own house and making most of its furniture. He fought all his life to abolish slavery, and his bill banning the slave trade was finally passed in 1808. As President, he negotiated the Louisiana Purchase, doubling the size of the USA overnight, and worked to open up the continent, making peace with Amerindians. In his 80s he supervised the creation of the University of Virginia, selecting staff, planning buildings and even devising the curriculum.

Unsurprisingly, there is a library-ful of books about Jefferson. His *Autobiography* and *Letters* exist in many editions, and are main sources, though somewhat formal and stiff to read: Jefferson put ease of manner into his life, not into his writings. Carl Binger, *Thomas Jefferson: a Well-Tempered Mind* (1970) and Thomas Fleming, *The Man from Monticello: an Intimate Life of Thomas Jefferson* (1969) are good overall accounts, free from the hero-worship which affects many biographers, and from others' strenuous attempts to find Jefferson's faults. Fawn M. Brodie, *Thomas Jefferson: an Intimate History* (1974) is a majestic book on Jefferson's personality: not so much his mind as his feelings and emotions. Other recommended books on specific subjects are John M. Allison, *Adams and Jefferson: the Story of a Friendship* (1966); Daniel Boorstin, *The Lost World of Thomas Jefferson* (1948); I.T. Frary, *Thomas Jefferson, Architect and Builder* (1931); and Sarah N. Randolph, *The Domestic Life of Thomas Jefferson* (1958).

⋅> **READ ON**
Alistair Cooke, *America* (contains a superb chapter on Jefferson).

JEKYLL, Gertrude (1843–1932) English gardener

Jekyll was one of the best-loved figures in English gardening, both a creator of gardens and a prolific journalist and writer. She developed the concept of the 'English cottage garden' for

⋅> **READ ON**
Beverley Nichols, *Merry Hall* (contented, restful story of how Nichols took over a big house and garden which had run wild, and restored them).

rich people with large plots. Her gardens had brick-paved paths, ponds, arbours, lawns and nooks. The plants were arranged in natural-looking but skilfully organized beds of contrasting colour, height and type. Her best-known gardens were made for houses designed by the architect Edwin Lutyens, and a 'Lutyens house with a Jekyll garden' was, in the 1880s–90s, the ambition of every member of the country-loving middle class. Many of Jekyll's gardens still survive, but more importantly, her ideas on plant choice and layout have influenced most ordinary gardens since: she is where present-day English gardening begins. Betty Massingham, *Miss Jekyll* (1966) is an affectionate biography, good on the plants, and has illustrations which will fill every gardener's head with good ideas.

JENNER, Edward (1749–1823) English doctor

Jenner, a country GP, worked for 20 years to show that if you gave people a dose of the mild disease cowpox, you could build up immunity in their bodies against the more deadly smallpox. In 1796 he gave the first 'vaccination' in England, and it was successful. The rest of his life was spent like a missionary for medicine, spreading his message throughout Europe, convincing sceptics and basking in adulation: an ordinary person pitchforked into celebrity and loving every minute. Dorothy Fisk, *Dr Jenner of Berkeley* (1959), the standard biography, makes an enthralling book from his story, not least because she enlivens it with Jenner's own comments, and with quotations from newspapers, letters and even laudatory poems of the time.

⋗ **READ ON**
Richard B. Fisher, *Joseph Lister* (biography of the surgeon who pioneered antiseptic practice in hospitals).

JOAN OF ARC (c1412–31) French soldier, later canonized

The story of the 'Maid of Orleans', who heard saints' voices telling her to deliver France from the English and who was betrayed, burned at the stake and later made a saint, has been a religious and heroic legend for the last five centuries. There have been thousands of books, plays (including *Shakespeare's Henry VI Part I* and *Shaw's Saint Joan*), films, paintings and religious tracts. *Vita Sackville-West, *Joan of Arc* (1973), a straightforward popular biography, recounts the facts clearly and elegantly. Marina Warner, *Joan of Arc, the Image of Female Heroism* (1981) is tougher but fuller, not only telling the story of Joan's life (making use of contemporary accounts, from everyone from her prosecutor to the soldiers she inspired) but coming to terms with her legend in art, literature, religion, war and gender studies. Warner's prose can be donnish, but her book (a classic study) is full of insights and provocative ideas.

⋗ **READ ON**
Thomas Keneally, *Blood Red, Sister Rose* (historical novel: powerful religious and military atmosphere). W.S. Scott (ed. and trans.), *The Trial of Joan of Arc* (transcript of the original proceedings – source material for every book and play since then).

JOHN, Gwen (1876–1939) English painter

John painted delicate, uncluttered pictures of serious-faced people (chiefly young women), and a few trim landscapes. She felt eclipsed by the talent of her more extrovert brother Augustus, and was shy of exhibiting or selling her work. It was not till after her death that her true talent (greater than her brother's) became apparent. She lived much of her life in France, where she earned a living as an artist's model, and had pasionate, if quiet, affairs with (among others) Rodin and Rilke. On the surface, her life seems as discreet as her art, but Susan Chitty, *Gwen John* (1981) makes it absorbing, not so much because of artistic interest as because she makes us feel that we know John intimately, as a warm, dignified, endlessly mysterious friend.

◇ READ ON
Cecily Langdale and David Fraser Jenkins, *Gwen John, An Interior Life* (superb reproductions of all John's major paintings). Michael Holroyd, *Augustus John*.

JOHNSON, Amy (1903–41) English air pioneer

Johnson took up endurance flying after an unhappy love affair, and in 1930 made the first solo flight from England to Australia. Her subsequent trips, from England to South Africa and back, and across the Atlantic, were headline news – as was her marriage to her former rival, 'playboy of the air' Jim Mollinson. In 1938 her marriage broke up, she began drinking and lost her concentration. When the Second World War broke out she worked delivering planes from factories to airfields, and in 1941, bailing out in mysterious circumstances (the plane was never found), she drowned in the River Thames. Constance Babington-Smith, *Amy Johnson* (1984) is good on her character and her film-star-like tabloid legend, and is excellent (not to say vertigo-inducing) about her flying.

◇ READ ON
Doris L. Rich, *Amelia Earhart*.

JOHNSON, Dr Samuel (1709–84) English writer

Johnson's own *Lives of the Most Eminent English Poets* (1779–81) began life as a series of introductions to the work of 52 earlier English poets (including Donne, *Milton, Dryden and Gray), but was published as a set of essays on their own. They are biased, factually dubious and wonderfully insightful. His other works include *Dictionary of the English Language*, an edition of *Shakespeare, essays, poems and the prose romance *Rasselas*.

Johnson survives not only for his own work, but because of *James Boswell, *The Life of Samuel Johnson* (1791), an account, unparalleled by any other biographer of any other subject, of Johnson's character and conversation. The book's extraordinary detail comes from the fact that it proceeds for the most part day by day, describing Johnson's meals, meetings, moods and

◇ READ ON
R.W. Chapman (ed.), *Samuel Johnson: Correspondence* (letters, in three fat volumes). *James Boswell, *The Journal of a Tour to the Hebrides with Samuel Johnson* (a kind of appendix to the *Life*: a straightforward travel journal, except for the light it sheds on Johnson's character, provoked by contact with scenery he admired and people he disliked).

above all his brilliant, devastating remarks on every subject under the sun. The book is long (1,400 pages), but irresistibly beckoning, an example of how to pile up trivia until they make an Alp. Good modern biographies, inevitably better on the background to Johnson's life, but (equally inevitably) far less fascinating on the man himself: Joseph Wood Krutch, *The Life of Samuel Johnson, LlD* (1945); John Wain, *Samuel Johnson* (1974); W.J. Bate, *Samuel Johnson* (1978).

JOHNSON, William (*c*1715–74) Irish/American soldier

Few true stories could sound less likely, yet every word is verified. Johnson could trace his ancestry back to St Patrick (one wonders how). He emigrated to America at 22 to trap fur-animals, became a Mohawk Indian (under the name Warraghiyagey), was a general during the French-Indian War, and after it persuaded the Mohawks to side with the British. He introduced European farming methods, and built a mansion at which he entertained as many as 1,000 British dignitaries at a time, guiding them on Amerindian affairs. He is reputed to have sired 600 children. The British rewarded his political work with a baronetcy, and he lived the rest of his life simultaneously in two worlds: as an elegant, powdered-wigged squire in a beautiful Georgian manor in Albany County, Massachusetts, and as a skin-clad, feather-headdressed Amerindian chief. James Thomas Flexner, *Lord of the Mohawks* (1979, an updating of the earlier *Mohawk Baronet*), despite scholarly notes and bibliography, still reads like a Fenimore Cooper novel, with a surprise on every page.

> **READ ON**
> Lovat Dickson, *Wilderness Man* (about another westerner who 'became' an Amerindian (*Grey Owl, though under different circumstances and with very different results).

JOHNSTON, George (1912–70) Australian writer

Johnston was a noted journalist, war correspondent and novelist, married to the writer Charmain Clift. In the 1950s–60s they left Australia for Europe, lived for 10 years on the Greek island of Hydra – a doomed, hippy attempt to find paradise on Earth – and then returned home, burnt-out and ill. Garry Kinnane, *George Johnston, A Biography* (1986) is a sympathetic study of both of them, the cautionary tale not only of this particular marriage but of a whole generation and its dreams.

> **READ ON**
> Geoffrey Dutton, *Kenneth Slessor, A Biography* (study of the journalist and war correspondent, a few years older than Johnston, who went on to become one of Australia's leading poets).

JONES, John Paul (1747–92) Scottish/American sailor

Jones joined the merchant navy at 13, and by the time he was

> **READ ON**
> Robert de la Croix, *John Paul Jones* (swaggering French biography).

21 he was a captain, in charge of his own slave-ship. He spent another six years in the slave trade, plying between Britain, Africa and the West Indies. Then, in 1775, he threw in his lot with the American colonists, and spent 13 years in what amounted to piratical raids on the British fleet, harrying them off the Scottish islands, the Cumberland and Yorkshire coasts and in what they took to be safe harbour in Belfast Lough. In 1788, denied the promotion he thought his due, he joined *Catherine the Great's Russian navy to fight the Turks, and then settled in Paris, where he died. His body was returned to the USA in 1913, and he is now a national hero. Samuel Eliot Morison, *John Paul Jones* (1960) is a wonderfully bluff biography, by a Rear-Admiral who became a professor of US history and who has no time for 'ifs' and 'maybes' but likes to get in every 'brave nor'easter', brace and jib he can find, and is equally breezy about Jones' amorous adventures and dubious money-making deals.

JOPLIN, Janis (1943–70) US singer

'The queen of rock', Joplin was a major, and characteristic, star of the 1960s. Her music was harsh, loud and raucous, and the words of her songs were a mixture of hippy mysticism and furious protest typical of the times. She seemed (to outsiders at least) to be permanently high on drink and drugs and to stand for everything that was nihilistic and self-destructive about her generation, a view which seemed confirmed when she died, apparently of a heroin overdose. Myra Friedman, *Janis Joplin: Buried Alive* (1974), by Joplin's assistant manager in her last two, tragic years, is acclaimed not only as a biography of Joplin herself but as a study of the 'lost soul' generation for whom she was such an important symbol, most of whom are now happily settled, ordinary people in early middle age.

> **READ ON**
> Albert Goldman, *Ladies and Gentlemen, Lennie Bruce* (about another 1960s figure, just as emblematic and just as tormented – this time a comedian not a singer).

JOYCE, James (1882–1941) Irish writer

Thousands of scholars have made Joyce their lives' work, pouring out books and articles on what he wrote and what it means. In the midst of all this learning, they often forget that Joyce had a life outside his work, and that it, too, is worth attention. Even Richard Ellmann, *James Joyce* (second ed. 1982), the standard biography, though it deals exhaustively with Joyce's literary friends and acquaintances, and with his writing, is thin on how he lived each day, what he thought about his students (he taught English in Trieste), his relationship with his family, his feelings about going blind. The best glimpses of Joyce the man are as co-star with his mistress, muse and (later) wife *Nora Barnacle in Brenda Maddox, *Nora* (1988), and in such

> **READ ON**
> Richard Ellmann (ed.), *Selected Letters of James Joyce*. James Joyce, *Portrait of the Artist as a Young Man* (autobiographical novel: schooldays and university life in late 19th-century Dublin. Nothing like Joyce's later books for difficulty, but their equal for atmosphere and observation of character).

memoirs as Stanislaus Joyce, *My Brother's Keeper* (1958) and
Mary Colum and Padraic Colum, *Our Friend James Joyce*
(1959). Even so, heresy though it may seem to Joyce scholars,
there is a crying need for a new biography which puts Joyce the
man in the forefront rather than Joyce the pen.

K

KAHLO, Frida (1907–54) Mexican artist

Kahlo grew up, and formed her political views, at the time of the Mexican Revolution. When she was 18 an accident left her unable to bear children and haunted by the images of childbirth, blood and death which fill her pictures. She was a Communist, and believed that art should be used for political purposes, to awaken and inform the people. She married the mural-painter Diego Rivera, had affairs with several other men including Trotsky, and was a founder of the Mexican feminist movement. Hayden Herrera, *Frida* (1983) tells her life with gusto and interprets her paintings. Many portraits, mainly of herself, are reproduced with borders and backgrounds using the fantastical colours and designs of folk art. The comments sometimes seem to tell more of the biographer than the subject, but this is the only blemish in a book as lively and surprising as the events of the life it tells.

> ⊹ **READ ON**
> Bertram D. Wolfe, *The Fabulous Life of Diego Rivera*.

KAYE, Danny (Daniel Kaminski) (1913–87) US comedy actor

For 20 years, from the moment when he upstaged Gertrude Lawrence in *Lady in the Dark* to the mid-1950s, when he was acclaimed as the greatest entertainer in the world, Kaye triumphed at everything he undertook, in films, on stage, conducting orchestras, even flying early jets. He was a childlike genius who needed to be the centre of attention on-stage and off, and whose icy misbehaviour when this failed to happen was a cross borne by all who worked with him. In the end, devastated by falling popularity, he seems simply to have lost the will

> ⊹ **READ ON**
> Freedland is a specialist in the revealing showbiz biography, and his other books are as fascinating as this one. Particularly recommended: *Al Jolson*; *Dino* (the Dean Martin Story); *So Let's Hear the Applause* (a study of Jewish entertainers).

to be funny, and became prey to stage fright. Michael Freedland, *The Secret Life of Danny Kaye* (1985) tells his story, summoning up Kaye's performances in words as if you were seeing them for the first time, and giving a sympathetic but not starry-eyed account of his personal problems and rebarbative personality.

KAZIN, Alfred (born 1915) US writer

Kazin's Russian-Jewish parents emigrated to the USA after the Revolution. He grew up in New York, and became a leading literary critic and editor. His first volume of autobiography, *Walker in the City* (1951), is an evocation of growing up in the Jewish immigrant area of New York between the wars, and of the delights of education – a familiar story, but wittily and gracefully told. The second volume, *New York Jew* (1978), describes his life during and after the Second World War. He writes about the politics of atomic warfare, the state of Israel, the Iron Curtain, the troubles of the 1960s, his travels in Europe and above all his work as a teacher, writer on American literature and a friend, enemy or colleague of such people as *Arendt, Bellow, Frost, *Mailer, *Plath and Wilson.

·> **READ ON**
Walker in the City: Nicholas Gage, *A Place for Us* (similar story, but about Greek immigrants in the 1950s and 1960s). Jerome Weidman, *Fourth Street East*; *Tiffany Street* (autobiographical novels). To *New York Jew*: Edmund Wilson, *Upstate*.

KEAN, Edmund (1787–1833) Irish actor

Kean was the finest tragic actor of his day: *Coleridge said that watching him was 'like reading Shakespeare by flashes of lightning'. He was a 'Romantic' in the mould of *Byron or *Berlioz – extrovert, neurotic, self-destructive – who wenched, drank, took drugs and squandered fortunes as if snapping his fingers at the gods. It is hard to describe the work of a memorable actor; to write about one long-dead, and to capture the stage ambience of his or her times, is a triumph of biography. Raymond FitzSimons, *Edmund Kean: Fire from Heaven* (1976) does this magnificently; the book's gusto rivals Kean's own, and FitzSimons has especial fun describing Kean's scandalous US tours. There is a good bibliography. Giles Playfair, *The Flash of Lightning* (1983) talks about Kean's life, but is particularly good at analysing his acting, quarrying contemporary critics to reveal what Kean did onstage.

·> **READ ON**
Maurice Willson Disher, *Mad Genius* (biographical novel). J.M.D. Hardwick (ed.), *Emigrant in Motley* (letters of Kean's son Charles and his wife Ellen (Tree) as they sought theatrical fortune touring the USA and Australia in the 1860s).

KELLER, Helen (1880–1968) US writer and lecturer

Blind, deaf and dumb from the age of 19 months, Keller was rehabilitated by Annie Sullivan (1866–1936), who gave her the confidence and skills to cope with life. Keller graduated from

·> **READ ON**
Helen Keller, *Helen Keller's Journal*. Nella Braddy, *Anne Sullivan Macy* (by Keller's literary helper and adviser from 1927 to 1960 who after Sullivan's death had a bumpy

college, learned to speak, became a lecturer and writer, first about disablement, then about poverty and women's rights, and finally about her religious belief, Theosophy.

Keller's own books include *The Story of My Life* (second ed. 1976), *Midstream, My Later Life* (second ed. 1968) and a memoir of the woman she called 'Teacher', *Teacher: Anne Sullivan Macy* (1955). Joseph P. Lash, *Helen and Teacher* (1980), the standard biography, is 811 pages long and spectacularly detailed, using hundreds of documents and reminiscences by people who knew Keller and Sullivan and their circle. Lash is dispassionate about Keller's and Sullivan's relationship (so close that when Sullivan married John Macy, it was Macy who moved into the Keller-Sullivan household), about the vaudeville appearances, the films and the ballet which featured Keller, and above all about Keller's political work, which earlier writings play down or distort. Anyone wanting to pursue the legend will find Lash's bibliography useful; anyone interested in the truth need look no further than Lash's book itself.

KELLY, Margaret ('Miss Bluebell') (born 1912) Irish dancer

It would take a PhD thesis to explain why people should so enjoy watching a line of identically (skimpily) dressed girls, all more than usually tall and wearing feather headdresses, high-kicking and goose-stepping in precise synchronization with the music's beat. Eroticism without risk (safety in numbers)? A glorious parody of military drill? Certainly the act reached its peak of popularity in Europe between the two World Wars and into the 1960s. Kelly ('Miss Bluebell') recruited, choreographed and supervised dozens of such troupes, first at the *Folies-Bergère* and then throughout the world. George Perry, *Bluebell* (1986) tells her story and also sheds as much light as one may ever need on such matters as how to become a Bluebell Girl, what one has to do to remain one, what sort of living the job offers and the pitfalls one must avoid. There are serious chapters on the occupation and liberation of Paris, but otherwise, all is for kicks.

KELLY, Michael (1762–1826) Irish singer and actor

As a young man Kelly had sensational European success, creating roles in operas by a dozen composers. He was, for example, Don Basilio in *Mozart's *Marriage of Figaro*, and (as he tells the tale) gave Mozart a hint or two on comic technique. Later, he managed the Theatre Royal, Drury Lane in London, and was a friend of *Sheridan and the Prince Regent (who called him 'my

relationship with the rest of Keller's entourage).

⊹ **READ ON**
Lynn Haney, *Naked at the Feast* (biography of *Josephine Baker, arguably the finest *Folies-Bergère* artist of this century – and a good deal more besides).

⊹ **READ ON**
*Lorenzo da Ponte, *Memoirs*.
Jane Williamson, *Charles Kemble, Man of the Theatre*.

dearest Mick'). His *Reminiscences* (1826), also called *Solo Recital*, are typical theatre memoirs, stuffed with good stories (in most of which the author stars) and with gushing testimonials to friends in the business and rivals he admires. The 18th-century perspective gives added zest: the cast of these anecdotes includes 'Emperor this', 'His Majesty that', 'Her Ladyship the other', not to mention a host of famous names from music and the stage, ranging from Sarah Siddons to Salieri, from Haydn to *Edmund Kean.

KELLY, Ned (1854–1880) Australian bushranger

Kelly turned to crime in his teens, and led a gang which terrorized the area between Victoria and New South Wales, robbing banks, rustling cattle, hijacking and outraging the bourgeoisie. He was eventually caught and hanged, but survives as the hero of a thousand folk-tales, a cross between Billy the Kid and Robin Hood. Max Brown, *Ned Kelly: Australian Son* (rev. ed. 1980) is the standard biography. Charles Osborne, *Ned Kelly* (1970) is a witty, slightly novelized account (full of dialogue) written to coincide with a film in which Kelly was played by Mick Jagger of the Rolling Stones. Both books are huge fun, disentangling fact from legend but making it seem just as extraordinary, and conveying the feel of the lawless, empty Australian bush and the pursed-lipped, puritanical burghers of Kelly's time.

> **READ ON**
> Pat F. Garrett, *The Authentic Life of Billy the Kid: the Noted Desperado of the Southwest, Whose Deeds of Daring and Blood Made his Name a Terror in New Mexico, Arizona and Northern Mexico.*

KENDAL, Geoffrey (born 1909) English actor

Anyone who has ever been stagestruck will recognize Kendal's condition instantly, and rejoice at his good luck. A leading juvenile in his local amateur group at 18, he turned professional, trod the boards in British repertory theatres and touring companies for 15 years, served in ENSA during the war, then settled in India as actor-manager of a company which played everything from *Dracula* to *King Lear* wherever an audience could be found. *Shakespeare was particularly popular (the casket scene from *The Merchant of Venice* never failed with schoolgirls, for some reason), and at one point in the 1950s Kendal's company was touring no fewer than 13 of his plays at once. The film *Shakespeare Wallah* was based on their Indian experiences, and now Kendal's autobiography (with Clare Colvin) *The Shakespeare Wallah* (1986) fills in the gaps. There is nothing earth-shattering about it: it is simply a happy book by a man who always knew what he wanted to do in the world, and found a way to do it.

> **READ ON**
> Micheal MacLiammoir, *Each Actor on his Ass* (hilarious memoirs of a 'jobbing actor' who was also a considerable star).

KENNEDY family

The Kennedys have played a major part in 20th-century US politics and a smaller one in world affairs. Rich and well placed in society, they have also had their fair share of tragedy. **Joseph Patrick (Joe) Kennedy** (1888–1969), founder of the dynasty, was a multi-millionaire banker and a moving force in the Massachusetts and national Democratic Party. In the late 1930s he was US ambassador in London, and is still controversial because of his efforts to persuade Roosevelt not to bring the USA into the Second World War. Richard J. Whalen, *The Founding Father* (1964) tells his life. **Rose Fitzgerald Kennedy**, his wife, wrote an autobiography, *Times to Remember* (1974), which also provides a group portrait of her and Joe's nine children. Gail Cameron, *Rose: a Biography* (1972) is revealing about the home life of all that brood. Joe and Rose had presidential ambitions for their sons: first for **Joseph Kennedy jr** (1915–44), then in turn for *John F. Kennedy** (1917–63), *Robert Kennedy** (1925–68) and **Edward Kennedy** (born 1932). This is a main theme of Doris Kearns Goodwin, *The Fitzgeralds and the Kennedys* (1987), which tells the family story from the courtship of Joe and Rose to John's inauguration in 1962. Lyn McTaggart, *Kathleen: The Untold Story of Jack Kennedy's Favourite Sister* (1984) is about **Kathleen Kennedy** (1920–48), who was widowed soon after her marriage and died in a plane crash (*see also* *Jacqueline Onassis).

READ ON
J. McCarthy, *The Remarkable Kennedys* (1962). Arthur Krock, *Memoirs: Intimate Recollections of Twelve US Presidents from Roosevelt to Nixon* (includes a memorable portrait of Joe Kennedy in full political-fixing sail).

KENNEDY, John F(itzgerald) (1917–63) 35th US president

Few biographers of Kennedy even pretend to be impartial. The authors of books written during his presidency seem to keep pinching themselves to make sure that 'Camelot' truly exists. Those writing in the mid- to late-1960s, after his death, are full of grief and anger for all that might have been. Later still, after a pause filled mainly with academic assessments of this or that aspect of his policy, came muck-rakers, and they in turn were followed by more sober reassessments. A sub-branch of Kennedy literature contains books about his actual assassination, 'proving' that it was done by everyone from the CIA to aliens from Mars.

Theodore H. White, *The Making of the the President* (1962) is a blow-by-blow account of the 1960 presidential campaign. William Manchester, *Portrait of a President* (1962, rev. ed. 1967) is a set of verbal snapshots of Kennedy in office, and Arthur M. Schlesinger jr, *A Thousand Days: John F. Kennedy in the White House* (1965) is a detailed account of his administration. Other books on this period, by Kennedy intimates, are Pierre

READ ON
Bill Harris, *John Fitzgerald Kennedy: A Photographic Documentary* (spectacular pictures, and good text if you can track it through the fancy layout). David Halberstam, *The Best and Brightest* (assessment of the Kennedy and Johnson administrations: complex but riveting for anyone interested in politics). Joan and Clay Blair jr, *The Search for J.F.K.* (leading 'bad news about Kennedy' contender: details of the glamorization of his war record, of his womanizing, of how he was presented as the picture of health when he was in fact battling illness, and much more).

Salinger (his press secretary), *With Kennedy* (1966), and Evelyn Lincoln (his personal secretary), *My Twelve Years With John F. Kennedy* (1966).

William Manchester, *Death of a President* (1967) is a grief-filled book about the assassination and its aftermath, still agonizing to read for anyone alive at the time. Michael Eddowe, *November 22: How They Killed Kennedy* (1976), and David Lifton, *Best Evidence: Disguise and Deception in the Assassination of John F. Kennedy* (1980) are more dispassionate, trawling a mass of evidence including the Warren Commission Enquiry (1964) and Mark Lane, *Rush to Judgement: a Critique of the Warren Commission Enquiry* (1966).

Arthur M. Schlesinger jr, *The Imperial Presidency* (1974) is a measured, historical assessment by an earlier biographer. William Manchester, *One Brief Shining Moment* (1983) is a moving celebration of Kennedy's life, ending with an emotional evocation of why and how people remember him. Lord Longford, *Kennedy* (1976) is a good, brief biography, and Reg Gadney, *Kennedy* (1983), the book of a TV series, is an objective account, neither overlooking nor fawning over unpleasant facts and with an excellent bibliography (*see also* *Jacqueline Onassis).

KENNEDY, Robert (1925–1968) US politician

Robert was the third of his generation of *Kennedys to be groomed for the US presidency, and he came close enough to cause continuing conjecture about whether he would have made it and what he would have done if he had. Though his Democratic thinking was different from that of his brother *John F. Kennedy, he worked selflessly as his Attorney General, making a reputation and many political enemies in the process. William V. Shannon, *The Heir Apparent* (1967) and David Halberstam, *The Unfinished Odyssey of Robert Kennedy* (1968) are excellent accounts of his political growth (the Shannon written before his assassination, but still useful). Arthur Schlesinger jr, *Robert Kennedy and His Times* (1978), by a leading Kennedy admirer, is persuasive: long and full of notes, but still compulsive.

⬦ **READ ON**
Robert Kennedy, *Thirteen Days: a Memoir of the Cuban Missile Crisis.* Arthur Krock, *Memoirs: Intimate Recollections of Twelve US Presidents from Roosevelt to Nixon* (the Kennedy chapter gives a remarkable taste of the hostility Bobby could arouse).

KILVERT, Francis (1840–79) English clergyman and diarist

Kilvert was a curate in the border country between Wales and England, about as cut off from the rest of the UK as it was then possible to be. His life was placid, but he had the gift of finding something unique in even the most humdrum events. He wrote thousands of words each day, describing the weather, the countryside, the people he met, the activities of farmers,

⬦ **READ ON**
*Dorothy Wordsworth, *Journals* (written in different circumstances, but with a similar mood and appreciation both of home life and of the landscape, flora and fauna outside the door).

townsfolk, servants and fellow clerics, and his general contentment with his life. His *Diary*, discovered and published some 60 years after his death, is a minor classic, as evocative of its time and place, and of the personality of its writer, as *Pepys' is of his. William Plomer (ed.), *The Diary of Francis Kilvert* (second ed. 1961) is complete (in three volumes) and has thorough, fascinating notes. William Plomer (ed.), *Kilvert's Diary 1870–1879* (1944) is a one-volume selection, a splendid sample. Frederick Grice, *Francis Kilvert and his World* (no date) is an affectionate biography, good on Kilvert's church work.

KING, Martin Luther jr (1929–68) US civil rights campaigner

A Baptist minister and lawyer, King spent his life – and lost it to an assassin – campaigning to win equal civil rights for all in the USA. His public profile was high, and his charisma and authority were crucial to the movement, one of the main ingredients in its success. His private life was a blend of politics, warm family life and steadfastness against horrendous physical and verbal attacks by white extremists.

David L. Lewis, *Martin Luther King: a Critical Biography* (1970) was one of the first books about him published after his death, and blends rawness of grief for the man with jubilation over his achievement. Stephen B. Oates, *Let the Trumpet Sound* (1982) is a more objective, scholarly account by a historian who specializes in the story of racial equality in the USA. David J. Garrow, *Bearing the Cross: Martin Luther King jr: a Personal Portrait* (1987), already the standard biography, has new material and looks at the old with a fresh eye. If one book alone were to stand about King's life and political importance, this would be it. Coretta Scott King, *My Life with Martin Luther King, jr* (1969) is a moving book by his widow, seeing the struggle from the family point of view, so to speak, and dealing compassionately with King's attempts to balance public mission and private life.

⋄ **READ ON**
Martin Luther King sr (with Clayton Riley), *Daddy King: an Autobiography* (by King's father). Ralph David Abernathy, *And the Walls Came Tumbling Down* (autobiography, melodramatically written but engrossing, of the man who was, in the blurb's words, 'Joshua to King's Moses' in the 1960s, and who led the civil rights movement after King was killed).

KINGSLEY, Mary (1862–1900) English explorer

Until Kingsley was 30, she nursed her invalid mother. Then she gave herself up to her passion: travel in 'darkest Africa'. Dressed in a long skirt, a starched, high-necked blouse and button boots, she crossed the jungles of West Africa, climbed Mount Cameroon and explored the Congo and Ogooue rivers, keeping her eyes open for plant species to collect for Kew Gardens and folk customs and religions to add to what was known of the peoples of the region. She wrote a bestselling account of her travels (*see* Read On), fell disastrously in love,

⋄ **READ ON**
Mary Kingsley, *Travels in West Africa* (wonderfully witty. Who else would compare a charging hippo to 'a furniture van in hysterics', or comment, on being told by a native guide that she would see more bare skin in Cameroon than on a regiment of Grenadiers, 'I worried for a *week* at the awfulness of the pun'?). Pat Barr, *A Curious Life for a*

and finally died of typhoid while nursing in Cape Town during the Boer War. Olwen Campbell, *Mary Kingsley: a Victorian in the Jungle* (1957) eclipsed all earlier biographies, making full use of unpublished letters and other primary sources. It still reads well, but has itself been overtaken by Katherine Frank, *A Voyager Out* (1986), which is good not only on Kingsley's travels (which Frank herself repeated a century later), but also on her early life, her love affair and her time in South Africa.

Lady (about Isabella Bird, an equally robust western traveller in the Far East).

KIPLING, Rudyard (1865–1936) English writer

Poet, short-story writer, author of *The Jungle Book* and the *Just So Stories* – and, some say, arch-propagandist for British jingoism at its worst, Kipling wrote an autobiography, *Something of Myself* (1937), which should have been entitled *Practically Nothing at All about Myself*. Later authors have made up for his reticence. Angus Wilson, *The Strange Ride of Rudyard Kipling* (1977) is objective and thorough about Kipling's whole life, but especially good on his time in India. Marghanita Laski, *From Palm to Pine* (1987) is well illustrated, uses family material withheld from previous biographers, and pulls no punches about Kipling's wretched final years, plagued by illness, loneliness and grief for the death of his son – and of the Imperial dream – in the First World War.

⋗ **READ ON**

Neil Philip (ed.), *The Illustrated Kipling* (extracts from Kipling's works, each relevant to one part of his life, framed with relevant drawings and photos. Superb photo-research; well-chosen passages; an unusual and satisfying book).

⋗ KITH AND KIN

Ronald W. Clark, *The Huxleys*
Amabel Clough-Ellis, *All *Stracheys Were Cousins*
Daphne Du Maurier, *The Du Mauriers*
Percy Fitzgerald, *The Lives of the *Sheridans* (two volumes)
*Rose Gamble, *Chelsea Child*
Doris Kearns Goodwin, *The Fitzgeralds and the *Kennedys*

Jonathan and Catherine Guinness, *The House of *Mitford*
F. Morton, *The Rothschilds*
John Pearson, *The Ultimate Family: the Making of the House of Windsor* (*Royal Family)
Brian Roberts, *The Mad, Bad Line* (Marquess of Queensbury and Family)
Desmond Seward, *Napoleon's Family*
Clarissa Young Spencer, *Brigham Young at Home*
Barbara Boyd *Wedgwood and Hensleigh Wedgwood, *The Wedgwood Circle 1730–1897*

KOKOSCHKA, Oskar (1886–1980) Austrian artist

In the 1900s–10s Kokoschka was a leading member of the Viennese avant-garde, who admiring *Sigmund Freud and *Jung, experimented with presenting dream-states and the unconscious in paint on canvas. He also wrote poems and plays and designed stage sets. Denounced by the Nazis, he travelled widely between the wars before settling in Britain and continuing to paint portraits and dream-landscapes in his own unsettling expressionist style. His autobiography *My Life* (Eng. ed. 1974) is fascinating on Vienna before the First World War, his war-service and his travels, but unique in what it tells of his inspiration, the way he sought hallucination and drove himself to the brink of physical and mental breakdown, plundering his psyche to make his art. The strange subject matter is balanced by a simple, lucid style, as if a grandfather is telling bedtime stories. Frank Wishford, *Oskar Kokoschka* (1986) is more objective about Kokoschka's life, and good on his paintings (which are, alas, reproduced only in black and white).

> **READ ON**
> Karen Monson, *Alma *Mahler, Muse to Genius* (biography of Kokoschka's long-time mistress and inspiration).

KORDA, Alexander (1893–1956) Hungarian film-maker

Korda worked in the film industries of Paris, Berlin and Hollywood before settling in London in the early 1930s and setting out to create a British film industry – and a studio system – equal to any he had known abroad. He succeeded: among the hundreds of films he masterminded are *The Private Life of Henry VIII*, *The Four Feathers*, *The Thief of Baghdad* and *The Third Man*. *Churchill wrote scripts anonymously for him, *H.G. Wells and *Beaverbrook were close friends, and his stars included *Laughton, *Olivier and Merle Oberon, whom he also married. Karol Kulik, *Alexander Korda: the Man Who Could Work Minacles* (1975) is the standard biography, thorough and detailed. Paul Tabori, *Alexander Korda* (1959) is more starry-eyed, full of juicy anecdotes. The most enjoyable account of all is Michael Korda, *Charmed Lives* (1979), a 'family romance' about Alexander and his two brothers, and, in passing, a funny and perceptive study of the rise and fall of the British film industry.

> **READ ON**
> Michael Balcon, *A Lifetime of Films* (autobiography by Britain's other main film mogul of the 1930s–60s, Korda's rival and the creator of Ealing Studios).

KRISHNAMURTI, Jiddu (1895–1986) Indian mystic

When Krishnamurti was 15 the theosophist *Annie Besant declared him the reincarnation of Lord Maitreva, Teacher of

> **READ ON**
> Jiddu Krishnamurti, *Krishnamurti's Journal*; *Krishnamurti to Himself* (two of the simplest, most accessible, of his many books). Radha

the World. He was educated in England, and led the Star of the East mystical movement until 1929, when he disbanded it and renounced his claim to be a Messiah. Ever since then he preached and taught his own mystical philosophy and way of life, transcending national culture, class or creed. Mary Lutyens, *Krishnamurti* (1976–88), the authorized biography, is in three volumes: *The Years of Awakening, The Years of Fulfilment* and *The Open Door*. It is readable and (seemingly) objective, telling Krishnamurti's life and presenting his thought in a way which should appeal to those who know nothing about him, but without alienating devotees. (For anyone interested in reading further, the third volume includes a useful list of Krishnamurti's writings.)

Rajagopal Sloss, *Lives in the Shadow with J. Krishnamurti* (the author gives her personal memories of a childhood spent with Krishnamurti as a kind of second father).

L

LAFAYETTE, Marquis de (1757–1834) French Revolutionary

Despite, or because of, his aristocratic background, Lafayette was one of the most convinced radicals of his time. Trained as a soldier, he sailed for America in 1777 and became one of *Washington's youngest generals. His advocacy persuaded the French to fight on the American side, and he was involved in the capture of Yorktown. In the early months of the French Revolution he was commander of the National Guard, and acted as mediator between the King and the Revolutionaries. This earned him the distrust of both sides, and he spent the next few years in exile (and some of them in prison). He took no part in politics during *Napoléon's reign, but afterwards returned to Paris and served for 12 years as a left-wing member of the Chamber of Deputies. Peter Buckman, *Lafayette* (1977) is engrossing, lively, and has particularly good sections on Lafayette's part in both the American and French Revolutions.

⊹> **READ ON**
Louis Gottschalk, *Lafayette Comes to America* (typically thorough and magisterial book from a multi-volume biography by the US scholar who made Lafayette his life work).

⊹> LARGER THAN LIFE

Virginia Childs, *Lady Hester Stanhope, Queen of the Desert*
Johanna Johnston, *Mrs Satan* *Victoria Woodhull
Peter Noble, *The Fabulous *Orson Welles*
Frederic Raphael, *Byron*
Philip Singerman, *Red Adair: an American Hero*
G. Skelton, *Richard and Cosima *Wagner*
N. St Barbe Sladen, *The Real *Le Queux*

LAUGHTON, Charles (1899–1962) English actor

Generations of comedians have parodied Laughton's hammy performances in two film roles: the Hunchback of Notre Dame and Captain Bligh. This is unfair to the memory of one of the most versatile character actors in film, whose parts ranged from *Henry VIII and Rembrandt to the drunken northern English bully of *Hobson's Choice* and the florid southern US senator of *Advise and Consent*. The best book about Laughton's work is by another actor, Simon Callow, *Charles Laughton, a Difficult Actor* (1987). Charles Higham, *Charles Laughton* (1976) is excellent on the details of Laughton's life, and Elsa Lanchester, *Charles Laughton and I* (1938) is a no-holds-barred account of genius at work by his wife, written shortly before they moved to Hollywood.

⋗ READ ON
Simon Callow, *Being an Actor* (autobiography, full of fascinating analyses and comments on the craft of acting, and the 1970s–80s English theatre scene).

LAUREL and HARDY

Stan Laurel (Arthur Stanley Jefferson), (1890–1965) and **Oliver Hardy** (1892–1957) divide opinion. To their fans they are one of the finest, best-loved, double acts in comedy; other people fail to see what all the fuss is about. Their private lives were complicated – Laurel, for example, was married five times – and the backstage circumstances of their film-making are fascinating. Laurel conceived and co-directed most of their films, which they previewed and re-edited extensively. After 1940 their career collapsed, and they seemed powerless to stop it. But since all books about them seem to be written by fans for fans, little of this gets into print: an objective biography is still to come. In the meantime, the books which do exist concentrate on their work, to glorious effect. John McCabe, *Mr Laurel and Mr Hardy* (1961) is an affectionate account of their partnership, and John McCabe and Al Kilgore, *Laurel and Hardy* (1975) is an addict's delight: a photographic record, sometimes sequence-by-sequence, of every film.

⋗ READ ON
John McCabe, *The Comedy Mind of Stan Laurel* (interesting book about Laurel as a conceiver of comic routines; includes the script for his and Hardy's stage tour of the world in the 1950s); *Babe: The Life of Oliver Hardy*.

LAWRENCE, D(avid) H(erbert) (1885–1930) English writer

Lawrence believed that 20th-century human beings were losing touch with the natural world, and with their own nature. To rediscover this quality in life, we should be open and direct about our feelings, as innocent as Adam and Eve. This outlook, and the plain way he expressed it, caused him problems. His paintings were banned because they showed pubic hair, two of his novels were prosecuted for obscenity (*see* Read On), and

⋗ READ ON
D.H. Lawrence, *Letters*. Martin Green, *The Von Richthofen Sisters*. H. Montgomery Hyde (ed.), *The 'Lady Chatterley's Lover' Trial* (wonderfully absurd: English legal and literary grandees locking horns in court to discuss whether Lawrence's novel is pornography or a work of 'literary merit'). (*See also* *Dorothy Brett and *Helen Corke).

many people rejected his work as both uncomfortable and un-couth. Similar rawness affected his private life. He eloped with his professor's wife (Frieda von Richthofen, cousin of the First World War air ace), though the marriage was stormy because both partners believed in free love, and yet were passionately jealous of each other's affairs. He travelled the world, easing his TB symptoms by visiting warm countries – and yet was constantly drawn back to damp England and his disapproving critics.

Jeffrey Meyers, *D.H. Lawrence* (1990) is a straightforward bi-ography, concentrating chiefly on Lawrence's character and on what he did. Keith Sagar, *D.H. Lawrence: Life into Art* (1985) discusses Lawrence's work, showing how his experiences were transformed into art. Anthony Burgess, *Flame into Being* (1985) does both jobs in a single book, and is excellent on Lawrence's travels and his tussles with the literary establishment. Harry T. Moore and Warren Roberts, *D.H. Lawrence and His World* (1966) is an efficiently written, dazzlingly illustrated brief 'life'. Moore also wrote a fat, scholarly biography, published in 1954 as *The Intelligent Heart* and revised and reissued as *The Priest of Love* (1974). Richard Aldington, *Portrait of a Genius, But . . .* (1950), although old, is an invigorating (and none too polite) appraisal of Lawrence's behaviour and personality.

LAWRENCE, T(homas) E(dward) (1888–1935)
English soldier and writer

Lawrence learned Arabic as an archaeologist in what is now Iraq, and later served in the First World War, commanding the 1917 Arab revolt against the Turks. In the 1920s, his book *The Seven Pillars of Wisdom* brought him enormous fame, which he hated. He changed his name, enlisted as a ranker in the RAF, and tried to live in obscurity despite the efforts of such well-meaning friends as *Shaw and *Graves. *The Seven Pillars of Wisdom* is a mixture of autobiography, military memoir (about the desert campaign against the Turks) and philosophical re-flection: *Churchill called it one of the greatest books ever written in English. Early biographies, including Robert Graves, *Lawrence and the Arabs* (1927), depict Lawrence as a romantic war-hero (much as in David Lean's 1960s film *Lawrence of Arabia*). Richard Aldington, *Lawrence of Arabia* (1955) shattered the image, concentrating on Lawrence's homosexuality and the way he used heroics to mask personal inadequacy. More recent books, striking a fairer balance, include Phillip Knightley and Colin Simpson, *The Secret Lives of Lawrence of Arabia* (1969) and the magisterial, 1,200-page Jeremy Wilson, *Lawrence of Arabia* (1990).

⋄ READ ON
David Garnett (ed.), *The Letters of T.E. Lawrence*. '352807 A/C Ross' (Lawrence, under his RAF number, rank and name), *The Mint* (a 'documentary' about the misery of service life, published after his death). Reader Bullan, *The Camels Must Go* (autobiography).

LEAKEY, Louis (1903–72) English/Kenyan anthropologist

Leakey spent his life investigating the ancestors of the human race. The family lived in Kenya, and Louis, his second wife Mary and their children (most notably Richard) excavated at Olduvai Gorge. Their discoveries revolutionized our knowledge of how, where and when the human race evolved. Sonia Cole, *Leakey's Luck* (1975) gives a 'warts and all' picture of Leakey: his unconventional time at Cambridge, his early scientific squabbles (he was accused of faking evidence), his unplacid domestic life, and above all his 40-year career as anthropologist, curator of the National Museum and founder of the Kenya National Parks. A particularly fascinating section tells of Leakey's research, for the British government, into the Mau Mau in the early 1950s, at the start of the Kenya independence struggle.

> **READ ON**
> Richard Leakey, *The Making of Mankind* (account, by Leakey's son, of early humanity: good on the work not only of Leakey senior, but of other researchers including Mary Leakey and Richard himself).

LEAR, Edward (1812–88) English writer and artist

Author of such poems as *The Jumblies*, *The Dong With the Luminous Nose* and *There Was an Old Man with a Beard*, Lear was a beloved friend to many people, like a benevolent, eccentric uncle. He earned his living as a painter (at one time, he taught Queen *Victoria), and travelled widely to make landscape paintings, writing and illustrating accounts of his journeys to Albania, Crete, Spain, Corsica and India. John Lehmann, *Edward Lear and His World* (1977) is a good, brief 'life', illustrated by Lear's own work. Fuller accounts are Vivien Noakes, *Edward Lear: the Life of a Wanderer* (1968), the standard work, and Susan Chitty, *That Singular Person Called Lear* (1988), a sympathetic, lively study, outstanding on Lear's psychology.

> **READ ON**
> Holbrook Jackson (ed.), *The Complete Nonsense Verse of Edward Lear* (illustrated by Lear). Vivien Noakes (ed.), *Edward Lear: Selected Letters*.

LEE, Laurie (born 1914) English writer

Lee's *Cider With Rosie* (1959) is an evocative memoir of growing up in a remote country village in the 1920s. It describes a way of life, and habits of mind, which have utterly disappeared: Lee says that he was a chance witness of 'the end of a thousand years' life'. His style is poetic and reflective, as much meditation as description. *As I Walked Out One Midsummer Morning* (1969) is a harder-edged sequel, describing how he left the village for London, and tramped through Spain on the very brink of civil war.

> **READ ON**
> To *Cider With Rosie*: *Carl Nielsen, *My Childhood*. To *As I Walked Out One Midsummer Morning*: Patrick Leigh Fermor, *A Time of Gifts*.

LEE, Peggy (born 1920) US singer

Lee was discovered by Benny Goodman when she was 18, and became one of the best-known jazz and band singers of the century. At first sight, her autobiography *Miss Peggy Lee* (1990) looks like a typical showbiz catalogue of starry friends (*Crosby, Gleason, *Sinatra), superb successes and inexplicable flops. But her writing is so vivid and her vitality so extraordinary that it is hard to put the book down. The last chapters in particular, about her struggle to go on performing despite serious heart trouble, are indomitable and magnificent: if she had told them on stage instead of writing them down, we would be cheering in the aisles.

> **READ ON**
> *Phil Silvers, *The Man Who Was Bilko* (triumphs, and struggle with illness, of a similar kind but in a different branch of showbusiness).

LEE, Robert E(dward) (1807–70) US general

Lee became prominent in the Mexican War of 1846–8, was appointed commander of the US Military Academy, and led the soldiers who put down John Brown's rebellion at Harper's Ferry in 1859. During the Civil War he was general-in-chief of the southern forces, and after the surrender worked for unity between the opposing sides. A cultured, honourable and universally respected man, he ended his life as President of the Washington and Lee University at Lexington, Virginia. Clifford Dowdey, *Robert E. Lee* (1965), the standard biography, untangles the politics of the Civil War – a welcome service for non-US readers – and is excellent on the strategy of Lee's battles. It is that rare thing, a long, scholarly biography (750 pages) which never palls, and it outshines all competition.

> **READ ON**
> A.L. Long, *Memoirs of Robert E. Lee* (account of Lee published in 1886 by one of his faithful officers). Peter Earle, *Robert E. Lee* (brief biography; superb illustrations; excellent on Lee's battles).

LEES-MILNE, James (born 1908) English conservationist and writer

Lees-Milne worked for the National Trust, conserving and chronicling English country houses and their gardens. His profession brought him into contact with many of the 'great and good' of the time, and his eye for human foibles and amusing incidents is as sharp as his love for ordered architectural beauty. He kept a diary from 1942 onwards, and used it as the basis for several volumes of graceful memoirs. Typical books are *Another Self* (1970) (episodes from his childhood, including an account of his first arrival at prep school, as uproarious as any *Waugh or *Mitford short story), and *Ancestral Voices* (1975), about his London life during the blitz in the Second World War: interesting, gently indiscreet glimpses of such people as Nancy *Mitford, Emerald Cunard (*see* *Nancy Cunard) and Harold Nicolson, whose biography he later wrote.

> **READ ON**
> James Lees-Milne, *Prophesying Peace*; *Caves of Ice*; *Midway on the Waves*.

LEHMANN, Rosamond (1901–90) English writer

Lehmann wrote novels about the feelings and emotions of children and young women coming to terms with life: *Invitation to the Waltz*, *The Weather in the Streets*, *The Echoing Grove*. Her memoir *The Swan in the Evening* (1967) begins with a stunning evocation of childhood, written as it were jointly by the six-year-old and 66-year-old Lehmann (a strange style at first, but effective once you get used to it), and continues by describing her reactions to her beloved daughter's death in 1958. Lehmann, a mystic, believed that death is not final, and her book poignantly describes her certainty that her daughter was still alive in the spirit world, aware of her mother, and happy to continue their relationship. The book is heartfelt and poetic, apt to lie in the mind (especially of anyone recently bereft) long after you put it down.

> **READ ON**
> John Hillaby, *Journey Through Love* (moving story of how Hillaby came to terms with bereavement, partly through therapy and partly by walking in lonely parts of Britain and the USA). Rosamond Lehmann, *Rosamond Lehmann's Album* (album of photos, with commentary, of Lehmann's family, friends and lovers in the 1930s–40s).

LEIGH, Vivien (1913–67) English actress

Leigh had success in a range of roles from Scarlett O'Hara in *Gone With the Wind* to Lady Macbeth (opposite her then husband, *Laurence Olivier). In the 1940s and 1950s Leigh and Olivier were two of the world's most glamorous people, leaders in their profession and seemingly the model of a happily married showbiz couple. But there were hidden tensions, caused by overwork, by Leigh's increasing physical and mental illness, and in the late 1950s by Olivier's affair with Joan Plowright (who became his second wife after he and Leigh divorced in 1960). The 1960s were a dismal time for Leigh, as she struggled to rebuild her personal and professional life. There are dozens of books about her, ranging from fan-magazine adulation to scurrility. Hugh Vickers, *Vivien Leigh* (1988) is objective and intelligent. Vickers gives a good idea of what made people love Leigh so much, assesses her career and her relationship with critics, and neither shirks nor dwells on her problems. The bibliography is magnificent: over 250 books on Leigh, Olivier, their friends, colleagues, critics, fans and the Hollywood and London society of their time.

> **READ ON**
> Angus McBean, *Vivien Leigh: a Love Affair in Camera* (memoir of a friendship, in words and dozens of glorious photos). Roland Flamini, *Scarlett, Rhett and a Cast of Thousands* (behind the scenes of *Gone With the Wind*).

LEITCH, David (born 1937) English journalist

Leitch was adopted when he was eight days old, as the result of an advertisement placed by his mother in the *Daily Express*. He had a typical establishment upbringing at public school and Cambridge, wrote for several leading newspapers, and took part in the prize winning *Sunday Times* investigation of the Cam-

> **READ ON**
> *Richard Cobb, *A Classical Education*.

bridge spy-ring which later appeared in book form as *Philby, the Spy Who Betrayed a Generation*. He has written two volumes of autobiography. *God Stand Up for Bastards* (1973) described his early life, and included a plea to his natural mother to come forward and contact him if she was still alive. *Family Secrets* (1984) tells what happened when she did: how he grew to understand and love her, how his wife and children coped, and what happened when he discovered that he had two sisters, now middle-aged, whom he had never met. His story is moving and extraordinary, and his deadpan, witty style is ideal for telling it (*see also* Rosie Boycott: Leitch's wife).

LENNON, John (1940–80) English musician

Lennon fronted the Beatles, wrote (with Paul MacCartney) most of their songs, and set their style, both in their flip, self-mocking early days and in the hippie late 1960s. Ray Coleman, *John Lennon* (1984), the authorized biography, benefits from the author's long friendship with Lennon and from interviews with his family, friends, fans and detractors. It was originally published in two volumes: *John Winston Lennon*, about Lennon's early years and the rise and apotheosis of the Beatles, and *John Ono Lennon*, about the change in Lennon after he met Yoko Ono, the disbanding of the Beatles and Lennon's last ten years. It is a cliché to say that a person symbolizes an entire era, but for once, and especially for anyone who lived through the 1960s and 1970s, that opinion seems absolutely true. Albert Goldman, *The Lives of John Lennon* (1988), though scorned by Beatles fans as muck-raking and sensationalist, is actually well-researched, wittily written and gives the general reader a superb pen-picture of the excesses and triumphs of Lennon and all he stood for. Its real crimes, for Lennon's admirers, are probably Goldman's openness about the drugs, and his readiness to criticize Lennon, Ono and everyone else. A roller-coaster book about a white-knuckle ride of a life.

⋄ **READ ON**
Ray Connolly, *Brian Epstein* ('the man who made the Beatles'). Cynthia Lennon (his first wife), *A Twist of Lennon*. Hunter Davies, *The Beatles* (authorized by the Beatles, published in 1968).

LENO, Dan (1860–1904) English comedian

In the 1890s and early 1900s 'Dan Leno' (George Galvin) was the highest-paid artist in British music-hall, famous for patter songs and as the star comic (usually Dame) in pantomime. His career declined tragically when he contracted a brain tumour, but in his day few performers were more idolized. Gyles Brandreth, *The Funniest Man on Earth* (1977) magnificently evokes both Leno himself and the kind of theatre show he starred in; the book quotes many of Leno's routines, which still stand up today. J. Hickory Wood, *Dan Leno* (1905) is an affectionate bi-

⋄ **READ ON**
John Fisher, *Funny Way to Be a Hero* (studies of a dozen British comedians, from Leno to Frankie Howerd, vividly recreating their acts and the vanished music-halls and variety shows they worked in).

ography by one of Leno's friends, the man who wrote most of the pantomimes he starred in.

LEONARDO DA VINCI (1452–1519) Italian artist

Leonardo's fame as a painter rests on 17 surviving works, including *La Gioconda* (*Mona Lisa*) and *The Last Supper*. He spent 17 years as the Duke of Milan's adviser on town-planning, fortifications and court entertainments, and during this time he also did extensive scientific research into, among other things, anatomy, plant biology, geology and mechanics. His multifarious mind and achievements tend to baffle one-volume biographers, and the best books on him specialize in this or that area of his interest. Carlo Maria Franzer, *Leonardo* (1969) is a useful, brief life, without illustrations but clear on how Leonardo did his work, day by day, and on the social and political life of Florence, Milan and Rome. *Kenneth Clark, *Leonardo da Vinci* is good on Leonardo's paintings, both completed and projected. (There are many editions; the newer they are, the better the illustrations are reproduced.) Ivor B. Hart, *The World of Leonardo da Vinci* (1961) describes Leonardo's scientific work thoroughly, lucidly and with 130 of Leonardo's beautiful drawings. Of all books on Leonardo, this one gives the best impression of the quality of his mind.

⊹ READ ON

M. Kemp, *Leonardo da Vinci* (best recent study of the man and his work, somewhat confusing on its own but illuminating when read after the three mentioned above).

LE QUEUX, William (1864–1927) English writer and spy

N. St Barbe Sladen, *The Real Le Queux* (1938) begins in characteristically pugnacious, dotty style: 'Amongst the many famous men whom I have known in almost every sphere of life was WILLIAM TUFNELL LE QUEUX . . . To those whose lips curl at the mere mention of his "spy" novels, to which I allude briefly, I must point out that his fiction writing was solely a means to an end, i.e. "pot-boiling", to enable him to defray, *inter alia*, the heavy expenses of his Secret Service activities and their necessary adjunct – foreign travel.' On every page of this sublime book, Le Queux 'scents a mystery', watches 'his majesty deal his ace' or is 'charged with a secret mission concerning armaments for the forthcoming war'. Le Queux knew everyone, from Bertie, Prince of Wales to Crippen, from *Mata Hari to *Rasputin – not to mention 'H.E. Count Chedomile Mijatovitch' and 'Harry De Windt, the Explorer', whose photos adorn the book. Spoof? No chance. Le Queux was real.

⊹ READ ON

William Le Queux, *Things I Know* (equally dotty memoirs: dogs, fillies, vintage port, mysterious veiled women, riffraff and royalty). *Reginald Teague-Jones, *The Spy Who Disappeared*.

> LETTER WRITERS

Wayne Andrews, *Germaine: a Portrait of Mme de Staël*
*Gertrude Bell, *Letters*
*St Jean de Crèvecoeur, *Letters from an American Farmer*
B. Dobrée (ed.), *The Letters of *Lord Chesterfield*
*Maria Edgeworth, *Letters from England*
Rudolf Elvers (ed.), *Felix Mendelssohn, a Life in Letters*
*Mary Wortley Montagu, *Letters*
Arvind Nehra, *Letters from an Indian Judge to an English Gentlewoman*
*Pliny the Younger, *Letters*
Madame de Sevigné, *Letters*
A. and M. Simpson, *I Too Am Here: Selections from the Letters of *Jane Welsh Carlyle*
*P.G. Wodehouse, *Yours, Plum*

LEWIS, C(live) S(taples) (1898–1963) Irish writer

Lewis, a don first at Oxford and then at Cambridge, is known for scholarly works, for books preaching Christianity (e.g. *The Screwtape Letters* and *Surprised by Joy*), for science fiction and for the 'Narnia' books for children. He was a friend of *Tolkien and shared his interest in heroic myth and fantasy. A.N. Wilson, *C.S. Lewis* (1990) is fascinating on Lewis' university life, his (at first unwilling) conversion to Christianity, his friends and family, the way he coped with fame, and his writing, especially the Narnia books. Brian Sibley, *Shadowlands* (1985) is the story of how Lewis, in his late 50s, fell in love with Joy Davidman, a divorcée who was terminally ill, courted and married her in defiance of church teaching on divorce. C.S. Lewis, *A Grief Observed* (1961) is a moving autobiographical account of how Lewis coped after his wife's death.

> **READ ON**
Humphrey Carpenter, *The Inklings* (about the group of Oxford friends which included Lewis and Tolkien). C.S. Lewis, *They Stand Together* (letters to Arthur Greeves, 1914–1963); *Letters to Children*. Walter Hooper, *Through Joy and Beyond: a Pictorial Biography of C.S. Lewis*.

LEWIS, G(eorge) H(enry) (1833–1911) English lawyer

> **READ ON**
H. Montgomery Hyde, *Carson*.

For 50 years Lewis was one of London's leading criminal solicitors. He worked for clients as diverse as *Whistler, Parnell, the pickpockets and prostitutes of the London slums and the police-framed son of the 'nigger vicar' of Great Wyrley, Staffordshire. His friends included *Gilbert and Sullivan, *Max Beerbohm and the Prince of Wales. The Baccarat Scandal happened at his house. He knew *Wilde, and if their friendship had lasted Wilde might have been steered away from prosecution. He fought for better rights for divorcées and unmarried women, and for a proper system of appeal. He was Victorian rectitude personified, a character out of *Dickens or *Trollope, and John Juxon, *Lewis and Lewis* (1983) relishes every minute of his life, his cases, his forays into the East End, his weekend and evening parties and his serene, affectionate family life.

LINCOLN, Abraham (1809–65) 16th US president

The son of settlers, Lincoln educated himself while working as ferryman, storekeeper, clerk and postmaster. He became a lawyer, specializing in land and criminal cases. In the 1840s he went into local politics, toured the country advocating the abolition of slavery, and was elected to the House of Representatives. He was one of the founders of the Republican Party, and became President in 1861. Opposition to his anti-slavery laws culminated in the Civil War, during which he spoke nobly of national reconciliation and of democracy and equality for all. After the war, the shock of his assassination, as nothing else, spurred his fellow Americans to follow his earlier advice and 'bind up the nation's wounds'.

There is a mountain of books on Lincoln: only *Napoléon outranks him as a subject for biography. The most accessible selection of Lincoln's own writings is Philip Van Doren Stern (ed.), *The Life and Writings of Abraham Lincoln* (1904). This includes W.D. Howells', *Life of Abraham Lincoln*, written for the 1860 election, and edited and annotated by Lincoln: the nearest thing to an autobiography, and the origin of the 'log cabin to White House' legend. Carl Sandburg, *Abraham Lincoln* is the standard biography, and it is of a standard hard to beat. Originally in four volumes, (1926–39), it is also available in a single, slimmed-down (to 800 pages) book, *Abraham Lincoln*, (1954). Sandburg's research is magisterial, his political and historical analysis persuasive, and his language (like Lincoln's own) echoes the cadences of the Bible and the Founding Fathers. It is a truly American book, mirroring the unaffected grandeur of its subject. Two shorter biographies, especially helpful for non-US readers, are Stephen B. Oates, *With Malice Towards None* (1978), good on Lincoln's political career, and avoiding Sandburg's temptation to turn Lincoln's life into some kind of seminal US myth, and Lord Longford, *Abraham Lincoln* (1974), which offers a clear-headed text and over 100 unusual and informative illustrations.

LIND, Jakov (born 1927) Austrian writer and artist

A Jew, Lind was evacuated to Holland in 1938, and spent his

> **READ ON**
> Ishbel Ross, *The President's Wife: Mary Todd Lincoln*. R.J.S. Gutman, *John Wilkes Booth Himself* (amazing story of the mad actor who assassinated Lincoln).

> **READ ON**
> Jakov Lind, *Numbers* (what happened next: Lind spends the 1950s as a kind of European super-tramp (*see also* *W.H.

early teens, like *Anne Frank, hiding in an attic to escape Gestapo searches. In the last years of the war he went into Germany, pretending Dutch identity, and worked as a spy. After the war he settled briefly in emerging Israel, and tried to make sense of his experiences by painting and writing. *Counting My Steps* (1969), the first volume of his autobiography, describes all this in Lind's usual ironic, bewildered style: it is as if Europe is an insane, Kafka-designed maze and he is staggering through it trying to find his identity and to work out why he exists, while the forces of darkness inexorably hunt him down.

Davies), still looking for his identity – and in the process enjoying sexual adventures that make *Frank Harris and *Henry Miller seem like amateurs).

LINDBERGH, Charles (1902–74) US air pioneer

In 1927 Lindbergh flew a monoplane single-handed across the Atlantic, the first person ever to do so. He became the best-known man in America, a position which led to tragedy five years later when his baby son was kidnapped and murdered. Embittered, Lindbergh left the US for Europe, and became a fervent and vociferous supporter of *Hitler. This caused him problems when the USA entered the Second World War, and he was banned from flying. In the 1950–60s he worked as adviser to the USAF and later PanAm, and he found a final, uncontroversial, role as a propagandist for animal conservation. Kenneth S. Davis, *The Hero* (1959) tells his story, and reflects on the American need for heroes, and on the effect this has on the people so renowned. Leonard Mosley, *Lindbergh* (1976) is outstanding on Lindbergh's politics and the latter part of his life generally.

⋄ **READ ON**
Charles Lindbergh, *Spirit of Saint Louis* (Lindbergh's own story of his flight); *The Wartime Journals of Charles A. Lindbergh* (published in 1970, with an introduction suggesting that Lindbergh's views had not mellowed at all in the intervening years). Anne Morrow Lindbergh (his wife), *Bring Me a Unicorn; Hour of Gold, Hour of Lead.*

LINDSAY, Jack (born 1900) Australian/English writer

The son of *Norman Lindsay, Jack Lindsay in his 20s was a classical scholar at Brisbane University, and a fiercely modernist poet. In 1926 he moved to Britain, where he lived at the hub of 1930s literary London. Personal tragedy made him give up that life, and after war service he spent his time quietly in the West Country. He wrote over 100 books: plays, novels, works on classical subjects, biographies (of, among others, *Cézanne, *Cleopatra and *Turner). *Life Rarely Tells* (1921), the first volume of his autobiography, is a beautifully written memoir of his childhood and his intellectual development at school and university. *The Roaring Twenties* (1960) is hilarious about life among the 1920s Australian avant-garde. *Fanfrolico and After* (1961) tells of his time in London, and also explains, in moving terms, the intellectual and emotional self-reassessment which led him to turn his back on the metropolis.

⋄ **READ ON**
To the Australia-set books: Graham McInnes, *The Road to Gundagai; Humping My Bluey* (memoirs of childhood and youth by a 'Pom' who settled in Australia in the early 1950s, aged 11).

LINDSAY, Norman (1879–1969) Australian artist and writer

When Lindsay sat down to write his autobiography *My Mask* (1970), he vowed 'to keep art, metaphysics and politics right out', and to confine himself 'simply to the entertainment', an ambition he fulfilled triumphantly. He is funny about his childhood among the old Gold Rush diggings, his Bohemian student days in Melbourne, his love affairs (which he says began at the age of seven), his years as a Sydney newspaperman, his travels to Europe and America, and his peaceful old age in his beautiful garden in the Blue Mountains of New South Wales. This is autobiography even more selective than most, but also funnier and wiser. One of Lindsay's best-known books is the children's story *The Magic Pudding*, and anyone who loved that will find the same exuberance, the same twinkly-eyed zest, here on every page.

‑> **READ ON**
Rose Lindsay, *Model Wife* (witty, scandalous memoirs by Lindsay's second wife, who modelled for some of the most talented, most extrovert artists of the time). Keith Wingrove (ed.), *Norman Lindsay on Art, Life and Literature* (packed anthology).

LISTER, Joseph (1827–1912) English surgeon

The greatest English surgeon of his time, Lister pioneered the use of antiseptics in operating rooms and recovery wards. He designed instruments and equipment, and was a renowned teacher and lecturer. Pictures show him as everybody's idea of a typical Victorian grandee: stiff-collared, sour-featured, prim. This may have been his public face, but in private he was relaxed, affable and charming, loved as well as admired by patients, colleagues and friends. Richard B. Fisher, *Joseph Lister* (1977) is good on this side of his personality (making excellent use of family letters and diaries), but also paints a grim picture of the hospitals of the time, and explains clearly what Lister did and how he did it.

‑> **READ ON**
Frank G. Slaughter, *Immortal Magyar* (tragic story of Ludwig Semmelweiss, who had similar ideas to Lister's in Vienna at the same time, but instead of being encouraged was hounded out of his job by the establishment and died in miserable, mysterious conditions in a lunatic asylum).

LISZT, Ferenc (Franz) (1811–86) Hungarian musician

Liszt was the finest pianist of his day, idolized not only by musicians but by fans who swooned, screamed and threw flowers throughout his performances. He had a string of lovers, and lived life at a gallop until he was 37, when he retired from the concert platform to become conductor of the court orchestra at Weimar. Here he experimented with musical Romanticism (the use of melody, harmony and orchestration to suggest and evoke emotion) and became a vital bridge between such early Romantics as *Beethoven or *Berlioz and composers such as *Wagner and Debussy.

Throughout his life Liszt refused to publish an autobiogra-

‑> **READ ON**
Mozelle Moshansky, *Liszt: His Life and Times* (lively pictorial biography). Charlotte Haldane, *The Galley Slaves of Love* (about Liszt's tempestuous, scandalous affair with Marie, Comtesse d'Agoult).

phy, saying that legend would serve his career far more than fact. This causes problems for biographers: they tend to plump either for musical complexity or for gossip about Liszt's public and private life. Ronald Taylor, *Franz Liszt* (1986) steers a course between these extremes, and offers insights (accessible to the general reader) into Liszt's character and the place of his work in the German Romantic tradition. Adrian Williams, *Portrait of Liszt: by Himself and his Contemporaries* (1990) is a huge, scholarly anthology of documents: all biographical work should start here.

LIVINGSTONE, David (1813–73) Scottish explorer

Livingstone worked as a textile labourer from the age of ten, educating himself in the evenings. He went as a Christian missionary to Africa when he was 27, but gradually abandoned Church work for exploration. David Livingstone, *Missionary Travels and Researches in South Africa* (1857) and *Journeys and Researches in South Africa* (1905) are spectacular accounts of the hardships and excitements of his life, and to modern readers an equally striking revelation of unconscious racism and cultural imperialism. Those themes are further covered in G. Seaver, *David Livingstone, His Life and Letters* (1957) and Oliver Ransford, *David Livingstone: the Dark Interior* (1978), the standard biographies. Edna Healey, *Wives of Fame* (1986) includes an account of Livingstone's wife Mary, who made equally far-ranging missionary journeys of her own, but loyally let her husband's fame engulf her life.

> **READ ON**
> *Henry Morton Stanley, *How I Found Livingstone*. I. Schapera (ed.), *David Livingstone Family Letters* (2 vols, 1959); *Livingstone's Private Journals, 1851–1853* (1960). Judith Listowel, *The Other Livingstone* ('feet of clay' book, making the case for four of Livingstone's fellow explorers, whose discoveries, the author says, Livingstone claimed as his own and whose names he tried hard to keep out of any records of his life).

LONDON, Jack (1876–1916) US writer

Before London was 20 he worked as mill-hand, sailor and oyster pirate, and took part in the Klondike Gold Rush. He began writing stories for newspapers, and was soon producing 1,000 words a day. His short stories and novels, notably *The Call of the Wild* and *White Fang*, brought him international fame, and he toured the world, meeting revolutionaries and writing savage descriptions of the victims of capitalism in such cities as London and Chicago. He wrote no official autobiography, but two of his novels are based on his own experience: *Martin Eden* about an ordinary man, a sailor, working to educate himself and become a writer, and *John Barleycorn* about a writer struggling against alcohol. His tormented private life and his uncompromising political views made him a favourite target for newspaper gossip, and his reputation as a hard-hitting, hard-drinking, womanizing wanderer was clinched in the 1930s by Irving Stone's lurid and bestselling biographical novel *Sailor on Horse-*

> **READ ON**
> King Hendricks and Irving Shephard (eds), *Jack London Reports*; (letters from Jack London) Joan London (Jack's daughter), *Jack London and his Times*.

back. Andrew Sinclair, *Jack London* (1978) sorts out fact from fiction, and is excellent on London's place in the tradition of US he-man literature.

◇ LONDON LIFE

P.Y. Betts, *People Who Say Goodbye*
*Charles Chaplin, *My Autobiography*
*Richard Church, *Over the Bridge*
Peter Conrad, *Charles Dickens*
*Rose Gamble, *Chelsea Child*
*Mrs Robert Henrey, *Spring in a Soho Street*
Christopher Hibbert, *The Road to Tyburn* (*Jack Sheppard)
*Samuel Pepys, *Diary*
Angela Rodaway, *A London Childhood*
Dorothy Scannell, *Mother Knew Best: an East End Childhood*
*Terence Stamp, *Stamp Album*
Phyllis Willmott, *A Green Girl*

LOOS, Anita (1891–1981) US writer

Beginning with the subtitles for *Intolerance* in 1916, Loos wrote over 250 films, including most of those starring Douglas Fairbanks senior, and the hilarious flapper-epic *Gentlemen Prefer Blondes*. Her autobiography *A Girl Like I* (1966) is funny, bitchy and starry-eyed about Hollywood, New York, every film star you've ever heard of and – last but not least – Loos' own sex life. It's hard to believe that anyone's life could fizz like pink champagne for 90 fun-packed years, but that's Loos' story and she tells for all it's worth.

◇ **READ ON**
Anita Loos, *Kiss Hollywood Goodbye*; *Cast of Thousands* (memoirs and anecdotes). Mrs D.W. Griffiths, *When the Movies Were Young* (wickedly wide-eyed account of behind-the-screen shenanigans in the very early days).

LOUIS XIV (1638–1715) French king (ruled 1643–1715)

The reign of the 'Sun King' was longer and more dazzling than any other in French history: a golden age. Nancy *Mitford, *The Sun King* (1966) conveys its glitter by intertwining a biography of Louis himself with the story of how he gradually transformed a former hunting lodge into the palace of Versailles. Mitford's writing bubbles with enjoyment, and she has an eye for every absurd or meaningful anecdote of court life. Fine illustrations rival, but hardly outshine, the text. Vincent Cronin, *Louis XIV* (1964) is a good book to read in tandem with Mitford's, filling in background and revealing about the politics

◇ **READ ON**
Ragnhild Hutton, *Louis XIV and his World* (brief, tiny type, well illustrated). Lucy Norton, *The Sun King and his Loves*. Harriet Ray Allenteuch, *Madame de Sévigné* (biography, crammed with gossip about Louis and his court, culled from Sévigné's sparkling *Letters*).

of Louis' reign. Philippe Erlanger, *Louis XIV* (Eng. ed. 1970) does little to explain the enigma of Louis himself, but is excellent on his court.

LUDWIG II (1845–86) Bavarian king (ruled 1864–86)

A lonely, unloved child, Ludwig found comfort in fairy tales and the work of such writers as Goethe, Poe and Hoffman. He was also one of the first-ever *Wagner addicts. When he was 18 his father abdicated, and Ludwig saw his chance to become one of the great artistic patrons of the century. He bankrupted the state for Wagner, financing him to write *The Ring of the Nibelung, Tristan and Isolde* and *Parsifal*. But the two men quarrelled, and Ludwig retreated into fantasy, spending his time building and furnishing fairy-tale castles on the banks of the Rhine. His ministers eventually had him declared insane, and soon afterwards he was found dead in Lake Starnberg, with nothing to prove whether it was murder or suicide. Wilfrid Blunt, *The Dream King* (1970) disentangles fact from fairy tale, and is magnificently illustrated with photos and paintings of Ludwig, his castles (interior and exterior) and the sumptuous sets (some based on his own equally stagy royal apartments) he financed for Wagner's operas.

> ⇢ **READ ON**
> Henry Channon, *The Ludwigs of Bavaria* (joint biography of Ludwig and his harsh, hardly less eccentric father).

LUNT, Lynn
LUNT, Alfred

Lynn Fontanne (English/US, 1887–1983) and her husband Alfred Lunt (US, 1893–1977) were two of this century's most distinguished US actors, both separately and especially together. They performed in plays as diverse as *Arms and the Man*, *The Brothers Karamazov* and *The Taming of the Shrew*, and were renowned for the sensitivity of their duet-playing: a double act as compulsive as their comic counterparts *Burns and Allen or *Laurel and Hardy. They continued working into their 80s, and were two of the few fellow actors who (in his own words) took *Olivier's breath away. Maurice Zolotow, *Stagestruck* (1964), a joint biography, was written while they were in their prime and is slightly gushy. But it captures the essence of their style on stage, is good on their war-work in Britain, and offers in passing a panorama of serious Broadway theatre in the middle years of this century.

> ⇢ **READ ON**
> Alfred S. Shivers, *Maxwell Anderson* (biography of the star 1930s Broadway playwright whose *Elizabeth the Queen* gave the Lunts one of their greatest triumphs).

LUTHER, Martin (1483–1546) German religious reformer

Books about Luther need to come to terms with his self-tormenting, dour personality and his harsh private life, but even more they should untangle the web of early Renaissance Church and state politics. The Church side of things is well covered in Roland Bainton, *Here I Stand* (rev. ed. 1978), which is also excellent on Luther's preaching and his day-to-day work as he translated the Bible. Heiko A. Oberman, *Luther* (1990), a dazzling historical biography, sets Luther in the context of Renaissance thought, comparing his cast of mind with Copernicus', for example, and is copiously illustrated. Although *John Osborne, *Luther* (1961) is a play, and fiction, it gives a believable view of Luther's personality, and of how what he did may have happened not just because of outside circumstances but from his own character: a controversial, personal companion to the other books.

> **READ ON**
> Martin Luther, *Table Talk*; *Letters*: *Sermons* (essential documents, somewhat hard to read but clear demonstrations of the dazzle of Luther's mind). T.H.L. Parker, *John Calvin*.

LUXEMBURG, Rosa (1870–1919) German revolutionary

'Red Rosa' was a leader in the uncomfortable politics of European revolution 80–100 years ago: a whirlpool of communists, socialists and anarchists. She spent the years of the First World War in prison for encouraging soldiers to desert rather than kill their fellow-proletarians. After the war she and Karl Liebknecht founded the Spartacists, dedicated to paralleling the Russian Revolution in Germany. Her uncompromising views, and the nature of her death (she and Liebknecht were murdered by state troopers sent to arrest them) have made her a kind of communist martyr-saint, an icon for left-wing revolutionaries. J.P. Nettl, *Rosa Luxemburg* (two volumes, 1966) is the authorized biography, full of detail on Luxemburg's politics (she wrote over 700 pamphlets, articles and books) and on her happy private life, unexpected in one whose political profile was so harsh and so high.

> **READ ON**
> K.W. Meyer, *Karl Liebknecht: Man Without a Country*.

M

MacARTHUR, Douglas (1880–1964) US soldier

MacArthur had a glittering service career, retiring in 1935 as US Chief-of-Staff. When the bombing of Pearl Harbor brought the USA into the Second World War he was appointed supreme Allied commander in the south-west Pacific, and supervised the defeat and surrender of Japan. In 1950 he was for a time US commander in Korea, but disagreements with President *Truman culminated in his being recalled to the USA. He is the subject of two epic, classic biographies. William Manchester, *American Caesar* (1978) is good on MacArthur's military career – the detailed comparison with *Caesar, for example, justifying Manchester's title, is alone worth the price of the book – and he writes with insight about the way MacArthur restructured Japanese constituional life after the war. But his main interest is MacArthur's tormented, complex personality, demonstrating that, as he puts it, 'for every . . . strength there was a corresponding weakness', and packing the book with anecdotes about MacArthur's notorious egotism: he was one of the few people on Earth who made *Montgomery seem a shrinking violet. D. Clayton James, *The Years of MacArthur* (three volumes, 1970–78) concentrates, by contrast, on MacArthur's public life, and is especially good on his pre-war years and the row between him and Truman. It is long but not hard to read, and makes a fine foil for Manchester. To get the measure of the subject, both writers should be read.

⋗ **READ ON**
Douglas MacArthur, *Reminiscences* (published when MacArthur was 84, but still fighting old feuds and feeding on grudges from 40, 50, 60 years before).

McCARTHY, Mary (1912–89) US writer

McCarthy put her own views and experiences into all her work: her reportage (*Vietnam*), novels (*The Groves of Academe, The*

⋗ **READ ON**
Mary McCarthy, *How I Grew* (more self-consciously factual account of the events in *Memoirs*

Group) and even her theatre criticism (*McCarthy's Theatre Chronicles*) are full of reworked autobiography. She worked once in the opposite way, producing autobiography tinged by fiction in *Memoirs of a Catholic Girlhood* (1957), an admired description of childhood and the growth of intellectual and political awareness.

MacDONALD, Betty (1908–58) US writer

At 18, MacDonald left Seattle to marry and live on a remote, upstate chicken farm. Running the farm, working at a marriage which she soon realized was a mistake, and bringing up two children with almost no conveniences are experiences she describes in her bestselling *The Egg and I* (1946). Returning to Seattle, she had to find a job during the Depression, and was supplied with many – mostly unsuitable – by her sister Mary, whose motto MacDonald used as the title of another book, *Anybody Can do Anything* (1950). During the search for jobs she contracted TB, and the time she spent in a strictly run sanatorium is the subject of *The Plague and I* (1948). In the first two books, mental and physical desperation, and in the third, death, are ever-present behind the humour. MacDonald's ability to convey this without labouring it, as well as her thumbnail sketches of people (her bossy sister, her vague, flappy mother, the martinet Charge Nurse at the sanatorium) still make the books leap to life.

MacDONALD, Finlay J. (1925–87) Scottish writer

Shortly after the First World War, a community of eight families was set up on the island of Harris in the Outer Hebrides. This new village was built on land that had been given to soldiers (such as MacDonald's father) returning from the war, and Finlay was among the first children to live there. His memoir *Crowdie and Cream* (1982) contrasts matter-of-fact accounts of the struggle to survive with more lyrical passages about the Hebridean environment and (his own) childhood innocence. He spoke only Gaelic until he was five, and his English still has a Gaelic fall and pace.

MacGREGOR, Robert ('Rob Roy') (1671–1734) Scottish bandit

Rob Roy ('Red Robert') was a 17th-18th century Scottish equivalent of a US 'wild west' cattle baron. He was a landowner and a notorious rustler who used his reputation to extort

of a Catholic Girlhood, making for fascinating comparisons).

⤳ READ ON
Betty MacDonald, *Who Me?* (anthology from all three books, arranged in autobiographical sequence); *Onions in the Stew* (about running a restaurant).

⤳ READ ON
Finlay J. MacDonald, *Crotal and White*; *The Corncrake and the Lysander* (sequels, the first about going away to school on the mainland, the second taking him into the Second World War).

⤳ READ ON
Leslie Frewin, *The Highland Rogue* (anthology of the folk legends about Rob Roy).

protection money from timid neighbours. When pursued by his enemies, the Dukes of Atholl and Montrose, or by the redcoats, he melted with his men into the hills round Loch Lomond and Loch Katrine. In English eyes, he compounded such Robin Hood-like behaviour by supporting the Jacobite cause. He died in bed at home, but his legend lived on, boosted in 1817 by Walter Scott's novel *Rob Roy*. That was quickly followed by the first 'factual' biography: Kenneth Macleay, *Rob Roy* (1818, rev. ed. 1881). M. Evans, *Rob Roy* (1972) and W.H. Murray, *Rob Roy MacGregor* (1982) give up-to-date, and far more sober, accounts, perhaps best read as restoratives after the other books' intoxicating brew.

MacKAY, Catherine Elliott (1900–60) Australian barmaid

❖ **READ ON**
*Helen Forrester, *Twopence to Cross the Mersey* (Depression life in Liverpool).

'Caddie', as she was universally known, was deserted during the Depression, and had to bring up two children alone and in dire poverty. Her autobiography *Caddie; the Autobiography of a Sydney Barmaid* (1953) is an evocation, in fresh, earthy prose, of the hardship and struggle of the time, and of Caddie's own indomitable, resilient character.

MACMILLAN, Harold (1894–1988) English Prime Minister

❖ **READ ON**
Harold Macmillan, *War Diaries: The Mediterranean 1943–1945*(much more revealing than his autobiographies).

One of the last great Tory grandees, Macmillan entered Parliament in 1924, served in *Churchill's and Eden's Cabinets, and was Prime Minister from 1957 to 1963. He wrote six volumes of memoirs: *Winds of Change* (1966), *The Blast of War* (1967), *Tides of Fortune* (1969), *Riding the Storm* (1971), *Pointing the Way* (1972) and *At the End of the Day* (1972). They are deliberately impersonal, concentrating on public events and leaving his private life to others. Alistair Horne, *Macmillan* (two volumes, 1988–9), the authorized biography, much of it written under Macmillan's own eye, takes up this challenge. It is interesting on Macmillan's character – private shyness and unhappiness contrasted with public unflappability and 'bufferishness' – and is good on Macmillan's view that Britain's 20th-century decline from Edwardian splendour was something both inevitable and desirable, and in both cases infinitely sad. Nigel Fisher, *Harold Macmillan* (1982) is less informative on his private life and character, but gives a livelier account than Horne of the public man, and of Macmillan's position in Conservative ideology.

McPHERSON, Aimée Semple (1890–1944)
Canadian preacher

Anyone who thinks that fundamentalist Christian media preachers are a late 20th-century phenomenon will find McPherson's story a revelation. She founded the Angelus Temple and the International Church of the Four Square Gospel. She preached to vast crowds, and made full use of the new medium of radio. She toured the USA, Europe and China, speaking to hundreds of thousands of people and gathering millions of dollars in donations. Her enemies said that when attention flagged and funds dwindled, she created scandals to draw 'tabloid' attention – not least, it is claimed, when she disappeared in 1926, and the outcome was a sensational kidnap trial. She wrote three volumes of autobiography: *This is That* (1923), *In the Service of the King* (1927) and the composite *The Story of My Life* (1951). The last, in particular, reads as if St Francis of Assisi had collaborated with *Phineas T. Barnum: 'colourful' is the word.

> **READ ON**
> Lately Thomas, *The Vanishing Evangelist* (about the 1926 disappearance; based on trial reports and millions of words of newspaper accounts).

MAHLER, Alma (1879–1964) Austrian hostess

Alma's father was a landscape painter. After his death, her mother married Carl Moll, a founder-member of the Viennese *Sezession* (an avant-garde movement led by Gustav Klimt). In 1901 Alma married Gustav Mahler, the leading Austrian conductor and composer of the day. He was besotted by her, and this love inspired many of his finest works. After his premature death Alma married the architect Walter Gropius (founder of the Bauhaus). At 50, she married Franz Werfel (author of *The Song of Bernadette*). She had love affairs with the musicians Zemlinsky and Gabrilovich, the dramatist Hauptmann and (into ripe old age) the painter *Kokoschka, who called her a 'wild brat'. She was a leading Viennese hostess, encouraging and supporting such people as Berg, Kandinsky, Klee and Schoenberg. She also devoted herself to Mahler's memory, encouraging the publication and performance of his music, editing his letters and jealously guarding his manuscripts and other papers. Karen Monson, *Alma Mahler: Muse to Genius* (1984) tells her story, which despite the avant-garde severities of some of its characters, comes over like the plot of a Ken Russell film.

> **READ ON**
> Alma Mahler, *Gustav Mahler: Memories and Letters* (rev. ed. in English, 1975).

MAILER, Norman (born 1921) US writer

Mailer shares *Hemingway's two-fisted view of life, an aggressively macho outlook which has earned him no favours from

> **READ ON**
> Norman Mailer, *Advertisements for Myself* (cockily titled anthology of fiction, reviews and essays, with a linking

feminists. Boxing, boozing, brawling, standing for election as mayor of New York, marching on the Pentagon to protest against the Vietnam War, knifing one of his wives, publishing ecstatic eulogies of *Marilyn Monroe, he has consistently made headlines. His novels, such as *The Naked and the Dead* and *An American Dream*, and his non-fiction, *The White Negro*, *Armies of the Night* and *The Executioner's Song*, are among the crucial books of their era, forming the character of 1960s–80s America as much as charting it. Hilary Mills, *Mailer* (1982) is a perceptive biography, unflinching in its detail of Mailer's life, good on his work, and cool (though fair) about his attitudes to the world and to himself. Peter Manso, *Mailer: His Life and Times* (1985) is a brilliant idea: a 'biography' made from interviews by Mailer's relatives, friends, colleagues, lovers, enemies and detractors – a sensational, and sensationalist, collage in which Mailer himself gets to speak, commenting, embroidering or putting the record straight.

autobiographical commentary).

MANDELA, Nelson (born 1918) South African civial rights leader and politician

A lawyer and leader of the African National Congress, Mandela has worked from his mid-20s against the apartheid policy of the white South African government. In 1961, after speaking out against the Sharpeville massacre, he was arrested, tried and imprisoned as a terrorist. He remained in prison for 28 years, until ever-increasing international pressure forced the government to free him in 1990. At once he resumed his political leadership, working to resolve the tensions between black and white and between black and black. Fatima Meer, *Higher than Hope* (second ed. 1990) tells his story. The first edition was written while he was still in prison, but the second edition was updated and revised with the help of Mandela himself: it is as much his political testimony as his biography.

> **⋄ READ ON**
> Donald Woods, *Biko* (about the life and death of Steve Biko, a black activist 'ill-treated' to death by the white South African security police).

MANSFIELD, Katherine (1888–1923) New Zealand writer

Mansfield saw herself as a typical 'new woman' of her time, abandoning convention to throw herself into Life and Art. Her literary career did indeed dazzle, but her personal life was hobbled by illness and by a series of volcanic and destructive relationships. She left her first husband, George C. Bowden, on their wedding day to run away with her childhood sweetheart. She had several affairs, with men and women, and then married John Middleton Murry. The relationships between her, Murry and Frieda and *D.H. Lawrence were crucial to all of them and read like the scenario for a particularly melodramatic

> **⋄ READ ON**
> Helen McNeish, *Passionate Pilgrimage* (letters to Murry from Mansfield in France, as she was dying, with McNeish's photographs of the places mentioned). John Middleton Murry (ed), *The Journal of Katherine Mansfield*. Margaret Scott and Vincent O'Sullivan (eds.), *The Collected Letters of Katherine Mansfield*. John Middleton Murry, *Between Two Worlds* (autobiography). For a strange, sad aftermath to

film. She delighted in playing herself as different characters to different people, even taking several names. After her death (from TB complicated by a debilitating venereal infection) Murry promoted her short stories as work of genius, a view now normally accepted.

Mansfield's complex personality, and the fact that despite her frantic lifestyle she was, as she put it, 'a secretive creature to my last bones' have made establishing biographical facts a long, slow job. Anthony Alpers, *The Life of Katherine Mansfield* (1982) untangles most of the mysteries, but its donnish style and Alpers' assumption that his readers will know Mansfield's work as thoroughly as he does may put some people off. Claire Tomalin, *Katherine Mansfield, a Secret Life* (1987) is written in far livelier English, blows away the smokescreens of those who knew Mansfield, and has a bibliography covering not only Mansfield but also Lawrence, *Virginia Woolf, *Ottoline Morrell, and many others Mansfield knew.

Mansfield's life, *see* *Colin Middleton Murry.

MAO TSE-TUNG (1893–1976) Chinese leader

A co-founder of the Chinese Communist Party, Mao led the revolutionary side during the civil war, and in 1949 became head of state in the new People's Republic of China. He retired in 1959, but remained Party chairman, and despite sanctioning the mass suppression of liberals and intellectuals during the 'cultural revolution' from 1967 onwards, was regarded as father of his country and inspirer of its people, the only figure in the Communist world whose stature rivalled Lenin's. Ross Terrill, *Mao* (1980) is a good recent biography, making full use of Mao's own words. Its 'bibliographical note' is outstandingly helpful. D. Wilson, *Mao, the People's Emperor* (1979) is good on the complex politics of 20th-century China.

◇ **READ ON**
Siao-Yu, *Mao Tse-Tung and I Were Beggars* (memoir by a scholar and painter who was Mao's childhood friend, and his intimate during the turbulent years which led up to the foundation of the Chinese Communist Party. Illustrated by the author's own scroll-poems, and with commentary by the historian Robert C. North). *See also* *Hsaio Ch'ien.

MARIE ANTOINETTE (1755–93) Austrian-born queen of France

Daughter of Maria Theresa, Empress of Austria, Marie Antoinette married the future Louis XVI of France. She was frivolous and empty-headed, and was savagely lampooned in France, her gaffes (real or imaginary) and extravagance feeding the hatred already seething towards aristocrats in general and her husband in particular. During the Revolution she behaved with a mixture of private bravery (especially to her children) and public stupidity, even at one point writing to ask her brother to send in the Austrian army. She died by the guillotine, facing her execution with considerably more dignity than she had ever shown before. John Hearsey, *Marie Antoinette* (1969) is a lively biography, good on Marie Antoinette's sudden

◇ **READ ON**
Vincent Cronin, *Louis XVI and Marie Antoinette* (good on the politics and vanities of that doomed reign). Frances Mossiker, *The Queen's Necklace* (colourful account of the scandal which triggered the Revolution).

change of character, from foolishness to determination, as the pincers of revolution began to close around her children. Manuel and Odette Kamroff, *Marie Antoinette* (1972) is brief, brisk and as vivid as a novel.

MARKHAM, Beryl (1902–86) English aviator

Markham lived in Kenya from the age of four. She grew up on her father's farm, playing and hunting with the local children and learning their languages. When she was 18 her father left for Peru, but she stayed to become the first woman in Africa licensed to breed and train racehorses. In the 1930s she took up flying. She flew mail, passengers and supplies all over Africa, acted as aerial spotter for safaris, and in 1936 made headlines by being the first person to fly the Atlantic solo from east to west. Her autobiography *West With the Night* (1942), about her life until the outbreak of the Second World War, is a classic, with magnificent evocations of Africa and of the thrills of flying, and insight into the ways of both the white settlers and the Africans who worked with them.

⊹ **READ ON**
To the African chapters: *Elspeth Huxley, *The Flame Trees of Thika*. To the flying: *Charles Lindbergh, *The Spirit of Saint Louis*.

MARLBOROUGH, Duke and Duchess of

John Churchill (1650–1722), first Duke of Marlborough and ancestor of *Winston Churchill, was the most dazzling soldier of his day. For his victory over the French at the battle of Blenheim, he was rewarded with an estate and the money to build Blenheim Palace (a huge house modelled on *Louis XIV's palace at Versailles). His wife **Sarah Churchill** (1660–1744) was Queen Anne's confidante and friend, and one of the wittiest, freshest letter-writers of her time. Winston Churchill, *Marlborough, His life and Times* (two volumes, 1933) is good on Marlborough's career, both military and political. A.L. Rowse, *The First Churchills* (1956) and Kate Fleming, *The Churchills* (1975) concentrate on John and Sarah, but also investigate other twigs and branches of the family tree. David Green, *Sarah Duchess of Marlborough* (1967) is a well-documented biography, but should be complemented by Iris Butler, *Rule of Three* (1967), about the relationship between Queen Anne, Sarah and Sarah's relative Abigail Hill, who displaced her as the Queen's favourite.

⊹ **READ ON**
Sarah, Duchess of Marlborough, *Letters* (many volumes; letters between 'Mrs Morley' (Queen Anne) and 'Mrs Freeman' (Sarah) recommended). Gilbert Burnett, *History of his Own Times* (lively autobiography which also deals with the politics of the time, from the Restoration to the Jacobite Rebellion).

MARLEY, Bob (1945–1981) Jamaican reggae singer

The huge explosion in recent years of interest in Jamaican music, and its importance as a symbol of political and religious identity, begins with Marley. He was the first Jamaican pop

⊹ **READ ON**
John Henrik Clark and Amy Jacques Garvey, *Marcus Garvey and the Vision of Africa*. Joseph Owens, *Dread: the Rastafarians of Jamaica*.

superstar, and his songs united his people throughout the world, drawing on Rastafarian religious teaching and the political ideas of *Marcus Garvey. Timothy White, *Catch a Fire* (1983), although somewhat adoring in tone, is authoritative about the music, good on the religion and politics, and above all recreates the feeling of excitement which hovered round Marley like a flame, and made some of his followers talk of him as not just a musician but as some kind of saint.

MARSHALL, Alan (1902–84) Australian writer

Marshall is known for short stories, and for the classic childhood memoir *I Can Jump Puddles* (1955). He contracted polio at the age of six, and this book describes his small-town upbringing, with parents determined not to be over-protective despite his handicap, and schoolfriends who ignored his disabilities and expected him to play a full part in their schoolyard and after-hours exploits.

> **READ ON**
> On coping with childhood disability: Rosemary Sutcliffe, *Blue Remembered Hills*. On high old times in childhood: *Laurie Lee, *Cider With Rosie*.

MARX, Eleanor (1855–98) English social reformer

Eleanor ('Tussy') was *Karl Marx's daughter, and a friend and confidante of (the much older) Engels. She learned socialism, so to speak, at her father's knee, and spent much of her adult life trying to put his ideals into practice, speaking, working and writing on behalf of the Victorian underclass. She was instrumental in the rise of British socialism, and is one of its best-loved figures. Yvonne Kapp, *Eleanor Marx* (in two volumes, *Family Life 1855–1883*, (1972); *The Crowded Years 1884–1898*), the standard biography, is a monument of political biography; it is hard to see how Eleanor's life could be more thoroughly or readably described.

> **READ ON**
> Edna Healey, *Wives of Fame* (includes a memorable picture of the Marx household when Eleanor was a child).

MARX, Groucho (Julius) (1890–1977) US comedian

Groucho was the grease-moustached, frock-coated, loping leader of the Marx Brothers, and later had a long solo career as the (outrageously rude) presenter of a TV quiz show. His writings are as pungent and witty as anything he ever said on stage or screen. They include two books of comic 'memoirs', *Groucho and Me* (1959) and *Memoirs of a Mangy Lover* (1964), and *The Groucho Letters* (1967), correspondence with everyone from Warner Brothers to *T.S. Eliot. Arthur Marx (Groucho's son), *Life With Groucho* (1956) and *Son of Groucho* (1972) are part biography, part autobiography, and are laced with tart footnotes

> **READ ON**
> Richard Anobile and Groucho Marx, *The Marx Brothers Scrapbook*. Harpo Marx, *Harpo Speaks!* (autobiography by Harpo, who in real life was a wit and a member of the Algonquin set, as well as a prankster just as anarchic as he was on film).

by Groucho himself. Charlotte Chandler, *Hello, I Must Be Going* (1978) is a sad account of Groucho's last years, as he lapsed gradually into senility – intensely depressing for anyone who loves the life-enhancing art of the man in his prime.

MARX, Jenny (1814–81) German housewife

Jenny von Westphalen married *Karl Marx when she was 29, and devoted the rest of her life to him. She went with him from city to city in Europe, harried by debt and political persecution; she bore him seven children; she kept house, maintaining peace and quiet for Karl in two-room lodgings filled with their family; she begged from her aristocratic relatives; she discussed Marx's ideas with him, made neat copies of his books and endlessly wrote letters in his support. For the sake of 'a higher ideal', and because she loved him, she put up with his philandering, his smell (he seldom washed), and, in later years, his appalling, boil-covered body. If ever there was a power behind a throne she was it: Marx relied on her determination and selflessness as if they were his own. Her story is well told in Edna Healey, *Wives of Fame* (1986), which also contains biographies of Mary Livingstone and Emma Darwin. Heinz Frederick Peters, *Red Jenny* (Eng. ed. 1986) is less elegantly written, but gives a fuller account of Jenny's political support for Karl.

⋅> **READ ON**
Jenny Marx, *Short Sketch of an Eventful Life* (memoirs to 1860, especially good about the effects on the Marxes' life of the 1848 Revolution in France).

MARX, Karl (1818–1883) German social philosopher

The author of *The Communist Manifesto* ('Workers of the world, unite!') was a fiery thinker but an inept activist, forever being moved on by the authorities until he settled at last in London to work on his huge tome *Capital*. Practical incompetence also ruled his family life: he relied on his wife *Jenny Marx to run the household, bring up the children, manage the accounts, organize his papers and fend off supporters and over-attentive political police. As a thinker, Marx needed, and got, precisely the kind of bourgeois, male-centred domesticity he rejected intellectually – not the only paradox in his complex, prickly nature.

The difficulty of Marx's thought, and the diverse ways other people have found of implementing his ideas in various 20th-century societies, make him a minefield for biographers. Isaiah Berlin, *Karl Marx: His Life and Environment* (1939) is still, after half a century, the most accessible short account. David McLellan, *Karl Marx, His Life and thought* (1973), the standard work, is donnish and needs concentration, but repays the effort as it is politically neutral and complete and contains a good bibliography. The clearest accounts of Marx the man come in

⋅> **READ ON**
Franz Mehring, *Karl Marx, the Story of his Life* (by a friend and amanuensis: one of the first biographies, weak on domestic matters but good, if partisan, on Marx's ideas). G. Mayer, *Friedrich Engels*. G.D.H. Cole, *What Marx Really Meant*.

books about other members of his family, notably the section on Jenny in Edna Healey, *Wives of Fame* (1986) and the first volume of Yvonne Kapp, *Eleanor Marx* (1972). Terrell Carver, *Marx and Engels* (1983) is a study of the main intellectual relationship in Marx's life, again, not an easy read but thorough and sensible.

MARY I (1516–58) English queen (ruled 1553–8)

Mary refused to follow her father *Henry VIII in renouncing Roman Catholicism, and was initially denied the succession until the death of her younger half-brother Edward VI. As Queen she presided over anti-Protestant persecution (which earned her the nickname 'Bloody Mary') and the loss of Calais, England's last possession in continental Europe. Her private life was dominated equally by religious fervour and by aching, unfulfilled longing for a child. In outline, her life could hardly be more grim. It is a pleasure, therefore, to say that the standard biography, Carolly Erickson, *Bloody Mary* (1978), is written with such pace and warmth that it matches any novel. It is historically impeccable, but research never gets in the way: we are given an unforgettable picture of Mary forlornly struggling to find inner tranquillity amid the noisy pageant of Tudor court life, and trying to cope with other people's devious, unscrupulous political manoeuvrings. At 500 close-printed pages, it may seem a hefty read. In practice, few biographies can match it.

❖ READ ON
Hester Chapman, *Lady Jane Grey* (tragic story of Edward VI's Protestant heir, dispossessed by Mary).

MARY STUART, 'Queen of Scots' (1542–87) Queen of Scotland

For four centuries Mary's life has been treated, rightly or wrongly, as if it were the plot of a romantic novel: poor wee lass, queen at one week old, shipped to France to escape Protestant knives, back at 16, marries, bears son, implicated in murder of husband, imprisoned for 20 years by *Elizabeth I, condemned to death, executed after comforting tearful staff and echoing Christ's last words as she commends her soul to God. This legend persists whatever research throws up in the way of political naivety, lovers, Papist plots (or Protestant ones), or a streak in Mary of that conviction in one's own God-given invulnerability which later marked her grandson *Charles I. Antonia Fraser, *Mary Queen of Scots* (1969; illustrated ed. 1978) tells the story in gushy, romantic prose, with stormy skies mirroring the characters' emotions and adjectives like 'tragic' and 'bewildered' to guide our reactions on every page. Propaganda rather than biography (why, when the issues are so dead?), it is nevertheless a one-sitting read. Jenny Wormald, *Mary Queen of Scots: a Study in Failure* (1988) is more balanced and objective,

❖ READ ON
Arthur Salusbury MacNalty, *Mary Queen of Scots: the Daughter of Debate*. M.H. Armstrong-Davidson, *The Casket Letters*. Humphrey Drummond, *The Queen's Man*. Margaret Irwin, *The Gay Galliard* (novel). *See also* *Bothwell.

and paradoxically, by stripping away romanticism, presents someone who is both more recognizably human and far more sympathetic.

'MATA HARI' (1871–1917) Dutch/French dancer and spy

'Mata Hari' ('eye of dawn') was the stage name of Margarete Zelle. As a teenager she left her middle-class Dutch family to become an exotic dancer in France, in music-halls, cabarets and private parties (eventually before the crowned heads of Europe). Her love affairs (real or imaginary) were the talk of France. During the First World War, while dancing in Paris, she spent much time with German officers, and was eventually arrested and shot as a spy. Later, the authorities claimed that she was actually a double agent, thus adding to the air of exotic mystery which has surrounded her ever since. Erica Ostrovsky, *Mata Hari* (1985) is a well-documented, well-illustrated biography; the goings-on it describes make most subsequent spy-fiction seem tame.

⋄ **READ ON**
H. Holdredge, *Lola Montez* (about the 1840s dancer and courtesan who bewitched, among others, the eccentric King Ludwig I of Bavaria).

MAUGHAM, W(illiam) Somerset (1874–1965) English writer

One of the most popular playwrights and novelists of the 1920s–50s, Maugham was also famous as a waspish recluse (who nonetheless loved visitors), a 'three-quarters homosexual' whose marriage and companionships were notoriously stormy, a savager of other glitterati such as *D.H. Lawrence and *T.S. Eliot, and (not least) as a mysterious agent for British Intelligence after the Russian Revolution. In his eighties be became the very emblem of the malicious 'Grand Old Party' of English letters, and this reputation still blinds some people to his actual work (for example the fine autobiographical novel *Of Human Bondage*). His actual autobiography, *The Summing Up* (1938), written at the height of his success, tells all about his public life but practically nothing about private matters. Frederic Raphael, *Somerset Maugham* (rev. ed. 1989) is a brief, stylish biography, good on the the complexities of Maugham's character. The standard biographies are Ted Morgan, *Maugham* (1980), which takes a sharp view of Maugham's behaviour, and Robert Calder, *Willie* (1989) – 'the case for the defence' – which draws on conversations with Alan Searle (Maugham's companion in later life), and is consequently good on the last years, as well as on Maugham's secret service work and his many (hitherto unknown) acts of private generosity and kindness.

⋄ **READ ON**
Robin Maugham, *Conversations With Willie* (witty, admiring glimpses of Maugham during his last 20 years, by his nephew, the novelist and travel writer).

MAXWELL, Gavin (1914–69) Scottish writer

Maxwell is best remembered for *Ring of Bright Water*, a double story of his life in a remote Highland bay and his absorbed relationship with a pair of otters, and for travel books such as *A Reed Shaken by the Wind*, about a year spent with the Marsh Arabs of Iraq. His memoir *The House of Elrig* (1965) describes his childhood on a 'huntin', shootin' and fishin'' Highland estate (where he was more interested in watching wildlife than killing it), his lonely prep-school days and his happy time at public school, interrupted by illness. He writes in a style of total recall, recording conversations and emotions as if they had happened just yesterday. His evocation of prep-school life and of the unfocused panic of adolescence leads what, in British autobiography, is a crowded field.

❖ **READ ON**
Richard Frere, *Maxwell's Ghost: an Epilogue to Gavin Maxwell's Camusfearna* (follow-up to *Ring of Bright Water*). Anthony Powell, *Infants of the Spring* (first book in Powell's four-volume autobiography, about prep-school and Eton). W.H. Hudson, *Far Away and Long Ago* (account of naturalist's boyhood in South America: despite the very different location, parallels Maxwell's sensitivity to the natural world and to the feelings of childhood).

MEAD, Margaret (1901–78) US anthropologist

Convinced that primitive cultures should be researched and recorded before they disappeared, Mead went to work in the South Seas, and published *Coming of Age in Samoa* (1928), describing an Eden-like existence in which adolescent sex and free love were entirely without guilt. The book made her world-famous (as it also did, not surprisingly, anthropology and Samoa), and she went on, while continuing an honour-laden academic career, to become a guru on sex, race, culture, child-rearing and education. Some of her critics even blamed her personally for 1960s sexual permissiveness and the challenge to 'traditional values' which (they say) has so undermined western civilization. Jane Howard, *Margaret Mead: a Life* (1984) is a superb book, based on interviews with some 300 people who knew Mead, on reading what seems like every word written by or about her, and on journeys to all the societies she described. A triumph of US biography, it eclipses all earlier accounts, not least for its objectivity towards Mead and its readable, lively style.

❖ **READ ON**
Margaret Mead, *Blackberry Winter: My Earlier Years* (childhood memoirs). Derek Freeman, *Margaret Mead and Samoa: the Making and Unmaking of an Anthropological Myth* (1983 debunking of Mead, claiming that the Samoans realized early on what sort of sensational material she was after, and told her exactly what she hoped to hear).

MEDICI family

Medici power rested on a banking fortune built up by **Giovanni de' Medici** (1360–1429) and his son **Cosimo de' Medici** (1389–1464). Under Cosimo, the family also built up political influence, in Florence and beyond, to dwarf those of many monarchs elsewhere. Its authority continued for 200 years, most gloriously under **Lorenzo de' Medici** (1449–92), nicknamed 'The Magnificent', and **Cosimo II** (1519–74), Grand Duke of Tuscany. The Medici sponsored scientists and writers, and employed many of the artists and architects who

❖ **READ ON**
Judith Hook, *Lorenzo de' Medici*. E. Ewart, *Cosimo de' Medici*. Jean Héritier, *Catherine de' Medici*. Iris Origo, *The Merchant of Prato*. J. Lucas-Dubreton, *Daily Life in Florence in the Time of the Medici*. *Benvenuto Cellini, Autobiography*.

built the Florence we know today. They were bankers to the
Catholic Church, and the family provided two Popes and two
queens of France. Their enterprise, energy, despotism and patronage were emblems of their age: more than almost any other
dynasty, the Medici were like the Renaissance itself made flesh.
Marcel Brion, *The Medici* (1969) is a family biography, concentrating on magnificence. Christopher Hibbert, *The Rise and Fall
of the House of Medici* (1974) goes into murkier areas, showing
that the Medici, like any other powerful dynasty, had cupboards
stuffed with skeletons.

‣ MEDIEVAL LIVES

Richard Barber (ed.), *The Pastons: A Family in the Time of
the Wars of the Roses*
F. Barlow, *Thomas Becket*
George Faludy, **Erasmus of Rotterdam*
Peter Munz, *Frederick Barbarossa: a Study in Medieval
Politics*
P.H. Newby, **Saladin in His Time*
Guy Paget, *The Rose of Raby: a Life of Cecily Nevile*
Helen Waddell, **Peter Abelard*
Marina Warner, **Joan of Arc*

MEHTA, Ved (born 1934) Indian/US writer

Born in India, Mehta moved to the US when he was 15, and
eventually became a staff writer on the *New Yorker*. He has
been blind since the age of four, and the way he copes with this
is a recurring theme in his half-dozen volumes of autobiography, his major work. The first two books, *Daddyji* (1972) and
Mamaji (1979) are about his parents. The second two, *Vedi*
(1982) and *The Ledge Between the Streams* (1984), describe his
childhood in India. *Sound-Shadows of the New World* (1986) is
about his years in a US college for the blind, and is good not
only on adolescence but on the clash of cultures and religions.
Stolen Light (1989) takes him to university: Pomona College,
Oxford and Harvard. Multi-volume autobiographies, in which a
single afternoon's events can inspire whole chapters, can be tedious. Mehta is anything but: he writes with a winning combination of modesty, candour and *New Yorker* sharpness, and his
circumstances give him an objective but inside view of both
eastern and western cultures, a major pleasure in his work.

‣ **READ ON**
*R.K. Narayan, My Days
(parallels Mehta's books on his
childhood in India).

MEIR, Golda (1898–1979) Israeli politician

Born in the Ukraine, educated in the USA, Meir settled in Palestine in 1921. She worked as a teacher, but soon became absorbed in politics, both local (workers' welfare) and Zionist. After the state of Israel was established in 1948 she was Minister of Labour, Foreign Minister and finally Prime Minister, one of the first women to hold such an office anywhere in the world. Her autobiography, *My Life*, was published in 1975, and a somewhat idolizing biography, Peggy Mann, *Golda: the Life of Israel's Prime Minister*, appeared in 1972. Ralph G. Martin, *Golda Meir: the Romantic Years* (1988) comes as a delightful surprise after all this official stiffness. It is Meir's story from 1898 to the Siege of Jerusalem in 1948: a romantic saga of friendships, love affairs, political machinations, feminism, and the unfaltering belief in the working class movement and the justice of Israel's cause which motivated Meir not just in these 'romantic years' but throughout her life: a mini-series of a book.

⊹ **READ ON**
Robert Slater, *Golda: the Uncrowned Queen of Israel* (good text, especially on the politics; superb photos).

MELBA, Nellie (1861–1931) Australian singer

When opera-lovers talked of 'canary-fancying' 100 years ago, Melba's was the kind of voice they meant: sweet, pure, soaring above the orchestra but still able to wring the heart in the most dramatic, tear-stained roles in the repertoire. She was an international celebrity, living it up on three continents: two particular weaknesses were for peaches with raspberry sauce and for famous violinists as lovers. Joseph Wechsberg, *Red Plush and Black Velvet* (1961) is a starry-eyed biography, which begins 'The prima donna is still with us – and long may she live! Without that fascinating creature a night at the opera would be as dull as a bottle of flat champagne', and goes even further over the top with every word that follows. Thank goodness, one feels, for Melba's common sense, in the midst of all those popping corks. 'I was fond of Paderewski,' she said once. 'I'd have married him, but alas, he never asked.'

⊹ **READ ON**
Nellie Melba, *Melodies and Memories* (splendidly showbizzy autobiography). *Rita Hunter, *Don't Let Poor Nellie Starve* (autobiography of a modern prima donna).

MELBOURNE, William, Lord (1779–1848) English politician

Melbourne was an able and humane politician, chiefly remembered for the way he guided young Queen *Victoria in statecraft. Two scandals marked his private life: the love affair between Lady Caroline Lamb (his wife) and *Byron, and he himself being cited as co-respondent in a divorce case at the age of 57. His story thus opens a fascinating window on both public and private lives of Britain's 'great and good' in the first

⊹ **READ ON**
Philip Ziegler, *Melbourne* (brisker than Cecil, but just as good on the statecraft). A. Cecil, *Queen Victoria and her Prime Ministers*.

half of the 19th century: he was, in all respects, a figure of his time. The standard biography is David Cecil, *Melbourne* in two volumes: *The Young Melbourne* (1939) and *Lord M* (1954), the latter outstanding on Melbourne's relationship with Victoria. Good on the scandals are Henry Blyth, *Caro – the Fatal Passion* (1973) and Alice Acland, *Caroline Norton* (1948).

MENDELSSOHN(–BARTHOLDY), Felix (1809–47) German composer

Mendelssohn was a child prodigy: he could have made careers as linguist, painter, writer, scientist or musician – he chose music. He composed, played the piano and became an eminent conductor. He was beloved as son, brother, husband, father and friend (notably of Queen *Victoria and Prince Albert). He wrote some of the best-loved classical works of his time – *A Midsummer Night's Dream* music (including the famous *Wedding March*), the *Hebrides* overture, *Elijah* – works noted for the same kind of untroubled sunniness as marked his life. Herbert Kupferberg, *Felix Mendelssohn, His Life, His Family, His Music* (1972) describes exactly what the title promises. George R. Marek, *Gentle Genius* (1972) is good on the work.

> ✧ **READ ON**
> Rudolf Elvers (ed.) *Felix Mendelssohn, a Life in Letters* (delightful: Mendelssohn's flair for the happy phrase was as marked in words as in music). Wilfred Blunt, *On Wings of Song.* David Jenkins and Mark Visocchi, *Mendelssohn in Scotland.*

MERRICK, Joseph Carey (1862–90) English 'Elephant Man'

Merrick suffered from neurofibromatosis, a wasting disease which deforms the bones, and which twisted his skull grotesquely out of shape. For years, in unfeeling Victorian England, he was exhibited at fairs and freak shows as 'Half a Man and Half an Elephant', enduring agonies of soul which no one suspected. Then Frederick Treves, a surgeon interested in deformity, rescued him, treated him kindly and befriended him. Michael Howell and Peter Ford, *The True History of the Elephant Man* (1980) tell the story with sympathy and without sensation. Their illustrations include photos of the people concerned, playbills, engravings and other memorabilia of the 'entertainment' subculture of the time. It also contains Merrick's own autobiography, a dignified, tragic document two pages long, and Treves' account, from *The Elephant Man and Other Reminiscences* (1923).

> ✧ **READ ON**
> Ashley Montagu, *The Elephant Man: A Study in Human Dignity.* Frederick Treves, *The Tale of a Field Hospital* (about his experiences as an army doctor in the Boer War).

MICHELANGELO (Buonarroti) (1475–1564) Italian artist

Michelangelo worked in Florence and Rome, and his patrons included the *Medici and *Borgia families. His ambition was to

> ✧ **READ ON**
> Irving Stone, *The Agony and the Ecstasy* (magnificently detailed novel, centring on Michelangelo's obsessive self-questioning, and evocative on the

recreate ancient Greek styles and forms, using Biblical subjects, and his works include the Sistine Chapel ceiling, the Medici Chapel, numerous individual statues including those of Moses and David, and the final design for the dome of St Peter's in Rome. He was a mystic and a self-hater (particularly in old age, when he was racked by the thought that his homosexuality might have earned him Hell). He wrote poetry and letters full of domestic detail which leaps across the centuries. Irving Stone and Jean Stone (eds.), *I, Michelangelo, Sculptor* (1962) is an excellent selection of these, arranged in autobiographical sequence. Georg Brandes, *Michelangelo: His Life, His Times, His Era* (1921; Eng. ed. 1963) is one of this century's most admired biographies, good on Michelangelo's life and superb on his work, both artistic and literary. Ascanio Condivi, *Michelangelo* (Eng. ed. 1976) is a good modern biography.

physical effort required to do his work).

MILLER, Henry (1891–1980) US writer

Miller spent his early life bumming round Europe, living a self-consciously anarchic life free from all moral or philosophical restraint, trying everything. He wrote a series of books about it, part autobiography part fiction, packed with anecdotes and heady with his views on religion, politics, personal freedom and above all sex (about which he was one of this century's major boasters). His books – they include *Tropic of Cancer* (1934), *Tropic of Capricorn* (1939) and the 'Rosy Crucifixion' trilogy *Sexus*, *Plexus* and *Nexus* (1949–60) – were banned for years, though they became essential reading for the 1960s Beat generation, and were savaged by 1970s feminists for their relentlessly macho view of the human race and its relationships.

❖ **READ ON**
Miller's letters: **Lawrence Durrell and Henry Miller, a Private Correspondence*; *Letters to Anaïs Nin*; *Letters of Henry Miller and Wallace Fowlie*. Henry Miller, *My Life and Times* (unorthodox, back-to-front autobiography, illustrated with photos and many of Miller's own colourful, surreal paintings). Kate Millett, *Sexual Politics* (in which Miller's gender limitations are mercilessly exposed).

MILLIGAN, Spike (Terence) (born 1918) Irish humorist

In the 1950s Milligan wrote and performed in *The Goon Show*, a radio series which set standards of surrealist humour in Britain for a generation. He went on to write a score of books, including *Adolf Hitler: My Part in his Downfall* (1971), *Rommel? Gunner Who?* (1973), *Monty: His Part in My Victory* (1976) and *Mussolini: His Part in My Downfall* (1978). These are war memoirs, treating Milligan's army career as black farce, *The Goon Show* in uniform but with every bad pun and music-hall routine intact.

❖ **READ ON**
**Roald Dahl, *Going Solo*.

MILTON, John (1608–74) English poet

Most books about Milton tend to deal with his writing at the expense of his life and personality. Was he the greatest English

❖ **READ ON**
**Robert Graves, *Wife to Mr Milton* (historical novel, the 'autobiography' of Milton's

poet after *Shakespeare, or someone who wrote English (in
*T.S. Eliot's phrase) 'as if it were a dead language'? What is
the value of his political, religious and legal pamphlets? A.N.
Wilson, *The Life of John Milton* (1983) touches on these matters, but is chiefly about Milton the man: his dazzling student
years, his friendships, marriages and methods of work, the ways
he coped with fame and with blindness. John Arthos, *Milton
and the Italian Cities* (1968) describes (slightly donnishly) one of
the most formative events in Milton's life, his trip to Italy in
1638–9. Christopher Hill, *Milton and the English Revolution*
(1977) is a historical study of Milton as politician.

first wife).

⋄ MISTRESSES

F. Fraser, *Beloved Emma: the Life of Emma, Lady Hamilton*
Nerin E. Gun, *Eva Braun, *Hitler's Mistress*
Lucy Hughes-Hallett, *Cleopatra*
Roy MacGregor-Hastie, *Nell Gwyn*
*Nancy Mitford, *Madame de Pompadour*
Marquise de Montespan, *Memoirs*
M.B. Neumann, *Mistress to Kafka* (Milina Jesenka)

MITCHELL, Margaret (1900–49) US writer

Mitchell spent ten years researching and writing *Gone With the
Wind*, and another 13 years trying to prevent its huge fame, as
book and film, from destroying her privacy, eating her life. After she died, in a car crash, her family burnt all her private
papers in their possession, and refused to give interviews. This
fanned rather than dampened fascination in the Mitchell legend, a fascination now served by Anne Edwards, *The Road to
Tara* (1983), the definitive biography. Edwards is herself a novelist, and indulges at times in somewhat breathless speculation
about Mitchell's feelings and emotions. But her book recreates
the stuffy provincial world of Atlanta, Georgia, in Mitchell's
lifetime, documents her work on the novel and is especially
good on what happened after it was published and before, during and after the making of the film.

⋄ **READ ON**
Richard Harwell (ed.), *Margaret
Mitchell's Gone With the Wind
Letters, 1936–1949* (from
archives not destroyed by
Mitchell's family). Roland
Flamini, *Scarlett, Rhett and a Cast
of Thousands* (about the making
of the film).

MITCHISON, Naomi (born 1897) Scottish writer

Mitchison was born Haldane, a member of one of Britain's
leading left-wing intellectual families. She has written over 80
books, ranging from historical novels to poetry, from African
history to autobiography. *Small Talk* (1973) is a child's-eye view
of life in Edwardian Edinburgh, Oxford and the Highlands. *All

⋄ **READ ON**
Naomi Mitchison, *Among You
Taking Notes . . .* (selections from
Second World War diaries). Jill
Benton, *Naomi Mitchison: a
Century of Experience in Life and
Letters*.

Change Here (1975) is the story of her adolescence, her blissful years at Oxford, her friendships and love affairs, her marriage, and her experiences in the First World War. It and *Small Talk* are available in one volume entitled *As It Was. You May Well Ask* (1979) tells of her busy 1930s life: writing, travelling, lecturing, entertaining the legal, literary and socialist intelligentsia of the day. The book is tinged throughout with forebodings about Fascism and the coming war, and ends as the stormcloud breaks. *Mucking Around* (1984), about Mitchison's travels, is especially fascinating about her close relationship with a remote pastoralist community in Africa.

MITFORD family

The best-known Mitfords were daughters of Lord and Lady Redesdale: **Nancy Mitford** (1904–73), **Diana Mitford** (born 1910), **Unity Mitford** (1914–48) and **Jessica Mitford** (born 1917). Nancy Mitford wrote semi-autobiographical comic novels, and Selena Hastings, *Nancy Mitford* (1985) traces a number of real people who became characters in *Love in a Cold Climate*, *The Pursuit of Love* and *Don't Tell Alfred*. Hastings' book glitters with Nancy's wit (funny and hurtful), and with the dazzling and talented people she knew, but the ever-present shadows of Nancy's snobbery and loneliness also make it a sombre read. Jessica Mitford, *Hons and Rebels* (1906) is a merry, factual account of family life (many events are the same as in Nancy's *Love in a Cold Climate*), until Jessica elopes with Esmond Romilly. *A Fine Old Conflict* (1977) tells of her later life: she married an American after Romilly's death, was a member of the US Communist Party, a leading journalist and a scourge of undertakers. David Pryce-Jones, *Unity Mitford, a Quest* (1976) tells the sad story of Unity, who was dazzled by *Hitler, went to live in Germany, and crippled herself by a shot in the spine when the Second World War began. Diana Mitford (Lady Mosley, *see* *Oswald Mosley), *A Life of Contrasts* (1977) is a defiant autobiography.

⊹ READ ON
Jonathan and Catherine Guinness, *The House of Mitford* (story of the whole family, starting with the sisters' grandparents. Jonathan, Diana Mosley's son by a previous marriage, had access to all the family papers. He is also a politician, and some readers may be irritated by the undeclared bias of almost every phrase he writes).

MONROE, Marilyn (1926–62) US film star

30 years after Monroe's death, the presses still churn out books; not about her luminous, beautifully crafted performances, but full of sleazy details and speculation about her private life. Did she sleep with every *Kennedy in sight? Did she commit suicide or was she murdered? Was she goddess, bitch, nymphomaniac, lesbian or waif, a high-class whore or a butterfly broken on the wheels of the studio system and press intrusion? David Robinson and John Kobal, *Marilyn Monroe: a Life on Film* (1974) is excellent on her actual work,

⊹ READ ON
James Spada with George Zeno, *Monroe: her Life in Pictures* (marvellous photographs). Marilyn Monroe, *My Story* ('as told to' autobiography). W.J. Weatherby, *Conversations With Marilyn Monroe*. Ted Jordan, *Norma Jean: a Hollywood Love Story* (Jordan claims that his wife, strip-queen Lili St Cyr, taught Monroe all she knew,

and almost unique in concentrating on that side of her. Fred Lawrence Guiles, *Legend: the Life and Death of Marilyn Monroe* (1985) and Anthony Summers, *Goddess: the Secret Lives of Marilyn Monroe* (1985) are well-documented, reasonably (though not entirely) untabloid biographies, offering answers to many of the questions asked above. Summers' bibliography trawls a score of reasonable books from the sea of trash. *Norman Mailer, *The Life of Marilyn Monroe* (1973) is as much a hymn to Mailer's own fantasies about Monroe as an account of Monroe's life: a hypnotic oddity.

that he, Jordan, was Monroe's most intimate friend and lover, that Peter Lawford . . . and so on and so on. 'Sensational' is how the publishers describe this book, and they are right).

MONTAGU, Mary Wortley (1689–1762)
English writer

Montagu was rich, well-educated and witty. Until she was 50 she was happy to follow the conventions of the time, acting as hostess for her husband first in Turkey (where he was a diplomat) and then in London. But she wrote beady-eyed, no-quarter accounts of everything she saw (chiefly in letters to her daughter), and was the centre of a circle of poets, painters and wits-about-town. She published (anonymously) pamphlets on politics and feminism, and conducted a running feud with Alexander Pope, who began by adoring her and ended by savaging her in print. In 1739 she left her husband and spent the rest of her life in Europe, chiefly in Italy, still writing letters about the places she visited and the manners and absurdities of the people she met. Robert Halsband, *The Life of Lady Mary Wortley Montagu* (1956), the standard biography, deals especially well with her years in Turkey and in Europe, and uses letter-extracts to show both the charm and the ice in her character.

⋗ **READ ON**
Robert Halsband, *Complete Letters of Lady Mary Wortley Montagu*. Madame de Sévigné, *Letters* (equally witty and lively, about court life at Versailles under *Louis XIV).

MONTGOMERY, Bernard (1887–1976) English soldier

Montgomery's position, as one of the most successful generals of the Second World War, was due partly to his strategic thinking and partly to his relationship with his men. He radiated certainty: in himself, his soldiers, their country and its cause. He seldom found need to praise, or indeed to show much human warmth of any kind, but his absolute straightness, the feeling that he was on their side and that was all that need be said, made him beloved by those who served under him, if not by his superiors.

After the war, in retirement, while his men returned to real life, to loving friends and families, Montgomery found himself famous but without a role. Self-certainty gradually turned to bluster, bluster to arrogance, arrogance to vanity, vanity to ego-

⋗ **READ ON**
Brian Montgomery (Montgomery's brother), *Monty: a Life in Photographs*. Ronald Lewin, *Monty as a Military Commander* (concentrates on the battles and the conflicting claims of various generals, but does not neglect Montgomery the man). D. Montgomery, *Monty's Grandfather, G.C.S.I. K.C.B. L.L.D. – a Life's Service for the Raj* (biography of Montgomery's grandfather Robert Montgomery).

ism and egoism, by the end, to megalomania. This is the judgement, and 'vanity', 'egoism' and 'megalomania' are the words of his principal biographer Nigel Hamilton, whose three-volume study (*Monty: the Making of a General*, 1981; *Monty: Master of the Battlefield*, 1983; *Monty: The Field-Marshal*, 1986) is unstuffy, scrupulously fair, excellent on every aspect of Monty's military career and merciless (or desperately sad, depending on your point of view) about his declining years. Nigel Hamilton, *Monty: the Man Behind the Legend* (1987) is a well-illustrated single volume, including contributions from many people who knew Montgomery personally.

MONTGOMERY, L(ucy) M(aud) (1874–1942) Canadian writer

Montgomery wrote the 'Anne of Green Gables' novels – autobiographical, people say, in outlook if not in actual events. She was secretive about her own real life – her journalism, her 13 years spent caring for a widowed grandmother, her self-effacing marriage – and her only book of memoirs, *The Road to Yesterday* (1974), was not published until 30 years after her death. Mollie Gillen, *The Wheel of Things* (1975) fills in the gaps, and is the fruit both of many years' research and of magnificent chance: the discovery of a trunkful of previously unknown letters. The Montgomery story, and the Montgomery character, as Gillen writes about them, are just as fascinating as anything to do with Anne.

⋄ READ ON
Wilfrid Eggleston (ed.), *The Green Gables Letters*. Gene Stratton Porter, *The Life and Letters of Gene Stratton Porter*.

MOORE, Henry (1898–1986) English artist

Moore's sculptures ('people with holes in them') are some of the most admired artworks made this century. He was a quiet man, who kept out of the limelight but nevertheless knew everyone: a central figure in British art. William Packer, *Henry Moore* (1985) is a superb illustrated biography, full of quotations from letters, reviews, essays and other documents, and with pictures not only of Moore's work but of his family life, friends, studios and the places he knew.

⋄ READ ON
Henry Moore and John Hedgecoe, *Henry Moore*. Philip James (ed.), *Henry Moore on Sculpture*. Roger Berthoud, *The Life of Henry Moore*.

MOOREHEAD, Alan (born 1910) English writer

Moorehead is known for books about *Darwin, Burke and Wills, 19th-century African explorers and the desert campaigns of the Second World War. His memoir *A Late Education: Episodes in a Life* (1970) is set during his time as a war correspondent in Cairo in 1940. War is the backcloth; Moorehead's book is about the beginning, growth and tragic end of his

⋄ READ ON
*Richard Cobb, *A Classical Education* (different circumstances, and different kinds of friendship, but similar mood and style).

friendship with another young journalist, Alex Clifford. Intimate accounts of friendships (as opposed to sexual relationships) are rare, and those of male friendships rarer still. Anyone who has ever been formed a close and valued friendship in adult life will recognize the truth in what Moorehead writes, and every reader will warm to his unaffected, pared-down descriptions of what knowing Alex Clifford meant to him.

MORANT, Henry H. (1865–1902) Australian rider, writer and soldier

'Breaker' Morant was a cattle-drover who published rousing saloon-bar ballads about his work. In the Boer War he enlisted in the South Australian Mounted Rifles, and in 1902 he was executed by the British for shooting some prisoners. The Australian government cried 'foul', saying that Morant had only been obeying orders, and was being made the scapegoat for his superiors, and the British authorities, unused to being corrected by 'colonials', refused to listen and hushed up the case for decades. F.M. Cutlack, *Breaker Morant: a Horseman Who Made History* (1962) smashes it wide open, showing the spotty underbelly of British Imperial smugness, includes an account of Morant's life in the bush, and quotes some of his best verse.

⋗ **READ ON**
George Witton, *Scapegoats of the Empire* (memoirs of one of Morant's co-defendants: life in the 'bushveldt Carabineers', the incident with the prisoners, the trial, Witton's subsequent years as a 'lifer', picking oakum and breaking rocks in Parkhurst Gaol).

MORE, Thomas (1478–1535) English lawyer

More entered Parliament in 1504, and, after his succession, rapidly won favour with *Henry VIII. He was made Lord Chancellor (chief law officer) in 1529, and three years later Henry ordered him to arrange the dissolution of the King's marriage with Catherine of Aragon. More refused and resigned, and when Henry passed the Act of Supremacy, declaring himself head of the Church in England instead of the Pope, More's opposition earned him arrest and execution. He was canonized in 1935, and most early biographers (not to mention Robert Bolt's play *A Man for All Seasons*) make him seem a modest, otherworldly figure, not in accordance with the facts. Richard Marius, *Thomas More* (1984) deals well with his religious beliefs and with the politics of his quarrel with Henry, but also takes pains to show More as a human being: intellectually trapped between medieval and modern attitudes, and emotionally torn between loyalty to country, family, Church and King.

⋗ **READ ON**
Elizabeth F. Rogers (ed.), *Selected Letters of Sir Thomas More*. Bede Foorde (ed.) *Conscience Decides: Letters from Prison*. Jasper Ridley, *The Statesman and the Fanatic* (double biography: More and Wolsey). Ernest Reynolds, *Margaret Roper: Eldest Daughter of Sir Thomas More*.

MORGAN, Henry (c1635–88) Welsh pirate

All the legends about pirates – pieces of eight, 'yo ho ho and a

⋗ **READ ON**
John Ure, *The Quest for Captain Morgan* (entertaining mixture of biography and travel book: Ure

bottle of rum', cutlasses clenched in pearly teeth, everything but parrots on the shoulder and wooden legs – begin with Morgan. He treated the Spanish empire in the Caribbean and Central America as his private piggy-bank, looting ships, sacking cities, pillaging and terrorizing as the fancy took him. In 1674 Charles II appointed him Deputy Governor of Jamaica, either the reward for many years of loyal, if covert, service to the British or a shrewd attempt to turn a poacher into a gamekeeper. It was highly successful, as Morgan turned out to be just as good a local politician as he had once been buccaneer. Dudley Pope, *Harry Morgan's Way* (1977) splendidly mixes history and swashbuckle, redoubling Morgan's legend even as it debunks it.

set out to trace Morgan's footsteps, and found the Caribbean 'as full of rascals' as ever in Morgan's day).

MORGAN, John Pierpoint (1837–1913) US financier

Anyone who throws away the financial sections of newspapers as soon as they arrive can relax. There is not boredom here, but fascination. Morgan saw himself as the financial equivalent of Captain *Morgan the pirate, and didn't care who cared. He made fortunes from arms sales and gold speculation during the American Civil War, doubled them in the heyday of mergers between railway and shipping companies, and became so rich that he was able, single-handed, to cause or prevent the collapse of the US economy. He was a legendary art-collector, and owned a yacht nicknamed 'the floating palace'. Andrew Sinclair, *Corsair* (1981) tells his life as it was: that is, the origin of every soap opera and mini-series about the seriously rich, set in a 'never never land' (in every sense, except that in this case it was not fantasy but real).

·> READ ON
George Wheeler, *Pierpoint Morgan and Friends: the Anatomy of a Myth*. Edwin P. Hoyt, *The House of Morgan*. Ferdinand Lundberg, *The Rich and Superrich*.

MORRELL, Ottoline (1873–1943) English hostess

Ottoline Cavendish-Bentinck was expected to marry well, manage shooting parties and vote Conservative (her family had been active for *Disraeli). She did none of these things, marrying Philip Morrell, who became a Liberal MP, and running weekend parties at her house, Garsington Manor, where young high fliers in politics (especially Liberal), literature and art were helped on their way by the established and famous. Unlike other society hostesses, who were content to bask in the glow of their guest lists, she wanted active involvement with the people she knew. Sometimes this was sexual – her best-known lovers were Augustus John and *Bertrand Russell – but usually she confined herself to sponsoring their careers. The *Bloomsbury Group regularly stayed at Garsington, and wrote Morrell gushy

·> READ ON
Ottoline Morrell, *Memoirs* (glittering, but – so says Darroch – more wishful thinking than actual fact). Michael Holroyd, *Lytton Strachey* (good on the Bloomsbury Group and Garsington). Juliette *Huxley, *Leaves of the Tulip Tree* (autobiography of the Swiss governess of Morrell's daughter at Garsington, who later married Julian Huxley).

thank-you letters. When she discovered that they also wrote bitchily about her to one another, relations cooled, though *Lytton Strachey and *Virginia Woolf stayed friends. Morrell was also hurt to be pilloried in Aldous *Huxley's satires *Crome Yellow* and *Barren Leaves*, not to mention making a (disguised) appearance in *D.H. Lawrence's *Women in Love*. Sandra Jobson Darroch, *Ottoline* (1976) is good on all these feuds, and is a romp of a book, especially if you already know something of the milieu.

MORRIS, Jan (born 1926) Welsh writer

Morris was born 'into the wrong body', as she puts it: a boy who should really have been a girl. She lived for 40 years as James Morris, and was a successful writer (on travel and history) and journalist. Finally, when her children were old enough to cope with the situation, she took a course of hormones and underwent a series of operations, achieving her real identity at last. Her book *Conundrum* (1974) describes her thoughts and feelings with a simple directness which should speak to women and men equally. The last chapters in particular, about her slipping into femininity after the operations, have the radiance of an exile returning home at last.

> **READ ON**
> Jan Morris, *Pleasures of a Tangled Life* (essays on such subjects as Torcello, The Best Meal in the World and The Craft of Travelling).

MORRIS, William (1834–96) English writer and craftsman

Although Morris might have said that his life ran against the current of his times – he was a medievalist, craftsman and socialist in days of modernism, mass production and political paternalism – in retrospect he seems characteristically Victorian in his energy, his wide range of interests and his unquenchable optimism (though humanist, not Christian) that the human race was on an endless upward course of moral and material self-betterment. Jack Lindsay, *William Morris* (1975) is excellent on his thought, looking both backward to the Middle Ages and forward to a new millennium. Philip Henderson, *William Morris, His Life, Work and Friends* (1967) deals more with Morris' day-to-day life, his friendships and above all his political activities. It has two advantages over the earlier standard biography, J.W. Mackail, *The Life of William Morris* (1901): 60 years of political and technical hindsight and much more research into Morris' private papers.

> **READ ON**
> Philip Henderson (ed.), *The Letters of William Morris to his Family and Friends*. Gillian Naylor (ed.), *William Morris by Himself* (anthology of Morris' writings, with 200 sumptuously printed illustrations). Gay Daly, *Pre-Raphaelites in Love* (jolly joint biography).

MORTIMER, John (born 1923) English writer

Mortimer has had a charmed life. His upbringing was middle-

> **READ ON**
> John Mortimer *A Voyage Round my Father*, (autobiographical play, later made into a film). Penelope

class, cultured and idyllic. He enjoyed school and university, and spent the war not fighting but making propaganda films about British life. As a playwright he was a leader of the New Wave in the 1950s, and as a barrister he defended the 1960s 'permissive society' in cases as ludicrously British as anything in *Lewis Carroll. In the 1970s he became a popular TV playwright (notably for the 'Rumpole' series) and a leading interviewer and reviewer. He conceals hard work by pretending to bumble in an oh-so-amateur sort of way, and his autobiography *Clinging to the Wreckage* (1982) describes it with characteristic good humour and readability.

MOSLEY, Oswald (1896–1980) English politician

Mosley as politician, never mind leader of British Fascism in the 1930s, leaves one gaping at so much brilliance, so much wrong-headedness, so much waste. Oswald Mosley, *My Life* (1968) has very little about Mosley's private or family life: it is less an autobiography than a political testament, an exposition and justification of ideas which, then and now, set received thinking on its head. Robert Skidelsky, *Oswald Mosley* (1975) sets out not only to tell Mosley's life, but to pin down his place in British and European politics. While by no means an apologist for Mosley, Skidelsky is happy to confront received opinion. He claims, for example, that so far from being out of tune with British opinion, Mosley regularly anticipated it, among other things advocating Keynesian economics in 1925 and a European community in 1947, in each case long before anyone else supported them. Skidelsky is good on matters such as these, but bland on other, more central issues. Mosley's anti-semitism, for example, is not discussed but presented as some kind of aberration, the characteristic of a few followers in unrepresentative branches of the party.

MOUNTBATTEN, Lord and Lady

Louis, Lord Mountbatten of Burma (1900–79) was related to most of the royal families of Europe. He had a distinguished naval career, was Chief of Combined Operations during the Second World War and devised new equipment and strategies of deployment crucial to naval warfare at the time and still used today. After the war he served as the last viceroy of India (supervising the dissolution of the Raj), as NATO C-in-C Mediterranean, as First Sea Lord and as Chief of the Combined Defence Staffs. He was killed by a terrorist bomb in 1979. His wife **Edwina** (1901–60) was known for wealth, wit and a predatory, roving eye – questions were asked, for example, about her closeness to Nehru at the time of Indian independence. She worked tirelessly for the Red Cross and St John's Ambulance

Mortimer (Mortimer's first wife), *About Time.* *Peter Ustinov, *Dear Me.*

⊹ READ ON
Nicholas Mosley (Mosley's son), *The Rules of the Game; Beyond the Pale* (two-volume biography which sets out to be impartial about both Mosley senior and Mosley junior – who both followed a philosophy the author later came to detest – but is chiefly interesting for its agonizing over political ideas and for its picture of the growing apart of a devoted father and devoted son). Diana Mosley, née *Mitford (Mosley's wife), *A Life of Contrasts* (heavily political autobiography).

⊹ READ ON
Richard Hough, *Mountbatten, Hero of Our Time* (less gushy than the title suggests); *Louis and Victoria: the First Mountbattens* (about Mountbatten's parents). Antony Lambton, *The Mountbattens: the Battenbergs and Young Mountbatten* (no-holds-barred, as if Lambton is working off some undeclared grudge; but interesting on Mountbatten's antecedents and early years). Charles Smith, *Fifty Years With Mountbatten* (intimate memoir by his butler). *Mountbatten: Eighty*

Brigade in Europe, and for social welfare in India.

Philip Ziegler, *Mountbatten* (1984), the official biography, discusses Mountbatten's career, and is good on the way his unorthodoxy (he was, for example, that rare thing, a left-wing royal) opened doors unavailable to more hidebound officials. Ziegler finds obsessive vanity in Mountbatten, and says that he (Ziegler) had to make a desk note reading 'Remember, in spite of everything, he was a great man'. But his coolness breeds objectivity, an unusual and welcome ingredient in books about someone of Mountbatten's rank. Richard Hough, *Edwina, Countess of Burma* (1983) does a similar job for Lady Mountbatten, dealing with her public life without skimping and fearlessly dissecting her private life and character.

Years in Pictures (has no credited author, and its text is hero-worshipping, but the photos are superb).

MOZART, Wolfgang Amadeus (1756–91)
Austrian composer

Child prodigy and 'supreme genius of classical music', Mozart has been the subject of hundreds of books, most of them scholarly. The standard biography, Alfred Einstein, *Mozart: his Character, his Work* (fourth ed. 1960), is outstanding both on the man and the music, but technical in parts. H.C. Robbins Landon, *Mozart's Golden Years* (1990) and *Mozart's Last Year* (1989) are accessible and enthusiastic, and the latter convincingly untangles the controversy about Mozart's death. Both books have useful bibliographies. All modern writers on Mozart make use of Emily Anderson (ed.), *The Letters of Mozart and His Family* (third ed. 1985): Mozart was a lively, affectionate correspondent, and his letters (especially to his father) shed light on his creative processes, his family life and his character.

‹› **READ ON**
E. Valentin, *Mozart: a Pictorial Biography*. Eric Blom, *Mozart's Letters*. Stanley Sadie, *Mozart*. Michael Levey, *The Life and Death of Mozart*. H.C. Robbins Landon, ed., *Mozart and Vienna* and *The Mozart Compendium*.

MUGGERIDGE, Malcolm (1903–90) English journalist

Throughout his life, as foreign correspondent, editor of *Punch* and radio and TV pundit, Muggeridge delighted in controversy: he was at his best challenging other people's opinions or putting forward seemingly outrageous ideas of his own. In the 1930s he was one of the few European socialists to visit the USSR and return convinced that the system would never work. He had pungent things to say about Fascism, superpower diplomacy, multinational political leagues and unions and the British royal family. Once a scathing critic of religious belief, he became a fervent Christian convert. His autobiography *Chronicles of Wasted Time* (two volumes, 1972–3) catches the flavour of the man once nicknamed (possibly by himself) 'the gadfly of English letters'.

‹› **READ ON**
Ian Hunter, *Malcolm Muggeridge: A Life* (book which must have delighted Muggeridge, as it is that ultimate paradox, a biography which misses as much as it reveals). Malcolm Muggeridge, *Tread Softly, For You Tread on my Jokes*; *Things Past* (articles and essays). Richard Ingrams, *God's Apology* (chronicle of the friendship of Muggeridge, Hugh Kingsmill and Hesketh Pearson).

MUIR, John (1838–1914) Scottish/US naturalist

As a child in Scotland, Muir had knowledge beaten into him by teachers who believed that 'there was a close connection between the skin and the memory, and irritating the skin excited the memory to any required degree'. When he was 12 his family moved to Wisconsin, where he escaped from his father's bigoted Christianity (another case of beating: hammering into his children the idea that God was Love) by discovering the beauties of the wilderness. He studied science at university, but left to wander the USA. He was the first European to describe the wonders of Yosemite, and explored as far north as Alaska and as far south as the Gulf of Florida. He began the National Parks movement and the Sierra Club, whose purpose was to preserve the natural environment. His memoir *The Story of My Boyhood and Youth* (1913) is a classic account of the awakening of a child's soul to nature, and also contains unblinking reports of his brutal Scottish childhood and the efforts of his benighted father to wrestle his all-too-human son into love of God.

> ❖ **READ ON**
> John Muir, *A Thousand Mile Walk to the Gulf*; *My First Summer in the Sierras* (travel books aglow with the beauties of the American wilderness – hard to find, but well worth tracking down). W.H. Hudson, *Far Away and Long Ago* (awakening to nature). *Edmund Gosse, *Father and Son* (fundamentalist Christian father at loggerheads with growing, questioning son).

MURRY, Colin Middleton (born 1926) English writer

Colin was the son of John Middleton Murry, whose first wife was *Katherine Mansfield, and whose second wife (Colin's mother) died when the child was not yet five. Murry senior then made a third marriage, to a woman obsessively jealous not just of everyone else he spoke to but of his two previous wives. She treated her stepchildren (Colin and his sister) with utmost vindictiveness, and Colin also felt isolated from his aloof, unhappy father. Stir in a miserable school life, and Colin Middleton Murry, *One Hand Clapping* (1975) becomes a memoir of a grim and despairing childhood. His *Shadows on the Grass* (1977) takes the story on to the death of Murry senior in 1957, and is chiefly concerned with events in the Second World War: Murry senior left his third wife, summoned his son to live with him and his (then) mistress, worked as a pacifist and ran a communal farm.

> ❖ **READ ON**
> Mary Gamble (Murry senior's mistress and eventually fourth wife), *To Keep Faith*. Katherine Middleton Murry (Colin's sister), *Beloved Quixote* (1986) (autobiography, recounting her and Colin's childhood suffering, but much more affectionate, not to say idolizing, about their father).

N

NABOKOV, Vladimir (1899–1977) Russian writer

According to taste, Nabokov (author of *Lolita* and *Pale Fire*) is either a literary magician or one of the archest show-offs who ever set pen to paper. He is at full stretch in *Speak, Memory* (rev. ed. 1966), an evocation, in sumptuous, poetic prose, of an idyllic childhood before the Russian Revolution. Typical is his description of riding a bicycle: ' . . . weaving between two flat leaves and then between a small stone and the hole from which it had been dislodged the evening before; enjoying the brief smoothness of a bridge over a brook; skirting the wire fence of the tennis court; nuzzling open the little whitewashed gate at the end of the park; and then, in a melancholy ecstasy of freedom, speeding along the hard-baked, pleasantly agglutinate margins of long country roads.' Andrew Field, *V.N.* (1987) is a lively biography, reviled as inaccurate by Nabokov's family but still engrossing and revealing — a fan's book, for fans.

> **READ ON**
> Alexander Pasternak, *A Vanished Present* (memoirs, by Boris Pasternak's brother, of a pre-Revolutionary childhood very like Nabokov's). Manya Harari, *Memoirs 1906–1969* (sections on childhood similar to *Speak, Memory*; the rest is an amazing story of life travelling through Europe in the 1930s and as a reporter in Israel soon after its foundation).

NAPOLEON I (1769–1821) French soldier and emperor

There are said to be half a million books about Napoléon and at least one (an unpublished novel) by him. Henri Lachouque, *The Anatomy of Glory: Napoléon and His Guard* (1978) is thorough, magisterial, scholarly and, a blessed bonus in such a weighty tome, magnificently readable. David Chandler, *Napoléon* (1973) is a well-illustrated, brief biography, and his *The Campaigns of Napoléon* (1967) is a standard work, fascinating for anyone interested in military strategy. Pieter Geyl, *Napoléon, For*

> **READ ON**
> Frances Mossiker, *Napoléon and Joséphine*. Guy Breton, *Napoléon and His Ladies* (zestful summary of a packed subject). Desmond Seward, *Napoléon's Family*. Anthony Burgess, *Napoleon Symphony* (complex but rewarding novel). Raymond Horricks, *Marshal Ney, the Romance and the Real* (biography of Napoléon's chief lieutenant, a military genius overshadowed

and Against (1965) is a no-holds-barred 'psychological biography', demonstrating that in the end it was only seeds of self-destruction in Napoléon's own character which stopped his being the greatest world conqueror since *Alexander the Great or Genghis Khan. Ben Weider and David Hapgood, *The Murder of Napoléon* (1982) describes Napoléon's last days on St Helena, and tackles one of the main mysteries of his life: did he die naturally (as his British gaolers claimed) or was he 'helped'?

only by his master). *See also* *Joséphine Beauharnais.

NARAYAN, R(asipuran) K(rishnaswami) (born 1907) Indian writer

Narayan's novels, set in the imaginary Indian town of Malgudi, are in a gentle, ironical style which conceals sharp criticism of Indian attitudes, past and present. His autobiography *My Days* (1975) has the same qualities: in Narayan's hands, fact is as simple and as resonant as fiction. The book is a quiet account of Narayan's childhood, his beginnings as a writer, his first marriage (ended by his wife's tragic death) and the farce which surrounded the filming of his book *The Guide*. Narayan's fans, recognizing these ingredients, will rush to read it. Anyone new to his work can look forward to a treat.

⊹ **READ ON**
R.K. Narayan, *The English Teacher/Grateful to Life and Death* (delicate, sad novel, partly autobiographical, about a young husband devastated by his wife's death).

NEAL, Patricia (born 1926) US actress

Neal worked her passage to stardom in the old Hollywood studio system, and won an Oscar in 1961 for *Hud*. She worked with such stars as *Bette Davis, Katharine Hepburn, Paul Newman and *Laurence Olivier, and had a memorable and notorious affair with Gary Cooper. She married *Roald Dahl, and had the children she had always longed for, only to see the marriage disintegrate and the children suffer accident and illness. She herself had three near-fatal strokes, and was forced to relearn from scratch how to walk and talk. Her autobiography (with Richard Deneut), *As I Am* (1988) describes all these events, and continues with her even more astonishing life in the 1980s, when she rebuilt her personal and public confidence (thanks to devoted friends, and to regular Roman Catholic retreats), and toured the world, fund-raising for neurological research.

⊹ **READ ON**
Barry Farrell, *Pat and Roald*.

NELSON, Horatio (1758–1805) English Admiral

During Nelson's life he was called 'The Hero', and his tragic death, at the very moment of victory at Trafalgar, had a similar effect in Britain to that of *John F. Kennedy in the USA some 150 years later. Nelson was an inspiring leader, and an innova-

⊹ **READ ON**
Tom Pocock, *Nelson and His World* (good illustrations). F. Graser, *Beloved Emma: the Life of Emma, Lady Hamilton*. Winifred Gérin, *Horatia Nelson* (about the daughter of Lady Hamilton and

tive tactician who changed the whole nature of naval battles. In public he sometimes behaved in an arrogant manner, and this, coupled with the scandal of his affair with Emma Hamilton, earned him considerable disapproval.

Roy Hattersley, *Nelson* (1974) is outstanding on Nelson's battles, complementing non-technical accounts with clear maps and diagrams. The illustrations are excellent, and the book deals well with Nelson's private lives, his personal qualities and his tendency to self-dramatizing heroics. Tom Pocock, *Horatio Nelson* (1987) benefits from thorough research, including Pocock's visits to the places where Nelson lived and fought. Good discussion of early influences, from Nelson's Norfolk childhood. David and Stephen Howarth, *Nelson: the Immortal Memory* (1988) is good on Nelson's relationship with and effect on the Royal Navy. C.S. Forester, *Nelson* (1929) draws on few sources apart from the letters, but, as one might expect from the creator of Hornblower, it breathes life and an aura of greatness into the man: an unassuming treat.

Nelson, and excellent on the social atmosphere which made her consistently refuse to acknowledge Hamilton as her mother). Oliver Warner, *The Life and Letters of Lord Collingwood* (about Nelson's devoted second-in-command).

NERO (37–68) Roman emperor (ruled 54–68)

Gossip-writers of the time depicted Nero Claudius Drusus Germanicus as a monster. There are many legends about him, each more extraordinary than the last. They said for example that his rule was marked by the mysterious murders of every-one who seemed a possible threat, including his mother and his first wife. Sure that he was a god, equal to Jupiter, he ban-krupted the state to build a golden palace, with a bridge over the Forum so that he and Jupiter could pass over ordinary mortals' heads whenever they felt like chatting. He burned Rome to provide a backcloth while he recited his epic poem 'The Fall of Troy'. He devised the most appalling ways of tor-turing Christians to death. He was even said to have jumped on the stomach of his pregnant second wife until he killed her. In the end, faced with a palace coup, he committed suicide, mut-tering as he died 'What an artist perishes in me'. Michael Grant, *Nero* (1970) zestfully recounts these and other legends, under the guise of examining all the evidence. There are 100 photographs of artworks and buildings from Nero's time.

⋅> **READ ON**
Suetonius, *The Twelve Caesars* (chapter on Nero is the source of most of the juiciest stories about him). Lloyd C. Douglas, *The Big Fisherman* (historical novel about St Peter, with particularly graphic scenes set in Nero's Rome).

⋅> NEVER A DULL MOMENT

Mary de Bunsen, *Mount Up With Wings: Press Secretary at Heston Airport, War Services Civilian Ferry Pilot for RAF, Organic Gardening and the Soil Association, Travels as a Partial Invalid in the Far East and a Successful Heart Operation*

*Benjamin Franklin, *Autobiography*
Frederic Grendel, *Beaumarchais: the Man Who Was Figaro*
Arthur Gould Lee, *The Flying Cathedral: the Story of Samuel Franklin Cody, Texan Cowboy, Bronco-buster, Frontiersman, Barnstormer, Circus Sharpshooter, Horsetrack Racer, Showman, Man-Carrying Kite Inventor and Pioneer Aviator*
Elizabeth Gunn, *A Passion for the Particular* *Dorothy Wordsworth
Johanna Johnston, *Mrs Satan* *(Victoria Woodhull)
Frank McLynn, *Stanley: the Making of an African Explorer*
John Masters, *Casanova*
Patrick Morah, *Prince Rupert of the Rhine*
Arthur H. Nethercot, *The First Five Lives of *Annie Besant*; *The Last Four Lives of Annie Besant*

NEWBY, Eric (born 1919) English writer

Newby's books blend autobiography, travel and humour: he writes as if he is the only sane person in a world of gentle, obsessive lunatics. In *The Last Grain Race* (1956) he is a 19-year-old deck hand on a Swedish cargo ship powered by sail. In *A Short Walk in the Hindu Kush* (1958) he and a friend don big boots and long shorts and go tramping in the Himalayas. *Something Wholesale* (1962) is slightly less exotic (but only slightly): it describes Newby's years touring England's department stores as an executive in his father's dress business. *A Traveller's Life* (1982) pulls the whole thing together: it is an autobiography written as a series of travel stories, with such section-titles as 'The Baby as a Traveller', 'Journey Through Darkest Hammersmith', 'Snakes and Ladders' and 'Wimbledon to Italy By Bicycle'.

-> **READ ON**
Eric Newby, *Slowly Down the Ganges* (about India); *The Big Red Train Ride* (about China). John Preston, *Touching the Moon*.

NEWTON, Isaac (1642–1727) English scientist

Famous today for his scientific work (on the theory of gravitation, in optics, in mathematics), Newton was also known in his own time as a Member of Parliament, as master of the Royal Mint and as a controversial writer on the Apocrypha and the Biblical Book of Revelations. He was an austere, lonely man, perhaps because from childhood his chief relationship was with intellectual work, not people, and there has even been speculation about his sanity, along the lines of 'genius is next to madness'. Frank E. Manuel, *A Portrait of Isaac Newton* (1968) deals with all this, drawing on both published and unpublished evi-

-> **READ ON**
Robert Hooke, *Diary* (by a pathologically jealous rival of Newton, prone to claim that Newton's discoveries were plagiarized from his own unpublished work).

dence. Its prose is rather stuffy ('cognate problems'; 'such adulation was more than mere baroque extravagance'), but it gives a sympathetic account of Newton the man, and explains his science in a way which lay people can understand.

-> NEW YORK

*Helen Hanff, *Underfoot in Show Business*
Edwin P. Hoyt, *The Man Who Came to Dinner* (Alexander Woolcott)
*Alfred Kazin, *Walker in the City*
John Keats, *You Might As Well Live* *Dorothy Parker
R.W.B. Lewis, *Edith Wharton*
Peter Maas, *Serpico*
Damon Runyon, *Father's Footsteps*
Ultra Violet, *Famous For Fifteen Minutes: My Years with *Andy Warhol*
Richard Wright, *Black Boy: a Record of Childhood and Youth*

-> NEW ZEALAND

Mary Anne Barber, *Station Life in New Zealand*
Sonja Davies, *Bread and Roses*
D. Fingleton, *Kiri Te Kanawa*
*Janet Frame, *To the Is-Land*
*Edmund Hillary, *Nothing Venture, Nothing Win*
Lynley Hood, *Sylvia: Biography of Sylvia Ashton Warner*
Michael King, *Te Puea*
Frank McKay, *The Life of James K. Baxter*
Ngaio Marsh, *Black Beech and Honeydew*

NICHOLAS and ALEXANDRA

Nicholas II (1872–1918) and Alexandra (1872–1918) were the last tsar and tsarina of Russia, executed with their family during the Revolution. Robert Massie, *Nicholas and Alexandra* (1985) combines a joint biography with a study of the causes and events of the Revolution itself. Massie uses a vast amount of information, but deploys it skilfully and readably. His view is that the family might have survived if the Tsarina (already under suspicion because she was German) had not brought *Rasputin to court, favouring him above the nobles and fomenting dissensions and rivalries which left the governing class power-

-> **READ ON**
Victor Alexandrov, *The End of the Romanovs* (detailed account of the events in 1918). David Kurth, *Anastasia* (story of the woman who claimed, years after the massacre, to be the only one of the Imperial family to have escaped death, and therefore the rightful heir to the Russian throne). Paul and Beatrice Grabbe (eds.), *The Private World of the Last Tsar* (photos, with

less to face revolution. Virginia Cowles, *The Last Tsar and Tsarina* (1977) is shorter than Massie's book, but equally accomplished and excellently illustrated.

NICHOLSON, Renton (1809–59) English restaurateur and showman

'Lord Chief Baron Nicholson', as he called himself, was an irrepressible self-made London man. He lived in a world of pawnshops, gambling dens and brothels, and made his living by providing food and drink, organizing prize-fights, cockfights, card games and *poses plastiques* (nude shows). He founded a society to stage mock trials (spicy with sex, blasphemy and irreverence to authority), and this (even more than his other activities) brought him into contact with middle-class toffs and sensation-seekers, from the Lord Chief Justice down. His autobiography, *Rogue's Progress* (ed. John L. Bradley, 1965), is one of the least known, most energetic and self-admiring of all 19th-century books. It begins 'Exquisite reader, I have a right to believe you perfection. Let me shake hands with you . . . ', and from then on you know that you are being taken for a ride, that the experience will be exhilarating and that the company will be unforgettable. There are many roguish autobiographies, and autobiographies by rogues, but few beat this.

> **READ ON**
> brief linking text).
>
> Kellow Chesney, *The Victorian Underworld* (guide to the seedy, seductive world in which Nicholson so flourished). Lesley Blanche, *The Game of Hearts* (selection from the *Memoirs* of Harriet Wilson, the 'queen of courtesans' in Regency London – different circumstances, and employment, from Nicholson, but similar zest and turn of phrase).

NIELSEN, Carl (1865–1931) Danish composer

Nielsen wrote a classic childhood memoir: *My Childhood on Fyn* (1927; translated as *My Childhood*, 1953). He describes his boyhood in a poor farming family, his musical beginnings (playing violin for country dances) and his years as a pint-sized army bandsman. The book wonderfully evokes the smells and sounds of the Danish countryside in summer; it is unsentimental about poverty and funny, in a naive, child's-eye way, about some of the adults who moulded the growing boy. Its air of unpretentious happiness will appeal even to readers who know nothing of Nielsen or his music.

> **READ ON**
> Tove Jansson, *The Summer Book* (fictionalized memoir of a young child and her elderly grandmother on an idyllic summer holiday on an island in the Gulf of Finland).

NIEMOLLER, Martin (1892–1984) German pastor

A submarine commander in the First World War who beame a Lutheran pastor in 1924, Niemöller led the resistance to *Hitler in the 1930s, speaking out against anti-semitism in particular. He spent the war in concentration camps (including Dachau), and afterwards continued his fiercely principled

> **READ ON**
> Martin Niemöller, *From U-Boat to Pulpit* (1936 autobiography, updated in 1939 as *From U-Boat to Concentration Camp*); *The Gestapo Defied* (published in 1943, with a foreword by Thomas Mann). Mary Bosanquet, *The Life and Death of*

stance, preaching against the division of Germany, the cold war, the proliferation of nuclear weapons, racism and the denial of human rights. James Bentley, *Martin Niemöller* (1984) describes his life, quoting liberally from letters, diaries, sermons, and in one case, from the verbatim account of a face-to-face, stand-up row between Niemöller and Hitler.

Dietrich Bonhoeffer (biography of another 'turbulent priest', who spent three years in the German Resistance before being arrested and hanged).

NIGHTINGALE, Florence (1820–1910) English nurse

Rich, educated and middle-class, Nightingale used her advantages, and her formidable personality, to establish standards of hospital nursing now taken for granted. Her adrenalin seems to have been triggered equally by compassion for the patients, pleasure in out-arguing pompous (male) members of the medical establishment, and ramrod-backed insistence on the uniformed, quasi-military hierarchy she devised for her profession. Cecil Woodham-Smith, *Florence Nightingale* (rev. ed. 1969) is fat and succulent, a case of an ace biographer meeting an ideal subject. It quotes from documents, gives conversations wherever possible (many people remembered their words to Nightingale, and more especially hers to them, verbatim), and takes an approach to Nightingale and her Victorian times which is zestful, ironic and unstuffy.

⊹ READ ON
Elspeth Huxley, Florence Nightingale (shorter than Woodham-Smith's book, but just as exuberant, and with 100 apt illustrations). George Pickering, *Creative Malady* (biographical studies of six people, including Nightingale, whose creativity was linked, Pickering says, to psychological illness). Zachary Cope, *Florence Nightingale and the Doctors.*

NIJINSKY, Vaslav (1890–1950) Russian dancer

Arguably the greatest dancer in the history of ballet, Nijinsky revolutionized his art, and also created a kind of smoulderingly erotic, superstar stage presence which has influenced a thousand film and pop stars since. His story is also tragic: a few glittering years with *Diaghilev's *Ballets Russes*, followed by a lapse into madness and a miserable 30-year existence in spas, on luxury liners, on the twilight fringes of sanity. Richard Buckle, *Nijinsky* (1971), the standard biography, is excellent on backstage politics and the making, performance and reception of such ballets as *The Spectre of the Rose, L'Après-midi d'un Faune*, and *Stravinsky's *Petrushka* and *The Rite of Spring*. Romola Nijinska, *Nijinsky* (rev. ed. 1980), by Nijinsky's wife, is evocative but sad about his later years. Vera Krasovskaya, *Nijinsky* (Eng. ed. 1979) deals mainly with the early years, and despite its sometimes novelettish style ('Sighing, he took a dab of sallow, yellow paint and put it on his face . . . '), it describes Nijinsky's work from an insider's, a dancer's point of view – perhaps the best way to remember him.

⊹ READ ON
Richard Buckle, *Diaghilev.* Bronislava Nijinska (Nijinsky's sister), *Early Memoirs.*

NIVEN, David (1910–83) English film star and writer

Niven excelled at playing debonair English gentlemen – either heroes (as in *The First of the Few* and *Carrington, VC*) or crooks (as in *The Pink Panther* or *The Brain*, in which he masterminds the Great Train Robbery). He had a second career as a writer of sunny, hilarious memoirs of film-business life: *Round the Rugged Rocks* (1951), *The Moon's a Balloon* (1971), *Bring on the Empty Horses* (1975) and *Go Slowly, Come Back Quickly* (1981). Sheridan Morley, *The Other Side of the Moon* (1985) is an affectionate, well-illustrated biography.

▹ **READ ON**
Peter Haining, *The Last Gentleman* (biography, including thumbnail accounts of all Niven's films, both masterpieces and disasters).

NOBEL, Alfred (1833–96) Swedish scientist

Nobel invented dynamite: a blend of nitroglycerine and an inert material which could be handled without risk of accidental explosions. Naively, he envisaged only peaceful uses for his invention, and was horrified when the human race found more deadly applications. His foundation of the Nobel Prizes was the result: an attempt to reward each year's major advances in literature, medicine, physics, chemistry and the pursuit of peace which has been almost as controversial as his initial discovery. Erik Bergengren, *Alfred Nobel: the Man and His Work* (1962) is a straightforward biography, scrupulously avoiding controversy. Michael Evlanoff and Marjorie Fluor, *Alfred Nobel: the Loneliest Millionaire* (1969) deals well with Nobel's life and personality, and revels in all the issues.

▹ **READ ON**
Tony Gray, *Champions of Peace* (brief biography of Nobel, followed by a description of each of the winners of his Peace Prize, from its foundation to 1976 when the book was published).

NORMAN, Frank (1930–80) English writer

After a loveless childhood, Norman worked as fairground hand, Soho wide-boy and burglar before spending three years in gaol. His tough, funny book about prison, *Bang To Rights* (1958) made him a celebrity, and he went on to write several more books, TV scripts and plays including *Fings Ain't Wot They Used T'be*. His childhood memoir *Banana Boy* (1969) is a savage account of life in a Dr Barnardo's home, where for ten years he was denied even the use of his Christian name, and from which he tried twice to escape. His picture of the underside of British charity is horribly Dickensian – little changed, it seems, since Oliver Twist asked for more – but also horribly funny; you'll laugh until you cry.

▹ **READ ON**
*Leslie Thomas, *This Time Next Week*. *Philip Oakes, *Dwellers All in Time and Space*.

O

O'CONNELL, Daniel (1775–1847) Irish politician

Books about O'Connell tend to be over-weighted, on one side or the other, by the politics of the 'Irish question'. Since it was O'Connell's untiring work, over 20 years, which won emancipation from British rule, the politics certainly need to be described. But O'Connell's private life, his charming, caustically witty personality and his eccentric family and upbringing, not to mention his campaigns against slavery and to help the poor, are of equal interest, and demand attention to complete the picture. Charles Chenevix Trench, *The Great Dan* (1984) tells us all this, and in so doing presents 'the Liberator' convincingly as a man of his time, a contemporary in thought, energy and quality of mind to such people as *Paine, *Jefferson or *Bolívar.

∻ **READ ON**
Arthur Houston (ed.), *Daniel O'Connell, His Early Life and Journal, 1795–1806)* (published in 1906, but still the most accessible book of O'Connell's own writings). R. Dudley Edwards, *O'Connell and his World* (well-illustrated 'brief life'). Sean O'Faolain, *King of the Beggars* (authoritative on the life, passionate about the politics).

O'HARA, John (1905–70) US writer

In his 374 short stories and 18 novels O'Hara set out to 'tell it like it was': the events, manners and lifestyle of all kinds of US citizens from the 1920s to the 1960s. He was a writer-about-town, a member of the Algonquin set, a lover of big cars and expensive restaurants, a friend of *Dorothy Parker, *Fitzgerald and *Hemingway, and – in the words of Robert Benchley, to whom he apologized the day after a drunken fight – 'A shit . . . born a shit just as some people were born with blue eyes.' Frank MacShane, *The Life of John O'Hara* (1980) is wonderfully entertaining, exhaustively researched, full of good literary criticism, excellent on the atmosphere and feeling of each epi-

∻ **READ ON**
Matthew J. Bruccoli, *Selected Letters of John O'Hara.*

sode or relationship described, and leaving no stone unturned in O'Hara's gravel-strewn life.

O'KEEFFE, Georgia (1887–1986) US artist

O'Keeffe grew up in pioneer country, and her childhood gave her a feeling for Nature's vastness which affected all her art. She worked in New York at the height of the 1910s modernist fervour, campaigned for women's suffrage, and put over the female point of view, in art as in life, in a way closer to 1970s feminism than to the male chauvinist 1910s. She had a stormy marriage with the photographer Alfred Stieglitz, whose portraits of her are among the most numerous and obsessive in his output. She spent the latter part of her long life in New Mexico, remote from metropolitan artistic and sexual-political ferments.

O'Keeffe's autobiography, *Georgia O'Keeffe* (1976), appeared when she was 89, and since then there have been a dozen books by others. Roxana Robinson, *Georgia O'Keeffe* (1989) is the first to be granted the use of family documents. It is poorly illustrated, but makes up for this by the attention it pays to O'Keeffe's relationships and her polemical views on women's experience and on art. The bibliography is huge.

◇ READ ON
Jack Cowart, Juan Hamilton and Sarah Greenhough, *Georgia O'Keeffe: Art and Letters* (well illustrated). Sue Davidson Lowe, *Stieglitz: a Memoir/Biography*.

OLIVIER, Laurence (1907–89) English actor

The most acclaimed English actor of this century, 'Sir' starred in 150 stage plays, 50 films, two dozen TV plays and one TV commercial (for Polaroid). He was the first director of the British National Theatre, the first English actor to be made a lord, and the idol and terror of colleagues, great and small. Laurence Olivier, *Confessions of an Actor* (1982) is a slightly gushy autobiography. *On Acting* (1986) is Olivier reflecting on his own performances, with anecdotes, advice and technical comments – a treat. Anthony Holden, *Olivier* (1988) is the standard biography, already a classic, free of adulation or prurience, and excellent on both Olivier's mesmeric stage presence and his private personality. It is particularly moving about Olivier's last decade, a period naturally not covered in two earlier books, the best of a huge crop: Virginia Fairweather, *Cry God for Larry* (1969) (fine on Olivier's films) and John Cottrell, *Laurence Olivier* (1975).

◇ READ ON
Royal National Theatre, with Richard Olivier and Joan Plowright, *Olivier at Work* (collection of backstage memoirs, by Olivier's colleagues and friends, illustrated with candid photos). *See also* *Vivien Leigh.

OMAN, Carola (1898–1978) English writer

Oman wrote novels, children's books, and biographies of, among others, *Nelson and Garrick. Her memoir *An Oxford Childhood* (1976) is a delightful account of her first 16 years, in

◇ READ ON
Gwen Raverat, *Period Piece* (Cambridge childhood of much the same kind, from a generation earlier).

the Edwardian Indian summer which ended with the outbreak
of the First World War. Oman's father was a professor, and his
daughters grew up in the quintessential upper-middle-class
Oxfordian golden haze. They were bright, privileged, surrounded by interesting people and fond of house-parties, page-
ants, punting and trips to the London theatre to see Irving and
Benson in *Shakespeare. The lifestyle Oman describes has become something of a myth, but her writing is so good that she
makes it appear the most natural, as well as the most delightful,
way to pass one's formative years.

ONASSIS, Jacqueline Kennedy (born 1929) US socialite

Jacqueline Bouvier became world-famous as *John F. Kennedy's
First Lady and then as his widow, when she was the most
photographed, most gossiped about person in the USA. In 1968
she married the billionaire shipping tycoon Aristotle Onassis, notorious for a flamboyant affair with *Maria Callas and a bitter
divorce from his wife. This marriage redoubled interest in everything to do with her – how, for example, had she coped with
Kennedy's womanizing, which was just becoming public knowledge? She consistently refused to make public statements or to
acknowledge such speculation, which had the effect of turning it
into a major industry. The many 'tell all' biographies all recount
scandal of one kind or another, and each seems to find different
'facts'. Kitty Kelley, *Jackie Oh! An Intimate Biography* (1978) and
C. David Heymann, *A Woman Named Jackie* (1989) are typical of
this kind of book: sensational reads in every sense. Stephen Birmingham, *Jacqueline Bouvier Kennedy Onassis* (1979) is (slightly)
more sensitive, more sympathetic.

> **READ ON**
> John H. Davis, *The Bouviers*
> (about 'Jackie's' family). Frank
> Bray, *Onassis: an Extravagant
> Life.*

O'NEILL, Eugene (1888–1953) US playwright

One of O'Neill's best-known plays, *Mourning Becomes Electra*,
reworks the Greek myth about the doomed family of
Agamemnon, Electra and Orestes – and by hindsight, the idea
of a family curse seems an inevitable choice of theme for him.
His parents were talented but self-destructive; he himself was
neurotic and alcoholic; his beloved daughter Oona married
*Charles Chaplin, a man of whom he deeply disapproved; one
of his sons committed suicide, the other was a drifter and a
drug addict. Louis Sheaffer, *O'Neill, Son and Playwright* (1968)
and *O'Neill, Son and Artist* (1973) is the standard biography,
both monumental and readable. The first volume covers
O'Neill's tortured family relationships, especially with his
drunken, actor-manager father (the subject of O'Neill's own
play *Long Day's Journey Into Night*). The second volume is

> **READ ON**
> A. Boulton, (O'Neill's second
> wife), *Part of a Long Story.*

about O'Neill's career, his disastrous first marriage, his debilitating illness and his grief at his children's troubles. Croswell Bowen, *The Curse of the Misbegotten* (1960) tells the family story in a sympathetic if doom-laden way. Compulsive reading, it still makes one ask why we take such morbid interest in other people's misery.

◇ THE OPEN ROAD

Thomas Callaghan, *Tramp's Chronicle*
*W.H. Davies, *Autobiography of a Super-Tramp*
John Hillaby, *Journey Through Love*
Jack Kerouac, *Lonesome Road*
*Laurie Lee, *As I Walked Out One Midsummer Morning*
Patrick Leigh-Fermor, *A Time of Gifts*
Joseph Stamper, *Less Than The Dust: Memoirs of a Tramp*
Dorothy Strange, *Born on the Straw: a Romany Biography* (Tony Butler)
David Williams, *A World of His Own (The Double Life of George Borrow)*
Martin Frederick Wood, *In the Life of a Romany Gypsy*

OPPENHEIMER, Robert (1904–67) US scientist

It is a terrible distinction to have headed the team which created the first atomic bomb – and no amount of congratulation on ending the Second World War could lift the shadow from Oppenheimer's mind. He became a *cause célèbre* for the second time in the 1950s, when he was arraigned for Communist sympathies by the sinister Senator McCarthy. Americans still worry at his reputation, and he is a prime case-study for anyone studying the complex relationship between science and ethics. Nuel Pharr Davis, *Lawrence and Oppenheimer* (1968), the classic biography, is good on these issues, and prompts the sombre question, 'which is in charge, human will or the progress of events?' Peter Goodchild, *Robert Oppenheimer* (1980) is an illustrated biography, making good use of previously secret FBI material. Oppenheimer's own thoughts (both more guarded and scientifically more complex) are in *Science and the Common Understanding* (1954) and *Letters and Recollections* (ed. Alice Kimball Smith and Charles Weiner, 1980).

◇ **READ ON**
Leslie R. Groves, *Now It Can Be Told: the Story of the Manhattan Project*. Phillip M. Stern, *The Oppenheimer Case: Security on Trial*.

ORTON, Joe (1933–67) English writer

Orton wrote dazzling farces (including *Loot* and *What the Butler Saw*) satirizing the Establishment and outraging the bourgeoi-

◇ **READ ON**
*Kenneth Williams, *Just Williams* (autobiography by the comedian and first star of *Loot*, who was a

sie. He was one of the 1960s' most dazzling lights, and his reputation turned sensational when he was bludgeoned to death by his lover Kenneth Halliwell, who then committed suicide. John Lahr, *Prick Up Your Ears* (1978) is a glorious biography, enriched with quotations from Orton's work, and catching exactly the combination of hilarity, outrageousness and danger which was Orton's stock-in-trade. Joe Orton, *The Orton Years* (ed. Lahr, 1968) is tart and funny, though its accounts of endless sex may need to be taken one encounter at a time.

friend of Orton and Halliwell, and one of the few people Orton claims to have trusted and admired).

ORWELL, George (1903–50) English writer

'George Orwell' was the pen-name of Eric Blair, an Eton-educated non-conformer who began his adult life serving the British Empire in Burma, became a radical journalist in the 1930s and wrote some of the most savage indictments of political humbug ever published in English. His early novel, *Burmese Days*, and his non-fiction books, *Down and Out in Paris and London*, *The Road to Wigan Pier* and *Homage to Catalonia*, are autobiographical, dealing respectively with life in the Burma police, among tramps and derelicts in two European capitals, in a depressed working-class town, and in Spain during the Civil War. Bernard Crick, *George Orwell* (1980), the standard 'life', traces the relationship between fact and fiction in these books, is excellent on Orwell's schooldays and superb on his political journey from Edwardian middle-class conformity to the furious despair of *Animal Farm* and *1984*. The section on *1984* alone is worth the price of the book.

◇ **READ ON**
Sonia Orwell and Ian Angus (eds.), *George Orwell: Collected Essays, Journalism and Letters* (four volumes).

OSBORNE, John (born 1929) English playwright

Osborne's *A Better Class of Person* (1981) is a witty, bawdy autobiography, beginning with his childhood living in rented rooms with his mother, progressing to a boarding school (which he hated and from which he was expelled), early days in rep, and metamorphosis, with *Look back in Anger*, into the first of the 1950s' 'angry young men'. Osborne is characteristically merciless to people he knew, institutions he despised, journalists, bad actors and even his mother (something for which the book was much criticized). The book shares the tone of such plays as *Look Back in Anger* and *The Entertainer*: it is an unstoppable, vigorous, hilarious and slightly manic rant about England and the English, compulsive whether you warm to Osborne or disagree with every word he writes.

◇ **READ ON**
Peter Nichols, *Feeling You're Behind* (equally outrageous autobiography, by Osborne's contemporary). Philip Roberts, *The Royal Court Theatre*.

-> OUTSIDE THE LAW

Derek Bickerton, *The Murders of *Boysie Singh, Robber, Arsonist, Pirate, Mass-Murderer, Vice and Gambling King of Trinidad*
Max Brown, **Ned Kelly: Australian Son*
Pat F. Garrett, *The Authentic Life of Billy the Kid*
Christopher Hibbert, *The Road to Tyburn *(Jack Sheppard)*
John Kobler, *The Life and Work of Al Capone*
Dudley Pope, **Harry Morgan's Way*
Quentin Reynolds, *I, William Sutton, the Story of the Cleverest Bank Robber of Modern Times*
John Rollin Ridge, *The Life and Adventures of Joaquin Marieta, the Celebrated Californian Bandit*
Mark A. Stuart, *Gangster: the Story of Longy Zwillman, the Man who Invented Organised Crime*

P

PAINE, Thomas (1737–1809) English writer

In Paine's own day, his writings so annoyed people that he was imprisoned, fined and burnt in effigy, and even today the mere mention of his name is enough to make establishment-minded Englanders foam at the mouth. His *Common Sense* stated the arguments for independence from Britain which triggered the American Revolution. His *Rights of Man* defended the French Revolution. His *Age of Reason* claimed that even if God exists he has nothing to do with Christianity, and that the Bible is a hodge-podge of superstition, half-baked dogma and fairy tales. Not surprisingly, Paine's ideas made his life a switchback between being idolized and persecuted, and he spent much of his time on the run, either in America, France or Britain. Audrey Williamson, *Thomas Paine: His Life, Work and Times* (1973) is the standard biography: full, careful and remarkably objective considering Paine's power, still, to get under one's intellectual and political skin.

↔ **READ ON**
A.J. Ayer, *Thomas Paine* (enthusiastic, mellow account of Paine's life and thought – no comfort for those who disapprove of radicalism, but wittily written and with an unanswerable silkiness which equals Paine's own prose).

↔ PAINTERS

Sidney Alexander, *Marc Chagall: a Biography*
Robert Coughlan, *The Wine of Genius: a Life of Maurice Utrillo*
Laurence and Elizabeth Hanson, *The Tragic Life of* *Henri Toulouse-Lautrec
Jack Lindsay, *The Life and Work of* *J.M.W. Turner
Jean Renoir, *Renoir, My Father*
Meryl Secrest, *Salvador Dalí, the Surrealist Jester
See also Art and Artists

PANKHURST family

Emmeline Pankhurst (1858–1928) and her daughters Christabel Pankhurst (1880–1958) and **Sylvia Pankhurst** (1882–1960) were treated with vitriolic scorn by the male establishment of the 1900s–20s, and are still disdainfully described in many male-written reference books. Emmeline Pankhurst led the British suffragette movement, advocating direct action in a way which infuriated the authorities, delighted the tabloid press, and eventually won the day. Christabel Pankhurst was her mother's most ardent disciple, and when the cause was won she emigrated to the USA and became a revivalist preacher. Sylvia Pankhurst first intended to be an artist (and was a fine neo-impressionist painter), but devoted her time instead to the suffragette movement, to the betterment of working conditions, especially for women, and, from the 1930s onwards, to free Ethiopia from the Italians and raise standards of education and living there.

David Mitchell, *The Fighting Pankhursts* (1967) and *The Pankhursts* (1970) are good joint studies, with useful bibliographies. Emmeline Pankhurst, *My Own Story* (1914) is an 'as told to' autobiography, making a fascinating contrast with Sylvia Pankhurst, *The Life of Emmeline Pankhurst* (1935) (good on the suffragette struggle). David Mitchell, *Queen Christabel* (1967) devotes two thirds of its space to the struggle, but is then excellent on Christabel's religious work. Patricia W. Romero, *E. Sylvia Pankhurst* (1987) is good on Sylvia Pankhurst's political work, particularly after 1914, but weak on her painting, a deficiency made up for in a well-illustrated book by Sylvia's son: Richard Pankhurst, *Sylvia Pankhurst, Artist and Crusader* (1979).

‑> **READ ON**

Barbara Castle, *Sylvia and Christabel Pankhurst* (magnificent short study of their political work: 150 pages without a wasted or unclear word). Roger Fulford, *Votes for Women* (lively, sympathetic study of the whole suffrage movement, and especially of the workers who disagreed with the Pankhursts' methods).

‑> PARENTS AND CHILDREN

*Elias Canetti, *The Tongue Set Free*
Susan Chitty, *Now to My Mother* (*see* *Antonia White)
Gary Crosby, *Going My Own Way*
*Edmund Gosse, *Father and Son*
Lyndall P. Hopkinson, *Nothing to Forgive* (*see* *Antonia White)
*David Leitch, *Family Secrets*
*John Muir, *The Story of My Boyhood and Youth*
*Colin Middleton Murry, *One Hand Clapping*

> *Hal Porter, *The Watcher on the Cast Iron Balcony*
> *Margaret Powell, *My Mother and I; My Children and I*
> James *Roosevelt, *My Parents – a Differing View*
> Louis Shaeffer, *O'Neill, Son and Playwright*
> *Sarah Shears, *Tapioca for Tea*

PARKER, Dorothy (1893–1963) US writer

Parker was the tartest-tongued, and possibly funniest, member of the 'Algonquin set', a group of stage, film and literary people who met to swap witticisms in the Algonquin Hotel, New York (other luminaries were Robert Benchley, Robert Sherwood, Alexander Woolcott and Harpo Marx). Parker wrote screenplays, short stories, humorous verses and devastating reviews – as 'Constant Reader' in the *New Yorker* she dismissed *The House at Pooh Corner* in four words: 'Tonstant Weader Fwowed Up'. All the glitter was, however, intellectual and superficial: her emotional life was as messy as it was miserable. John Keats, *You Might As Well Live* (1970) tells the story, quoting Parker's own words wherever possible – a wise move for anyone writing her biography.

> ⊹ READ ON
> *Lillian Hellman, *An Unfinished Woman* (memoir of Hellman's own life, including accounts of Parker and her circle in New York, and of Parker in Hollywood).

> ⊹ PARTNERS AND FRIENDS
>
> Caryl Brahms, *Gilbert and Sullivan*
> John McCabe, *Mr Laurel and Mr Hardy*
> Jeanne MacKenzie, *A Victorian Courtship* (Beatrice Potter and Sidney Webb) (*Webb)
> Elisabeth Mavor, *The Ladies of Llangollen*
> *Alan Moorehead, *A Late Education*
> Joanna Richardson, *Victoria and Albert*
> James Dewey Watson, *The Double Helix*
> Maurice Zolotow, *Stagestruck* (*The Lunts)

PARTRIDGE, Frances (born 1900) English diarist

Frances Marshall was the sister-in-law of David Garnett, a member of the *Bloomsbury Group. She fell in love with and eventually married Ralph Partridge, who until then had lived in a *ménage à trois* with his first wife Dora Carrington and her lover *Lytton Strachey. The relationships were further complicated because both Partridge and Carrington had had other lovers, one of Carrington's being Partridge's friend Gerald

> ⊹ READ ON
> Julia Strachey, *A Portrait of Herself and Frances Partridge*.
> Gerald Brenan, *A Life of One's Own*; *Personal Record* (autobiographies). Ian Fielding (ed.), *Best of Friends: an Exchange of Letters between Gerald Brenan and Ralph Partridge*.

Brenan. Frances Partridge, *Memoirs* (1981) tells her life thus far, beginning with her childhood and ending with the deaths of Strachey and Carrington. Other volumes, based on her diaries, continue the story. *A Pacifist's War* (1978) is good about English country life during the Second World War, in which Ralph Partridge was a conscientious objector, and also tells how disagreement about the war soured the friendship between Ralph and Brenan (who still lived locally). *Everything to Lose* (1987) and *Hanging On* (1990) bring Partridge's life story up to date, including among other pleasures accounts of travel in Russia, Turkey, Mexico and India, begun when she was over 70. Like all her writings, they show her as a funny, sharp-tongued woman who, because of the follies of the society she lived in and the people she knew, sometimes seems like the only grown up at a particularly hysterical children's party.

PAUSTOVSKY, Konstantin (1893–1968)
Russian writer

Paustovsky, a leading literary journalist under Stalin, is remembered for his classic autobiography, *Story of a Life* (six volumes, 1964–70). *Childhood and Schooldays* describes his early life in Kiev and at Moscow University. *Slow Approach of Thunder* is about his service in the First World War, his political awakening and the approach of the Revolution. *In That Dawn* and *Years of Hope* cover his adventures during the Revolution and the civil war which followed. *Years of Hope* is a particularly memorable account of life in a city under siege (Odessa, beset by the White Russian army). *Southern Adventure* is about Paustovsky's days as a journalist in the Caucasus in the 1920s. *The Restless Years*, also set in the 1920s, describes Paustovsky's travels throughout Russia, and is good on such remote regions as the area between Astrakhan (on the northern shore of the Caspian Sea) and Murmansk (on the southern shore of the Barents Sea, in the Arctic Circle). We are used in the West to thinking about the Revolution as an affair of bloody politics and even bloodier repression. Paustovsky shows it as a farcical shambles, of the kind *Gogol or Hašek might have invented, and he magnificently describes the life and landscape of regions of the Soviet Union closed to westerners for half a century.

⋄ **READ ON**
Manya Harari, *Memoirs* (growing up in the last decades of Tsarist Russia). *Reginald Teague-Jones, *The Spy Who Disappeared*.

PEPYS, Samuel (1633–1703) English civil servant and diarist

After the Restoration of the monarchy in 1660, Pepys worked for the Navy Board, in charge of supplies. He was also Secretary, later President, of the Royal Society. His *Diary* runs from

⋄ **READ ON**
Geoffrey Trease, *Samuel Pepys and his World* (rather 'bufferish' text, as if written for children, but splendid illustrations). C. Marburg, *Mr Pepys and Mr Evelyn* (see *John Evelyn).

1660 to 1669, years which included the Fire of London, the Great Plague and the terrifying and unprecedented sight of a Dutch war fleet sailing up the Thames. Pepys describes all these, supplies news and gossip about court life, details his navy work, and gives endless accounts of meals eaten, theatres visited, conversations held and women lusted after. The definitive edition of his diary (R. Latham and W. Matthews eds., 1970–83) runs to 11 volumes; William Plomer (ed.) *Pepys' Diary* (1946) is a good one-volume selection. Arthur Bryant, *Pepys* (three volumes, 1933–38), for long the standard biography, is fascinating on the history, but is written in a style which present-day readers may find both laboured and patronizing. Richard Ollard, *Pepys* (1974) is an excellent one-volume account, good on the society of Pepys' time and on his voracious enthusiasm for books, plays and music.

PERON, Eva Duarte (1919–52) Argentinian politician

Eva Duarte was a star actress in radio soaps and films. After her marriage she invigorated her husband's flagging political career not just by personal appearances but by advice, guidance and – her enemies said – machinations behind the scenes. She was soon as powerful as he was, and while she lived his popular revolution (battling against the entrenched interests of the Church and the rich) hardly put a foot wrong. She worked for women's suffrage, and created the Eva Perón Foundation for Social Welfare to help the poor. After her death many witnesses claimed that her body remained unchanged, as beautiful as ever, and she was put forward as a candidate for sainthood. In the McCarthyite USA, by contrast, she was branded as a Communist Machiavelli. She is still a legend. Nicholas Fraser and Marysa Navarro, *Eva Perón* (1980) tells her story clearly and objectively, a rare achievement in books about her. J.M. Taylor, *Evita Perón, the Myths of a Woman* (1979) discusses her various legends (star, revolutionary, saint) and their sociological importance for Argentina.

> ⋄ **READ ON**
> Eva Perón, *My Mission in Life* (official autobiography and political testimony, published in 1952).

PETER I, 'the Great' (1672–1725) Russian tsar (ruled 1682–1725)

Until the rule of Peter the Great, Russia was less a united country than a group of feudal fiefdoms ruled by barons in medieval style. He brought it kicking and screaming into the Age of European Enlightenment, modernizing the navy, opening schools, centralizing administration, reducing the power of the Church, and building a new capital city (modern Leningrad) in the most glittering western style. His achievements, and his failures (re-

> ⋄ **READ ON**
> M.S. Anderson, *Peter the Great* (dry style, but good on the politics of Peter's reign).
> Christopher Marsden, *Palmyra of the North: the First Days of St Petersburg*.

tention of the serf-system; 'divide and rule' tactics with the barons, who promptly united against him; a hugely unpopular poll tax), are described in Robert K. Massie, *Peter the Great* (1981), an 800-page blockbuster which also deals well with Peter's time in the West and his foreign wars. Alex de Jong, *Fire and Water* (1979) and Henri Troyat, *Peter the Great* (Eng. ed. 1988) are shorter, and miss some of the detail. But they are both good on life in Peter's court, and are full of such unexpected, revealing touches as Peter's liking for performing animals and freaks, his love of gardening and his taste for drinking bouts as lavish, obscene and vulgar as any Roman orgy.

PICASSO, Pablo (1881–1973) Spanish artist

By working eight hours a day for 80 years, Picasso created some 20,000 works of art, of which 500 or so are acknowledged masterpieces – an achievement surpassed only by Rembrandt. For most of his life, he was the best-known artist of the century, a celebrity whose opinions, politics, marriages, arrivals and departures were headline news. There are hundreds of books about him, including one by *Gertrude Stein (*Picasso*, 1938). Jean-Paul Crespelle, *Picasso and His Women* (Eng. ed. 1969), despite its silly title, is a good, brief account of his life and personality which avoids art criticism throughout. Roland Penrose, *Picasso* (second ed. 1971) is weaker on the life – Penrose writes well only about the periods when he met Picasso personally – but outstanding on the art. Patrick O'Brien, *Pablo Ruíz Picasso* (1976) is objective and well illustrated.

> •> **READ ON**
> David Douglas Duncan, *Viva Picasso!* (magnificent picture book, with brief but helpful text). Françoise Gilot, *Life With Picasso* (by the woman who was his model, mistress, wife and the inspiration of some of his finest paintings, including *Weeping Woman* which, to hear her tell it, expresses exactly what her life with him was like. Gilot is also the author of *Matisse and Picasso: a Friendship in Art* in which she evocatively describes the relationship between the two artists as she witnessed it.) Arianna Stassinopoulos, *Picasso* ('feet of clay' biography, gossipy and anecdotal, especially about Picasso's later years. Much mocked, it's still hard to put down).

> •> PIONEERS
>
> Mary Durack, *To Be Heirs Forever*
> Lawrence Elliott, *Daniel Boone: the Long Hunter*
> George D. Lyman, *John Marsh: Pioneer. The Life Story of a Trail Blazer on Six Frontiers*
> *John Muir, *The Story of My Boyhood and Youth*
> Robert Reid, *Marie Curie*
> William Rodney, *Joe Boyle: King of the Klondyke*
> Constance Babington Smith, *Champion of Homeopathy* (Marjorie Blackie)
> Dorothy Clark Wilson, *Lone Woman* (Elizabeth Blackwell, first woman doctor)
> *See also* Beyond the Frontier; Brave New Worlds; Science and Mathematics

PLATH, Sylvia (1932–63) US writer

Plath committed suicide one month after the publication of her semi-autobiographical novel *The Bell Jar*, about a woman desperately trying to stay sane in what seems to her a predatory and hostile world. Apart from this book, she is known for poetry, much of it about love, illness and death. Since her death she has been claimed as one of the outstanding poets of her generation, and her tragic life has been seen as typical of the extremes to which a sensitive, well-educated woman can be driven in a male-dominated, male-orientated world. Books about her take sides, revealing as much about the authors' prejudices – and which side of the Atlantic they come from – as about Plath herself. Linda Wagner-Martin, *Sylvia Plath* (1988), though its American perspective on Plath's marriage to the poet Ted Hughes has been disputed, is generally admiring, good on Plath's state of mind (especially her self-punishing perfectionism) and on her poetry. Its bibliography is magnificent, even including a list of the books in Plath's personal library. Anne Stevenson, *Bitter Fame* (1989) is the English standard biography. Though it is reviled by other Plath experts because of its merciless approach to Plath's psychology and her relationship with Hughes, it is good on the links between her life and work.

⊳ **READ ON**
Sylvia Plath (ed. A.S. Plath), *Letters Home*.

PLINY THE YOUNGER (62–114) Roman politician

A career politician, Gaius Plinius Caecilius Secundus (called 'the Younger' to distinguish him from his uncle, who had the same names) worked for several Roman emperors and crowned his career by governing Bithynia (a turbulent province just south of the Black Sea). His *Letters* (ed. and trans. Betty Radice, 1963) are chatty, perceptive and full of delightful self-mockery. He tells of his daily life (revealing glimpses of the Roman upper class at work and rest), his villas, his hobbies (writing and dinner parties), his family and friends, recounts amazing events (for example the eruption of Vesuvius in 79 which engulfed Pompeii) and the gossip and scandal of the day. The last 100 letters are queries sent from Bithynia to the emperor Trajan, about how to deal with such unprecedented problems as creating a fire brigade or dealing with 'that depraved and foolish superstition' Christianity, and Trajan's patient, succinct replies.

⊳ **READ ON**
Seneca, *Letters* (similar class and period; similar contents, but more discursive and essay-like. Seneca, a philosopher who tutored the emperor *Nero, liked to ponder every issue, and loved to tell the world his thoughts).

POCAHONTAS (1595–1617) Amerindian princess

When Pocahontas (also called Mataoka) was 11, she saved the life of Captain John Smith, leader of the English settlers in Jamestown, Virginia. Five years later she married another settler, John Rolfe, and went back with him to London – the first Amerindian ever to visit Europe. Her story has since become the subject of children's books, poems, plays, paintings, operettas and ballets: one of America's most potent legends. Told straight, as historical narrative, it sheds light on the pre-Pilgrim European settlers in America, on Jacobean English attitudes to people of other races, and on the roots of the cultural incomprehension which later caused such bloodshed between settlers and native peoples in America. Philip L. Barbour, *Pocahontas and Her World* (1969) not only uses lively first-hand accounts of the English settlement in Virginia, but is excellent at seeing things from the Amerindian point of view. Frances Mossiker, *Pocahontas* (1976) covers the same ground in a similar way, but also – most entertainingly and enthusiastically – discusses Pocahontas' legend in its various manifestations, from dewy-eyed to racist, over the last four centuries.

‹› **READ ON**
Philip L. Barbour, *The Three Worlds of Captain John Smith* (wonderfully detailed account of the 'Jamestown adventure' and Smith's part in it).

‹› POINTS EAST

Kumit Chandruang, *My Boyhood in Siam*
Charlotte Haldane, *The Last Great Empress of China*
*Hsiao Ch'ien, *Traveller Without a Map*
Li Lu, *Moving the Mountain*
Siao-Yu, **Mao Tse-Tung and I Were Beggars*
*Han Suyin, *A Mortal Flower*
See also India

POLO, Marco (1254–1324) Venetian traveller

Polo, a Venetian merchant, travelled widely in Central Asia, became a confidant of Kublai Khan, and took home tales of adventures so exotic that people dismissed them as fairy stories. Henry H. Hart, *Marco Polo* (1967) is a detailed, scholarly biography, especially good on Polo's business connections and friends in Venice. Richard Humble, *Marco Polo* (1975) is shorter, good on the travels, and is illustrated with maps of the period, gorgeous pictures from early editions of Polo's book, and modern photographs of the places he visited. Both books are usefully read before Polo's own account, as they give historical and geographical sense, in modern terms, to what might

‹› **READ ON**
Gabriel Ronay, *The Tartar Khan's Englishman* (story of the English soldier and spy who worked for Genghis Khan two generations before Polo, when Mongol invaders swept west, conquering as far as the gates of Vienna).

otherwise seem as unconnected a sequence of wonder-tales as
The Arabian Nights. R.E. Latham (ed. and trans.), *The Travels of
Marco Polo* (1958) is a readable, well-annotated edition of
Polo's autobiography – and Humble's book supplies the one
missing ingredient: pictures.

POMPADOUR, Jeanne de (1721–1764)
Mistress of Louis XV

Pompadour, the beautiful daughter of a businessman, married
money, went to court, and in 1745 became the King's mistress.
Louis, unable to divorce his wife and marry her, stayed in love
with her for 20 years – largely because she worked so hard to
keep him amused and occupied. (In later years she even encouraged him to take other, shorter-term mistresses.) Nancy
*Mitford, *Madame de Pompadour* (1964) marshals vast amounts
of information about the Versailles court with verve and style,
and explains everything English readers might want to know
about France in Pompadour's time. Style – Pompadour's in
life, Mitford's in art – is of the essence here, and not a hair is
out of place.

> **READ ON**
> D.B. Wyndham Lewis, *Four
> Favourites* (includes Pompadour
> as one of four royal companions:
> the others are Godoy,
> *Melbourne and Potemkin).
> Olivier Bernier, *Louis the Beloved*
> (tiny type, but stylish and worth
> the effort).

POMPEY (Gnaeus Pompeius) (106–48 BC)
Roman general and statesman

Pompey was an inspired, unorthodox commander, beloved by
his troops and successful against every enemy except his lifelong rival, *Caesar. He was the second greatest soldier in ancient Rome; just as Caesar triumphed in the West, so he con-
quered the East. Although the two generals were warily
respectful of each other when apart, it was inevitable that ambition would lead them to fight for supremacy, and that the conflict would threaten Rome itself. Even then, Pompey might
have won if he had not been treacherously murdered by *Cleopatra as a love-gift for Caesar. Peter Greenhalgh, *Pompey: the
Roman Alexander* (1980) charts his dazzling career to 59 BC
(when he made an uneasy, short-lived political truce with
Caesar), and *Pompey: the Republican Prince* (1981) covers the
civil war. Greenhalgh's style is vivid, his scholarship is efficient
but unobtrusive, his descriptions of ancient battles and long-
past politics are as clear as if the events had happened yesterday.

> **READ ON**
> Julius Caesar, *The Civil War*. R.
> Seager, *Pompey: a Political
> Biography*.

PORTER, Hal (1911–84) Australian writer

Porter is known for short stories, novels, and *The Watcher on the
Cast Iron Balcony* (1963), the first volume of his autobiography.

> **READ ON**
> Hal Porter, *The Paper Chase*; *The
> Extra* (sequels). *Elias Canetti,
> *The Tongue Set Free* (about a

It is a stylish, even 'peacocky' account of his life to the age of 18, full of minute social detail of the 1920s, and a moving portrait of his beloved, scatterbrained mother, with whose death the book – and Porter's childhood – end.

European childhood 20 years before Porter's, but an equally striking account of the relationship between a young boy and his adored mother).

POTTER, Beatrix (1866–1943) English writer and artist

Generations of small children have loved Potter's books about Peter Rabbit, Mrs Tiggy-Winkle and others, with their meticulous illustrations of animals in tweeds and calico dresses, playing house in late-Victorian kitchens and withdrawing-rooms. The charm of Potter's work tends to stay with its fans well into adult life, and they – as well as other grown-ups immune to its tweeness – will be fascinated by her own story. She was a rebel, choosing to be a nature artist at a time when painting was considered no career for well-brought-up young women. Broken-hearted after the early death of her fiancé, she lived alone for 30 years, then made a late and very happy marriage. She kept out of London society, farming in the Lake District and supporting countryside causes – something which, in London literary circles if not in the real world, earned her the reputation as a recluse. There are two main biographies, equally affectionate and crammed with Potter's own pictures, so that there is little but the dates to choose between them: Margaret Lane, *The Tale of Beatrix Potter* (1946, rev. ed. 1984) and Judy Taylor, *Beatrix Potter* (1986).

⊰ **READ ON**
Judy Taylor (ed.), *The Journal of Beatrix Potter; Beatrix Potter's Letters.* Leslie Linder, *The History of the Writings of Beatrix Potter.*

POUND, Ezra (1885–1972) US writer

As a young man, Pound bullied or charmed all his friends into sharing his taste for way-out ideas in literature and art. He loved ancient Greek and Chinese writings on the one hand, and modernist experiment on the other. The poets he encouraged included cummings, *Eliot and *William Carlos Williams, and he was a friend of (among others) *Hemingway, *Stein and Yeats. In the 1920s he began to speak out for Fascism, and during the war he made broadcasts from Italy so pro-Nazi that he was nicknamed 'the Italian Lord Haw-Haw'. In a lunatic asylum in Pisa after the war, he finished the *Pisan Cantos*, described by some as masterpieces and by others as gibberish.

Pound was a troubled man, and his trouble was typical of one kind of intellectual questing – not to mention intellectual arrogance – during this century. Noel Stock, *The Life of Ezra Pound* (1970) is the standard biography, and Peter Conrad, *Ezra Pound and His World* (1980) is a good introduction to both man and work. Other interesting books, by people who knew

⊰ **READ ON**
D.D. Paige (ed.), *The Selected Letters of Ezra Pound.* Dorothy Pound (his first wife), *Etruscan Gate.* Mary de Rachewiltz (his daughter), *Discretions.* Wyndham Lewis (fellow revolutionary), *Blasting and Bombardiering.* William Carlos *Williams, *Autobiography.*

Pound or tried to work out what made him tick, are Hugh Kenner, *The Pound Era* (1972); 'H.D.', *An End to Torment* (1979); Michael Reck, *Ezra Pound, a Close-up* (1967).

POWELL, Margaret (1907–84) English writer

In the 1960s Powell had great success with two books about her life in domestic service in the 1920s: *Below Stairs* (1968) and *Climbing the Stairs* (1969). She followed them with *The Treasure Upstairs* (1977), about how she educated herself at night school, and became a successful author and TV personality. They are in an outspoken, witty style: 'how naive we all were then' autobiographies laced with common sense.

> **READ ON**
> Margaret Powell, *My Mother and I*; *Albert and I*; *My Children and I*. Jean Rennie, *Every Other Sunday* (harsher-toned account of similar life and times).

POWELL, Violet (born 1912) English writer

Powell is known for biographies, including the best selling *The Irish Cousins* (1970), about Somerville and Ross, the authors of *Some Experiences of an Irish R.M.* and *Further Experiences of an Irish R.M.*. She has also published several volumes of autobiography. *Five Out of Six* (1960) is about growing up in a large, upper-class Anglo-Irish household – a delightful example of the 'big house full of eccentric relatives' school of autobiography. *Within the Family Circle* (1976) is equally funny about her relatives, but this time counterpoints their antics with darker themes: the Depression, the Slump, the atmosphere of frantic self-indulgence and political humbug as Europe lurched towards the Second World War.

> **READ ON**
> Jessica Mitford, *Hons and Rebels*. Anthony Powell (Violet's husband), *To Keep the Ball Rolling* (sequence of memoirs).

> THE POWER BEHIND THE THRONE

Paul F. Boller, *Presidential Wives*
Anthony Bridges, *Theodora
Iris Butler, *Rule of Three* (Abigail Hill, Queen Anne and Sarah, *Duchess of Marlborough)
Molly Hardwick, *Mrs Dizzy* (Mary Anne Disraeli)
Edna Healey, *Wives of Fame* (Emma Darwin, Mary Livingstone, *Jenny Marx)
Kitty Kelley, *Nancy Reagan: The Unauthorized Biography*
Anny Latour, *Uncrowned Queens* (women who moulded the society they lived in: Isabella d'Este, the French literary hostesses, the Bluestockings, Princess Belgiojoso, *Gertrude Stein . . .)
Phyllis Lee Lewis, *Abigail Adams
Carola Oman, *Napoléon's Viceroy* (*JosephineBeauharnais)

> Vera Weizmann, *The Impossible Takes Longer* (the memoirs of the wife of Israel's first president)

PRESLEY, Priscilla (born 1942) US actress

Priscilla Beaulieu met Elvis Presley when she was 14, was infatuated by the time she was 16, and married him at 24. Priscilla Beaulieu Presley (with Sandra Harmon), *Elvis and Me* (1985) is an honest account of their relationship, which ended in divorce because she felt that she could never live up to the image he had of her, and that his drug habit was taking him beyond her reach. It is, however, neither a 'sleaze and tease' book nor a story for anyone who thinks Elvis next best thing to God. The prime feeling it gives is of perfectly ordinary people, deeply in love, one of whose personality is torn in two because he is a global superstar. One could pick up this book for entirely the wrong reason (to see the dirty linen of the great and famous being washed in public?), and end up both surprised and moved.

> **‹› READ ON**
> Michael Edwards, *Priscilla, Elvis and Me* (about how a glamorous male model began an affair with Priscilla Presley after Elvis' death, only to find career, other lovers and – as he puts it – 'Elvis' ghost' driving them apart). Albert Goldman, *Elvis* (definitive 'dirty linen' biography of Elvis).

PRITCHETT, V(ictor) S(awdon) (born 1900) English writer

Pritchett's father was a religious bigot and a domestic bully in the most heavy-handed Victorian style. The boy escaped at 15 into the leather trade, then to France where he worked in a photography studio before becoming a journalist and writer. As well as novels and short stories he has written two volumes of elegant, ironical autobiography. *A Cab at the Door* (1968) describes his Edwardian childhood and adolescence, a story of genteel poverty, first job and sexual awakening. It is very like *H.G. Wells' tales of the youth of such characters as Kipps or Mr Polly – except for the ever-present, overbearing figure of Pritchett's father. *Midnight Oil* (1971) deals with Pritchett's life between the two World Wars, and is excellent on his travels in Ireland, France and Spain, his literary progress and his reaction to the Spanish Civil War.

> **‹› READ ON**
> V.S. Pritchett, *You Make Your Own Life and Other Stories* (short stories set among the same kind of people as those in *A Cab at the Door*).

PROUST, Marcel (1871–1922) French writer

All biographies of Proust stand in the shadow of his own work, the enormous novel *Remembrance of Things Past*. Each of its seven sections is self-contained, and the first and last (*Swann's Way* and *Time Regained*) are especially autobiographical, describing respectively the childhood and old age of a rich, sensitive man-about-town in French aristocratic society before the First World War. George Painter, *Marcel Proust: A Biogra-*

> **‹› READ ON**
> Céleste Albaret, *Monsieur Proust* (intimate memoir by Proust's housekeeper, who nursed him for his last, bed-ridden nine years, and – as she tells it – discussed every detail of his novel with him as he wrote it). George Pickering, *Creative Malady* (about how psychological

phy (1959–65; one volume ed. 1983) magnificently, magisterially recreates Proust's own life, linking it to passages in the novel. It is as long, and as absorbing, as Proust's own book. Ronald Hayman, *Proust* (1990) is shorter (though still 564 pages long), more readable, and outstanding on Proust's personality and other literary and social grandees in the France of his time.

illness was vital to the work of well-known people: the Proust chapter is particularly illuminating).

PU-YI (1906–67) Chinese emperor (ruled 1908–12)

Enthroned at three years old, Pu-Yi was plunged straight into the rigorous but meaningless political charades of the imperial court. After the proclamation of the Republic in 1912 he was held pawn by one side or the other, and was imprisoned by the Russians from 1945 to 1950. He returned to China as a model Communist. Brian Power, *The Last Emperor* (1986) recounts his life in the style of itinerant Chinese storytellers. At first the book reads stiffly, but its gentle, hypnotic rhythms soon become compulsive. Power's main concession to western-style biography is a descant of despair at the way foreigners and the Chinese ruling class consistently misread or ignore the feelings of ordinary Chinese. Neville John Irons, *The Last Emperor* (1983) is a more orthodox biography, drawing on a wider range of sources, good on Pu-Yi's feelings, both as child and adult, and more partisan than Power on his behalf.

⋅> READ ON
Pu-Yi, *From Emperor to Citizen* (heavily party-line 'autobiography' published in 1964). Reginald F. Johnston, *Twilight in the Forbidden City* (autobiography by the child emperor's Scottish tutor). Brian Power, *The Ford of Heaven* (account of the author's life in Tientsin, where Pu-Yi lived in seclusion for several years). *See also* *T'zu-Hsi.

R

RALEGH, Walter (c1552–1618) English courtier

Handsome, witty and a dandy, Ralegh became *Elizabeth I's favourite almost as soon as he went to court in 1582. She gave
him titles, land and money; he financed expeditions to the New
World and against the Spanish. He fell out of favour when the
Queen discovered his love for her maid-of-honour Elizabeth
Throckmorton, and when James I came to the throne, anxious to
make peace with Spain, Ralegh was condemned to death and
imprisoned in the Tower. He spent 13 years there, writing and
doing scientific experiments, then was freed (to make a last expedition to the Caribbean), only to be rearrested and beheaded
on his return. He was one of the most brilliant lights of the English Renaissance, and his fall was also typical of the intrigue and
arbitrariness which also characterized that dazzling age. R. Irwin,
That Great Lucifer (1960) is good on this (*and see* Read On). J.H.
Adamson and H.F. Follard, *The Shepherd of the Ocean* (1969) is
outstanding on Ralegh's seafaring. Andrew Sinclair, *Ralegh and
the Age of Discovery* is an excellent modern biography.

⋗ **READ ON**
Stephen J. Greenblatt, *Sir Walter
Ralegh* (biographical study
claiming that Ralegh, like many
Renaissance grandees, tried to
live his life as if it were a work
of art. Unusual, well-written
book, shedding light on several
areas of Ralegh's life, and on his
complex relationship with that
other play-actor, Elizabeth).

RANSOME, Arthur (1884–1967) English writer

A journalist, Ransome had one of the scoops of the century: he
was in Moscow when the Russian Revolution began, and
covered it for the *Daily News*. On his return to England he
settled to a quieter life of sailing, fishing and walking. He is
remembered for the series of children's books beginning with
Swallows and Amazons, and for *The Autobiography of Arthur Ransome* (1976), whose centre-piece, flanked by sections on his
youth and his middle age, is a lively account of his time in Russia, almost breathless with excitement. Hugh Brogan, *Arthur

⋗ **READ ON**
Christine Hardiment, *Arthur
Ransome and Captain Flint's
Trunk*(account of the real people
and places behind *Swallows and
Amazons*– an addicts' treasure-
trove).

Ransome (1984) beautifully catches the way Ransome seemed able to switch in an instant from boyishness to worldliness, from shyness to garrulousness, on all kinds of abstruse and fascinating lore – a quality not only of the man but of his books.

RASPUTIN, Grigoriy Efimovich (1871–1916) Russian seer

Rasputin ('debauched one') began his hypnotic, mystical career before puberty, seeing visions and 'healing' animals by the laying-on of hands. In his teens he added seduction to his repertoire, claiming that spiritual and sexual ecstasy were linked and that he was a vehicle for both. His hold on the Russian court was due either to his power to help the Crown Prince's haemophilia, or to sexual enslavement of the Tsarina. What you believed depended on your politics, so that nobles, for example, who felt that Rasputin (a commoner) was displacing them as imperial adviser/puppet-master, sought his death. 'Mad monk' or true visionary, his story is as absorbing as it is sordid, and the truth of it is elusive, the evidence incomplete. R.J. Minney, *Rasputin* (1972) tells what is known, with a mixture of historian's wariness and wide-eyed relish which ideally suits the subject and the times.

> ⬦ **READ ON**
> Prince Youssoupoff, *Rasputin: His Evil Influence and His Murder, by One of the Men Who Killed Him* (lurid 1927 'biography', chief origin of the 'mad monk' legend and full of self-congratulation by the author). Maria Rasputin (Rasputin's daughter, a circus lion-tamer), *Rasputin, The Man Behind the Myth* (novelettish style, gushy dialogue and sexual explicitness make up for lack of historical completeness or objectivity. One of the oddest books any daughter can ever have written about her father).

RATUSHINSKAYA, Irina (born 1954) Russian poet

A Christian and a dissident in the dying days of Brezhnev's USSR, Ratushinskaya was imprisoned in 1983, and was freed only after months of campaigning by friends and fellow writers in the West. She emigrated just before the coming of *glasnost* – an ironical twist to a dismal tale. She has written two books of autobiography, *In the Beginning* (1990), about her childhood and that of her future husband, already rebelling against the party line taught in schools, and *Grey is the Colour of Hope* (1988), about her struggle with the authorities, her imprisonment and her release. Dick Rodgers, *Irina* (1987) is a good, if biased, account of her life so far.

> ⬦ **READ ON**
> Alexander Solzhenitsyn, *One Day in the Life of Ivan Denisovich*(grim, autobiographical novel set in a prison camp a generation before Ratushinskaya).

RAY, Man (1890–1976) US artist

From his teens Ray was a modernist, eagerly trying each new movement (Cubism, Dadaism, Surrealism) as it came along. With Duchamp and Picabia, he introduced Dadaism to a startled New York in 1915; in the 1920s he worked with *Picasso, *Dalí and others in Paris, and in the 1930s he had a hilariously bumpy time in Hollywood. He was a leading photographer, and

> ⬦ **READ ON**
> Roland Penrose, *Man Ray* (biographical study, notably good on Ray's relationship with the Surrealists).

pioneered techniques of 'solarizing' photographs to produce unique effects of contrast and composition. *Self Portrait* (1963) is a lively biography, with clear accounts of how he worked and zestful, quirky descriptions of the people he knew: he claims for example to have all but fainted with bewilderment when he first met Matisse (who looked like a French bank manager), because he had previously known him only in a self-portrait with a neatly trimmed green beard. The 1990 edition of this book, with an afterword by Ray's wife Juliet, is crammed with illustrations, many published for the first time and all extraordinary.

❖ REFLECTIONS OF THEIR AGE

Peter Brent, *The Edwardians* (includes *Horatio Bottomley, Marie Lloyd, E. Nesbit, Rolls and Royce)
*Benvenuto Cellini, *Autobiography*
April FitzLyon, *The Libertine Librettist* (*Lorenzo da Ponte)
Leonard Mosley, *Lindbergh*
*Pliny the Younger, *Letters*
Keith B. Poole, *The Two Beaux* (*Brummell and Nash)
*Gertrude Stein, *The Autobiography of Alice B. Toklas*
*Lytton Strachey, *Eminent Victorians* (Manning, *Nightingale, Arnold, Gordon)
John Sugden, *Sir Francis Drake*

RENOIR, Auguste (1841–1919) French painter

Renoir was a leading Impressionist, known especially for his nudes: he found more, and more sensuous, flesh tones than almost any other artist. Jean Renoir, *Renoir My Father* (Eng. ed. 1962) is a classic: a warm, poetic memoir by his son, the film director. It is part biography, part autobiography, outstanding on atmosphere and on the excitement and difficulties of developing one's own artistic personality while living with a genius. Most editions are illustrated with well-chosen family photos and with Renoir's paintings of his wife and children. M. Drucker, *Renoir* (1944) is a more objective, art-historical biography.

❖ **READ ON**
Jean Renoir, *My Life and My Films* (autobiography, good on conditions in wartime France, on Renoir's time in India and Hollywood, and about work on such masterpieces as *The Grand Illusion* and *Rules of the Game*).

RICHARD III (1452–85) English king (ruled 1483–85)

Biographies of Richard either follow the propaganda put out by Henry Tudor (who supplanted him) which formed the basis of *Shakespeare's play, or take a briskly contrary view. The Tudor line on Richard – deformed monster, murderer of the

❖ **READ ON**
James Gardner, *History of the Life and Reign of Richard III* (1878 'anti-Richard' book which reopened the controversy in modern times. Clements Markham, *Richard III, His Life and Character* (1906 counterblast

Princes in the Tower – is forcefully presented in A.L. Rowse *Bosworth Field* (1966). Books taking the opposite view, that Henry was a usurper and may himself have had a hand in the Princes' murder, range from Paul Murray Kendall, *Richard III* (1955), a scholarly biography, to Josephine Tey, *The Daughter of Time* (1951), a modern detective story in which the sleuth 'solves' the historical mystery from his hospital bed. P.W. Hammond and Anne F. Sutton, *Richard III: The Road to Bosworth Field* (1985) is a weighty historical study, quoting source documents in medieval spelling: fascinating for anyone interested in Richard and who knows the other books. Jeremy Potter, *Good King Richard* (1983) tells the story of the historians' view of Richard, and in passing discusses the whole question of sources, traditions and their interpretation. Potter, chairman of the British Richard III society, is hardly impartial, but gives everyone a hearing, from *Thomas More to Horace Walpole and *Jane Austen.

and Character(1906 counterblast to Gardner). Rosemary Horrox, *Richard III: a Study of Service* (academic study of the times, from the point of view of the noblemen who served or opposed Richard. A remarkable insight into medieval concepts of kingship and service).

ROBESON, Paul (1898–1976) US singer and actor

The US people never forgave Robeson for combining three things in one person: he was talented, black and a Communist. For a time, in the 1930s, they tolerated his colour and his politics because of his enormous success in musicals (such as *Showboat*) and stage plays (*The Emperor Jones* and *Othello*). But as soon as he began to use his position to champion integration and to speak out against poverty and the hysterical anti-Communism of the McCarthy era, they turned on him. The story of how he coped, and of what it cost him in terms of career, health and happiness, is tragic and shaming: he was like a colossus destroyed by ants. Martin Bauml Duberman, *Paul Robeson* (1989) is a large, magnificently documented biography, and it will make you weep – for Robeson, and for America.

◇ **READ ON**
Paul Robeson, *Here I Stand* (combined autobiography and political manifesto, published in 1958 to enormous, stage-managed press hysteria, and still uncomfortable to read today).

ROB ROY: *see* MacGREGOR, Robert

◇ ROCK AND POP

Massimo Bonanno, *The Rolling Stones Chronicle*
Ray Coleman, *John Lennon*
John Densmore, *Riders on the Storm: My Life with Jim Morrison and The Doors*
Myra Friedman, *Janis Joplin: Buried Alive*
*Bob Geldof, *Is That It?*
Albert Goldman, *Elvis*

> Dylan Jones, *Dark Star* (Jim Morrison)
> Bruce Thomas, The Big Wheel
> Ivan Waterman, *The Life and Death of a Rock Legend* (Keith Moon)
> Bill Wyman, *Stone Alone*

RODGERS, Richard (1902–79) US songwriter

Rodgers' autobiography *Musical Stages* (1975) is the story of a man blessed by the gods, able to write songs as fluently as other people sign their names, an expert craftsman of musical shows who was successful from the moment he left college for over 50 years. He worked with the greatest names on Broadway and in Hollywood, and his book reads like a catalogue of US showbusiness – not to mention telling us all the backstage/ backscreen gossip about the creation and production of such hits as *On Your Toes, Babes in Arms, Pal Joey, Oklahoma!, Carousel, South Pacific, The King and I* and *The Sound of Music.*

◇ **READ ON**
Dorothy Hart (ed.), *Thou Swell, Thou Witty: the Life and Lyrics of Lorenz Hart.*

ROLFE, Frederick William (1860–1913) English writer

Literary England knew Rolfe as an eccentric, minor novelist, whose best-known book was *Hadrian the Seventh* (1904), about an ordinary man (a reject for the priesthood) who is unexpectedly made Pope. But Rolfe was also 'Fr Rolfe' and 'Baron Corvo', conmen preying on the well-heeled in Europe (especially Venice) and enjoying numerous homosexual adventures. Or were these characters too inventions of Rolfe's overheated brain? The man would be a footnote in the history of the Gay Nineties were it not for A.J.A. Symons, *The Quest for Corvo* (1934), a biography of Rolfe written with such zest, and unearthing such bizarre characters and incidents that it reads itself like one of the wilder fictions of that steamy, Beardsleyan age.

◇ **READ ON**
Arthur Symons, *Aubrey Beardsley.*

ROMMEL, Erwin (1891–1944) German soldier

Partly because of his dazzling African campaigns, and partly because he was implicated in the 1944 plot against *Hitler and was forced to commit suicide, the 'Desert Fox' had, and has, a greater hold on British imagination than any other German commander of the Second World War. Charles Douglas-Hume, *Rommel* (1973) and Ward Rutherford, *Rommel* (1981) are absorbing, well-documented accounts of his life and campaigns. Both are copiously illustrated, Rutherford in black and white, Douglas-Hume in colour. David Irving, *The Trail of the Fox: the Life of Field Marshal Erwin Rommel*(1977), in addi-

◇ **READ ON**
Basil Liddell Hart (ed.), *The Rommel Papers. See also* *Montgomery.

tion to telling Rommel's life, discusses the reasons for his reputation at home and abroad, and is interesting to read in tandem with Rutherford, as it often interprets the same events (for example the 1944 plot) in a completely different way.

ROOSEVELT family

Theodore Roosevelt (1858–1919) became the 26th US president when McKinley was shot in 1901. He was a red-blooded, Republican patriot, who did much to push the USA centre-stage in world affairs. He published a typically zestful *Autobiography* (1913). Edmund Morris, *The Rise of Theodore Roosevelt* (1979), is written in portly prose, but even so, Roosevelt's extraordinary personality comes bursting through. He was a man of enormous physical energy, hunting, fishing, Japanese-wrestling in the White House library. He was also intellectually tireless, a linguist, historian, ornithologist and voracious reader of books of any and every kind.

However remarkable 'Teddy' was, even he pales beside his cousin 'FDR': Franklin Delano Roosevelt (1882–1945), the Democrat who served a record four terms as President. James MacGregor Burns, *Roosevelt: the Lion and the Fox* (1956), first of a magisterial two-volume biography, is good on Roosevelt's character and on his 1930s efforts (still controversial) to pull the USA from economic disaster to a prosperity befitting their status as a leading world political power. Burns' second volume, *Roosevelt: the Soldier of Freedom* (1970) continues Roosevelt's story, as he led his country in the Second World War. Joseph Alsop, *The Life and Times of Franklin D. Roosevelt* (1982) is good not only on the politics, but also on the Roosevelt family background to which Alsop himself belonged.

Eleanor Roosevelt (1884–1962), FDR's cousin and wife, worked tirelessly on her husband's behalf, masking private sternness with public compassion and warmth of character. When she discovered that FDR had been unfaithful, she started to live her own life, and continued it long after his death: travelling, campaigning against war, and working for a host of good causes and organizations, including the UN. Joseph P. Lash, *Eleanor and Franklin* (1971) and *Eleanor: the Years Alone* (1972) is by a leading US Roosevelt scholar who was Eleanor's friend. Roosevelt herself published two volumes of memoirs (*The Lady of the White House*, 1938; *On My Own*, 1959) and an *Autobiography* (1962).

ROSSETTI, Christina (1830–94) English poet

Sickly, reclusive and melancholy, Rossetti wrote poems which seem to hint at a much more vibrant, energetic interior life, a

-> **READ ON**
Elliott Roosevelt and James Brough, *An Untold Story – The Roosevelts of Hyde Park*; *A Rendezvous with Destiny – The Roosevelts of the White House*; *Mother R. – Eleanor Roosevelt's Untold Story* (memoirs, in slightly 'tabloid' English, by one of the Roosevelt children). James Roosevelt (with Bill Libby), *My Parents – a Differing View* (exactly what the title says, and interesting on the advantages and drawbacks of a White House upbringing, both in his own and other presidential families). James Roosevelt, *Affectionately, FDR: a Son's Story*.

-> **READ ON**
Margaret Sawtell, *Christina Rossetti, Her Life and Religion* (short, selective, persuasive). S. Weintraub, *Four Rossettis* (good

secret which biographers seek to unlock with the help of clues from her everyday existence. Her Christian faith is one such 'deeper current' (as her brother D.G. Rossetti put it); another is sexual timidity or frustration (perhaps caused by an unrequited love affair). Lona Mosk Packer, *Christina Rossetti* (1963) is the standard biography, linking life and work, with expert criticism of Rossetti's poems. Georgina Battiscombe, *Christina Rossetti* (1981), supplementing the same evidence with the results of research done since Packer's book was published, reaches somewhat different conclusions. Either Rossetti yields up her secrets (if you accept either of these accounts) or keeps them; whatever the case, the evidence is fascinating.

on Christina's relationships with her erratic, talented family. *See also* *Dante Gabriel Rossetti).

ROSSETTI, Dante Gabriel (1828–82) English artist and poet

Rossetti's paintings and poems are a characteristically Pre-Raphaelite blend of mysticism and mock-medieval (some say coy) stylistic simplicity. His private life similarly blended bohemianism with a self-tormenting, very Victorian view of his own sexual and creative drives. He was a passionate, haunted man – and knowing it, playing the part to the hilt, was vital to his life. Oswald Doughty, *A Victorian Romantic*(1960) is a classic of biography, 700 pages of lucid prose based on research so thorough that it seems to leave nothing more to say. It has evocative illustrations and a full bibliography. Rosalie Glynn Grylls, *Portrait of Rossetti* (1964), one third as long, is necessarily faster-moving, but is good on Rossetti's character and quotes generously from letters. Brian and Judy Dobbs, *Dante Gabriel Rossetti: an Alien Victorian* (1977) treats Rossetti as a historical and psychological case-study: a man of his times who fought against those times.

⟶ READ ON
Gale Pedrick, *Life With Rossetti* (entertaining account of life in the Rossetti household, centred on Harry Treffry Dunn, who lived with the Rossettis for 20 years, beginning as their house-guest, ending as Rossetti's business manager, art assistant and curator of his private zoo). Gay Daly, *Pre-Raphaelites in love* (zestful group biography). *See also* *William Morris, *Christina Rossetti.

ROSSINI, Gioacchino (1792–1868) Italian composer

Rossini lived two entirely separate lives. Until 1829 he was a leading opera composer, producing one or two new works each year and supervising their production – and playing his full part in the attendant backstage scandals – in theatres all over Europe. He retired at 37, and spent the rest of his life as a *bon viveur* and elder statesman of music, composing little but salon pieces, and famous for his waspish tongue ('Wagner's music has wonderful moments, but terrible quarters of an hour'). Nicholas Till, *Rossini, His Life and Times*(1983) catches the spirit of both the man and his times, and is marvellously illustrated. Herbert Weinstock, *Rossini* (1968) is more sober about

⟶ READ ON
Stendhal, *Life of Rossini* (extraordinary document, first published in 1824: not so much a biography as a scream of rage about opera styles of the time: a fiery issue. Of mainly specialist interest, but wonderful for specialists).

Rossini's personality and public life, but goes deeper into his music.

ROTHSCHILD family

Meyer Amschel Rothschild (1743–1812), founder of the dynasty, foresaw that fortunes could be made by bankers and investors during the various European wars and revolutions of his time. From his base in Frankfurt, he sent his sons to set up banks in various European capitals, and by 1815 (when Nathan Meyer Rothschild I (1777–1836) made £1 million by speculating, with insider information, on the result of the Battle of Waterloo) the family was established at the heart of European finance. Shrewd investment in new industries (for example railways) vastly increased their wealth, as did the negotiation (for which they were uniquely well placed) of international, inter-governmental loans. They poured their money back in philanthropic gestures, and have been especially vigorous for Jewish causes. F. Morton, *The Rothschilds* (1962) is a fascinating family history – not to mention a study of international politics, business, philanthropy, scientific experiment and art patronage in the last two centuries.

> **·> READ ON**
> Miriam Rothschild, *Dear Lord Rothschild* (affectionate biography, by his niece, of **Lionel Walter Rothschild** (1868–1937), an expert on insects who set up a world-renowned Natural History Museum at Tring, Hertfordshire, and whose research did much to advance the cause of Darwinism. He also served as an MP and was one of the main instigators of the 1917 Balfour Declaration which promised British support for a Jewish homeland in Palestine).

ROUSSEAU, Jean-Jacques (1712–78) French writer

Reviled in Britain for 150 years for his advocacy of revolution as the best way for the downtrodden to cast off their political and social shackles, Rousseau has recently been rehabilitated as one of the most amusing, enlightened and spirited people of his time. His *Confessions* (1781) are egocentric and none too truthful, but give a lively picture of his early years (from the time when he was abandoned by his father, to his finding a post as a rich woman's footman and 'toy boy'), his intellectual awakening, especially to music, his life in the theatre, his love-affair with Thérèse Lavasseur, and his constant struggle against political reactionaries. Maurice Cranston, *Jean-Jacques* (1983), covering Rousseau's first 42 years, is outstanding on the development of his thought and its relationship to attitudes of his time, but – such is the man's nature – it also reads like a more than usually juicy 18th-century novel: *Tom Jones*, perhaps, reset in Switzerland and France.

> **·> READ ON**
> Maurice Cranston, *The Noble Savage* (second volume, covering 1754–62, the high peak of Rousseau's work for intellectual and political revolution). Joseph Shearing, *The Angel of the Assassination* (study of Corday, Marat, Lux: three 'disciples' of Rousseau).

THE ROYAL FAMILY

(Biographies of the British Royal Family)
So many books have been written about the main members of the British royal family (Queen, Queen Mother, Prince and

> **·> READ ON**
> Caroline Latham and Jeannie Sabel, *The Royals* (irreverent titbits, alphabetically arranged). *See also* *Edward VII, *Windsor.

Princess of Wales) that the basic material is stretched to transparency. There are dozens of books about lesser royals: even babies, dogs and vehicles have inspired 'biographies'. Some writers are so anxious to uphold the whole institution of royalty that their chosen people are presented like beings from some germ-free, not to say character-free, never-never-land. Other books shamelessly retell private conversations verbatim, usually making the royals speak 'tabloidese'. Most books are magnificently illustrated, and several authors specialize in royal books. There is, in short, plenty for every taste, and we have listed only books with something extra to offer, books which stand out from the crowd.

HM the Queen	Robert Lacey, *Majesty* (1977); Elizabeth Longford, *Elizabeth R* (1983)
Prince Charles	Anthony Holden, *Charles, Prince of* Wales (1979); *Charles*(1988)
Princess Diana	Robert Lacey, *Princess* (1982); Susan Lowry, *The Princess in the Mirror* (1985)
Prince and Princess of Wales	Graham and Heather Fisher, *Charles and Diana* (1984)
Queen Mother	Elizabeth Longford, *The Queen Mother*(1981); Patrick Montague-Smith, *Queen Elizabeth the Queen Mother* (1985)
Princess Royal	Brian Hoey, *Anne the Princess Royal: Her Life and Work*(1989); John Parker, *The Princess Royal* (1989)
Duke of Edinburgh	John Parker, *Prince Philip*
Whole family	John Pearson, *The Ultimate Family: The Making of the House of Windsor* (1986)

RUBINSTEIN, Artur (1888–1982) Polish pianist

Rubinstein's concert career lasted for 80 years, and he was still playing 100 concerts a year in his 90s. Off the platform, although he withdrew periodically from public life to recoup his mental energies by meditation and musical study, in general he had a high old time. He knew everyone, from presidents to racecourse touts, society designers to film stars. He travelled, gambled, gossiped, seduced women and basked in being lionized (and in outsmarting other kings of the jungle, for example famous conductors) wherever he went. His memoirs are a feat to rival even his concert-giving: their 1,000 lively pages were dictated from memory in his late 80s. They tell his life, one day at a time, in a gossipy, buttonholing way which describes everything: each encore played, each one-liner delivered, each smoked-salmon sandwich and bottle of champagne. Rubinstein the raconteur could give Rubinstein the pianist a run for his money any day, and these memoirs will delight lovers of music and anecdote alike. *My Young Years* (1973) deals with his youth in Poland, his education (including stormy sessions with Pader-

⊳ READ ON

George Antheil, *The Bad Boy of Music* (more 'they don't make 'em like that any more' memoirs, this time by a leading 1920s avant garde composer-about-town).

ewski) and his early triumphs. *My Many Years* (1980) covers the inexhaustible, gaudy pageant of the rest of his life. Where did he find the energy?

RUPERT, Prince of the Rhine (1619–82) German/English prince

After growing up in a Germany torn by the Thirty Years War (in which one of the first losers was his father, the Elector Palatine Frederick V), Rupert went to England at 16 to fight for his uncle *Charles I in the Civil War. He was a dazzling tactician, inventing a new kind of cavalry charge, but inexperience still lost him the only battle he actually commanded, Marston Moor. After Charles' death he turned to piracy, commanding a privateer on the Spanish Main, in the Atlantic and the Mediterranean, before being recalled to Britain at the Restoration and acting as Admiral in the Dutch Wars. On retirement from active service he busied himself learning languages, supporting the newly formed Royal Society, doing scientific research and enjoying the company of such people as *Evelyn, Locke and *Wren. He invented, among many other things, mezzotint engraving, a gunpowder many times more powerful than any used before, an early form of machine gun and new kinds of water pump. Patrick Morah, *Prince Rupert of the Rhine* (1976) – using and acknowledging Eliot Warburton, *Memoirs of Prince Rupert and the Cavaliers* (three volumes, 1849) – is outstanding on both the man and his times: a long book which may still be a one-sitting read.

> **READ ON**
> George Malcolm Thomson, *Warrior Prince* (1976) (excellent short account). Josephine Ross, *The Winter Queen* (biography of Rupert's equally characterful mother Elizabeth, Queen of Bohemia and daughter of James I). *See also* *Charles I and *Cromwell.

RUSH, Len (born 1908) English pigeon-fancier

The son of a Fenland farmworker, Rush spent his childhood crow-scaring, hay-making and looking after the huge horses which pulled the ploughs. From the age of eight he was fascinated by racing pigeons, and he became one of the leading breeders and racers in the Fancy. In 1962 Queen *Elizabeth II (one of whose summer palaces was just up the road at Sandringham) appointed him Royal Lofts Manager, setting the seal on the career of a gentle, happy man. Len Rush, *Captain of the Queen's Flight* (1987) is a placid autobiography, fascinating both for what it tells of long-vanished country life and for its detail about the Fancy. It was co-authored by Joy Chamberlain, and reads as if spoken, not written, in a ruminative Norfolk burr, punctuated by pipe-puffs and sips of good, strong tea.

> **READ ON**
> Sheila Stewart, *Lifting the Latch* (about the life of Rush's contemporary Mart Abbott, an Oxfordshire farmboy, labourer and shepherd). *Carl Nielsen, *My Childhood* (rural Denmark 120 years ago, but similar anecdotes and a similar feel for country ways).

RUSSELL, Bertrand (1872–1970) English philosopher

By training, Russell was a mathematician and philosopher who wrote (with Alfred Whitehead) a pioneering work on mathematical logic, *Principia Mathematica*. In private life he vociferously championed several things hated by the Establishment: atheism, free love, pacifism, Communism, nuclear disarmament. He was a popular speaker and broadcaster, partly because he looked and sounded like everyone's idea of an Oxbridge professor, and partly because what he said contradicted this, being passionate, witty, often outrageous, and easy to understand. These are also qualities of *The Autobiography of Bertrand Russell*(three volumes, 1967–9), dictated with huge gusto when he was in his late 80s. Ronald Clark, *Bertrand Russell* (1975), the standard biography, is drier, but manages the rare trick of explaining to readers exactly what a towering intellect is thinking about, and what that thinking means. It is also good on Russell's political mischievousness, and on his busy sex life.

‹› **READ ON**
Ronald Clark, *Bertrand Russell and his World* (brief, well-illustrated biography). Alistair Cooke, *Six Men* (memorable portrait of Russell, among Cooke's other friends). Katharine Tait, *My Father, Bertrand Russell.*

RUSSELL, Dora (born 1894) English campaigner

A pioneer of women's liberation, Russell took a Cambridge degree in 1915, was one of the first women to stand for the British Parliament, and fought for birth-control, maternity leave and sexual reform. Married to *Bertrand Russell for a time in the 1920s, she founded with him a progressive school whose methods are still far ahead of educational practice (to most children's loss). She believed passionately in political *détente*, was one of the first westerners to visit the USSR after the 1917 Revolution, and in the 1950s and beyond spent much time visiting Communist China and eastern Europe, paying particular attention to the status of women and children in the Marxist system. Her autobiography *The Tamarisk Tree* (three volumes, 1977–85) describes her childhood, education, her work for children and for women's rights in the 1920s–30s, and what she did in the Second World War and afterwards, campaigning against nuclear weapons and leading the worldwide Women's Peace Movement.

‹› **READ ON**
Dora Russell, *The Dora Russell Reader: 57 Years of Writing and Journalism.*

-> RUSSIAN CHILDHOODS

Scholem Aleichem, *The Great Fair: Scenes from my Childhood*
*Maxim Gorki, *My Childhood*
Valentin Katayev, *A Mosaic of Life*
*Vladimir Nabokov, *Speak, Memory*
*Konstantin Paustovsky, *Childhood and Schooldays*
Galina Vishnevskaya, *Galina, a Russian Story*
*Taya Zinkin, *Odious Child*

S

SACKVILLE, Victoria (1862–1936) English hostess

The illegitimate daughter of an English diplomat and a Spanish dancer, Sackville had no education until she was 16, when her mother died and she was sent to a convent in France. She left at 18 and went to Washington to become hostess for her father who was British Ambassador. She was a vital, charming woman, attracting many proposals of marriage, including one from President Arthur. Susan Mary Alsop, *Lady Sackville* (1978) chronicles this heady early life, and goes on to tell of Sackville's passionate marriage to her cousin, her love for the Sackville country-house Knole, and the upbringing of her daughter, *Vita Sackville-West.

◇ **READ ON**
Vita Sackville-West, *Pepita* (biography of Sackville's mother, the author's grandmother); *Knole and the Sackvilles* (about the family house and garden).
*Henry Adams, *The Education of Henry Adams* (superb picture of 1880s Washington high society, with glimpses of Sackville).

SACKVILLE-WEST, Vita (1892–1962) English gardener and writer

In her day Sackville-West was celebrated not only as hostess, gardener, poet and biographer, but also for her marriage to Harold Nicholson (documented each day by letters and diaries) and her passionate friendships – to put it no higher – with, among others, *Violet Trefusis and *Virginia Woolf. Victoria Glendinning, *Vita* (1983) is critical but fair, and draws on all the literary material. The only drawback, at least for gardeners, is that the magnificent garden at Sissinghurst, Sackville-West's creation, is mentioned only in passing. Nigel Nicolson, *Portrait of a Marriage* (1971) is a joint study of Sackville-West and Harold Nicolson (the author's parents), and was the first book to state publicly that both partners were also attracted to their own sex.

◇ **READ ON**
Vita Sackville-West, *Diaries*; *Letters*; *Pepita* (biography of her Spanish-dancer grandmother).
*James Lees-Milne, *Harold Nicolson* (account, by a close friend, of Nicolson's public life – first as diplomat and then as literary figure – and of his marriage). Harold Nicolson, *Diaries* (several volumes); *Letters*. See also *Victoria Sackville.

> ·> SAILORS
>
> J.H. Adamson and H.F. Follard, *The Shepherd of the Ocean* (*Ralegh)
> Roy Hattersley, **Nelson*
> Samuel Eliot Morison, *John Paul Jones*
> Dudley Pope, **Harry Morgan's Way*
> John Sugden, **Sir Francis Drake*
> Walter Magnus Teller, *The Search for Captain Slocum*

SALADIN (1137–93) Arab sultan and conqueror

In 1169 Salah-ed din Yussuf ibn Ayub succeeded his uncle as vizier of Egypt, and in 1174 he was appointed sultan of Egypt and Syria. He spent 13 years conquering the vast area between Damascus and the Persian Gulf, and then in 1187 moved west, besieging Jerusalem, and triggering the Third Crusade. Somewhat patronizingly, the Christians (led by Richard the Lionheart) always claimed that Saladin was a perfect gentleman, a flower of chivalry almost as fragrant as themselves. P.H. Newby, *Saladin in His Time* (1983) explores this opinion – somewhat scathingly comparing the degrees of 'enlightenment' of Saladin and the Christian warlords he fought – and is also excellent on Saladin's campaigns, in country Newby himself knows well.

·> **READ ON**
Stephen Runciman, *A History of the Crusades* (magnificent three-volume account, one of the century's most admired historical works. Volume three, relevant to Saladin, is superbly readable).

SAND, George (1804–76) French writer

If Sand had been a man, no one in 19th-century society would have thought twice about 'his' life: author of 100 works, ranging from travel books to slushy historical romances, conductor of 14 love-affairs, many involving elopements and stays abroad for months on end. Even such goings-on as cross-dressing might have been ignored. But Sand was a woman, Amandine Aurore Lucie Dupin, and whatever she did – whether running off with *Chopin or smoking cigars in public – outraged the bourgeoisie. Her husband asked for the *Légion d'honneur* for putting up with her, and amazingly, people sympathized with him. Noel B. Gerson, *George Sand* (1972) is an entertaining biography, spoiled only by determination to make Sand some kind of prototype feminist virago. Ruth Jordan, *George Sand* (1976) is more sober, but also more sensible, pointing out that it was the society Sand lived in, not Sand herself, whose attitudes were bizarre.

·> **READ ON**
George Sand, *Story of My Life* (abridged; the complete book runs to seven volumes); *Letters to and from Flaubert*; *Winter in Mallorca* (about her stay there with Chopin, who was sick and very grumpy).

‹› SANDS OF THE DESERT

Reader Bullard, *The Camels Must Go*
Stanton Hope, *Born to Adventure: the True Story of Haji*
Williamson, Sea-rover and Desert Nomad
James Lunt, *Glubb Pasha*
Elizabeth Monro, *Philby of Arabia*
*Wilfred Thesiger, *Arabian Sands*
Jeremy Wilson, *Lawrence of Arabia* (*T.E. Lawrence)

SARTRE, Jean-Paul (1905–80) French writer

Philosopher, playwright, novelist and political guru, Sartre was
one of France's best known intellectual heavyweights for 40
years. All his writings, including his autobiography *Words*
(1964), are dense with philosophical reasoning, putting forward
the Existential view of life which he worked out with his friend
and companion *Simone de Beauvoir. Earlier biographies, for
example A.J. Belkird, *Jean-Paul Sartre* (1970), tend to concentrate on his public and intellectual lives; later ones, for example
Ronald Hayman, *Writing Against* (1986), also go into his private
life, a mixture of grandeur, conceit, depression and indiscrimi-
nate sexual energy. Annie Cohen-Solal, *Sartre* (1987) takes the
middle course, doing its best to rehabilitate Sartre's intellectual
reputation without glossing over his faults.

‹› **READ ON**
Jean-Paul Sartre, *Nausea The*
Roads to Freedom (three volumes)
(novels, heavily autobiographical,
about young people awakening to
politics and philosophy in the
1930s and 1940s, and being
forced to relate their ideals to
outside circumstances, such as
resistance work in German-
occupied France in the Second
World War). Deirdre Bair,
Simone de Beauvoir.

SAVONAROLA, Girolamo (1452–98) Italian religious and political reformer

Appalled by the worldly wealth and corruption of such leading
families as the "Borgias and "Medici, Savonarola preached a
return to the self-denying Christian lifestyle laid out in the letters of St Paul: making this life a preparation for the next. Acclaimed by his followers, he went further, leading a political
coup which established Florence as a puritan Christian republic, and organizing a 'bonfire of the vanities' at which people
were encouraged to burn their rich clothes, gold, silver and
other baubles. Savonarola's aristocratic enemies, not unnaturally, resisted, and he was eventually hanged and burned. P.
Villari, *Savonarola* (1861; Eng ed 1918), the standard scholarly
biography, will fascinate anyone with some understanding of
the intricacies of Renaissance Church and secular history. R.
Ridolfi, *Life of Girolamo Savonarola* (1959) is more accessible to
general readers.

‹› **READ ON**
*George Eliot, *Romola* (novel set
in the Florence of Savonarola's
time).

SAYERS, Dorothy L(eigh) (1893–1957) English writer

Sayers won fame for her detective novels starring Lord Peter Wimsey (prime examples of what her fellow writer Colin Watson called the 'snobbery with violence' school). In later life she was a Christian apologist, known especially for her radio play *The Man Born to be King*, and she translated Dante. She was an obsessively, pugnaciously private person, and her prickly secretiveness fuelled speculation over what it was she had to hide. *Janet Hitchman, *Such a Strange Lady* (1975) peels away the layers of Sayers' life and work in search of the inner heart: a classic piece of literary and biographical detection. It is still fascinating, but has been superceded by James Brabazon, *Dorothy L. Sayers* (1981), the authorized biography, which uses primary sources not available to Hitchman, and spends less time on Sayers' crime writing, to good effect. Hitchman makes Sayers seem a very odd person indeed; Brabazon also shows that she was consistent, human and vulnerable.

⋄ READ ON
Jane Aiken Hodge, *The Private World of Georgette Heyer* (biography of a similarly reclusive popular writer, of the same period and milieu).

⋄ SCANDAL

Richard Berkeley, *The Road to Mayerling* (Rudolph, Crown Prince of Austria)
Mandy Rice Davies and Shirley Flack, *Mandy*
Barbara Goldsmith, *Little Gloria... Happy at Last* (*Vanderbilt family)
H. Montgomery Hyde, *The Trials of *Oscar Wilde*
David Yallop, *The Day the Laughter Stopped: The True Story of Fatty Arbuckle*

SCHLIEMANN, Heinrich (1822–90) German archaeologist

Modern scholars pooh-pooh Schliemann's credentials as an archaeologist, saying that his methods were unsound and that because he went excavating to prove a point rather than to see what he could find, he ignored or destroyed anything which failed to fit his ideas. He may have been no scientist, but his story is one of the great romantic sagas of archaeology: millionaire has bee in bonnet that Homer's Troy and Agamemnon's palace were not legend but real, goes digging and finds both places, stuffed with treasure. Leo Deuel, *Memoirs of Heinrich Schliemann* (1977), a dazzling 'autobiography' compiled from Schliemann's articles, letters and excavation notes, gives insight

⋄ READ ON
Leonard Cottrell, *The Lion Gate/ Realms of Gold* (good historical and archaeological account of Mycenae, scientifically accurate but written for lay people).
Irving Stone, *The Greek Treasure* (novel).

into Schliemann's character. It is full of passion and conviction, as single-minded as a fundamentalist sermon, and fond of phrases like 'the mystery of Troy' or 'the glory that was Greece'. Lynn and Gray Poole, *One Passion, Two Loves* (1967) is an equally starry-eyed joint biography of Schliemann and the wife he idolized, reproducing photographs of her, for example, in ancient jewels Schliemann claimed had belonged to Helen of Troy. Robert Payne, *The Gold of Troy* (1960) is more sceptical about Schliemann's claims, but even so is tinged with wonder at what he actually achieved.

◇ SCHOOLS

*Roald Dahl, *Boy*
*Finlay J. MacDonald, *Crowdie and Cream*
*Gavin Maxwell, *The House of Elrig*
Alan Paton, *Towards the Mountain*
Anthony Powell, *Infants of the Spring*
'Miss Read', *Time Remembered*
Robert Roberts, *A Ragged Schooling*
Phyllis Taylor, *Buckskin and Blackboard*
Phyllis Willmott, *A Green Girl*
See also Teachers and Teaching

SCHUBERT, Franz (1797–1828) Austrian composer

Almost universally beloved, Schubert was the centre of a circle of friends who met regularly for party games, musical evenings and earnest political and artistic discussions in what British people might think a particularly Victorian way. He lived at the height of Biedermeier Vienna: a mixture of primness and giggliness, repression, licence and middle-class cosiness which is fascinating in itself. He was ambitious to write operas as famous as *Rossini's, and to emulate *Beethoven in symphonies and chamber works – but in fact his compositions (600 songs and dozens of piano works as well as orchestral and chamber pieces) radiate the same kind of geniality as people find in his life. Maurice J.E. Brown, *Schubert: a Critical Biography* (1958) is the standard scholarly work, dry but accessible, and Charles Osborne, *Schubert and His Vienna* (1985) sets Schubert well in the context of Biedermeier Vienna. Peggy Woodford, *Schubert, His Life and Times* (1978) is a well-illustrated 'brief life', with some technicality.

◇ **READ ON**
John Reed, *Schubert: the Final Years* (good on Schubert's fine, late music, and on the illness – probably syphilis – which killed him). Otto Eric Deutsch, *Schubert: Memoirs by his Friends* (intimate glimpses, culled from Deutsch's monumental scholarly anthology *Schubert: A Documentary Biography*).

SCHUMANN, Clara (1819–96) German pianist and composer

‹› **READ ON**
Alan Walker, *Robert Schumann,
The Man and His Music.*

Less attention is usually paid to Clara Schumann than to the compositions, music criticism and descent into madness of her husband Robert. But Clara's story is just as remarkable. Trained by her single-minded father from the age of six, she became one of the leading concert pianists of her century, and was a good, if uninspired, composer. She fell in love with Schumann when she was 11 (he lodged in the family home), outfaced parental opposition, eventually eloped with him and devoted herself to him and their enormous brood of children. After he died (she was 37) she continued her concert career, spending six months each year touring and the other six on family life, supported by her lifelong friendship with the composer Brahms. Nancy B. Reich, *Clara Schumann, the Artist and the Woman* (1985) is excellent on these later years, and refreshingly tells the story of Clara's and Robert's marriage from Clara's point of view. Joan Chissell, *Clara Schumann, a Dedicated Spirit* (1983) sees Clara far more as Robert's appendage, but is better than Reich on her musical achievements.

SCHWEITZER, Albert (1875–1965) German musician, doctor and theologian

‹› **READ ON**
Erica Anderson, *The Schweitzer
Album* (picture study). Clara
Urquhart, *With Doctor Schweitzer
in Lambarene.* George N.
Marshall, *An Understanding of
Albert Schweitzer.*

In the 1930s–50s Schweitzer seemed an unassailable candidate for Christian sainthood: a musician and philosopher of dazzling gifts who gave it all up to run a leper colony in Africa; a thinker and mystic whose life was a beacon in torn and troubled times. In the 1960s reaction set in, and he was criticized for paternalism, racism, unhygienic medical practices and determined unworldliness. (The last charge surfaced, in the USA especially, when he joined *Einstein in condemning nuclear weapons). Although the final verdict may simply be that he was a good man who lived beyond his time, the jury is still out, and books about him reflect this.

Schweitzer's own autobiographical books include *Memoirs of Childhood and Youth* (Eng. ed. 1924), *My Life and Thought* (Eng. ed. 1933) and *From My African Notebook* (Eng. ed. 1938). Gerald McKnight, *Verdict on Schweitzer* (1964) is a good summary of the 'case against'. George N. Marshall and David Poling, *Schweitzer* (1971) puts the case 'for', and is endorsed by Schweitzer's daughter Rhena. James Brabazon, *Albert Schweitzer* (1975) is thorough and objective, presenting all Schweitzer's human contradictions and fallibility – and paradoxically making clear just how he might seem, as his more intemperate admirers claim, to be nothing less than 'the noblest figure of the century'.

✦ SCIENCE AND MATHEMATICS

Peter Brent, *Charles Darwin: a Man of Enlarged Curiosity*
Laura Fermi, *Atoms in the Family* (*Enrico Fermi)
Martin Goldman, *The Demon in the Aether* (James Clerk Maxwell)
Peter Goodchild, *Oppenheimer: the Father of the A-bomb*
*Otto Hahn, *My Life*
Andrew Hodges, *Alan Turing: The Enigma*
Frank E. Manuel, *A Portrait of *Isaac Newton*
Peter Michelmore, *Einstein, Profile of the Man*
Robert Reid, *Marie Curie*
W.J. Sparrow, *Knight of the White Eagle* (Benjamin Thompson, Count Rumford)
James Dewey Watson, *The Double Helix*

SCOTT, Robert Falcon (1868–1912) English explorer

A naval captain, Scott led several polar explorations culminating in a race with Roald Amundsen to be first to reach the South Pole. Amundsen won by a month, and Scott and his four companions struggled back towards their base, dying after extreme hardship almost within sight of safety.

For half a century, Scott was portrayed as a great British hero, the epitome of endurance and endeavour. Typically enthralling accounts are L. Huxley (ed.), *Scott's Last Expedition* (1913), based on Scott's own diaries, found after his death, and Apsley Cherry-Garrard, *The Worst Journey in the World* (1922), superb on the challenges and hardships of Antarctic survival. In the 1970s, people began questioning Scott's leadership. Would he have succeeded if he had been more willing to listen to those more experienced in polar survival and less reliant on theory? The standard 'debunking' account is Roland Huntford, *Scott and Amundsen* (1979), as lively as it is controversial.

SCOTT, Walter (1771–1832) Scottish writer

Scott's poetry and novels, drawing on Scottish history and legend, inspired generations of Romantic artists, writers and musicians, from *Turner to *Arthur Conan Doyle, from Donizetti (several of whose operas are based on Scott) to *Robert Louis Stevenson, Anthony Hope (*Prisoner of Zenda*)

✦ **READ ON**
R.E.G. Amundsen, *My Life as an Explorer*. *Elspeth Huxley, *Scott and Amundsen*. Sue Limb and Patrick Cordingley, *Captain Oates, Soldier and Explorer*.

✦ **READ ON**
Walter Scott, *Journal* (ed. W.E.K. Anderson, 1972).

and Baroness Orczy (*The Scarlet Pimpernel*). J.G. Lockhart, *The Life of Sir Walter Scott* (1837–38) is one of the most renowned of all literary biographies, equal in reputation to *Boswell's *Johnson* or Froude's *Carlyle*. Its style is as slow-paced as Scott's own, and its blurring of uncomplimentary facts has been criticized, but it remains both monumental and mesmeric. Two later books make zestful cases for Scott, and are as enthusiastic for the man as they are for his work. John Buchan, *Sir Walter Scott* (1932) plays the Scottish card on every page, showing a sensitivity to lochs, heather and stormy skies as Romantic as Scott's own. A.N. Wilson, *The Laird of Abbotsford* (1980) is by a self-confessed addict, and its raves about Scott's personality, his work, even his houses and his dog, will delight fellow admirers and may persuade even the most flinty-hearted non-devotees to try again.

⋄ SCOTTISH CHILDHOODS

David Daiches, *Two Worlds: an Edinburgh Jewish Childhood*
Lavinia Derwent, *A Breath of Border Air*
Lucy, Lady Fairfax, *Hebridean Childhood*
*Finlay J. MacDonald, *Crowdie and Cream*
Angus MacVicar, *Salt in My Porridge*
*Naomi Mitchison, *Small Talk*
*John Muir, *The Story of My Boyhood and Youth*
Donald Sutherland, *Butt and Ben: a Highland Boyhood*
*Molly Weir, *Shoes Were for Sunday*

SEACOLE, Mary (1805–81) Jamaican nurse

The daughter of a Scottish sailor and a Jamaican hotel-owner, Seacole worked as a nurse in the Caribbean and Central America until 1853, when she travelled to London to volunteer for the Crimean War. Rejected because of her colour, she went nevertheless as a private person, and worked alongside *Florence Nightingale. Returning to London, she wrote a bestselling autobiography, *Wonderful Adventures of Mrs Seacole in Many Lands* (1857; rev. ed. 1984), which is still as zestful and as full of surprises as on the day it first appeared.

⋄ **READ ON**
Margaret Goodman, *Experiences of an English Sister of Mercy*.
*Elspeth Huxley, *Florence Nightingale*.

> SECOND WORLD WAR

Dianna Dewar, *Saint of Auschwitz*
Joyce Grenfell, *The Time of My Life: Entertaining the Troops*
Etty Hillesum, *Diary 1941–43*; *Letters from Westerbork*
Robert Kee, *A Crowd is Not Company*
Stella King, *Jacqueline: Pioneer Heroine of the Resistance*
Marianne MacKinnon, *The Naked Years*
François Maspers, *Cat's Grin*
Peter Padfield, *Himmler, Reichsführer SS*
Albert Speer, *Inside the Third Reich*
Joan Wyndham, *Love is Blue*
See also Women; Children at War

SHAARAWI, Huda (1879–1947) Egyptian feminist

Shaarawi led the movement to give women equal rights in Egypt: she was one of the first women to flout Islamic dress law, and fought for suffrage and changes in the laws on marriage, contraception and property ownership. Her memoir *Harem Years* (Eng. ed. 1986) deals with her childhood, upbringing and beginnings of dissent. It has been crudely topped and tailed by an over-political feminist editor, but Shaarawi's own writing is simple, atmospheric and moving, making its case without need of polemic. It sets a common story in an unfamiliar location, and one of the points it makes most strongly – one for some reason ignored by her editor – is how its people's feelings and human relationships, whatever their customs, are little different from our own.

> **READ ON**
Ellen Chennells, *Recollections of an Egyptian Princess by her Governess* (published in 1893, and detailing the kind of harem conditions which had lasted unchanged for centuries, and which Shaarawi was determined to change).

SHAKA ZULU (1787–1828) Zulu leader

The story of the Zulus, the warrior-nation of Southern Africa, is known to westerners chiefly – and distortedly – through epic films and 'great white hunter' novels in the tradition of *King Solomon's Mines*. In fact it is a tale of usurpation, conquest, cunning and betrayal as complex and bloody as any struggle for dominance in European or Asian history. Shaka Zulu, uniter and founder of the nation, comes over like a cross between Geronimo and Genghis Khan. E.A. Ritter, *Shaka Zulu* (1955) is by a white man who learned Shaka's story as a child, from his Zulu nurse. The book blends folk-tale-like narrative – incantatory and hypnotic – with comments and reflections from

> **READ ON**
Peter Becker, *Path of Blood* (biography of Mzilikasi, founder of the Matabele nation). C.T. Binns, *The Life and Death of Cetshwayo*.

historical hindsight and from a different point of view, that of the British overlords who dispossessed Shaka's descendant Cetshwayo and ruled South Africa. Unusual; enthralling.

SHAKESPEARE, William (1564–1616) English playwright and poet

Shakespeare seems to dazzle other writers, so that books about his work tend to be scholarly and pernickety (far harder to understand than the works themselves), and biographers tend to fuss about small and often half-invented details. Who was the Dark Lady? Was Shakespeare bisexual? Did someone else actually write his plays? The really interesting questions – what was Shakespeare like, what happened in his life and under what conditions did he work? – are seldom dealt with. Martin Fido, *Shakespeare* (1978) is the exception. By treating Shakespeare like any other subject for biography, Fido brushes away the dust of centuries and shows us a believable human being in the context of his time. Paradoxically, the effect is to make Shakespeare seem an even more startling genius. But he can cope with that. E.A.J. Thompson, *Shakespeare: the 'Lost Years'* (1985) does a similar job on Shakespeare's youth, proving, among other things, that he was brought up as a Roman Catholic and that, like many writers before and since, he started his working life as a reluctant schoolteacher.

▸ **READ ON**
Gareth and Barbara Lloyd Evans, *Everyman's Companion to Shakespeare* (encyclopedia of facts about Shakespeare's life, his plays, performances down the centuries, and how Stratford-on-Avon today compares with the town Shakespeare knew). G.L. Hosking, *The Life and Times of Edward Alleyn* (about Shakespeare's star actor and partner). Caryl Brahms and S.J. Simon, *No Bed for Bacon* (uproarious comic novel spoofing every imaginable legend of Shakespeare's life and times).

SHAW, Eliza (1794–1877) English settler

Shaw and her husband, an army captain who had fought at Waterloo and was now on half-pension, decided in 1829 to emigrate. With six children, two servants, some livestock, and far more enthusiasm than knowledge, they sailed to the Swan River Valley in Western Australia. They were not the only settlers: the area had been widely advertised as a 'second Paradise' in the English press, and there were quite a few takers. The following years were a story of hard work, problems with the Aborigine owners whose land had been parcelled out to the settlers, and the joys and problems of raising a large family in pioneer conditions. Mary Durack, *To be Heirs Forever* (1976) tells the Shaws' story, much of it based on Eliza's chatty, detailed letters home.

▸ **READ ON**
Mary Durack, *Sons in the Saddle* (memoir of the cattle-ranchers and cowherders of 19th-century Western Australia, one of whom was Durack's own father).

SHAW, George Bernard (1856–1950) Irish writer

Shaw's first career was as a critic (of drama, art and music) and lecturer (on social conditions and politics); he was in his late 30s when his first plays were produced. All his life he loved

▸ **READ ON**
M. Peters, *Bernard Shaw and the Actresses*. Janet Dunbar, *Mrs G.B.S.*. George Bernard Shaw, *Collected Prefaces*. Dame Felicitas Corrigan, *The Nun, the Infidel*

controversy, and poured out speeches, letters and essays, wittily holding forth on every subject under the sun, from Nietzsche to naturism, from the USSR to the perils of drinking tea.

Shaw's gadfly brilliance, and his beautiful prose – some of the most readable English written this century – overshadow anyone who writes about him. The standard biography (Michael Holroyd, *George Bernard Shaw*, three volumes 1988–91) is fat with facts and comments, but lacks the mischievous Shavian sparkle of an earlier work, Hesketh Pearson, *George Bernard Shaw* (rev. ed. 1961), which Shaw read (and in part rewrote) himself. Shaw's letters are published complete, but also in selections such as C. St John (ed.), *Ellen Terry and Bernard Shaw: a Correspondence* (1931) and A. Dent (ed.), *Bernard Shaw and Mrs Patrick Campbell: Their Correspondence* (1952), charting, among other things, a heady love affair. Dan H. Laurence (ed.), *Shaw's Music* (1983) collects some of Shaw's funniest, most discursive journalism, as much about Shaw's own quirky life in 1880s–90s London as it is about sonatas and symphonies.

and the Superman (letters on faith and atheism, between the Benedictine nun Dame Felicitas and two other correspondents, of whom the 'Superman' is Shaw).

SHEARS, Sarah (20th century) English writer

Sarah Shears, *Tapioca for Tea* (1971), the story of her childhood, is dedicated to and dominated by her mother, who coped with rural poverty, a large family and a feckless, absentee husband. *Gather No Moss* (1972) begins when Shears is 21 and determined to travel. It tells how she achieved this, working as a nanny, a ship's stewardess, a wartime ministry clerk in London and a housemaid in a hostel for aircraft workers. Her style is sometimes breathless, but the books should delight anyone who enjoys her novels.

▷ **READ ON**
To *Tapioca for Tea*: Phyllis Willmott, *Growing Up in a London Village*. To *Gather No Moss*: Lucilla Andrews, *No Time for Romance*.

SHELLEY, Mary (1797–1851) English writer

Daughter of one flouter of convention (*Mary Wollstonecraft) and wife of another (the poet *Percy Bysshe Shelley), Mary Shelley seemed doomed to spend her life overshadowed by relatives. She idolized her husband, agreeing to a *ménage à trois* with him and *'Claire' Clairmont, living the bohemian life with him in Italy, and cherishing his reputation after his death. But she was a busy author in her own right, publishing novels (including *Frankenstein*), biographies and travel books. Frederick L. Jones (ed.), *Mary Shelley's Journal* (1947) and *The Letters of Mary W. Shelley* (1946) are the main sources for her life. R. Glynn Grylls, *Mary Shelley* (1938) is the standard biography, dry but full. Jane Dunn, *Moon in Eclipse* (1978) is livelier, though some readers may dislike the author's habit of telling us people's thoughts, even when (as Shelley was towards the end)

▷ **READ ON**
Christopher Small, *Ariel Like a Harpy: Shelley, Mary and 'Frankenstein'* (about the possible psychological effects of Mary's life on her best known book).

they are mute and paralysed by strokes. Muriel Spark, *Child of Light* (1951) is a shout of rage at the way other people's reputations stood in Shelley's way.

SHELLEY, Percy Bysshe (1792–1822) English poet

In both life and work, Shelley was passionate about freedom. He wrote savage essays about such subjects as democracy, religion, free love and the 'Irish question'. His poetry and plays are as much about politics and personal liberty as they are lyrical. He spent eight years in a *ménage à trois* with his wife (*Mary Shelley) and mistress (*'Claire' Clairmont).

After Shelley's death, his family suppressed evidence of his freethinking, and promoted his lyric poetry above everything else he wrote. This view filters into earlier books about him, for example Edward Dowden, *The Life of Percy Bysshe Shelley* (1886). Later biographies, more balanced, include Newman Ivy White, *Shelley* (two volumes, 1947), the standard work, dry but thorough, and Richard Holmes, *Shelley, The Pursuit* (1974), excellent on his life. Claire Tomalin, *Shelley and His World* (1980) is short, enthusiastic and well illustrated. Shelley's politics are dealt with in K.N. Cameron, *Young Shelley: Genesis of a Radical* (1951) and *Shelley: the Golden Years* (1974). Edward E. Williams, *Shelley's Friends: Their Journals and Letters* (1951) is a good anthology.

> **⋗ READ ON**
> Frederick L. Jones (ed.), *Shelley's Letters*. David Lee Clark (ed.), *Shelley's Prose*. Marion Kingston Stocking (ed.), *The Journals of Claire Clairmont*. Edward J. Trelawney, *Records of Shelley, Byron and the Author. See also* *Byron.

SHEPHERD, Dolly (1886–?) English woman of action

Shepherd's memoir *When the Chute Went Up* (with Peter Hearn and Molly Sedgwick, 1984) is a find. Published when she was 98, it recounts her heady 20s and 30s as a stunt parachutist. She was part of a team which went round the country giving shows, ascending in hot-air balloons or in rickety, primitive planes, jumping out with parachutes and sometimes working with trapezes slung underneath. The book is breathless with excitement, telling of skin-of-the-teeth' adventures in the air and no less amazing escapes on the ground. Like all the women in the troupe, Shepherd was as pretty as a pin-up, wore a figure-revealing jumpsuit, and was mobbed by stage-door johnnies (or whatever the parachuting equivalent is) every time she fell to land.

> **⋗ READ ON**
> Hanna Reitsch, *The Sky My Kingdom*.

SHEPPARD, Jack (1702–24) English highwayman

> **⋗ READ ON**
> Daniel Defoe, *The History of the Remarkable Life of John Sheppard;*

For four years, from his 18th birthday until he was hanged at Tyburn before 200,000 spectators, Sheppard's robberies were the sensation of London for their daring, their style and for Sheppard's own good looks: at one point it was almost fashionable to be robbed by him. He inspired ballads, operas (for example *The Beggar's Opera*), novels and pantomimes, and until the mid-19th century his fame as a folk hero rivalled even Robin Hood's. Christopher Hibbert, *The Road to Tyburn* (1957) takes his mouthwatering story and makes a meal of it, using contemporary newspaper accounts and other documents to give a picture not just of Sheppard himself but of the whole 18th-century English underworld.

A Narrative of all the Robberies, Escapes, etc, of John Sheppard (published to cash in on Sheppard's death: 18th-century gutter journalism of genius).

SHERIDAN, Richard Brinsley (1751–1816) Irish writer

As playwright, theatre manager and politician, Sheridan moved in some of the most brilliant London circles of his time: his friends included Garrick, Sarah Siddons, Charles James Fox and the Prince Regent, and his enemies included every rival theatre-owner and politico in town. Oscar Sherwin, *Uncorking Old Sherry* (1960) is as lively as its title, though its use of the present tense throughout may irritate. It is particularly good on the theatre and gaming-house society of Sheridan's time, and the carousing which was his favourite relaxation and which proved his downfall. Stanley Ayling, *A Portrait of Sheridan* (1985) is more purse-lipped at Sheridan's excesses, but notably good on his political career. Eliza M. Butler, *Sheridan, a Ghost Story* (1931) deals well with Sheridan's sad last years. Thomas Moore, *Memoirs of the Life of Richard Brinsley Sheridan* (two volumes, 1825) is a delight: gossipy, hero-worshipping, talk-filled, as if Sheridan himself were in the room.

⋄ **READ ON**
William Lefanu (ed.), *Betsy Sheridan's Journal* (letters by Sheridan's sister: demure, commonsensical, like a cold compress after the feverish goings-on of Sheridan and his friends).

⋄ SHOWBIZ

Larry Adler, *It Ain't Necessarily So*
Gyles Brandreth, *The Funniest Man on Earth* (*Dan Leno)
*George Burns, *The Third Time Around*
Denis Castle, *'Sensation' Smith of Drury Lane*
Hermione Gingold, *How to Grow Old Disgracefully*
James Harding, *Cochran*
Charles Higham, *Ziegfeld*
Mary Martin, *My Heart Belongs*
Ethel Merman, *Don't Call Me Madam*
Sheridan Morley, *A Talent to Amuse* (*Noël Coward)

Giles Playfair, *The Prodigy: a study of the Strange Life of Master Betty*
Harry Secombe, *Twice Brightly*
Dodie Smith, *Look Back with Gratitude*
See also Applause! Applause!

SHUTE, Nevil (1899–1960) English/Australian writer

Many of Shute's heroes are ordinary men with a background in aviation and/or engineering. In his autobiography *Slide Rule* (1954) he shows how this reflects his own life. He talks briefly about writing, but it takes distinctly second place to his other activities. The book first tells of Shute's childhood, during which his father was head of the Post Office in Ireland (Shute was a passer-by in Dublin when the Post Office was taken in the Easter Rising of 1916). Shute goes on to describe how, as a young aircraft engineer, he worked on the R100 airship, and how he set up and ran his own aircraft company, Airspeed Ltd.. Throughout, as in Shute's novels, his plain, gripping prose makes compulsive reading from quite ordinary events and people.

⋗ READ ON
Nevil Shute, *No Highway* (novel, based on experience, about an engineer travelling in a passenger plane who realizes that it is about to break up because of metal fatigue – and no one will listen).

SIDIS, William (1897–1944) US intellectual

Child prodigies usually shine at just one skill – maths, chess, music, sport. But Sidis was multi-talented, one of the finest minds ever assessed. His IQ was 50–100 points higher than *Einstein's (the previous highest ever recorded). He began talking at six months old, could read at 18 months, studied Homer in Greek when he was three and spoke seven languages by the time he was six years old. At 11 he went to Harvard to read maths, and graduated at 16. Then puberty struck, and his life collapsed. His subsequent attempts to balance intellectual and emotional needs, and to avoid the attentions of the press, are the subjects of an absorbing biography, Amy Wallace, *The Prodigy* (1986). It hardly explains what made Sidis so unusual – though it has harsh things to say about his parents, firm advocates of the 'superbaby' theory – but it is excellent, and moving, about what happens to child geniuses once hormones, not brain-cells, rule.

⋗ READ ON
Norbert Wiener, *Ex-prodigy* (sad memoirs of another Harvard prodigy, a few years ahead of Sidis, with some pointed comments on the nature of genius generally, and the Sidis case in particular).

⋗ THE SILVER SCREEN

Luis Buñuel, *My Last Breath*
Marlene Dietrich, *Marlene Dietrich: My Life*

*Anita Loos, *A Girl Like I*
John McCabe, *Babe: the Life of Oliver Hardy* (*see* *Laurel and Hardy)
Norman MacKenzie, *The Magic of Rudolf Valentino*
Arthur Marx, *Everybody Loves Somebody Sometime (Especially Himself)* (Dean Martin)
Lynn Tornabene, *Long Live the King* (*Clark Gable)
Mae West, *Goodness Had Nothing to Do With It*
See also Film Stars; Hollywood

SIMENON, Georges (1903–89) Belgian novelist

Simenon wrote some 400 novels: psychological thrillers and crime stories starring Chief Inspector Maigret. His *Intimate Memoirs* (Eng. ed. 1984) is a tormented autobiography, triggered by the suicide of his daughter and ending with a lacerating series of letters, poems and reflections on her death. In the rest of the book, and in his earlier autobiography *When I Was Old* (1970), Simenon talks of his childhood, his days as a journalist, his travels, his writing and his private life – if 'private' is quite the word, in view of his claim to have made love to 10,000 women in 70 years.

> **READ ON**
> Georges Simenon, *Pedigree* (atmospheric novel about a boy growing up in Belgium before the First World War: fictionalized autobiography).

SINATRA, Frank (born 1915) US singer and actor

Books about Sinatra fall, even more than with most entertainers, between 'raves' and 'put-downs'. Raves concentrate on the stream of success which is his performing life, as singer, film star, dancer and producer. A good example, bubbling with enthusiasm and excellent on the music, is John Rockwell, *Sinatra: an American Classic* (1984). Put-downs concentrate on his stormy offstage, offscreen life: his love-affairs, marriages, political activity and alleged connections with the Mafia. Kitty Kelley, *His Way* (1986) is typical of these. Based on interviews with 800 people (many of whom had no reason to like Sinatra), it is an immensely readable, 'warts above all' portrait of the man which failed to please Sinatra and will not amuse his fans. John Howlett, *Frank Sinatra* (1980) is the most balanced biography so far: more careful than the others – and perhaps therefore not half so much fun.

> **READ ON**
> Gene Ringold and Clifford McCarthy, *The Films of Frank Sinatra*. Herb Sanford, *Tommy and Jimmy: the Dorsey Years* (evocative biography of the bandleaders with whom 'The Voice' had his first success).

SINCLAIR, Ronald: *see* TEAGUE-JONES, Reginald

> ❖ SINGERS
>
> Brian Adams, *La Stupenda* (Joan Sutherland)
> D. Fingleton, *Kiri Te Kanawa*
> Myra Freedman, *Burned Alive* (*Janis Joplin)
> *Rita Hunter, *Wait Till the Sun Shines, Nellie*
> *Michael Kelly, *Reminiscences/Solo Recital*
> M. Lang, *Édith Piaf*
> David A. Low (ed.), *Callas as They Saw Her*
> John Rockwell, *Sinatra: An American Classic*
> Michael Scott, *The Great Caruso*
> Joseph Wechsberg, *Red Plush and Black Velvet* (*Melba)
> *See also* Jazz; Rock and Pop

SINGH, John 'Boysie' (1908–57) Trinidadian gangster

Derek Bickerton, *The Murders of Boysie Singh, Robber, Arsonist, Pirate, Mass-Murderer, Vice and Gambling King of Trinidad* (1962) is one of those books whose title says it all – except that for once, the book is just as good as the title promises.

❖ **READ ON**
*Joseph Bonanno, *A Man of Honour*.

SITTING BULL (1834–90) Amerindian chief

One of the rawest wounds in the US psyche is the mutual incomprehension of native Amerindians and the settlers who displaced them. In the mid-19th century, Sitting Bull was in the eye of the storm, as he fought to defend Sioux lands from invasion. His defeat of General Custer at Little Big Horn (1876) was the climax of his success; the following years were a catalogue of compromise, intimidation and treachery by the government, which used assimilation to conquer where brute force had failed. Alexander B. Adams, *Sitting Bull* (1973) writes with sympathy for both sides and a remarkable feeling for the land and landscape all the fuss was about.

❖ **READ ON**
Alexander B. Adams, *Geronimo* (an almost exactly parallel and – for whites – equally shaming tale). P. and D. Goble, *Custer's Last Battle*. Dee Brown, *Bury My Heart at Wounded Knee* (bleak, general account of the clash between whites and Amerindians).

SITWELL family

Edith Sitwell (1887–1964) and her brothers **Osbert Sitwell** (1892–1969) and **Sacheverell Sitwell** (1897–1988) were at the hub of literary London for 50 years. Edith was an experimental poet and editor of anthologies. Sacheverell was a biographer (notably of *Mozart and *Liszt) and travel writer. Osbert (by far the most talented) wrote novels, poems, plays, travel books and memoirs.

❖ **READ ON**
Sacheverell Sitwell, *Journey to the Ends of Time* (memoirs). Osbert Sitwell, *Tales My Father Told Me* (anecdotes left out of his autobiography). Edith Sitwell, *English Eccentrics* (wonderful skeletons from the murkier cupboards of the English

The best account of the Sitwells' lives, friends and enemies is in Osbert Sitwell's four-volume autobiography *Left Hand! Right Hand!*. The books (*Left Hand! Right Hand!*, 1945; *The Scarlet Tree*, 1946; *Great Morning!*, 1948; *Laughter in the Next Room*, 1949) are packed with anecdotes of eccentric ancestors, of Osbert's childhood in Derbyshire, life at Eton and Oxford, war service, and enjoyable years as man-about-literary-London. What feuds the Sitwells fought! What triumphs they had! They were the original glitterati, and Osbert catches their passionately serious, butterfly public style in prose which turns soufflé into art. Victoria Glendinning, *Edith Sitwell: A Unicorn Among Lions* (1981) is good on the queen bee of the Sitwell hive, and deals well with the idea (encouraged not least by Sitwell herself) that she was one of our leading 20th-century poets. John Pearson, *Façades* (1978) is a family biography, a dossier of high old times and far-out, full-throttle eccentricity.

aristocracy).

SLEEMAN, William Henry (1788–1856) English soldier

For many centuries travellers in India had mysteriously disappeared on long journeys. Sleeman, a soldier and administrator for the British East India Company, realized that these disappearances were the work of organized gangs who joined the groups, waited till their companions trusted them, then strangled them, robbed them and buried their bodies. These criminals were the Thugs ('deceivers'). By sending in spies and amassing great amounts of evidence, Sleeman defeated them. Francis Tuker, *The Yellow Scarf* (1961) tells the story, drawing on Sleeman's own account (*see* Read On). Tuker is over-eager to show the British presence in India in a good light, but this is the only blemish in a fast-moving, extraordinary tale.

> ⋅> **READ ON**
> W.H. Sleeman, *Rambles and Reflections of an Indian Official* (autobiography). John Masters, *The Deceivers* (novel, using invented characters but based on Sleeman's life).

SMITH, Bruce (1855–1942) English stage designer

'Sensation' Smith designed sets for Drury Lane Theatre. As his nickname suggests, he specialized in astounding the audience: his stage effects included burning buildings, earthquakes, balloon ascents, submarines, sinking ships, even the Derby and the chariot-race in *Ben Hur* staged with real galloping horses. He designed for *Shaw, Pinero, *Gilbert and Sullivan, *Dan Leno, Irving, Pavlova, Harry Lauder, *Melba and *Beecham, and for eight royal command performances. In his spare time he did charity work, was an army reservist (rising to the rank of major) and had a love-affair with a Brighton barmaid which was one of the scandals of the age. Dennis Castle, *'Sensation'*

> ⋅> **READ ON**
> W. MacQueen Pope, *Theatre Royal Drury Lane*; *The Footlights Flickered* (feasts of theatrical nostalgia). John Wade, *The Trade of the Tricks* (how some of the most sensational stage illusions were done).

Smith of Drury Lane (1984) is one of those 'smell of the grease-paint, roar of the crowd' theatre books which delight fans but baffle everyone else. It is wonderful not only on Smith himself (the author's grandfather) but on the brash, irresistible world he served.

SMITH, Harry (1787–1860) English soldier

As a career army officer, Smith played his part in every significant British battle from the Peninsular War almost to the Crimea. On retirement he was appointed Governor of South Africa, with orders to reconcile Boers, Britons and Zulus. Joseph Lehmann, *Remember You Are an Englishman* (1977) is fascinating, but less for accounts of battles or the running of one corner of the Empire than for its picture of Smith's whole-hearted, brave and cheerful personality.

✦ READ ON
Jane Eliza Masted, *Juana: the Gentle Amazon* (biography of Smith's equally remarkable wife, who was 14 when she met him at the siege of Bajadoz; she married him two days later, followed the colours wherever he went, and is commemorated by the town Ladysmith in Natal). *Georgette Heyer, *The Spanish Bride*; *An Infamous Army* (novels, based on Smith's early career).

SMITHSON, Harriet (1800–54) Irish actress

Smithson is chiefly remembered as the actress who captivated *Berlioz, seeming to him the incarnation not just of *Shakespeare's heroines but of Beauty and The Eternal Feminine themselves. They married; the marriage failed; she turned to drink. She never had success at home or in England to equal the effect she made in France, but that effect was extraordinary, not just on Berlioz but on the entire French literary and theatre establishment. Peter Raby, *Fair Ophelia* (1982) tells her story, in prose as evocative of Romanticism and the theatre of the time as his well-chosen illustrations. The book's bibliography is a treasure-store for anyone interested in 19th-century acting.

✦ READ ON
Robert Baldick, *The Life and Times of Frédérick Lemaître* (lively biography of the leading French actor of Smithson's time). David Cairns, *Berlioz 1803–1832: the Making of an Artist*.

SMYTH, Ethel (1858–1944) English composer

Even today, comparatively few women become composers of classical music, and in Smyth's day it was even rarer. She was determined to rival *Beethoven and *Mendelssohn, and bullied her family into letting her study in Europe. Militant for women's rights, she spoke at rallies, wrote songs with heavily political words for women's choir, and was imprisoned in 1911 (an event which distressed her gaolers more than it did her). In later life she was famous as a crusty old party, snappish and out of sympathy with modern music and modern times. She had lesbian affairs, including one (it was rumoured) with *Virginia Woolf. Her volumes of memoirs, notably *Impressions That Remained* (1919, about her student days in Europe) and *As Time*

✦ READ ON
Ethel Smyth, *A Three Legged Tour in Greece*; *Streaks of Life*; *A Final Burning of Boats*; *Female Pipings in Eden*; *Beecham and Pharaoh*; *Inordinate (?) Affection*; *What Happened Next*. A selection of her writings can be found in *The Memoirs of Ethel Smyth* (Roland Crichton and Jovy Bennett, eds.).

Went On... (1936, about her tussles to have her music performed in Britain) are merciless to everyone who failed to see the worth of her work, and give unexpected glimpses of such luminaries as the Bensons, Brahms, *Queen Victoria and Henry James. Louise Collis, *Impetuous Heart* (1984) is zestfully written, sympathetic to her ideas and full of affectionate malice at her eccentricities.

SOYINKA, Wole (born 1934) Nigerian writer

Soyinka, a Nobel prize-winning poet and playwright, thinks that the world's different cultures should not stand aloof, but should cross-fertilize each other. He is known especially for presenting Yoruba myths with the same kind of resonance as Homer or Aeschylus gave to those of ancient Greece. He has also written two evocative memoirs; *Aké* (1988), about his early childhood, his discovery of the world around him and the world of myth, and *Isara* (1990), about his father (a provincial schoolteacher) and a group of like-minded people, trying to balance their own inherited culture with that of the world outside wartime Nigeria.

> ·> **READ ON**
> Wole Soyinka, *The Man Died* (a powerful account of his imprisonment in 1967–69, at the time of the Nigerian Civil War).

SPEER, Albert (1905–81) German architect

Speer was *Hitler's architect, designing among other things the Nuremberg Stadium and the first autobahn system. He was also a senior member of the Nazi party, and Minister of Armaments from 1941. Tried after the war, he admitted the failings of the régime, but pleaded that he was a technician and not a politician. He repeated these claims in his book *Inside the Third Reich* (1970), asserting that he had no knowledge of Nazi atrocities and indeed was a covert enemy of Hitler, the 'last rebel'. The book was taken at face value in its time, and seems to be the chilling account, by a fly, of life in a spider's web. However, Matthias Schmidt, *Albert Speer, the End of a Myth* (Eng. ed. 1985) takes Speer's self-justifications apart sentence by sentence, almost comma by comma, showing that he knew and approved of everything that was going on, and that he falsified the record, and lied in every word he wrote or said afterwards, either from self-delusion or to save his skin.

> ·> **READ ON**
> Albert Speer, *Spandau: the Secret Diaries* (more self-justification, written during Speer's 20-year imprisonment for war crimes, and seeking to pin the blame for Nazi atrocities on everyone else.)

·> SPIES AND SECRET LIVES

Lory Adler and Richard Dalby, *The Dervish of Windsor Castle*
R. Deacon, *C: A Biography of Maurice Oldfield*

> Derek Hudson, *Munby, Man of Two Worlds*
> Edna Nixon, *Royal Spy: the Strange Case of the Chevalier d'Éon*
> Erika Ostrovsky, *Eye of Dawn: the rise and fall of *Mata Hari*
> Barry Penrose and Simon Freeman, *Conspiracy of Silence: the Secret Life of Anthony Blunt*
> *Reginald Teague-Jones, *The Spy Who Disappeared*
> Hugh Trevor-Roper, *Hermit of Peking: the Hidden Life of *Sir Edmund Backhouse*
> June Rose, *The Perfect Gentleman* (*James Barry)
> N. St Barbe Sladen, *The Real *Le Queux*
> Anne Taylor, *Laurence Oliphant*
> *See also* Derring-Do

STALIN, Joseph (1879–1953) Soviet dictator

Stalin's career follows the pattern (alas) standard for dictators: impeccable revolutionary credentials, a combination of bravery and cunning during the coup, a period of consolidation and a long decline into paranoia and murderous excess. No one in 20th-century history – few people in all human history – created a mightier nation or caused so many deaths. Books about him tend to reflect the view held internationally about him at the time of writing. David Cole, *Stalin, Man of Steel* (1942) depicts him as revolutionary hero and staunch wartime ally. Robert Payne, *The Rise and Fall of Stalin* (1965), the most readable general biography, takes a more jaundiced view, though full revelation is still hampered by lack of access to official Soviet papers. Alex de Jonge, *Stalin and the Shaping of the Soviet Union* (1986) combines a 'warts and all' (warts and warts) picture of Stalin the man with a historian's analysis of what he was trying to achieve – and even it has been overtaken by events. Other books of interest include Leon Trotsky, *Stalin, an Appraisal* (1947), Edward Ellis Smith, *Stalin: the Early Years* (1968) and Budu Svanidze, *My Uncle Joe* (1952).

⊹ READ ON
Achmed Amba, *I Was Stalin's Bodyguard*. Svetlana Alliluyeva (Stalin's daughter), *Twenty Letters to a Friend* (published in 1967, after her sensational emigration to the USA and before her equally sensational return to the USSR).

STAMP, Terence (born 1940) English actor

Stamp's three-volume autobiography (*Stamp Album*, 1987; *Coming Attraction*, 1988; *Double Feature*, 1989) tells how a working-class Cockney boy, whose teachers predicted a great future for him as manager of Woolworths, became a heart-throb film star, one of the icons of the sixties, and what happened when times – and fashions in film stars – changed. He writes with a mixture of wryness and straightforwardness: just as the cocky adolescent was a suave ladykiller at heart, so the adult actor,

⊹ READ ON
*Kenneth Williams, *Just Williams* (similar childhood, ambitions and writing style, but a very different career).

mixing with celebrities in the world's most glamorous niteries, never once lost his streetwise, blitz and Bow Bells cheekiness.

STANHOPE, Hester (1776–1839) English traveller

Loftily dismissed by men as an 'eccentric' both during and after her lifetime, Stanhope was actually someone who chose to live by her own rules instead of those of the stuffy conventions of her time. Until she was 30, she lived demurely enough, even acting as housekeeper for her uncle, Prime Minister William Pitt the Younger, for which she was given a sizeable official pension. In 1810 she settled in what is now Lebanon, building herself an oriental palace, taking a Syrian lover, intervening (sometimes effectively, sometimes disastrously) in the politics of the area, and using her money to help the local people. The story, alas, ends tragically: the authorities in London cut off her pension, and she died in poverty. Her *Memoirs* (ed. C.L. Meryon, 1945) are witty, cockily self-admiring and merciless to others. Virginia Childs, *Lady Hester Stanhope, Queen of the Desert* (1990) is a well-illustrated biography, and although it offended some (male) critics because of its approval of Stanhope and disgust at the way people treated her, it is as witty and exuberant as, by all accounts, she was herself.

◊ **READ ON**
Duchess of Cleveland, *Lady Hester Stanhope: Life and Letters* (1913: 'life' outdated; letters unbeatable). *See also* Jane Digby.

STANLEY, H(enry) M(orton) (1841–1904) Welsh/US explorer

The flamboyant Stanley ran away from the workhouse at 15, emigrated to America, fought on both sides in the Civil War, worked as a journalist in Egypt and Abyssinia, was sent to find *Livingstone and forthwith became an explorer in his own right. Later, he retired to Britain to write his memoirs, and became a Unionist Member of Parliament. His own books tell his story with appropriate dash, zip and absence of false modesty (or indeed modesty of any kind): *How I Found Livingstone* (1872); *Through the Dark Continent* (1878); *In Darkest Africa* (1890); *Autobiography* (1909). A good modern biography is Frank McLynn, *Stanley* (1989–91).

◊ **READ ON**
H.M. Stanley, *My Early Travels in America and Asia.*

STARK, Freya (born 1893) English traveller

Stark began travelling in her 20s, and continued until she was over 90. She specialized in the Middle East, and wrote books (illustrated with her own photos and drawings) on Iran, Iraq, Southern Arabia, Syria and Turkey. Her travel books (for example, *The Southern Gates of Arabia*, 1936, and *The Lycian*

◊ **READ ON**
Caroline Moorhead (ed.), *The Selected Letters of Freya Stark.* Alexander Maitland, *A Tower in a Wall* (memoir of Stark in old age, including many conversations in which Maitland encouraged her to talk about her

Shore, 1956) are partly about landscape, people and history, partly about herself; her autobiographies (for example, *Traveller's Prelude*, 1950) cover the same ground, so to speak, from the opposite direction, concentrating on herself. Caroline Moorhead, *Freya Stark* (1990) is a good, brief biography, putting Stark's own writings into clear perspective.

STEIN, Gertrude (1874–1946) US writer

From 1903 Stein lived in France, where her friends included Braque, *F. Scott Fitzgerald, *Hemingway, Matisse and *Picasso. She wrote over 500 works, many in an avant-garde style, without syntax or punctuation (or, if the mood took her, without adjectives, verbs or nouns). Stein published three autobiographical books. *The Autobiography of Alice B. Toklas* (1933) is not what it seems (an autobiography of Stein's lesbian companion) but a fictionalized memoir of Stein herself, as if by Toklas. *Everybody's Autobiography* (1937) is more straightforwardly about herself, and *Wars I Have Seen* (1945) is chiefly about Paris under German occupation. Janet Hobhouse, *Everyone Who Was Anybody* (1975) is a biography so colourful that it reads like a fairy story scripted by *Dalí. But that, it seems, is exactly how things were.

STEINBECK, John (1902–68) US writer

Steinbeck worked as builder, house-painter, caretaker, fruit-picker and reporter before becoming a full-time writer at 33. He specialized in books about the poor and inadequate – the mentally subnormal Lennie in *Of Mice and Men*, exploited share-croppers in *The Grapes of Wrath* – and built several novels on legendary or Biblical themes: *East of Eden*, for example, updates the story of Cain and Abel. Jackson J. Benson, *The True Adventures of John Steinbeck, Writer* (1984) is a well-researched critical biography, and Elaine Steinbeck and Robert Wallsten, *Steinbeck: a Life in Letters* (1975) uses Steinbeck's own words, to good effect.

STENDHAL (1783–1842) French writer

'Stendhal' was the pseudonym of Marie Henri Beyle, who served as a soldier under *Napoléon I and later worked as a consul in Italy. He wrote biographies (including an argumentative one of *Rossini), travel books and novels such as *The Red and the Black*, a bitter satire on post-Revolutionary French society. He felt that his life was a progression of disasters, and his work is full of grumbles and worked-off grudges. Something of a 'case', he is a splendid subject for literary biography, and

life and ideas). *See also* *Gertrude Bell.

❖ **READ ON**
Alice B. Toklas, *What is Remembered* (real memoir by the real Toklas). Donald Gallup (ed.), *The Flowers of Friendship* (letters written to Stein). Samuel M. Seward (ed.), *Dear Sammy: Letters from Stein and Alice B. Toklas*.

❖ **READ ON**
John Steinbeck, *Travels with Charley in Search of America* (a mixture of travel, autobiography and social commentary); *Journal of a Novel: the East of Eden Letters*.

❖ **READ ON**
Stendhal, *Journal* (dealing chiefly with 1801–15, the peak – or trough – of Beyle's army career); *The Life of Henri Brulard*; *Memoirs of an Egoist* (fictionalized autobiographies).

Robert Adler, *Stendhal* (1980) does him proud, mingling life and work in a way which sends you hurrying back to Stendhal's books. Joanna Richardson, *Stendhal* (1974) is lighter on literary criticism, but livelier on Stendhal's personality, seeing him as a kind of 'modern', 50 years before his time.

STEPHENSON, George (1781–1848) English engineer

Stephenson was a pioneer of the Industrial Revolution in Britain, and particularly of railways. Everyone knows that, because Samuel Smiles' biography (*see* Read On) put him into every Victorian school curriculum. But the detail of his life, his pugnacious character and his unpopularity with colleagues are less often heard about. Hunter Davies, *George Stephenson* (1975) is a lively account of his life and character, good on industrial conditions at the time. L.T.C. Rolt, *George and Robert Stephenson* (1960) is chiefly about the railway work, and is fascinating on the technology.

⊹ READ ON

Samuel Smiles, *Life of George Stephenson*; *Lives of the Stephensons* (huge, uplifting tomes presenting the Stephensons as heroes of Victorian industry). Terry Coleman, *The Railway Navvies* (grim account of the lives of the Irish immigrant workers who actually built the railways: a savage counterpart to Smiles' notion that everything depended on temperance, hymn-singing and elbow-grease). Jack Gould, *Thomas Brassey, 1805–1870* (biography of one of the Stephenson's main successors as a builder of railways).

STEVENSON, Robert Louis (1850–94) Scottish writer

Stevenson's ambition, to be an engineer like his father, was dashed by ill-health. He graduated as a lawyer, but was seduced by theatre and literature. He travelled widely, for the sake of his health, settled in Samoa in 1888, and died there six years later. He published a book of memoirs, *Memories and Portraits* (1887), and wrote thousands of letters, of which a good selection is Sidney Colvin (ed.), *Selected Letters of R.L. Stevenson*, (four volumes, 1911). David Daiches, *Robert Louis Stevenson* (1947), the standard scholarly biography, is drily written, but relates Stevenson's work and life in interesting, often unexpected ways. Jenni Calder, *RLS: a Life Study* (rev. ed. 1990) is good on the complexities of Stevenson's character. James Pope Hennessy, *Robert Louis Stevenson* (1974) tells Stevenson's life in prose as vivid as Stevenson's own – a scholarly book which enthrals like fiction.

⊹ READ ON

David Daiches, *Robert Louis Stevenson and His World* (well-illustrated, 'brief life'). Fanny and Robert Louis Stevenson, *Our Samoan Adventure*. J.C. Hart (ed.), *From Scotland to Silverado* (collection of Stevenson's writings about his three years in the USA). J.C. Furnas, *Voyage to Windward* (biography, good on Stevenson's travels).

STOPES, Marie (1880–1958) English scientist

A brilliant scientist, Stopes triumphed over anti-woman prejudice first to study for university degrees, then to lecture on

⊹ READ ON

Ruth Hall (ed.), *Dear Doctor Stopes* (anthology of touching, furious, hilarious and desperately

palaeobotany (the study of fossil plants). In her 30s she began a more controversial campaign, against sexual prudery. She wrote books proclaiming that women had as much right as men to enjoy sex, and describing techniques of sex and love; she advocated birth control and opened clinics to give advice. Ruth Hall, *Marie Stopes* (1977) describes all this, and is particularly good on the gender politics and moral tunnel-vision of the time. The book is superb on Stopes' character: her combination of iron certainty of purpose with fluffy, Romantic dottiness, aptly summed up by the cover photo which shows her galumphing ecstatically about in flowing, transparent draperies, like an overweight, undertalented Martha Graham.

sad letters by people who asked Stopes' advice or wanted to tell her what their sex lives had been before and after they discovered her work).

STRACHEY, Lytton (1880–1932) English writer

Strachey is remembered as a pivotal member of the *Bloomsbury Group, and as author of *Eminent Victorians* (1918), a set of elegant historical and psychological case-studies (of *Florence Nightingale, Cardinal Manning, Doctor Arnold and General Gordon) which blew away forever the cobwebs of awe Britons had felt about their immediate past. He spent the last 16 years of his life in a three-part relationship with Ralph Partridge and Partridge's wife Dora Carrington – a relationship which, like everything else to do with Bloomsbury, has been picked over and written about by others connected with the Group (*see* *Frances Partridge). Michael Holroyd, *Lytton Strachey* (two volumes, 1968) is one of the most influential biographies of the second half of this century, ushering in the 'modern' method (like police evidence, using documents and interviews to build up the picture) just as Strachey's work was seminal 50 years before. (Holroyd is fascinating on the different approaches.) Not the least of Holroyd's achievements is to disentangle the Bloomsbury relationships, so that his book is a study of the whole phenomenon as well as of one of its most distinguished and stylish members.

⊹ READ ON
Lytton Strachey, *Eminent Victorians* (illustrated edition, with foreword by Frances Partridge). Annabel Strachey, *All Stracheys Were Cousins* (autobiography of Strachey's cousin, who married the architect Clough Williams-Ellis). Gretchen Gerzina, *Carrington*. David Garnett (ed.), *Carrington: Letters and Extracts from her Diary*.

STRAUSS family

For over a century, the Strauss family provided Imperial Vienna with musical diversion. They organized dances, wrote and conducted the music for them, played for balls, parties and firework displays and ran a music-publishing empire. The most talented member of the dynasty, **Johann Strauss II** (1825–99) composed over 400 waltzes (including *The Blue Danube*), polkas and other orchestral items, and 16 operettas including *Die Fledermaus*.

Jerome Pastene, *Three Quarter Time* (1951) and Joseph Wechsberg, *The Waltz Emperors* (1973) are studies of the whole

⊹ READ ON
Henry Pleasants (ed.), *Vienna's Golden Years of Music* (setting the Strausses in the context of such other Vienna-lovers as *Mozart, *Schubert, Brahms and Mahler). *Frances Trollope, *Vienna and the Austrians* (as they appeared to a beady-eyed visitor in 1838, their heyday).

family, as people and as a business phenomenon. Wechsberg's book is beautifully illustrated – a real bonus in studies of this particular subject and period. Hans Fantel, *Johann Strauss* (1971) is a joint biography of the founder of the dynasty, **Johann Strauss I** (1804–49), and his more famous son. Egon Gertenberg, *Johann Strauss* (1974) is a biography with political stiffening: it paints the Strausses, and Johann II in particular, as purveyors of a kind of fake 'Vienneserie', attractive but little to do with the real corruption and decadence as the Austro-Hungarian Empire danced towards collapse.

STRAUSS, Richard (1864–1949) German composer

Strauss is known for songs, orchestral works (including *Don Juan* and *Till Eulenspiegel*) and operas (especially *Der Rosenkavalier*). He spent his 70s and early 80s in uneasy co-existence with the Nazis, alternately being idolized as Germany's greatest composer and reviled because he insisted on working with Jewish musicians and writers the authorities ordered him to drop. Few composers are better served by biographers. Kurt Wilhelm, *Richard Strauss, an Intimate Portrait* (Eng. ed. 1989) is a well-illustrated account of his personal life, especially good on his relations with his family, on his character and his politics, and moving about his old age. Norman del Mar, *Richard Strauss* (three volumes, 1962–72) is definitive, though technical, about the music. Alan Jefferson, *The Life of Richard Strauss* (1973) is a handy half-way house: a brisk introduction to Strauss' life and music with especially interesting chapters on the writing and production of his operas.

⋗ **READ ON**
Richard Strauss, *Recollections and Reflections* (collected articles). Richard Strauss and Hugo von Hofmannstahl, *Correspondence* (one of the most famous exchanges in musical literature, working letters between Strauss and the librettist of several of his finest works). Lotte Lehmann, *Singing With Richard Strauss* (memoir by one of his favourite opera-stars).

STRAVINSKY, Igor (1882–1971) Russian composer

For most of his long life, from his riotous successes with *Diaghilev's Ballets Russes, through his flirtation with Hollywood to his waspish, *Groucho-Marxish old age, Stravinsky made headline news. He was the modern composer whose music everyone loved to hate, but also the creator of one of the most popular works of the 20th century, the *Firebird Suite*, which he himself – just one conductor among hundreds – directed over 1,000 times, an average of once every three weeks throughout his working life. His autobiography, *Chronicles of My Life* (1936), is chiefly of interest to musicians, as is the best of all the books about him, Eric Walter White, *Stravinsky, The Composer and His Works* (second ed. 1978), which discusses in (technical) detail every piece he wrote. Robert Craft, *Stravinsky*

⋗ **READ ON**
Igor Stravinsky and Robert Craft, *Conversations with Igor Stravinsky; Memories and Commentaries; Expositions and Developments; Dialogues and a Diary* (in which Stravinsky, prompted by Craft, remembers with gusto, comments with malicious wit on everything from Diaghilev's love-life to the faults of Karajan's recording of *The Rite of Spring*: for musicians and non-musicians alike, easily the most enjoyable of all books by or about Stravinsky). Robert Craft, *Stravinsky in Pictures and Documents*.

(1986) is dry, but describes Stravinsky's life rather than his music, and is accessible to the general reader. Interesting reminiscences by people who knew Stravinsky in later life are Paul Horgan, *Encounters With Stravinsky* (1972) and Lillian Libman, *And Music at the Close* (1978).

STRINDBERG, August (1849–1912) Swedish writer

Strindberg pioneered many ideas of modern experimental theatre, and wrote plays, poems, novels and memoirs. He was a self-tormentor, swinging between exhilaration, despair and madness. Three disastrous marriages hardly helped his mental state, but gave him material for plays such as *The Father* and *Miss Julie*, in which women humiliate and dominate men. From time to time he published autobiographical fragments, which pick at his obsessions and neuroses in a revealing but largely fictional way: *Son of a Servant* (1886), about his childhood; *A Madman's Manifesto* (1887), about his second marriage; *Inferno* (1897), about going mad in Paris. Olof Lagerkrantz, *August Strindberg* (Eng. ed. 1984) combines a brisk account of Strindberg's life with sensitive discussion of his character and work. Michael Meyer, *Strindberg* (1985) is longer, and takes a day-to-day approach which can be tedious. But it omits nothing, and gives background useful to English-speaking readers.

⋄ **READ ON**
August Strindberg, *From an Occult Diary* (selections from the diary of occult happenings which Strindberg kept for 20 years: a window into the darkest corners of his mind). Frida Strindberg, *Marriage With Genius*.

STRZELECKI, Paul Edmond (1797–1845) Polish/English explorer and/or adventurer

Strzelecki left Poland in his mid-20s, either under a cloud or because he failed to win the rich girl he was courting (the evidence is doubtful). He went on several expeditions to South America and the Pacific, publishing accounts of his discoveries many of which later scholars have not been able to verify. In the 1830s he went to Australia, where he knew Sir John Franklin and did much genuine exploring in the interior, mapping mountains. He named one mountain Kosciusko, proclaiming it a monument to his country's heroic 1790s struggle against the Russians. This act seems to be the main reason why, during Polish resistance to the Nazis in the Second World War, he came to be regarded as a national hero, particularly among expatriates. The difficulty of establishing true facts about his character and life makes him a glorious biographical challenge. Geoffrey Rawson, *The Count* (1954) takes him at face value, calling him 'explorer and scientist' and concentrating on his years in Australia. H.M.E. Heney, *In a Dark Glass* (1961) is less starry-eyed, suggesting (without ever stating directly) that

⋄ **READ ON**
Kathleen Fitzpatrick, *Sir John Franklin in Tasmania*.

Strzelecki's story involves not only triumph but good old-fashioned roguery.

STUART, Charles Edward (1720–88) Scottish prince

'Bonnie Prince Charlie' was the grandson of King James II, who was replaced on the throne by William and Mary because of his Roman Catholicism. In 1745 Charles made an abortive attempt to win his grandfather's throne, but was defeated and fled to Europe, where he lived in exile until he died. Few people since Robin Hood have had such a hold on British popular imagination. Charles' landing in the Hebrides, the gathering of the clans, the glorious deeds at Prestonpans, the massacre at Culloden, Flora MacDonald and the escape to Skye – this is tragedy, melodrama and romance, all rolled into one. The legend is enthusiastically told (and well illustrated) in Eric Linklater, *The Prince in the Heather* (1930) and Rosalind K. Marshall, *Bonnie Prince Charlie* (1986). A less starry-eyed account, good on Charles' military strategy and wonderfully evocative of Highland landscape and lifestyle, is Fitzroy Maclean, *Bonnie Prince Charlie* (1986). Susan MacLean Kybett, *Bonnie Prince Charlie* (1986) presents a completely different Charles: spoiled, virtually illiterate, arrogant and – in his later years – alcoholic and paranoid. Frank McLynn, *Charles Edward Stuart* (1986) is a dispassionate historical assessment. In these, and in hundreds of other books about Charles, the debate continues. What we make of the evidence depends, more than with most historical figures, on our emotional response to Charles.

⊹ **READ ON**
John Prebble, *Culloden* (grim account of the brutality of the battle and its aftermath). Walter Scott, *Waverley* (novel set during the Jacobite rebellion).

SULLIVAN, Annie: *see* KELLER, Helen

SULLIVAN, Arthur: *see* GILBERT AND SULLIVAN

SUYIN, Han (born 1917) Chinese writer

Suyin's mother was European and her father was Chinese (an unheard-of alliance in 1910s China). Suyin herself studied medicine, worked in Singapore and Malaya, and became world-famous in the 1950s when her novel *A Many-Splendoured Thing* was filmed. She has written several books of memoirs, jumping backwards and forwards in time and blending personal and family reminiscence with descriptions of the Chinese landscape and history. *The Crippled Tree* (1965), the story of her grandparents and parents, is set in the half century before and after the 1913 Revolution. *A Mortal Flower* (1967) is about her

⊹ **READ ON**
Han Suyin, *Destination Chungking* (novelized account of Suyin's first marriage, and of her life as a midwife in the Second World War); *A Share of Loving* (about how she and her family cared for her stepson Vincent, after brain damage from an illness turned him into a kind of middle-aged child); *Tigers and Butterflies* (essays). *Hsiao Ch'ien, *Traveller Without a Map*

own childhood and adolescence in the turbulent 1920s–30s. *Birdless Summer* (1968) continues her story through the Second World War and Chinese Civil War. *My House Has Two Doors* (1980) takes us to 1979, and includes memorable scenes as Suyin revisits China, reflecting on events since the Communist takeover and the rule and overthrow of the 'Gang of Four'.

(different view of the same period and events, by a journalist fascinated by the cultural interaction between his own country and the West).

T

TALBOT, William Henry Fox (1800–77) English scientist

Talbot is best known as a pioneer of photography. In particular, he devised the first ways of making prints on paper, removing the need for the long exposures required by rival systems. His main scientific work was as one of a team repeating and extending *Newton's experiments on the physics of light, and his work on spectra is still valuable. His other interests included palaeolinguistics (he helped to decipher the cuneiform tablets found at Nineveh) and politics. H.J.P. Arnold, *William Henry Fox Talbot* (1977) is superbly detailed, crammed with first hand documents, and illustrated with dozens of photographs, including all Talbot's own most important work.

▷ READ ON
Alexander Wood, *Thomas Young: Natural Philosopher* (biograpy of 'Phenomenon Young', whose interests and career closely paralleled Talbot's). H. and A. Gernsheim, *L.J.M. Daguerre* (good on the excitement of early photography).

TALLEYRAND-PERIGORD, Charles Maurice de (1751–1838) French diplomat

Talleyrand was a weathercock: by looking at where he was pointing you could see where the political wind was blowing. Trained as a priest, he became a bishop, only to resign as soon as the French Revolutionaries were clearly about to set up a secular state. As Foreign Minister of the new republic, he worked to bring *Napoléon I to power. As Napoléon's Foreign Minister he plotted his master's downfall, and served the restored monarchy until the day he died. He was – he would have to have been – as charming as he was unscrupulous, and even his dupes, we are told, found his company a pleasure. His *Memoirs* (five volumes, 1891–92) deal largely with political matters, and are as self-laudatory and self-justifying as one might

▷ READ ON
Annette Jolson, *Courtesan Princess* (story of Catherine Grand, the sexual adventuress who became Talleyrand's mistress when he was Bishop of Autun, and later married him and vastly complicated his private and diplomatic life by her promiscuous behaviour).

expect. J.F. Bernard, *Talleyrand* (1973), the standard biography, sets the record straight, and is also excellent on Talleyrand's personality and private life.

TANGYE, Derek (born 1920) English writer

Tangye, a successful journalist, knew many of the 'great and good' in the years after the Second World War. In the early 1950s he and his wife left the bright lights to run a flower farm in Cornwall. Since 1961, Tangye has written a score of bestselling books about their life there and the animals on their farm. They include *A Gull on the Roof*, *Cottage On a Cliff*, *A Donkey in the Meadow*, *The Winding Lane* and *The Evening Gull*. Derek Tangye, *The Way to Minack* (1968) and *The Cherry Tree* (1986) are autobiographies, and *Jeannie* (1988) is a biography. Delicate, gentle writing: the essence of English rural life, distilled in prose.

> ·> **READ ON**
> Denys Val Baker, *A Family for All Seasons* (family life in Cornwall). Beverley Nichols, *Merry Hall* (evocative writing about renovating an old country house and especially its garden).

TAYLOR, Elizabeth (born 1932) US film star

Taylor has had more rubbish written about her than almost any other person this century. Her films, marriages, clothes, weight, tastes in food, drink and exercise, fascinate almost as much as the regularly recurring, never properly answered question 'What is the private person like behind the hype?' Brenda Maddox, *Who's Afraid of Elizabeth Taylor* (1977) is good about her films, especially those made in the 1960s when she was only twice out of the list of the ten biggest box-office stars. Kitty Kelley, *Elizabeth Taylor, the Last Star* (1981), a compelling read, is good on Taylor's private life, if anything lived in such a glare of myth-making publicity can be described as 'private'. The book is, however, full of conversations, quoted word for word: a sure sign that people's memories, or the author's imagination, have been working overtime.

> ·> **READ ON**
> Melvyn Bragg, *Rich* (biography of Richard Burton: contains a more thoughtful, less sleaze-ridden account than most other books do of Burton's relationship with Taylor).

·> TEACHERS AND TEACHING

*Edward Blishen, *Roaring Boys*
*Helen Corke, *The Light of Common Day*
A.S. Neill, *Neill of Summerhill*
Alan Paton, *Towards the Mountain*
Frederick G. Rea, *A School in South Uist: Reminiscences of a Hebridean Schoolmaster*
Phyllis Taylor, *The Noiseless Foot*
See also Schools

TEAGUE-JONES, Reginald (1889–1989)
English adventurer

As a young man, Teague-Jones was a soldier and spy; in the First World War he ran British Intelligence operations in the Persian Gulf. In 1918, accused by Trotsky of ordering the death of 26 commissars in Baku during the Revolution, he changed his name to Ronald Sinclair, joined the British consular service and spent the rest of his life out of the public eye. In 1988 (aged 99) he published *Adventures in Persia*, about the hazards of driving from Beirut across Iran to India in a 'model-A' Ford in 1926 – a ripping yarn every word of which was true. After his death his true identity was revealed, and an even more extraordinary book was published, *The Spy Who Disappeared*, based on his own Baku diaries from 1918. Wonderful, blood-stirring stuff, the *Boy's Own Paper* come to life – but if this were invented, who would believe a word of it?

> ⊹ **READ ON**
> N. St Barbe Sladen, *The Real Le Queux* (*see* *William Le Queux).

TEILHARD DE CHARDIN, Pierre (1881–1955)
French priest and scientist

A Jesuit teacher and palaeontologist, Teilhard found that his scientific work seemed to contradict Bible accounts of the creation. His superiors made him give up science and concentrate on religion, but after his death several of his books were published, trying to unite the discoveries of science and religion, and assessing in particular why, in his view, the human race is a species like no other, particularly favoured by God. These writings caused new controversy in the Church, but made him a spiritual guide and philosopher for lay people throughout the world. Mary and Ellen Lukas, *Teilhard* (1977) is a sympathetic account of his character, his palaeontological work, his struggle with the religious authorities and his faith.

> ⊹ **READ ON**
> Pierre Teilhard de Chardin, *The Phenomenon of Man*. Peter Medawar, *The Future of Man* (scientific rebuttal of Teilhard's arguments).

TEMPLE, Shirley: *see* BLACK, Shirley Temple

THEODORA (c500–548) Byzantine empress

Theodora was a dancer, stripper and courtesan who became first the mistress and then the wife of the Emperor Justinian. Her subsequent role in Byzantine politics foreshadowed that of *Eva Perón in Argentina 1,400 years later, and most of the enlightened legislation of the time is credited to her. She advocated such things as equality for men and women, state aid for widows and orphans and, not least, religious tolerance, something which earned her the hatred of Christian writers for over 1,000 years. She was one of the most glittering figures in a

> ⊹ **READ ON**
> Procopius, *Secret History* (the original, and most scurrilous, of all the accounts of Justinian's and Theodora's reign, makes the murders and orgies of *Nero and his court seem like toddlers' picnics). Robert Browning (not the poet), *Justinian and Theodora* (dry but readable historical account). Stephen Runciman, *Byzantine Style and Civilization*.

dazzling age, and her life is well told in Antony Bridge, *Theodora* (1978), which also manages the difficult feat of making Byzantine politics not only understandable but as gripping as our own.

THESIGER, Wilfred (born 1910) English traveller

From boyhood, Thesiger was drawn to deserts and the people who live there. His books, *Arabian Sands* (1959, about living with the Bedu people of the Sahara), *The Marsh Arabs* (1964, about his time in Iraq) and *Desert, Marsh and Mountain* (1979, about travels in Kurdistan, Pakistan and Afghanistan) engrossingly blend travel writing, autobiography and philosophy. His actual autobiography, *The Life of My Choice* (1987), tells of his childhood in Addis Ababa, his years in the Sudan Political Service, his wartime service in the Western Desert in the SAS, and above all of his love for Ethiopia and his relationship with Haile Selassie. The mixture of 'stiff upper lip' heroics (*T.E. Lawrence and the characters of Buchan were boyhood idols) and poetic description of landscape is unique to Thesiger, and few writers have so memorably suggested the effects of desert life not just on the body but on the soul.

> ⬦ **READ ON**
> *Gavin Maxwell, *A Reed Shaken by the Wind*. Laurence van der Post, *The Lost World of the Kalahari* (about life among the Bush people of Southern Africa: lusher prose, woollier, more mystical and more romantic, but a match for Thesiger in descriptions of the desert and the people who make it home).

THOMAS, Dylan (1914–53) Welsh poet

There is controversy about whether Thomas' poetry is really work of genius, or merely sounded that way when he read it himself, in his sonorous, bardic bass. There is no doubt, however, about his self-destructive life (which he ended by drinking himself to death), or the quality of his prose writing, and especially the radio play *Under Milk Wood*. His book *Portrait of the Artist as a Young Dog* (1940) is a collection of short stories, partly autobiographical and to be recommended for its evocations of childhood. Paul Ferris, *The Life of Dylan Thomas* (1977) is the best of many biographies, sympathetic to Thomas' character (but not slavishly admiring) and good on his work for the fledgling BBC Third Programme and on his US lecture tours.

> ⬦ **READ ON**
> Caitlin Thomas (his wife), *Leftover Life to Kill* (heartbroken memoir written just after Thomas' death); *Caitlin* (written with George Tremlett in 1986 and far more vitriolic about her life with Thomas and the abominable way he treated her). Paul Ferris (ed.), *Dylan Thomas: the Collected Letters*.

THOMAS, Leslie (born 1931) Welsh writer

Thomas is known for a string of novels, including *The Virgin Soldiers* (a comic novel based on his National Service), *Dangerous Davies* and *That Old Gang of Mine*. His autobiography *In My Wildest Dreams* (1984) is in a relaxed, witty style, as if Thomas himself is at your side, pointing out the wryness or ridiculousness of every event he describes. Author-autobiographies are

> ⬦ **READ ON**
> Leslie Thomas, *This Time Next Week* (a more extended memoir of life in the Barnardo's home). *Michael Green, *The Boy Who Shot Down an Airship*; *Nobody Hurt in Small Earthquake* (different childhood; similar style and view of life).

ten a penny; this one stands out. The first part tells of Thomas' childhood in South Wales and of his days in a Dr Barnardo's home after his parents were killed in the Second World War. The second part recounts his search, as a National Service squaddie in the Far East, for some way – any way – to lose his virginity. The third part tells of his development as a writer, from cub reporter to international journalist to bestselling writer.

THOMPSON, Flora (1876–1947) English writer

Thompson was a country person: she grew up in Oxfordshire, later lived in Hampshire and Devon, and contributed nature notes and poems to several magazines and newspapers. She wrote an autobiographical classic, *Lark Rise to Candleford* (1939). Written in the third person (as if about a child called 'Laura'), this tells of growing up in Victorian rural Oxfordshire, and is a blend of refined nature writing, accounts of farming ways and practices long gone, and warm but beady-eyed pen-portraits of the adults and other children 'Laura' knew. Two sequels, *Over to Candleford* (1941) and *Candleford Green* (1943), were published in one volume with *Lark Rise* in the second edition of *Lark Rise to Candleford* (1945). Gillian Lindsay, *Flora Thompson: the Story of the 'Lark Rise' Writer* (1990) sets Thompson's childhood memories in context and is excellent on her adult life.

> **READ ON**
> *Laurie Lee, *Cider With Rosie*. Winifred Foley, *A Child in the Forest*. *Sarah Shears, *Tapioca for Tea*.

THURBER, James (1894–1961) US writer and artist

Thurber worked extremely hard, producing two dozen books and hundreds of drawings. But he always gave the impression of shambling through life, caring nothing for deadlines, having inconclusive love-affairs, hovering between being drunk and sober. Burton Bernstein, *Thurber* (1975) mercifully never tries to analyse what makes Thurber funny, but is content to quote. Bernstein gives a wonderful account of how Thurber did his work, what triggered his humour, and his shambolic, comic-tragic relationships, with women, with his family, with dogs and with his editor at the *New Yorker*, Harold Ross.

> **READ ON**
> Dale Kramer, *Ross and the New Yorker*.

> TO BOLDLY GO ... *(explorers)*
>
> Fawn M. Brodie, *The Devil Rides* (*Richard Francis Burton)
> Geoffrey Dutton, *Australia's Last Explorer – the Life of Ernest Giles*

Richard Hall, *Lovers on the Nile* (*Samuel and Florence Baker)
Roland Huntford, *Ernest Shackleton*
Alistair MacLean, *James Cook*
Frank McLynn, *Stanley: the Making of an African Explorer*
*Alan Moorehead, *Cooper's Creek* (Burke and Wills)
Bruce Norman, *Footsteps*
Oliver Ransford, *David Livingstone: the Dark Interior*
Andrew Sinclair, *Ralegh and the Age of Discovery*
Anthony Smith, *Explorers of the Amazon*
See also Beyond the Horizon

TOLKIEN, J(ohn) R(onald) R(euel) (1892–1973) English writer

Until *The Lord of the Rings* brought Tolkien worldwide fame in the 1950s, he was a devoted, somewhat eccentric Oxford don. After the book's success, he went on teaching but plunged ever deeper into his imagination, continuing to invent whole languages, mythologies and cycles of history. Humphrey Carpenter, *J.R.R. Tolkien* (1977) gives due weight to Tolkien's real life, but is outstanding both about the books and about the importance to Tolkien of fantasy, which seems to have been more real to him than reality itself.

⋗ READ ON
Humphrey Carpenter and Christopher Tolkien (eds.), *The Letters of J.R.R. Tolkien* (splendid stuff: Tolkien took for granted indications that some people found his created world emotionally compelling, and was irritable with those who thought it twee).

TOLSTOY, Leo (1828–1910) Russian writer

The life of the author of *War and Peace* and *Anna Karenina* was as fascinating as anything in his books. He was an aristocrat who believed in the equality of all human beings; he freed his serfs, set up schools and hospitals for his workers (something unheard of) and ended by renouncing all his property. He had a beloved wife and 15 children, but ended his life estranged and alone. He was a freethinker who became revered in his own lifetime as a kind of secular saint.

Tolstoy wrote a renowned three-volume autobiography, *Childhood* (1852), *Boyhood* (1854) and *Youth* (1856), and is the subject of one of the most acclaimed biographies ever written: Henri Troyat, *Tolstoy* (Eng. ed. 1965). This uses Tolstoyan style – leisurely, reflective prose, enlivened by brilliant word-snapshots of everyone involved, from children to servants, from serfs to tsars – and presents Tolstoy's life and thought as a kind of teeming, disorganized tapestry, so that it is only at the end that you realize that Troyat knew from the start exactly what he thought about Tolstoy, and that you tend to agree with

⋗ READ ON
Leo Tolstoy, *Diaries*; *Journals*; *Letters* (several volumes). Sofia Tolstoy, *The Diary of Tolstoy's Wife, 1860–1891*; *The Final Struggle: Countess Tolstoy's Diary for 1910*. Ilya Tolstoy, *Reminiscences of Tolstoy, by His Son*. Leo Tolstoy jr, *The Truth About My Father*. Anna Tolstoy, *Tolstoy, A Life of My Father*; *The Tragedy of Tolstoy*. Aylmer Maude (ed.), *Family Views of Tolstoy* (good introduction to all this material). Other books of interest: *Maxim Gorki, *Reminiscences of Tolstoy*; Tatiana Kuzminskaya, *Tolstoy as I Knew Him*.

him. A.N. Wilson, *Tolstoy* (1988) is shorter and more incisive about the links between Tolstoy's life and work.

TOULOUSE-LAUTREC, Henri de (1864–1901) French artist

Toulouse-Lautrec's personal life was shadowed by a riding accident at 14, which stunted his growth and left him the size of a child. He felt an outsider from society, incapable of love, and further complicated his alienation by drink and drugs. In his art, he became a kind of commentator on human activity – and the activities he chose were those of cabaret artists, prostitutes, drinkers and down-and-outs in Montmartre, Paris. The Hollywood idea of life as a kind of heartbroken cabaret observed by cynical, penniless artists of genius comes chiefly from his work – and the same spirit is marvellously caught in Lawrence and Elizabeth Hanson, *The Tragic Life of Toulouse-Lautrec* (1956). The book's only drawback is that all but one of its beautiful illustrations are in black and white.

◇ **READ ON**
Marcel Joyaut, *Henri de Toulouse-Lautrec* (good on the art).

TOUSSAINT L'OUVERTURE, Pierre (c1746–1803) Haitian revolutionary

Toussaint led a slave revolt on French-owned Haiti, and in 1794, when the French Revolutionary government in Paris abolished slavery throughout the empire, he was appointed commander-in-chief on Haiti. He defended the island vigorously against Spanish and English invaders, but then over-reached himself (in French eyes) by declaring it an independent republic. In 1802 *Napoléon I sent a large force to reconquer Haiti and dethrone Toussaint, who was taken to France and died in prison. C.L.R. James, *The Black Jacobins* (second ed. 1963) focuses on Toussaint, but is chiefly a historical account of the rebellion, one of several abortive attempts at this time, James says, to set up revolutionary states in the Caribbean, Central and South America. Wenda Parkinson, '*This Gilded African*' (1978) is a detailed, immensely readable biography, with unusual and evocative illustrations.

◇ **READ ON**
Charles Moran, *Black Triumvirate* (joint biography of Toussaint and his deputies and successors Dessalines and Christophe).

TRACY, Spencer (1900–67) US film star

Tracy made 100 films, projecting an image of steady, reliable niceness remarkably at odds with his troubled private persona. Some of his best roles were in films with his friend and lover **Katharine Hepburn** (born 1907): they include *Woman of the Year*, *Adam's Rib*, *Father of the Bride* and *Guess Who's Coming to Dinner*. Garson Kanin, *Tracy and Hepburn* (1970) is

◇ **READ ON**
Charles Higham, *Kate* (biography of Hepburn).

a loving memoir of their relationship, by the friend who wrote and directed two of their finest films, *Pat And Mike* and *Adam's Rib*. Larry Swindell, *Spencer Tracy* (1970) is sensitive about Tracy's life, enthusiastic about his films. Bill Davidson, *Spencer Tracy* (1986) is a splendid 'tell all' biography, perhaps a little over-keen on anecdotes about Tracy's drinking and his temper.

TRADESCANT family

John Tradescant I (c1570–1638) supervised the design and stocking of some of the finest gardens of the Elizabethan age, and worked to naturalize many plants brought to Britain by explorers from more exotic lands. His son **John Tradescant II** (1608–62) continued the work, going on collecting trips and introducing hundreds of shrubs, trees, vegetables and fruit (over 40 kinds of pear, for example). The Tradescants also set up the first public museum in Britain, 'The Ark', housing botanical, historical and anthropological curiosities from round the world (their collection is now in the Ashmolean Museum in Oxford). Tradescant senior also served as a soldier, notably against pirates in Algiers. Prudence Leith-Ross, *The John Tradescants* (1984), a joint biography, is stiffly written, but the sheer exoticism of the Tradescants' lives and work, and the detailed appendices listing plants and the contents of their museum, should absorb anyone fascinated with gardens, 17th-century London, or lives which, without being eccentric, are entirely outside the ordinary run.

⋅> **READ ON**
Elias Ashmole, *Memoirs* (in *Works*, ed. C.H. Josten, 1967).

⋅> TRAGIC LIVES

Richard Berkeley, *The Road to Mayerling* (Rudolph, Crown Prince of Austria)
*Andrew Bihaly, *The Journal of Andrew Bihaly*
Virginia Spencer Carr, *The Lonely Hunter: a Biography of Carson McCullers*
Myra Friedman, **Janis Joplin: Buried Alive*
Albert Goldman, *Ladies and Gentlemen, Lennie Bruce*
F.L. Guiles, *Norma Jean: the Life and Death of *Marilyn Monroe*
*Nancy Mitford, **Zelda Fitzgerald*
*August Strindberg, *From an Occult Diary: Marriage with Harriet Bosse*
Stephen Trombley, *'All That Summer She Was Mad';*
*Virginia Woolf and Her Doctors

TRAVERS, Ben (1886–1980) English playwright

In the 1920s–30s Travers wrote a series of smash-hit comedies, the Aldwych farces (named after the London theatre at which they played), and in the 1970s he had another triumphant decade beginning with the success of his play *The Bed Before Yesterday*, written in his late 80s. He published two books of memoirs, not just about the stage and London literary society, but about pioneer aviation, cricket, film-making, and what he calls his lifelong addiction, pretty girls. The first book was *Vale of Laughter* (1957); *A-Sitting on a Gate* (1978) updates it, adds new stories and embellishes the old ones: a benign performance by an 'old babbler' (as Travers calls himself), a funny old gentleman who is blissfully content with life and not afraid to say so.

> **READ ON**
> *P.G. Wodehouse and Guy Bolton, *Bring on the Girls* (similarly happy memoirs, about working on musical comedies in the 1920s).

TREFUSIS, Violet (1894–1972) English socialite

Violet Keppel's mother, mistress of *Edward VII, was well liked and the soul of discretion. When her daughter began an affair with *Vita Sackville-West (who had recently married the diplomat Harold Nicolson), Mrs Keppel and *Lady Sackville (Vita's mother) set to work to defuse the scandal, and Violet was married off to Denys Trefusis and went to live abroad. Years of misery followed, turning Violet from a romantic, talented girl to an unhappy eccentric. Henrietta Sharpe, *A Solitary Woman* (1981) is a sympathetic but clear-eyed account of her life, a welcome counterbalance to two gross fictional distortions, in *Virginia Woolf's *Orlando* and *Nancy Mitford's *Love in a Cold Climate*.

> **READ ON**
> Mitchell A. Leaska and John Philipps (eds.), *Violet to Vita: the Letters of Violet Trefusis to Vita Sackville-West*. Sonia Keppel (Violet's sister), *Edwardian Daughter* (good on the Keppel household, though discreet about the part 'Kingy' played in their mother's life). Nigel Nicolson, *Portrait of a Marriage* (a different perspective on the affair, by Sackville-West's son).

TROLLOPE, Anthony (1815–82) English writer

Son of a wastrel father and a writer (*Fanny Trollope), Trollope had a miserable childhood, and only found happiness in his mid-20s, as a GPO official in Ireland. He published his first successful novel, *The Warden*, when he was 40, and went on to become one of the most caustic (though seemingly cosy) analysts of the Victorian Establishment. His *Autobiography* (1883), though reticent about his private life, gives a fine picture of a man of letters of the time, working at books as a craftsman might make shoes or window-frames. It shocked members of the artistic establishment, for example Ruskin, who were convinced that novels should be works of genius, inspired by the Muses. Richard Mullen, *Anthony Trollope: a Victorian and*

> **READ ON**
> T.H.S. Escott, *Anthony Trollope: His Work, Associations and Literary Originals* (unsurpassed glimpses of Trollope in later life by a friend who was a literary journalist).

His World (1990) is massive (767 pages), authoritative (especially on Trollope's private life) and readable. C.P. Snow, *Trollope* (1975) is a brief, well-illustrated account of Trollope's Post Office work and his writing. James Pope Hennessy, *Anthony Trollope* (1971) is excellent on Trollope in Ireland and the West Indies.

TROLLOPE, Frances (1780–1863) English writer

Married to a wastrel, Frances Trollope began writing at 50 to support her family. She became famous for a scathing, funny account of trying to succeed in late 1820s America, *Domestic Manners of the Americans* (1832), and went on to write 114 books in all, including accounts of her travels in France, Austria and Italy, and several novels anticipating those of her son *Anthony Trollope. Frances Eleanor Trollope, *Frances Trollope, Her Life and Literary Work* (1895) is a fulsome but lively biography by her daughter-in-law (who never actually met her). H. Heinemann, *Frances Trollope* (1979) and J. Johnston, *The Life, Manners and Travels of Fanny Trollope: a Biography* (1986) are just as interesting, but more objective and far more accurate.

> ⬧ **READ ON**
> Thomas Adolphus Trollope, *What I Remember* (autobiography by Frances' son, husband of Frances Eleanor Trollope).

TRUMAN, Harry S. (1884–1972) 33rd US president

In 1944, when the presidency passed to Truman on the death of *F.D. Roosevelt, it seemed that he might be no more than a caretaker, a dull man trudging after genius. In the event he proved as decisive and radical as his predecessor. He was the last (so far) 'poor farmboy to White House' president, the embodiment of a particularly potent US myth. Almost as soon as he was elected he had to make major decisions: about the ending of the Second World War, the reconstruction of Europe and abandoning the USA's pre-war isolationism in favour of a major role in world affairs, for example in NATO and the United Nations. Roy Jenkins, *Truman* (1986) is brisk, perceptive, and makes US politics clear to non-Americans. Robert H. Ferrell, *Truman* (1984) does a similar job from the US point of view and like Jenkins, devotes over half its space to the presidency itself, the most interesting part (we assume) of Truman's life.

> ⬧ **READ ON**
> Margaret Truman, *Harry S. Truman* (affectionate, intimate portrait by his daughter). Merle Miller (ed.), *Harry S. Truman: Plain Speaking* (aural biography, assembled from Truman's own writing and speeches).

⬧ TRUST ME (FOOLS!)

Tom Cullen, *Maundy Gregory, Purveyor of Honours*
Roberto Gervaso, *Alessandro Cagliostro*

John Masters, *Casanova*
Russell Miller, *Bare-Faced Messiah* (*L. Ron Hubbard)
*Renton Nicholson, *Rogue's Progress*
John Symonds, *Madame Blavatsky*

TURNER, J(oseph) M(allord) W(illiam) (1775–1851) English painter

⊹ **READ ON**
M. Butlin and E. Joll, *The Paintings of Turner*.

People in the rest of the world consider Turner Britain's finest 19th-century painter, a giant of Romanticism and one of the forerunners of Impressionism. In Britain he still has the reputation of a 'wild man', and half his pictures are unexhibited. Biographers in the past were equally divided, either raving or tut-tutting without producing evidence. *Jack Lindsay, *The Life and Work of J.M.W. Turner* (1979) sets the record straight, and has become a classic. Lindsay uses Turner's verse jottings (he was an obsessive scribbler, in a style similar to *Blake's) and sketch-books to flesh out the picture of an awkward, withdrawn and uncooperative personality, and he also gives a magnificent account of the society and art world of Turner's time.

TUSSAUD, Marie (1761–1850) Swiss wax sculptor

⊹ **READ ON**
Francis Hervé (ed.), *Madame Tussaud's Memoirs and Reminiscences of France* (Tussaud's own anecdote-packed account, first published in 1838, of her years at court, the Terror and the establishment of her exhibition).

Tussaud learned modelling from her uncle, and made her first portrait bust (of *Voltaire) when she was 17. In the 1780s she worked for her uncle in Versailles, making models of the French court such as the famous tableau The Royal Family at Dinner. During the Revolution she was commissioned to make death masks of famous aristocratic figures (beginning with the King and Queen) executed on the guillotine, and soon afterwards she established a touring exhibition. She took it round Europe, finally settling in London in 1802 – and the rest, from Poe's macabre story *Death in the Wax Museum* to *Shaw's declaration that being modelled in wax for Madame Tussaud's was the proudest day of his life – is showbusiness. Anita Leslie and Pauline Chapman, *Madame Tussaud* (1978), the official biography, is crammed with history, anecdote and gossip, and its epilogue brings the story of Madame Tussaud's to the present day.

TWAIN, Mark (1835–1910) US writer

⊹ **READ ON**
Mark Twain, *Innocents Abroad* (funny, semi-autobiographical account of naive American tourists in Europe – a US parallel to Jerome K. Jerome's

'Mark Twain' was the pen-name of Samuel Langhorne Clemens. In old age he wrote a full-scale *Autobiography* (ed. Neider, 1960), but it is stiffer and less funny than the semifictional use he made of his life in such books as *Roughing It*

(1872), about gold-mining in Nevada, or his masterpieces *Tom Sawyer* (1876) and *Huckleberry Finn* (1884), about growing up on the banks of the Mississippi. Justin Kaplan, *Mr Clemens and Mark Twain* (1966) begins when Twain is 31, sensibly not trying to compete with Twain's own account of his youth and literary apprenticeship, but then leaves no leaf unturned, delving deeper and revealing more as Twain becomes ever more of a public figure and more reticent about what he really does, thinks and feels.

> ⋅> TWO CULTURES
>
> *(East meets West)*
>
> G. Adler, *Beyond Bokhara: William Moorcroft, Asian Explorer and Pioneer Veterinary Surgeon*
> Pat Barr, *A Curious Life for a Lady* (Isabella Bird)
> Pearl S. Buck, *My Several Worlds: A Personal Record*
> Katherine A. Carl, *With the Empress Dowager of China*
> Henry H. Hart, *Marco Polo: Venetian Adventurer*
> *Christmas Humphreys, *Both Sides of the Circle*
> Margaret Landon, *Anna Leonowens and the King of Siam*
> *Ved Mehta, *Sound-Shadows of the New World*
> *Alan Moorehead, *The Small Woman* (Gladys Aylward)
> John Pollock, *A Foreign Devil in China: the Story of Nelson Bell, a Surgeon in China*
> G.H. Preble, *The Opening of Japan*
> Profilla Kumar Sircar, *My Two Worlds: Vicar from India*

TZ'U-HSI (1835–1908) Chinese empress (ruled 1875–1908)

Although women were barred by tradition from ruling China, in practice Tz'u-Hsi held supreme power for 45 years, from 1861 unofficially for her son (who had succeeded to the throne when he was a boy of five), and as official regent from 1875 for her nephew (who also succeeded as a child). She was ruthless, arrogant ('I have often thought that I am the cleverest woman who ever lived'), expert at the minutiae of court politics, and contemptuous of men. So far as China was concerned, she was a disaster. Unable to cope with foreigners or dissidents in her own country, she shut her ears, becoming so lethal to messengers of bad news that finally none approached her. The country crumpled in her grasp, and imperial rule survived her death by only three years. Marina Warner, *The Dragon Empress* (1972) is an exhaustive account of her life and times (especially good on the times). Charlotte Haldane, *The Last Great Empress*

> ⋅> **READ ON**
> Katherine A. Carl, *With the Empress Dowager of China* (by a US artist who spent several months at court while painting Tz'u-Hsi in 1906, and made notes on all she saw and thought). *See also* Pu-Yi.

of China (1965) is simpler and easier for non-specialists: it makes welcome sense, for example, of all those Chinese names.

U

USTINOV, Peter (born 1921) English actor and writer

As a (somewhat elderly) child actor, Ustinov played one of Will Hay's 'boys' in the 1941 film farce *The Goose Steps Out*. In the Second World War he wrote, directed and acted in patriotic films, and afterwards made a starry career as an actor and a stage playwright of, for example, *The Love of Four Colonels* and *Romanoff and Juliet*. For Hollywood he played such memorable roles as *Nero, *Beau Brummell, a crooked slave dealer in *Spartacus*, a conman in *Topkapi* and *Agatha Christie's Hercule Poirot. From the 1960s onwards he was one of the world's favourite chat-show guests, a well of wit, dazzling anecdotes and impersonations. Reading his autobiography *Dear Me* (1978) is like listening to the man in your own living room: whether he is telling how he coped with British army snobbery in the war,

❖ **READ ON**
Robert Morley, *Robert Morley, Responsible Gentleman*. *David Niven, *The Moon's a Balloon*.

how he out-paused *Olivier on the set of *Spartacus* or how he almost caused an international incident by producing *Don Giovanni* at the Paris Opéra, he is uproarious good fun.

V

VAL BAKER, Denys (1917–84) English writer

Val Baker's good-humoured, happy books chart the ups and downs of family life in a converted mill in the Cornish countryside. Children, pets, neighbours, country life throughout the year, father's fads and fancies – all are reported with zestful, unfussy charm. Each book describes a single year, and many include holiday trips in the family's faithful motor boat *Sanu*, both in the Cornish coves and creeks and to such places as the Balearic Islands, Portugal, Greece and Turkey. Typical titles are *A Long Way to Land's End* (1977), *The Wind Blows from the West* (1978), *A Family for All Seasons* (1979) and *As the Stream Flows By* (1980). His first four books were republished in one volume, as the 'interim autobiography' *Adventures Before Fifty* (1969).

⊷ **READ ON**
Denys Val Baker, *Barbican's End* ('a novel of Cornwall'); *At the Sea's Edge* ('Cornish stories').

VAMBERY, Arminius (*c*1831–1913) Hungarian adventurer

Who was Vámbéry? Traveller, author, friend of royalty, British secret agent (who travelled in Central Asia disguised as a dervish), Bram Stoker's inspiration for the character of the Count in *Dracula* .... Lory Alder and Richard Dalby, *The Dervish of Windsor Castle* (1979), a biography as sparky as its title, does the man ample justice, and is full of revelations about the scaffolding of skulduggery and sleight-of-hand on which Britain's empire once depended. A reviewer of Vámbéry's memoirs (*see* Read On) said 'what is conspicuous from the first to last page

⊷ **READ ON**
Arminius Vámbéry, *Travels in Central Asia* (or, as it was retitled in other languages, *Travels of a Fake Dervish in Central Asia*); *The Story of My Struggles* (memoirs, best taken not so much with a pinch of salt as a stiff pink gin). *See also* *Le Queux, *Teague-Jones.

is . . . egotism' – and that applies not only to the man, but to the edifice he served.

VANDERBILT family

Cornelius Vanderbilt I (1794–1877) began running a ferry on the Hudson River when he was 16, and built it up into a worldwide steamship and railway business, source of the family fortune. His story is told in Edwin Palmer Holt, *Commodore Vanderbilt*. His children concentrated on commerce and philanthropy, in the manner of the time, and were one of the richest and most exclusive families in New York high society. But their descendants caught press attention less for wealth or social position than for a series of volcanic family feuds. Cornelius Vanderbilt III, *The Vanderbilt Feud* (1957) recounts one of them, begun when his father Cornelius II made a marriage which the rest of the family thought unsuitable.

Gloria Morgan Vanderbilt and Thelma, Lady Furness, *Double Exposure* (1958–59) is a joint autobiography (the authors wrote alternate chapters). Furness is fascinating about her life in English high society, her friends the *Duke of Windsor (with whom she had an affair) and Mrs Wallis Simpson (whom she rashly introduced to the Duke); Vanderbilt is interesting on the notorious court battle, one of the great scandals of 20th-century US legal history, she fought for custody of her daughter Gloria. Gloria Vanderbilt, *Once Upon a Time* (1985) is a gushy autobiography by the person in question, beginning in childhood and describing her growing up and adult life as heiress and fashion designer. Barbara Goldsmith, *Little Gloria, Happy at Last* (1980) is an objective account of the court case and its aftermath. Consuelo Vanderbilt Balsan, *The Glitter and the Gold* (1973) gives a chilling view of 1920s British high society, into which the author was pitchforked after a marriage of convenience to the ninth Duke of Marlborough: US cash wed British blue blood, and came hard up against the harsh divorce laws of the time.

VAN GOGH, Vincent (1853–90) Dutch painter

The details of Van Gogh's life are well known: self-tormenting genius cuts off ear, produces some of his finest work in a madhouse, sells only one picture in his lifetime and becomes, posthumously, one of the bestselling artists of all time. His *Complete Letters* (Eng. ed. 1958) open windows into his distracted, desperate world, and M. Shapiro, *Vincent Van Gogh* (1950) tells his life with sympathy and tact. David Sweetman, *The Love of Many Things* (1990) is a large biography, especially good on Van Gogh's paintings and what happened to them – and to his

⤏ **READ ON**
Cornelius Vanderbilt III, *Man of the World: My Life on Five Continents* (autobiography).
Arthur Vanderbilt II, *Fortune's Children: the Fall of the House of Vanderbilt* (full family history, telling how 'Commodore' Vanderbilt went from rags to become the richest person in the world, and how his descendants squandered the family wealth).

⤏ **READ ON**
Irving Stone, *Lust for Life* (novel).

reputation – after his death. Philip Callow, *Vincent Van Gogh: a Life* (1990) reads like a novel, full of domestic detail and giving us plentiful (and convincing) descriptions of the characters' thoughts and emotions. Good descriptions of the paintings Van Gogh was working on at each stage in his life.

VAN MEEGEREN, Han (1889–1947) Dutch artist

⊳ **READ ON**
Tom Keating, *Fake*.

Van Meegeren, who seemed to be a phenomenally untalented painter, became famous at the end of the Second World War when he was tried for selling Dutch art treasures to the Nazis, and defended himself by saying – and proving – that he had painted them all himself. The question of whether his six Vermeers and two Van Hooghs are masterpieces or not, now that they are known to be fakes, lies right at the heart of what 'great art' really means. It is one of the issues discussed in Lord Kilbracken, *Van Meegeren* (1967), a lively combination of biography, case study and trial report.

VICTORIA (1819–1901) English queen (ruled 1837–1901)

⊳ **READ ON**
Robert Rhodes James, *Albert, Prince Consort*. Virginia Surtees, *Charlotte Canning* (about one of Victoria's ladies-in-waiting, who went on to marry the first Viceroy of India). Dorothy Thompson, *Queen Victoria: Gender and Power* (fascinating view: that it was because Victoria was a woman that she was such a succesful monarch and national figurehead – and that she knew this, and ruthlessly exploited her femininity). *See also* *Edward VII, *Melbourne.

Victoria's vivacity as a young girl, her love-affair with Albert and her protracted widowhood make her fascinating as an individual. She was the longest-reigning of all British monarchs, and seemed to embody the qualities which gave 'Great Britain' and its empire their style at a particularly characterful period in their history.

First sources for all biographies of Victoria are her own diaries and letters: perceptive, unaffected and often humorous. A good selection is Christopher Hibbert (ed.), *Queen Victoria in Her Letters and Journals* (1984). Biographies range from historical assessments of Victoria's whole life (for example, Cecil Woodham Smith, *Queen Victoria*, 1972) to chatty accounts of particular events or relationships (Ursula Bloom, *Edward and Victoria*, 1977). Joanna Richardson, *Victoria and Albert* (1977) is good on the key relationship of Victoria's life, and the marriage which set the tone and style of British monarchy for generations. Two of the most readable of all books on Victoria are Elizabeth Longford, *Victoria R.I.* (1964) and Stanley Weintraub, *Victoria: Biography of a Queen* (1987), from an unusual US perspective. The volumes of Tyler Whittle's trilogy *Queen Victoria* (1971), *Albert's Victoria* (1972) and *The Widow of Windsor* (1974) are in the style of novels, full of invented conversations and personal reflections.

⋄ VICTORIANS

H.J. Arnold, *William Henry *Fox Talbot*
E.F. Benson, *As We Were: a Victorian Peepshow*
Caryl Brahms, **Gilbert and Sullivan*
Gyles Brandreth, *The Funniest Man on Earth* (*Dan Leno)
Stanley Chapman, *Jesse Boot of Boots the Chemist*
Susan Chitty, *That Singular Person Called Lear* (*Edward Lear)
Sarah Freeman, *Isabella and Sam* (*Mrs Beeton)
Michael Howell and Peter Ford, *The True History of the Elephant Man* (*Joseph Merrick)
Jerome K. Jerome, *Autobiography*
Susan Oldacre, *The Blacksmith's Daughter*
Hesketh Pearson, *Dizzy* (*Disraeli)
Geoffrey Stavert, *A Study in Southsea* (*Arthur Conan Doyle)
*Lytton Strachey, *Eminent Victorians*

VOLTAIRE (1694–1778) French philosopher

François Marie Arouet, known as Voltaire, is regarded today, especially outside France, as a man of somewhat forbidding intellect: scientist, political pamphleteer, contributor to Diderot's Encyclopedia, author of the social satire *Candide*, advocate of universal liberty and education which would free the human race from the tyrannies of religion, class and despotic government. In his lifetime he was known more as a poet, playwright, wit and scourge of anyone in authority. The first side to his personality is reflected in his own *Philosophical Letters/Letters Concerning the English Nation* (1734), a set of essays attacking aristocratic privilege and preaching universal tolerance. The lighter side is brilliantly shown in *Nancy Mitford, *Voltaire in Love* (1957), a sprightly but well-documented biography centring on his affair with the Marquise du Châtelet, whom he loved equally for her mind (they spent five years translating *Newton and duplicating all Newton's experiments) and her skill in bed.

⋄ **READ ON**
Theodore Besterman (ed.), *Voltaire's Love Letters to his Niece* (correspondence with the woman for whom Voltaire left his Marquise – amiably on both sides).

WAGNER, Richard (1813–83) German composer

Wagner's ambition was to write operas as grand as *Shakespeare's tragedies and as titanic as *Beethoven's symphonies. He pursued this goal ruthlessly, putting all human relationships second to the needs of his genius. He bullied, cajoled and begged to raise funds for a Wagner theatre at Bayreuth, a temple devoted exclusively to his works. He was a genius-superman, a megalomaniac, or both, and by the end of the 19th century no one interested in classical music, or stage drama, could ignore his work.

Richard Wagner, *My Life* (two volumes, Eng. ed. 1911), the selection of his diaries published as *The Brown Book* (Eng. ed. 1980) and John N. Burk (ed.), *Letters of Richard Wagner: the Burrell Collection* (1950) are essential source material. Ernest Newman, *The Life of Richard Wagner* (four volumes, 1933–47), a monumental biography, discusses every word and note of music Wagner wrote: essential for the Wagner-lover. Those new to the man may prefer Martin Gregor-Dellin, *Richard Wagner: His Life, His Work, His Century* (Eng. ed. 1983), which is objective about Wagner's character (no easy task), assumes no musical knowledge, is full of good anecdotes and is extremely readable. Charles Osborne, *Wagner and His World* (1977) makes up for a scrappy text with marvellous production photos from Wagner's works. *George Bernard Shaw, *The Perfect Wagnerite* (second ed. 1903) was written, quite simply, to make people share Shaw's idolatry of Wagner and his work. It is witty, discursive and persuasive, ideal for newcomers to Wagner and old devotees alike.

⇢ **READ ON**

If anything, Wagner's wife Cosima was even more daunting than he was, both during his life and for the 47 years she survived him, keeping the flame of his genius blazing. George R. Marek, *Cosima Wagner* is a good, brisk biography, and Geoffrey Skelton (ed.), *Cosima Wagner's Diaries* gives insight into Cosima's fervour for Wagner and the dragon-character which make her more fun to read about than she probably was to know.

WALEY, Alison (born 1901) New Zealand/ English writer

As a newcomer to London in 1929, Alison Grant fell in love with Arthur Waley, the leading Chinese scholar of his day. Her memoir *A Half of Two Lives* (1982) tells how she was his mistress for many years, only marrying him after the death of his long-time companion Beryl de Zoete, and how the relationship was affected by de Zoete's behaviour after she contracted the degenerative disease Huntington's chorea. Told in short, self-contained episodes, like film sequences, the book sheds merciless light not only on the Waley *ménage*, but on English manners of the time, and on the *Bloomsbury Group to which Arthur Waley was loosely attached.

·> READ ON
Ivan Morris (ed.), *Madly Singing in the Mountains: an Appreciation and Anthology of Arthur Waley*.
Gerald Brenan, *Personal Record*.
*Harold Acton, *More Memoirs of an Aesthete* (memoirs, including interesting portraits of the Waley *ménage*).

WARHOL, Andy (1926–88) US artist

Warhol began as a graphic designer, made his name with silkscreen multi-images of such famous people as *Marilyn Monroe and such cult objects as tins of tomato soup, and became one of the USA's best-known avant-garde eccentrics. His *Diaries* (1988) obsessively catalogue meetings with famous people (at which they said little and he said less), scanning newspapers and TV screens for stories about himself, snapping friends and acquaintances at the Studio (the heart of his empire), and buying roomfuls of art and junk. Victor Bockris, *Warhol: the Biography* (1989) tells his story, and tries to answer the question whether this blank-faced, sad-eyed man was a genius or the victim of the smart-art set's idea of what avant-garde life was supposed to be.

·> READ ON
Ultra Violet, *Famous for Fifteen Minutes: My Years With Andy Warhol*.

WASHINGTON, George (1732–99) First US president

As estate-owner, soldier and politician, Washington seems typical of the liberal, humane and bustling country gentlemen of his time: a mixture of 18th-century enlightenment and the Protestant work ethic. Over the years he has acquired a legend which most people seem to absorb with the air they breathe: everything from his wide-eyed, Pollyanna truthfulness as a child ('I cannot tell a lie') to his never smiling as an adult because of badly fitting, foul false teeth. Perhaps partly in compensation, books about him tend to be heavy historical or political tomes, accurate but cheerless, good on primary evidence but somehow losing sight of Washington as a human being: a good example is Douglas Southall Freeman, *George Washington* (seven volumes, 1948–54; one-volume abridgement 1970).

·> READ ON
John C. Fitzpatrick (ed.), *The Diaries of George Washington*.
Alice Curtis Desmond, *Martha Washington*.

Noemie Emery, *Washington* (1976) is more personal and more intimate. It makes equally good use of letters and other first-hand documents, but selects, shapes and presents the material to give a picture of Washington the man. It is especially good on his relationships with his wife Martha and his colleagues both during the War of Independence and in his years as President.

WATERTON, Charles (1782–1865) English naturalist

Waterton was eccentric: he bled himself three times a year, for example, releasing blood (and, he hoped, 'bad humours') from his body as one might bleed steam from a radiator. He toured North and South America, observing and collecting animals, and established a private zoo in his stately home (Walton Hall in Yorkshire). At 82 he was still quarrelling with every other scientist in sight, and exercising such jungle skills as shinning up trees barefoot. His book *Wanderings in South America, the North-West of the United States, and the Antilles* (1825; good modern ed. 1973, ed. David Snow) is a lively account of his collecting trips, wide-eyed with enthusiasm for the landscapes, flora and fauna of the New World. Gilbert Phelps, *Squire Waterton* (1976) is dull about the journeys, but fine both on Waterton's eccentricities and his painstaking work to give his zoo animals a suitable and unthreatening environment.

> **READ ON**
> R.A. Irwin (ed.), *The Letters of Charles Waterton* (learned, peppery, cranky – and the replies of some of Waterton's bemused correspondents). *Edith Sitwell, *English Eccentrics* (biographical essays by the greatest eccentric of them all: includes Waterton as a prize exhibit).

WAUGH, Evelyn (1903–66) English writer

After a typical 'bright young thing' Oxford career, Waugh became a society darling of the 1930s, spending his time partying with precisely the people he then sent up in his novels. He continued as a leading writer until the 1950s, when he became – or in public pretended to be – increasingly reactionary, snobbish, rude and self-tormenting. He wrote a funny-sad autobiography, *A Little Learning* (1964), and a series of *Diaries* (ed. Michael Davie, 1978), alternately self-lacerating and wicked about everyone else in sight. Christopher Sykes, *Evelyn Waugh* (1975), the standard biography, is good on Waugh's character and the events of his life, but was over-careful not to offend those of his contemporaries who were still alive when the book was written. Martin Stannard, *Evelyn Waugh* (two volumes, 1986, 1988) has fewer such restraints, and has also drawn on Waugh's diaries and letters (*see* Read On) published since Sykes' book was written. It is fascinating on Waugh's work and his travels, and makes good points about the character-quirk which made him so undermine his own talent, even as he flaunted it.

> **READ ON**
> Mark Amory (ed.), *The Letters of Evelyn Waugh*. Evelyn Waugh, *The Ordeal of Gilbert Pinfold* (novel about an alcoholic, boorish writer suffering hallucinations on a ghastly ocean cruise). Humphrey Carpenter, *The Brideshead Generation*.

⋅> THE WAY OF FAITH

Anne Arnott, *The Brethren: an Autobiography of a Plymouth Brethren Childhood*
Stanley Ayling, **John Wesley*
Sydney Block, *No Time for Tears: Childhood in a Rabbi's Family*
Dietrich Bonhoeffer, *Letters and Papers from Prison*
Stanley P. Hirshon, *The Lion of the Lord* (*Brigham Young)
*Christmas Humphreys, *Both Sides of the Circle*
Arthur H. Nethercott, *The First Five Lives of *Annie Besant*; *The Last Four Lives of Annie Besant*

⋅> THE 'WEAKER' SEX?

Mary, Duchess of Bedford, *The Flying Duchess, Her Diaries and Letters*
I.B. Bishop, *This Grand Beyond: the Travels of *Isabella Bird*
Katherine Frank, *A Voyager Out* (*Mary Kingsley)
Hanna Reitsch, *The Sky My Kingdom*
June Rose, *The Perfect Gentleman*
Dolly Shepherd, *When the Chute Went Up*

WEBB, Beatrice and Sidney

Beatrice Webb, née Potter (1858–1943) married **Sidney Webb** (1859–1947) on the rebound from a love-affair with Joseph Chamberlain (father of the future prime minister), who had imposed a condition on their relationship – her total subservience – which she rejected. The Webb marriage, between equals, lasted happily for 50 years. For most of this time they were leaders of left-wing British intellectual circles, founding the London School of Economics, *New Statesman* magazine and the Fabian Society. Sidney served as MP and member of the House of Lords; Beatrice worked as a lecturer, writer and committee member: a one-woman think tank.

Beatrice's autobiographies *My Apprenticeship* (1926) and *Our Partnership* (1948) are main sources for the Webbs' life, work and ideas. Kitty Muggeridge and Ruth Adam, *Beatrice Webb: A Life 1858–1943* (1967) is an excellent account of Beatrice's life, both public and private (Kitty Muggeridge was her niece).

⋅> **READ ON**

Jeanne MacKenzie, *A Victorian Courtship: the Story of Beatrice Potter and Sidney Webb* (what the title promises, plus brisk biographical topping and tailing). *Malcolm Muggeridge, *Chronicles of Wasted Time* (contains a beady-eyed portrait of the Webbs, and tart comments on their 1930s trip to the USSR and their rose-tinted reactions to what they saw there). *H.G. Wells, *The New Machiavelli* (novel, by the Webbs' one-time protégé and friend, parodying left-wing politics of the 1900s, and introducing a couple who work single-mindedly, blindly, to improve ordinary people's lives,

Since so much of those lives were spent with Sidney, the book serves as a useful joint biography. There is no satisfactory book about Sidney on his own.

WEDGWOOD family

From the days of their founder, the potter **Josiah Wedgwood** (1730–95), the Wedgwoods were one of the most enlightened families in Europe: model employers, patrons of science and the arts, political reformers and friends of such luminaries as James Watt, Joseph Priestley, Humphrey Davy, *Coleridge and *Wordsworth. *Darwin's mother was **Susannah Wedgwood** (1765–1817), and he later married another member of the family, his cousin **Emma Wedgwood** (1808–96). Darwin's niece **Snow Wedgwood** (1833–1913) had an affair with *Robert Browning (in his pre-Barrett years). Barbara Boyd Wedgwood and Hensleigh Wedgwood, *The Wedgwood Circle, 1730–1897* (1980) is a copiously illustrated account of this dazzling family, making vivid use of both published and private documents.

WEIR, Molly (born 1920) Scottish actress and writer

In the 1940s–60s Molly Weir's cheery Glaswegian voice was one of the best-loved sounds on radio, in such shows as *ITMA* (*It's That Man Again*) and *Life With the Lyons*. In the 1970s she wrote a set of bestselling memoirs. *Shoes Were for Sunday* (1970) describes her poverty-stricken childhood in Glasgow. *Best Foot Forward* (1972) and *A Toe on the Ladder* (1973) are about her early days on stage and in films. The books are breezy, unaffected and delightful, an exact reflection of the image people who heard Weir's broadcasts still have of her.

WELLES, Orson (1915–85) US actor and director

Welles started at the top in his 20s, with the radio programme *War of the Worlds* and the film masterpiece *Citizen Kane*. From then on his career mysteriously sagged: he had magnificent ideas, but was rarely able to raise the money to finance them. He spent his life alternately dazzling people (on film, for example, as Harry Lime; on stage as Othello) or squandering his talent in cameo appearances or advertisements for sherry and cigars. He was a passionate, witty extrovert, a lover of life shackled by the need to make a living. Barbara Leaming, *Orson Welles* (1985) was written to a plan of Welles' own, interspersing chapters of straight biography with interviews and reminiscences. Frank Brady, *Citizen Welles* (1989), already a

and who are unshakeably sure that whatever they think and say is a kind of holy writ).

‹› **READ ON**
Anthony Burton, *Josiah Wedgwood*. Robert E. Schofield, *The Lunar Society*.

‹› **READ ON**
Molly Weir, *Stepping Into the Spotlight* (chiefly about *ITMA*); *Walking Into the Lyons' Den* (chiefly about working with Bebe Daniels and Ben Lyon).

‹› **READ ON**
Peter Cowie, *A Ribbon of Dreams: the Films of Orson Welles*. Micheál MacLiammóir, *Put Money in Thy Purse* (hilarious memoir of working for Welles on *Othello*).

classic, casts its net even wider for its account of Welles' public career, is more coolly critical, and is outstanding on Welles' personality, especially in his depressed last years.

WELLINGTON, Arthur Wellesley, Duke of (1769–1852) English soldier and politician

Like many generals, Wellington found it hard to adapt to life away from the battlefield. The hero who defeated *Napoléon became one of the least popular, most ineffectual prime ministers the country has ever known, and made matters worse by his public character which, however warm and friendly he was in private, amply justified his nickname 'The Iron Duke'. Elizabeth Longford, *Wellington* (two volumes, 1969–72) is minutely researched (drawing in part on family papers: Longford is descended from Wellington's wife) and makes clear when speculation takes over from evidence, and why. Longford is especially interested in how such an unpromising boy, such a private man, should have become such a dazzler every time he took the field. The first volume, *Wellington: The Years of the Sword (1769–1815)*, traces Wellington's life to the battle of Waterloo, making sense both of his psychology and his battles. Volume two, *Wellington: Pillar of State*, describes and analyses his political career.

> **READ ON**
James Thornton, *Your Obedient Servant* (memoirs of Wellington's cook, edited and introduced by Longford, as revealing for what it omits as for what it says). G.C. Moore Smith (ed.) *The Autobiography of Lt. General Sir Harry Smith (see also *Harry Smith)*. Frederick Highet, *Peninsular General* (biography of Thomas Picton, who served with Wellington). Lesley Blanch (ed.), *The Game of Hearts* (memoirs of the courtesan Harriet Wilson, who informed Wellington that she would be publishing material which might embarrass him, and was roundly told to 'publish and be damned').

WELLS, H(erbert) G(eorge) (1866–1946) English writer

Wells was a utopian, convinced that if human beings set their minds to it, they could create an ideal society, fair to all. The means, he thought, were science: he was a tireless propagandist for the idea that science was a force for good. His private life was dominated by two factors of upbringing and nature: he came from the Victorian lower-middle-class, and never felt entirely at ease in 'polite' literary and social circles; and he was sexually voracious. His *Experiment in Autobiography* (1934) reveals little about his private life, but is fascinating on the early Fabians and about such friends as *Shaw and *Arnold Bennett. Norman and Jeanne Mackenzie, *The Time Traveller* (1973), especially good on Wells' character and public career, is balanced by the more intimate picture by his and Rebecca West's son, Anthony West, *Aspects of a Life* (1984).

> **READ ON**
Gordon N. Ray, *H.G. Wells and Rebecca West* (about the ten-year love-affair between Wells and West, conducted with the full knowledge of Wells' wife Jane: the book is based on over 800 surviving letters from Wells to West, by turns passionate, teasing and fizzing with ideas). *See also *Elizabeth von Arnim.

WESLEY family

John Wesley (1703–91), founder of Methodism, was 'born again' in 1738, and spent 50 years travelling, preaching and

> **READ ON**
John Pudney, *John Wesley and His World* (superbly illustrated brief biography).

converting. (He once calculated that he had ridden over 250,000 miles and preached 40,000 sermons.) His *Journals* give an idea of his mesmeric personality, the fervour of his sermons, and the terrible conditions travellers had to face in 18th-century England. John's devoted brother **Charles Wesley** (1708–88) wrote over 5,000 hymns, including 'Love Divine' and 'Jesu Lover of My Soul'. His son **Samuel Wesley** (1766–1837) and grandson **Samuel Sebastian Wesley** (1810–76) were celebrated organists and composers. Three notably good books were written about the Wesleys in the late 19th century: G.J. Stevenson, *The Wesleys* (1876); L. Tyerman, *The Life and Times of the Rev John Wesley* (three volumes, 1870–71); John Telford, *Charles Wesley* (1886). Maldwyn Edwards, *Family Circle* (1949) is good on early Methodism. Humphrey Lee, *The Lord's Horseman* (1954) and Stanley Ayling, *John Wesley* (1979) are splendid biographies of John.

WHISTLER, James McNeill (1834–1903) US artist

Intended for a service career, Whistler went to military college and then worked briefly in the US Coastguard, before going to France to become an artist. He stayed in Europe for most of the rest of his life, living first as a Bohemian in Paris and then as a member of the aggressively witty London circle which included *Oscar Wilde. In art he was a lifelong experimentalist, and his work as regularly outraged the public as it impressed and influenced fellow artists (notably the early Impressionists). His libel suit against the art critic Ruskin was one of the most notorious cases to pass through 19th-century English courts. He described the case and the issues behind it, with characteristic wit, in *The Gentle Art of Making Enemies* (1890). Gordon Fleming, *The Young Whistler, 1834–66* (1978) is outstanding on Whistler's youth in the USA and his years in Paris: a detailed, funny book. Hesketh Pearson, *The Man Whistler* (1952) deals well with Whistler's London life, a period on which Pearson was expert. Denys Sutton, *James McNeill Whistler* (1966) and *Nocturne* (1963) are good on Whistler's art.

‹› **READ ON**
*Arthur Ransome, *Bohemia in London*. Don Carlos Seitz, *Whistler Stories* (splendid anecdotes, collected in 1913).

WHITE, Antonia (1899–1979) English writer

In 1933 White published what became her best known book, the autobiographical novel *Frost in May*, about a girl educated (and psychologically maimed) in a horrendous convent school. For the next 25 years she was a member of the glitterati: translator of *Colette, friend of *Noël Coward, *Bertrand Russell and *Virginia Woolf. In the 1950s she published three more novels, and was 'rediscovered'. Her book *As Once in May*

‹› **READ ON**
Antonia White, *The Lost Traveller; The Sugar House; Beyond the Glass* ('autobiographical' novels, in which the heroine works as an actress, comes to terms with her demanding father and spends time in an asylum recovering

(1983), edited by her daughter Susan Chitty, contains short stories, articles and a childhood memoir, the first section of a never-finished autobiography. Susan Chitty, *Now to My Mother* (1985) is a merciless account of White, showing that her real life was nothing like the sensitive misery depicted in the 'autobiographical' novels, and in particular that she was a harsh and unloving mother to Chitty herself. Lyndall P. Hopkinson, *Nothing To Forgive* (1988), by White's other daughter, is a similarly lacerating account, but presents White from a totally different point of view. Both books need to be read to form any idea of White as a person. And what a person! She intimidates even at second hand.

WHITE, Gilbert (1720–93) English naturalist

A clergyman, White spent most of his life as curate of Selborne in the Hampshire countryside. He is remembered today for *Natural History and Antiquities of Selborne* (1788), a series of nature observations whose prose is a mixture of sensitive evocation and unsentimental, scientific description. The book is unique, much prized by White devotees, and White's own quizzical, unassuming character is one of its main pleasures. Richard Mabey, *Gilbert White* (1986) catches the flavour of both – and as all good biographies of writers should, it makes you hungry to get back to the pleasures of White's own work.

WHITTLE, Frank (born 1907) English inventor

Inventing the jet engine was easy. The hard part was persuading head-in-the-sand officials to take it seriously and finance its development. Whittle's autobiography, *Jet* (1953), deals with this period of his life, and standing as it does on the threshold of the jet age, makes fascinating reading now by hindsight, when his invention has changed almost every aspect of our lives and certainly our world view. John Golley, *Whittle: the True Story* (1987), written with Whittle's co-operation, fills in many details which Whittle was reluctant to publish in the 1950s. It describes his equally fascinating (and some would say, cantankerous) career, building up the air transport industry in the 1950s and pioneering a new drilling technique in the 1960s – again in the face of ineptitude, disbelief and downright hostility.

WILDE, Oscar (1856–1900) Irish writer

The tart-tongued darling of London society in the 1880s–90s, Wilde sued the Marquess of Queensberry for calling him a sodomite, lost, was counter-charged with gross immorality and

from mental illness).

✧ **READ ON**
W. Johnson (ed.), *The Journals of Gilbert White*.

✧ **READ ON**
Walter J. Boyne and Donald S. Lopez (eds.), *Forty Years of Jet Aviation* (for fans of specifications and technical descriptions, an Aladdin's cave). *See also* *Nevil Shute.

✧ **READ ON**
Rupert Hart-Davies (ed.), *The Letters of Oscar Wilde*. Brian Roberts, *The Mad, Bad Line* (biographies of Lord Alfred

spent two years in Reading gaol. It was sledge-hammering a butterfly, and he passed his last months in France, sick, alone and in despair.

Wilde's Icarus-like life has been well described in Hesketh Pearson, *The Life of Oscar Wilde* (1946) and Sheridan Morley, *Oscar Wilde* (1976). One of the most recent and widely available biographies is Richard Ellmann, *Oscar Wilde* (1987). H. Montgomery Hyde, *The Trials of Oscar Wilde* (1948) is a transcription of the court proceedings, showing Wilde throwing off epigrams, heedless of risk. Sad books about others caught up in his tragedy: Vyvyan Holland, *Son of Oscar Wilde* (1954); Maureen Borland, *Wilde's Devoted Friend* (1990) (about what happened to Wilde's former lover Robert Ross); Alfred Douglas, *Autobiography* (1929) (Douglas was 'Bosie', Queensberry's son and Wilde's lover – the youth all the fuss was about).

Douglas' eccentric family: 'Bosie' himself, his father who sued Wilde, his scandalous uncles, brothers, cousins and aunts). Micheál MacLiammóir, *An Oscar of No Importance* (account of the progress of the author's one-man show *The Importance of Being Oscar* – showbiz stuff on the surface, but some unexpected insights into Wilde's character and the way his work 'plays' in practice). Peter Ackroyd, *The Last Testament of Oscar Wilde* (novel).

> THE WILD FRONTIER

Rupert Croft-Cooke and W.S. Meadmore, *Buffalo Bill, the Legend, the Man of Action, the Showman*
William Cox, *Luke Short: Famous Gambler of the Old West*
Lovat Dickson, *Wilderness Man* (*Grey Owl)
Lawrence Elliott, *Daniel Boone: the Lone Hunter*
Pat F. Garrett, *The Authentic Life of Billy the Kid: the Noted Desperado of the South-West, whose Deeds of Daring and Blood Made His Name a Terror in New Mexico, Arizona and Northern Mexico*
*Alan Moorehead, *Cooper's Creek* (Burke and Wills)
Raymond W. Thorpe, *'Wild West' Doc Carver: Spirit Gun of the West; Plainsman, Trapper, Buffalo Hunter, Medicine Chief of the Santee Sioux, World's Champion Marksman and Originator of the American Wild West Show*

WILLIAMS, Kenneth (1926–88) English comedy actor

Famous for his flared nostrils, extraordinary voices and outrageous campery, Williams starred for 35 years on stage, radio and in films (especially the long series of 'Carry On' comedies). His autobiography *Just Williams* (1985) contrasts his extrovert public life with his fondness for bookish privacy, and is full of affectionate stories of such colleagues and friends as Ingrid Bergman, *Tony Hancock, Stanley Baxter, *Joe Orton, Maggie Smith and the 'Carry On' stars.

> **READ ON**
Kenneth Williams, *Acid Drops* (collection of insults, put-downs, personal anecdotes and bad reviews: the public Williams at his most unstoppable).

WILLIAMS, William Carlos (1883–1963) US writer

Williams was a quiet, humorous man who spent 40 years as a paediatrician among the poor, and whose writing career veered from wildly experimental poetry in his youth (he was a friend of *Ezra Pound) to wry short stories and simple descriptions of ordinary scenes and feelings in his old age. His *Autobiography* (1951) is a classic: gentle, ruminative, full of relaxed send-ups of the bizarre literary types he knew, reflections on how his two careers affected one another, ideas for poems and stories, and – especially – a kind of running dialogue with his own interior thoughts, as if he is talking not just to his readers but to himself.

↝ **READ ON**
Reed Whittemore, *Williams: Poet from Jersey*.

WINDSOR, Duke and Duchess of

Edward (1894–1972), eldest son of King George V, was determined to marry the divorcée **Wallis Simpson** (1896–1989), and when he was told that this was incompatible with being King Edward VIII, he abdicated. His action stunned the nation and still polarizes opinion half a century later, so that books about the 'crisis', and about the subsequent lifestyle of the Windsors (the title Edward and Wallis were given) are more frequent, and more controversial, than about any other members of the British royal family.

Frances Donaldson, *Edward VIII* (1974) draws not only on published memoirs, diaries and other writings, but on interviews with many of those in court and government circles at the time of the abdication. She quotes anonymously (promising that identities will be revealed only when all her sources are dead), and fascinatingly discusses the credibility of memory and the differing perspectives forced on people by royal and constitutional convention. Other biographers regard this book as the standard work, and it sets a benchmark for everyone writing about the Windsors. Philip Ziegler, *Edward VIII, the Official Biography* (1990) is the first account to be authorized by the Queen and to make use of royal papers. It and Donaldson between them make most other biographies redundant. Stephen Birmingham, *Duchess* (1981) is a US biography of the Duchess, good on her life before she met Edward and after he died.

↝ **READ ON**
Hector Bolitho, *King Edward VIII: His Life and Reign* (published in 1937, just after the event, and giving an excellent flavour of the mood of the times). Duke of Windsor, *A King's Story*; Duchess of Windsor, *The Heart Has its Reasons* (autobiographies). Michael Pye, *King Over the Water: the Windsors in the Bahamas 1940–45* (charting the Windsors' life during the Second World War, far from influence in London: Edward had favoured appeasement). Michael Thornton, *Royal Feud* (about the relationship between the Duchess of Windsor and the Queen Mother). Michael Bloch, *The Secret File of the Duke of Windsor* (one of many books by Bloch to make full use of the Windsor papers of which he is the official custodian – here using letters to show the Duke's sadness – but, as often with Bloch, dense to read and highly partisan). Robert Rhodes James (ed.), *'Chips'* (diaries of *'Chips' Channon; has an excellent chapter on the abdication). *See also* *Beaverbrook and *Churchill.

WODEHOUSE, P(elham) G(renville) (1881–1975) English/US writer

Author of over 120 comic novels (including the *Jeeves* and *Blandings* series) and 18 musical comedies, Wodehouse led a serenely happy life, except for one lapse in popularity after some injudicious broadcasts during the Second World War. His autobiographical writings, *Bring On the Girls* (with Guy Bolton, 1954), *Performing Flea* (1953) and *Over Seventy* (1957) (collected as *Wodehouse on Wodehouse*, 1957), are as effervescent as his novels, and the standard biography, Frances Donaldson, *P.G. Wodehouse* (1982), draws on these and on the reminiscences of friends and acquaintances to round out the picture of an unassuming, genial and endlessly creative man.

‹› **READ ON**
Richard Usborne, *Wodehouse at Work to the End*. Joseph Connolly, *P.G. Wodehouse: an Illustrated Biography*. Frances Donaldson (ed.), *Yours, Plum* (life-enhancing letters).

WOLLSTONECRAFT, Mary (1759–97) English writer

Wollstonecraft was one of the first English fighters for women's rights. She ran a girls' school, wrote novels highlighting the suffering of unmarried mothers and the lack of social and educational equality, and published two savage feminist pamphlets, *A Vindication of the Rights of Man* and *A Vindication of the Rights of Woman*. These caused fury in the conservative English society of the time, and she compounded it by her support of the French Revolution and her affair with the American writer Gilbert Imlay. Later she married the philosopher William Godwin; their daughter grew up to become *Mary Shelley. Claire Tomalin, *The Life and Death of Mary Wollstonecraft* (1974) supercedes all other biographies: it is passionate for its subject, thoroughly researched and good on both Wollstonecraft's intellectual views and her self-tormenting emotional life.

‹› **READ ON**
William Godwin, *Memoirs of the Author of A Vindication of the Rights of Woman* (published by Wollstonecraft's husband in the year after she died). G.R. Stirling Taylor, *Mary Wollstonecraft* (enthusiastic, readable and unpatronizing – unusual qualities considering its date, 1911, and the fact that its author is male).

‹› WOMEN AND CHILDREN AT WAR

*Janina Baumann, *Winter in the Morning: A Young Girl's Life in the Warsaw Ghetto and Beyond*
*Christabel Bielenberg, *The Past is Myself*
*Vera Brittain, *Diary 1939–45*; *Testament of Youth*
*Anne Frank, *The Diary of Anne Frank*
Joyce Grenfell, *The Time of My Life: Entertaining the Troops*
Trudi Kanter, *Some Girls, Some Hats and Hitler*

Agnes Keith, *Three Came Home*
Stella King, *Jacqueline*
*Anita Leslie, *A Story Half Told*
Zoe Polanska-Palmer, *Yalta Victim*
Joan Strange, *Despatches from the Home Front*
M. Wells, *Entertaining Eric*
Joan Wyndham, *Love Lessons*

WOODHULL, Victoria (1838–1923) US campaigner

In her heyday, the doings of Woodhull (nicknamed 'Mrs Satan') occupied more column inches in US newspapers than any event since the Civil War. She was Wall Street's first woman broker, making over a million dollars a year, and in her spare time ran a scandal-sheet which pilloried some of the most respectable people of the age. She campaigned for women's suffrage and for people's right to express their sexuality in any way they chose. She advocated birth control, abortion and free love, and put the last into practice by having a string of affairs, including one (it was juicily rumoured) with the clergyman husband of Harriet Beecher Stowe. She and her equally forthright sister Tennessee emigrated to England, but their reputation pursued them, so much so that Woodhull sued the British Museum, no less, for libel. Even when they retired to the country in their 70s they kept fingers in every pie, queening it at fêtes and flower shows and terrorizing local farmers with their views on advanced methods of agriculture. Johanna Johnston, *Mrs Satan* (1967) is a deadpan biography, but its characters are so rollicking and its events crowd in so busily that it should take even the fittest reader's breath away.

> **READ ON**
> Brian Matthews, *Louisa* (hardly less frantic biography of the Australian feminist Louisa Lawson).

WOOLF, Leonard and Virginia

Leonard Woolf (1880–1969) worked for the British Colonial Service in Ceylon before marrying **Virginia Woolf** (née Stephen) (1882–1941) and settling in London as publisher, essayist and Fabian Society activist. During Virginia's lifetime, he devoted himself to her, protecting her against the world and herself or promoting her work as necessary. She wrote essays (chiefly on feminist topics and literature), biography and novels blending description of ordinary events with reverie-like sections revealing their characters' inner thoughts and emotions. She suffered from nervous illness, and died by suicide.

George Spater and Ian Parsons, *A Marriage of True Minds*

> **READ ON**
> Joan Russell Noble (ed.), *Recollections of Virginia Woolf by Her Companions* (essays and reminiscences by a dozen Bloomsberries, by people on the fringes of the group and more disinterested parties such as the Woolfs' housekeeper). Stephen Trombley, *All That Summer She Was Mad* (on Virginia's illness). Jean Moorcroft, *Virginia Woolf, Life and London* (short, lucid biography geared round the

(1977) discusses both Woolfs, and is copiously illustrated: a good introduction to all other books by or about them. The Woolfs were main members of the *Bloomsbury Group, and like many Bloomsberries, wrote extensively about themselves: Leonard Woolf, *Autobiography* (four volumes, 1960–67; two volumes, 1969); *Letters* (ed. Frederick Spotto, 1990); Virginia Woolf, *Letters* (six volumes, ed. Nigel Nicolson, 1978); *Diaries* (five volumes, ed. Anne Olivier Bell, 1978; see also *A Passionate Apprentice: the Early Journals 1897–1909*, ed. Mitchell A. Leaska). Quentin Bell, *Virginia Woolf* (two volumes, 1972), the standard biography, is by another member of the group, her nephew. Lyndall Gordon, *Virginia Woolf: A Writer's Life* (1984) makes extensive use of Virginia's letters and diaries, relating the people in them to characters in her novels, and is particularly interesting on her standing as a feminist author. Duncan Wilson, *Leonard Woolf: a Political Biography* (1978) concentrates on an equally important strand in Leonard's life: his work for the British Labour movement.

places Woolf lived in, both in London and elsewhere). Noel Annan, *The Godless Victorian* (biography of Sir Leslie Stephen, the critic, biographer, editor of the first 26 volumes of the *Dictionary of National Biography*, and father of Virginia Woolf and Vanessa Bell, two of the founding members of the Bloomsbury Group). For a study of the two Stephen sisters see *A Very Close Conspiracy: Vanessa Bell and Virginia Woolf* by Jane Dunn.

WORDSWORTH, Dorothy (1771–1855) English writer

From childhood, Dorothy Wordsworth selflessy devoted her whole being to her brother *William Wordsworth. She ran his Lake District home, saw that he was given the quiet essential to his work, fended off such friends as *Coleridge and *De Quincey, walked with him, talked with him, gave him constant admiration and made fair copies of his works as he wrote them. Had she not chosen this existence, she might have been a formidable writer in her own right: her letters and journals show a feeling for nature equal to William's (her words often uncannily anticipate ideas and turns of phrase in his poems), and a sense of humour which he almost entirely lacked. The family life was chaotic, with unruly servants, even less ruly visitors (Coleridge, for example) and some kind of domestic disaster every day (often caused by Dorothy's obsessive desire to cocoon William from anything which might interrupt his work). Elizabeth Gunn, *A Passion for the Particular* (1981) catches all this magnificently, and also suggests reasons why Dorothy should have found satisfaction in such an apparently self-denying role.

⬩ **READ ON**

Hunter Davies, *William Wordsworth*. Mary Moorman, *William and Dorothy Wordsworth*. Sue Limb, *The Wordsmiths of Gorsemere* (a merciless spoof).

WORDSWORTH, William (1770–1850) English poet

In youth a traveller (and fervent supporter of the French Revolution), Wordsworth became something of a recluse in later life,

⬩ **READ ON**

Mary Wordsworth (William's wife), *Letters*. Émile Legouis, *The Early Life of William Wordsworth*.

settling in his beloved Lake District at the hub of a devoted family group, and writing verse in which human feelings and observation of Nature are linked more simply and gracefully – 'emotion recollected in tranquillity' – than by almost any other English poet.

Wordsworth's life and character are vividly recalled in the journals of his sister *Dorothy Wordsworth and in memoirs by two of his friends: *Samuel Taylor Coleridge, *Biographia Literaria* and *Thomas de Quincey, *Recollections of the Lake Poets*. His and Dorothy's *Letters* are available, and revealing. His poetry (especially the autobiographical *The Prelude*) and his *Prose Works* give unrivalled insight into his cast of mind. Mary Moorman, *William Wordsworth: a Biography* (1957–65) is a scholarly, objective modern biography. Hunter Davies, *William Wordsworth* (1980) bubbles with enthusiasm both for its subject and for the Lake District landscape: if any biography is a one-sitting read, this is.

⋄ WORKING THE LAND

Alan Bloom, *Prelude to Brassingham*
Joyce Fussey, *Milk My Ewes and Weep*
*Colin Middleton Murry *Shadow on the Grass*
Clifton Reynolds, *Glory Hill Farm – First Year* (and sequels)
P. Street, *My Father, A.G. Street*
Sheila Stewart, *Lifting the Latch*

WRAY, Fay (born 1907) US filmstar

Wray began playing small parts in Hollywood when she was 13, and by her mid-20s was starring for Erich von Stroheim. In the 1930s she became famous as 'the scream queen': the beautiful heroine forever being menaced by mad scientists, psychopaths and monsters. Her best known part was as the girl beloved by King Kong in 1933, but she made over 75 films altogether, and was one of Hollywood's hardest-working and best-liked actors. Her autobiography *On the Other Hand* (1989) is full of the usual kind of Hollywood stories, covering the entire history of the industry, but is chiefly interesting because it is not the usual glitzy, starry story. Wray never trod the peaks of fame, never relied on temperament or bitchiness: she got on with the work in a methodical, professional way, and had an even-tempered, wonderful time.

⋄ **READ ON**
Peter Underwood, *Horror Man* (biography of a similarly hard-working, gentle person, whose screen parts belied his real-life personality. Doris Karloff).

WYNDHAM, Joan (born 1922) English writer

When the Second World War broke out in 1939, Wyndham was a 17-year-old student in Chelsea. Her memoir *Love Lessons: a Wartime Diary* (1985) firmly puts the war into second or third place behind the excitement of being a student and the nagging quandary about whether, and with whom, to lose her virginity. Wyndham exactly, wryly, catches two main features of adolescence: the panic and thrill of growing up, and blithe ignorance of what the adult world (and in this case war) is really all about.

⋄ **READ ON**
Love is Blue (takes up the story when she joins the WAAF at 19 and is faced with another quandary: which of the men she knows is she really in love with?).

Y

YOUNG, Brigham (1801–77) US religious leader

Young was an early convert of the Mormon founder Joseph Smith, and succeeded him as leader. Under threat of prosecution for polygamy, and guided by a vision, he led his people, Moses-like, into the wilderness, and founded a settlement, Salt Lake City, in Utah. By contracting with the government to build roads, bridges and rail tracks through Mormon territory, he enriched his community, and his adoption of the latest farming methods 'made the desert bloom'. He defied the polygamy law to the end of his life, and was survived by 27 wives and 56 children. Clarissa Young Spencer, *Brigham Young at Home* is an account, by one of Young's daughters, of day-to-day life in the Young household: a kind of cast-of-thousands *Little House on the Prairie*, but filled with the presence and spirit of Young himself. Among recent biographies of Young is Leonard J. Arrington, *Brigham Young: American Moses* (1985).

YOUNG, Thomas (1773–1829) English scientist

Young was so multi-talented that his Cambridge contemporaries nicknamed him 'Phenomenon'. His main interest was the physics of light, and his contributions to the discussion on whether it consists of waves or rays were an essential bridge between *Newton's theories and modern mathematical physics. As a medical spin off from this work he produced a new theory about colour vision and how it may be impaired. He was also a linguist, one of the team who deciphered the Rosetta Stone, working out the meaning of ancient Egyptian hieroglyphics.

> ∗ **READ ON**
> H. Hartley, *Humphry Davy* (biography of another early 19th-century scientist, doing different work but of similar energy and enterprise).

Young was a Quaker, serene by temperament, and Alexander Wood, *Thomas Young: Natural Philosopher* (1954) catches this quality, making us feel that we know the man and are better for his company, as well as lucidly explaining both the science and the linguistics.

Z

ZINKIN, Taya (born 1918) Russian/English writer

Born to emigrés from the Russian Revolution, Zinkin grew up in Switzerland, the Côte d'Azur and Paris. The language was Russian, the religion was orthodox Jewish and the manners and talk of her family and their friends were all of the Old Country. It was, as Zinkin says, like living in a *Chekhov play, and she describes it wittily and aromatically in *Odious Child* (1971) and *Weeds Grow Fast* (1973), classic memoirs of childhood and adolescence. In many ways, the adults were the ones who remained children, forever recreating a world of past innocence to live in; the worldly wise child, watching and listening, missing nothing, seems far more grown-up than they would ever be.

·> **READ ON**
*Vladimir Nabokov, *Speak, Memory* (account of his privileged pre-Revolutionary childhood on the family estate). Isaac Bashevis Singer, *In My Father's Court* (memoir of his youth, as the son of a Warsaw rabbi at the beginning of this century).

INDEX